MANAGING INFORMATION FOR THE COMPETITIVE EDGE

Edited by Ethel Auster and Chun Wei Choo

Neal-Schuman Publishers, Inc.

New York   London

Published by Neal-Schuman Publishers, Inc.
100 Varick Street
New York, NY 10013

Copyright ©1996 by Neal-Schuman Publishers

Printed and bound in the United States of America

Library of Congress Cataloging-in-Publication Data

Managing information for the competitive edge / edited by Ethel
 Auster and Chun Wei Choo.
     p.   cm.
   Includes bibliographical references and indexes.
   ISBN 1-55570-215-5
   1. Information technology—Management.   2. Information
 resources management.   3. Management information systems.
 I. Auster, Ethel.   II. Choo, Chun Wei.
 HD30.2.M363   1996
 658.4′038—dc20   96-31251
                                                                      CIP

Contents

Preface

Information has become a uniquely strategic resource for any organization, as vital as land, labor, or capital, and yet imbued with its own special properties that enhance its importance. Labor or capital are depletable assets—the more one uses them, the less one has. Information on the other hand is a regenerative resource that not only grows with use, but can be used over and over again in different contexts to create value in multiple ways. Within an organization, the exchange of information and ideas among knowledgeable members can result in new insights that are more powerful than the individual pieces of information. Between organizations, the sharing of information and data can synergize relationships to dramatically improve the performance of the sharing parties. At the same time, the unmanaged spread of information can have debilitative consequences. Gossip and rumor can break the spirit of a healthy organization. Information dependencies between organizations can allow stronger partners to dominate the weak. In a sense then, information is also a risk-laden resource—there is so much information available, but one must be careful not to be misled by spurious information; there is much to be gained by sharing information, but one must be selective about what information to give away and what to hold back. The message seems clear: information offers both risks and riches, and the outcome depends on how well the organization manages its information resources.

Information management is the harnessing of the information resources and information capabilities of the organization in order to create and reinvent value both for itself and for its clients or customers. While information management is hard to define, there is no difficulty in spotting an organization that has managed information effectively. An information-savvy organization is an intelligent, learning organization that is skilled at creating, acquiring, organizing, and sharing knowledge, and that is able to adapt its goals and behavior to reflect the new knowledge. It thrives by the principle that the only sustainable competitive edge is that based on continuous learning and constant innovation. The information-savvy organization pursues information management as one of its core competencies. Information management enables collective learning in the organization. It develops know-how about the effective coordination and integration of the multiple streams of information, expertise, and knowledge that flows in an organization. It provides the memory and the foresight for the organization to adapt to and evolve with changing environments, and to continually renovate its activities and offerings. Information management as an organization's core competency is also difficult for competitors to imitate. While there are general principles guiding good information management, each organization must strike its own complex harmonization of its information assets. In practice, the task of information management is to plan, design, and develop the organizational structures, resources, and processes to realize these objectives. Ultimately, information management is concerned with nothing less than the creation of the brain of the organization.

The purpose of this book is to bring together a balanced selection of readings that address what we believe are some of the most salient issues in information management today. Are there systematic ways of apprehending the information needs of an organization? How do managers behave as information users? What strategies and tactics may be used to develop information management into the organization's core competency? How do organizations measure the value of information and information systems? How can the roles of information practitioners be re-engineered for the new information milieu? The book offers approximately equal servings of the theoretical and the practical—theoretical reviews summarize and synthesize our current understanding of information management while practical cases and strategies may be used to guide action and implementation. Reading the book should benefit information managers, practitioners, and specialists working in a broad range of settings, from libraries and information centers to any organization whose products, services, and activities are information-intensive. Students and instructors in library and information science schools, as well as business administration or management faculties should also find the volume useful.

Managing Information for the Competitive Edge is divided into six parts. Each part addresses a major theme, and is preceded by an introduction that summarizes each article, places them in the broader context of the topic under discussion, and recommends sources for further reading.

Part I presents two review articles that provide a theoretical background for the rest of the book. By drawing widely from the literatures of organization theory, management information systems, and management of information technology, they summarize where we are in our attempts to develop information models of organizational behavior. Many of the issues raised in this part form continuous threads that run through the other parts of the book.

Information management must be guided by a holistic understanding of the information requirements and information uses of the organization. The three articles in Part II attempt this: the first article by the guru of competitive strategy discusses how information is used in key organizational processes to create a competitive advantage; the second offers a comprehensive framework to analyze the information needs of groups of information users in an organization; and the third discusses user-centered models of information needs and uses and their implications for the provision of information services.

Part III looks at an important group of information users—the managers. The articles in this part reveal clearly that managers are a distinct group of information users whose information behaviors are constrained and shaped by the contingencies of managerial work. The relentless pace and inherent uncertainty of managerial work condition managers to simplify and limit their information search based on experience and familiarity, and to seek solutions that are good enough rather than optimal.

The five articles in Part IV discuss a number of strategies for managing information resources and capabilities more effectively. Information and communication audits allow an organization to assess the fit between its information assets and communication structures and the organization's goals and functions. A practical technique for mapping the organization's information resources is also described. After taking stock of information assets, organizations should develop shared information networks to prevent information hoarding and encourage collective information processing. Many organizations failed at information management because they did not manage the politics of information—an effective strategy requires a political model of information management that best matches the organizational culture. Finally, in order to survive in an increasingly complex and competitive environment, organizations need to set up an intelligence system to capture accurate and timely information about the external environment.

Part V introduces concepts and techniques for assessing the value of information and information services in organizations. Both quantitative and descriptive approaches are discussed, including a number of ways that libraries and information services can add value to the information they provide; an instrument for determining the priorities of organizational users, that can be used to set criteria for ranking information service options and evaluating existing services; and an integrated set of measures, models, and methods that essentially quantify the value of information in terms of time and dollar savings, and quality and productivity improvements.

Part VI presents two case studies of information management—one is Nippon Steel Corporation, the largest steel manufacturer in the world, and the other is the British pharmaceutical industry. Nippon Steel has weaved an intricate web of information structures and processes that is completely integrated into the operations of the firm. The information managers of ten British drug firms relate their successes and frustrations as they tried to provide competitor intelligence to their companies. Two other articles call for a redefinition of the role of information professionals in the new information organization—information professionals need to expand their repertory of skills to act as overseers of networks that link up information from internal and external, personal and impersonal sources.

With the widespread recognition that effective information management is the key to organizational innovation and productivity, it is perplexing to observe that information professionals in general have not been accorded the high status that one would expect given their training and skills in acquiring, organizing, analyzing and disseminating information. Perhaps this is in part because of the vision the information professionals have of themselves and their roles in the information organization. Many believe that their work is reactive, waiting for users to come to them with their information requests. Many believe that their contribution stops at providing information access, and shy away from involvement in decision making or problem solving. They are unwilling or unable to know and understand the detailed decision making situations in which information will be used. It would appear that information professionals have cast themselves in passive supporting roles on the organizational stage. To reinvent their roles, information professionals would need to break out of this mindset, and to move from being information custodians to information champions who have the entrepreneurial energy, the business knowledge, and the specialized skills to unleash the power of information. This attitudinal shift and role redefinition must take place in a framework of a deeper and more complete understanding of how organizations create, process, and use information. At the same time, we need to know how to show and quantify the worth of information and information services to the organization. Information is not the domain of a single profession but is the result of a confluence of multiple areas of expertise. Paradoxically, we are concerned about the viability of the information professions in the information age. Surely information professionals who succeed in enabling their organizations to manage information for competitive edge would also have succeeded in ensuring the growth and survival of their own professions.

Acknowledgements

From the time an idea for a book is first conceived to the day when it is finally published, scholars are dependent upon the encouragement, patience, and expertise of many people. It is with pleasure and gratitude that we acknowledge the help of those without whom we could not have created this volume.

Our search for the best articles to include led us to the literatures of Britain, Canada, the United States, and beyond. The reception our copyright and permission requests received from publishers and authors was unfailingly polite and prompt. We thank them all for their foresight in laboring in these areas of interest and for their generosity in sharing the fruits of those labors. In locating the original materials, the collection and staff of our Faculty's Library were, of course, invaluable. It is hard to imagine compiling a volume like this without such a superb resource at hand.

It is equally difficult to contemplate undertaking such a venture without the day-to-day help of a competent and reliable assistant. Shauna Taylor, a doctoral student, took charge of the myriad chores involved in the publishing process. Her devotion, good humour, and superb management skills kept us on track and moving forward. Knowing we could rely on her totally relieved us of much of the stress that accompanies any serious creative endeavour.

We are also grateful to the Faculty of Information Studies, University of Toronto, for providing a hospitable working environment and flexible administrative arrangements which enabled us to keep distractions to a minimum.

I
Information Models of Organizations

I
Information Models of Organizations

INTRODUCTION

Information used to be the invisible ether that permeated an organization—everyone was enveloped in information, but no one knew the complete story of where it came from, where it was going, and how it was really being used, if at all. Three developments changed the role of information in organizations. In their normal functioning, organizations accumulated at an alarming rate more as well as more detailed information, partly because of the growth of population and markets, and partly because of governmental and institutional requirements. At the same time, the proliferation of information technologies that capture, store, process, and transmit data extended the scope of information collection and greatly increased the speed and range at which information may be exchanged and shared. The final, and perhaps most significant development was that organizations began to learn how to ride the waves of the information deluge. Information is now seen as an economic resource that is as vital as land, labor, or capital. Time and again, organizations have proved that the strategic, intelligent use of information can lead to dramatic improvements in performance and profitability. Yet information has its own unique attributes different from any other economic good, and the proper handling of information as a strategic resource calls for a new paradigm of information management. Conceptually, information has to be managed at multiple levels—information as *content* (facts, ideas, knowledge, experience); information as *tools* (databases, files, libraries, repositories); and information as *processes* (information needs, information seeking, and information use).

If we are to manage information effectively, we need a holistic understanding of how organizations behave as information-seeking, information-creating, and information-using systems. In other words, we need models to reveal how the various information processes in an organization are connected to each other and may be managed to work together towards goals and objectives. Such models will take time to evolve as we ascend the learning curve of organizational information management. A crucial part of the education is to periodically take stock of what we have learned, to deepen our understanding in incremental steps, to apply the extant knowledge in practice, and to point out new priorities for study. The research on information in organizations has at least two related lineages, one situated in organization theory, and the other, more recent tradition in management theory and information systems.

The two review articles in Part I provide a theoretical background to frame our discussion of information management. We seek conceptual answers to some basic questions: What shapes the information needs of organizations? How do organizational members obtain and process information? What are the dominant modes of information use in organizations? The first article by Chun Wei Choo surveys the organization theory literature, juxtaposing the major theoretical frameworks that have been used to examine the information behavior of organizations. The second article by Marianne Broadbent and Michael Koenig provides an analytical guide to the general business literature on information and information technology in organizations.

A common theme in organizational research has been the treatment, often explicit but sometimes implied, of organizations as information-processing systems—organizations seek information; store, retrieve and transmit it; and use it to interpret events, solve problems, and make decisions. Organization theory is therefore a logical starting point in our attempt to apprehend the purpose and scope of information management. The article by Choo summarizes the work of Herbert Simon, James March, Richard Cyert, Jay Galbraith, Oliver Williamson, William Ouchi, Karl Weick, and many others whose work spans five decades. Several unifying lines of thought about the use of information are brought together in a tentative information model of the organization. In the model, an organization needs information for two general reasons—to reduce uncertainty, and to reduce equivocality. Uncertainty is the lack of information needed to perform organizational tasks, and information to reduce uncertainty is therefore information that is used typically in decision making and problem solving. Equivocality is created by the ambiguity of the messages received, and information to reduce equivocality is therefore information to enable an organization to make sense of its environment, and to learn rules and schemas that can be used again to interpret future signals. Information is acquired and processed by individual members, and they do so subject to their cognitive limitations and personal preferences, as well as the biases that are formed as a result of their belonging in an organization. The eventual use of information can pursue both rational and non-rational goals. Apart from decision making, problem solving, and organizational learning, information may also be deployed as a social or cultural symbol, as a political resource, as a means to legitimize the existence of the organization, and so on. It is this richness and complexity that create the unique challenges of information management in organizations.

While Choo's article concentrates on information-based organization theories, Marianne Broadbent and Michael Koenig review the general business literature on management information, information technology and information systems. They conclude that there has been a remarkable convergence of management attention on information and information technology in recent years. The information model of the organization that emerges appears to be characterized by several features. First, organizations seek to use information to win strategic and tactical advantage in an environment where information and information technology have intensified and redefined competition between organizations. Second, organizations, more than ever, recognize the need of relevant information, especially good external intelligence, in order to enable their managers to make effective strategic decisions. Third, organizations are concerned about the successful planning and design of computer-based information systems. The concern begins with the correct determination of the critical information needs of top management and other members, and extends to the methods and techniques that will transform these information needs into information systems. Fourth, information management in organizations needs to treat information as an economic resource that is as strategic as the traditional factors of production such as capital or labour. Fifth, information management in organizations evolves through distinct stages, driven by the growth of information technology, and by the changing functional context of applying the technology. A pressing information management task is the integration of currently separate enclaves of information resources and technologies into a coherent whole. As a result of their analysis, Broadbent and Koenig suggest that the top three information management issues would be:

(1) How to create competitive advantage through the strategic use of information and information technology;
(2) how to manage the archipelago of disparate islands of information

      resources and services that are scattered all over an organization; and

(3) how to analyze the information requirements of the organization as a whole, beginning with the information needs of top management.

The literature on information in organizations goes back several decades and adopts many different perspectives. The list of additional readings at the end of Part I is necessarily selective, but hopefully still gives a sense of the range and energy that move this research.

Towards an Information Model of Organizations

Chun Wei Choo

INTRODUCTION

A growing number of organization theories include an analysis of the role of information in organizations. The use of information is typically examined in the context of some other organizational activity such as decision making, problem solving, or interpreting environmental changes. An information model of the organization, on the other hand, would focus on the acquisition and use of information in organizations, and directly address issues such as:

- What determines the information needs of organizations?
- How do organizational members acquire and process information?
- What purposes motivate the use of information in organizations?

This paper compares a selection of perspectives on information in organizations so as to identify some conceptual elements that could be used to construct an information model of the organization.

MODELS OF ORGANIZATIONAL INFORMATION PROCESSING

The information-processing approach to organizational analysis seeks to understand and predict how organizations receive stimuli, interpret them, store, retrieve and transmit information, generate judgments, and solve problems (Larkey and Sproull 1984). Although there

Reprinted by courtesy of the Canadian Association for Information Science from *The Canadian Journal of Information Science/Revue canadienne des sciences de l'information* 16(3): 32–62.

is no unified theory of organizational information processing, the field has two main research themes: organizational participants as information processors, and organizational systems and structures that contribute to information processing. The accelerating interests in the information-processing view is driven by the deficiencies of theoretical views that ignore information-processing behaviours, the rapid diffusion of information-processing technologies, and the increasing information-processing content of organizational tasks.

For the purpose of this review, we differentiate between two broad streams of research. The first stream views organizations as rational decision-making systems, and analyses organizational decision-making behaviour in terms of information-processing activities. This decision-making perspective was developed by Herbert Simon, James March, and Richard Cyert, and became very influential in organization theory. Starting from this theoretical foundation, Jay Galbraith, Oliver Williamson, and William Ouchi proposed organizational models in which information processing was a central component. The second stream views organizations as loosely coupled systems whose individual actors create or enact the organizational environments and process information to resolve equivocality in the information inputs from the environment. This "enactment" perspective was suggested by Karl Weick, who together with Richard Daft later proposed a model of organizations as interpretation systems. Weick's view has similarities with that proposed by James March and his associates on the ambiguity and anarchy of organizational information processing.[1]

Although the two points of view are almost diametrically opposite, as will become clear in the ensuing discussion, Daft and Lengel (1984, 1986) attempted an integration in their information richness model.

The Principle of Bounded Rationality

The cornerstone of organizational decision-making theories developed by Simon and his associates at the then Carnegie Institute of Technology is the principle of *bounded rationality*. Simon, who formulated the principle, states it in this way:

> The capacity of the human mind for formulating and solving complex problems is very small compared with the size of the problems whose solution is required for objectively rational behavior in the real world—or even for a reasonable approximation to such objective rationality. (Simon 1957, 198)

What precisely constitute the bounds that limit the capacity of the human mind? Simon defines a "triangle of limits": the individual is limited by skills, habits, and reflexes; by values or conceptions of purpose that may diverge from organizational goals; and by the extent of knowledge and information possessed (Simon 1976, 40–41, 241). As a result, the individual of limited rationality, or the administrative man, behaves in two distinctive ways when making decisions. First, the administrative man *satisfices*—looks for a course of action that is satisfactory or good enough. Second, the administrative man constructs a simplified model of the real world in order to deal with it—the simplification is acceptable because most of the facts of the real world have no bearing on the particular situation being faced (Simon 1976, xxviii–xxx).

There is a larger consequence of the administrative man's bounded rationality:

> It is only because individual human beings are limited in knowledge, foresight, skill, and time that organizations are useful instruments for the achievement of human purpose; and it is only because organized groups of human beings are limited in ability to agree on goals, to communicate, and to cooperate that organizing becomes for them a "problem." (Simon 1957, 199)

The organization can therefore alter the limits to rationality of its members by creating or changing the organizational environment in which the individual's decision making takes place. One of Simon's major propositions is that the organization influences its members' behaviours by controlling the *decision premises* upon which decisions are made, rather than controlling the actual decisions themselves (Simon 1976, 223). A fundamental problem of organizing is then in defining the decision premises that form the organizational environment: "The task of administration is so to design this environment that the individual will approach as close as practicable to rationality (judged in terms of the organization's goals) in his decisions" (Simon 1976, 240–41).

Bounded Rationality in Organizations

The implications of the individual's bounded rationality for the organization are further pursued in March and Simon (1958). Here, the theme is that the basic feature of organization structure and function derive from the characteristics of human problem-solving processes and rational human choice. Because of the limits of the human mind, decision making in organizations requires "simplifications."

The simplifications have a number of characteristic features:

(1) Optimizing is replaced by satisficing—the requirement that satisfactory levels of the criterion variables be attained.
(2) Alternatives of action and consequences of action are discovered sequentially through search processes.
(3) Repertories of action programs are developed by organizations and individuals, and these serve as the alternatives of choice in recurrent situations.
(4) Each specific action program deals with a restricted range of situations and a restricted range of consequences.
(5) Each action program is capable of being executed in semi-independence of the others—they are only loosely coupled together. (March and Simon 1958, 169)

The key simplification is in the use of action or *performance programs*. These programs guide the decision behaviours of individuals: while some of these programs that deal with repetitive situations can be routinized, others that deal with novel situations will have to be developed through problem-solving activities that first construct a definition of the situation and then develop appropriate new programs. In any case, much of the decision making in organizations is driven by performance programs. To elaborate:

> . . . an environmental stimulus may evoke immediately from the organization a highly complex and organized set of responses. Such a set of responses we call a *performance program,* or simply, a *program.* For example, the sounding of the alarm gong in a fire station initiates such a program. So does the appearance of a relief applicant at a social worker's desk. So does the appearance of an automobile chassis in front of the work station of a worker on the assembly line . . . Most behavior, and particularly most behavior in organizations, is governed by performance programs. (March and Simon 1958, 141–42)

Organizational Decision Making

Expanding on the work of Simon, Cyert and March (1963) have placed their focus on the processes of organizational decision making. They seek to answer the question: how does a firm behave as an information-processing and decision-making system? To start with, an organization is not monolithic, but acts like a continuously shifting multiple-goal coalition. Managers, workers, shareholders, suppliers, customers, bankers, tax collectors, and so on all have a stake in the firm, but their goals or preferences about what should be done differ. Organizational goals are set by a negotiation process that occurs among members of the *dominant coalition.* An organization consists of various groups, each seeking to further its own interests or goals, without any single group being able to completely determine what goals the organization should pursue. Group members thus look for allies in those groups whose interests are similar, and they negotiate with those groups whose interests are divergent but whose participation is essential. Each negotiated agreement between groups places constraints on what the organization can regard as an acceptable course of action: the goals themselves become complex preference statements that summarize the multiple conditions that any acceptable choice must meet. It is not surprising, then, that managers spend much of their time managing the coalition, as decisions cannot be taken without taking into consideration all the diverse and often conflicting interests.

The decision-making process itself is characterized by four concepts that together form a theory of how these decisions are arrived at: (1) quasi resolution of conflict, (2) uncertainty avoidance, (3) problemistic search, and (4) organizational learning.

Because an organization is a coalition of conflicting interests, it has to resort to a number of methods to resolve conflict. These methods do not actually achieve consensus, but enable the organization to continue to operate despite unresolved divergencies. The devices for the *quasi resolution of conflict* are: "local rationality" (the subunit solves problems rationally within its own specialized domain); "acceptable level decision rules" (rules that are acceptable to all interests rather than being optimal overall); and "sequential attention to goals" (organization attends first to one goal, then another in sequence).

All organizations must face uncertainty—uncertainty about the market, suppliers, shareholders, government agencies, and so on. Organizations act to avoid *uncertainty* by two main strategies. They use decision rules that emphasize short-run reaction to short-run feedback rather than try to anticipate long-run uncertain events. They arrange for a negotiated environment through the imposition of plans, standard procedures, industry tradition, and contracts on the environment (Cyert and March 1963, 119).

Problemistic search is the means by which organizations determine what choices are thought to be available. Search is "motivated"—the occurrence of a problem initiates the search for ways to solve it, and once a way is found, then the search stops. Search is "simple-minded"—when a problem occurs, search for a solution is concentrated near the old solution. Search is "biased"—it reflects the training, experience, and goals of the participants.

Finally, *organizational learning* takes place in the decision-making process through the individual members of the organization.

Goals are adapted by assessing past experience and comparing with other organizations. Changed goals lead to adaptation in attention, whereby different sets of events or problems would now need to be addressed.

Organizations as Information-Processing Systems

Building on the work of Simon, March, and Cyert, Galbraith (1973, 1977) proposes the theory that an organization processes information in order to reduce task uncertainty, defined as the difference between the amount of information required to perform the task and the amount of information already possessed by the organization. Organization structures must then be designed so that they have the information-processing capability required to perform the task to the desired level of performance.

Galbraith presents a hierarchy of alternative organization structures that provide interesting capabilities to process information in the face of increasing task uncertainty. Starting with a bureaucratic organization, its first strategy is to specify the necessary task execution behaviours in advance in the form of *rules or programs.* As uncertainty and complexity increase, the second strategy is for managers in the organizational *hierarchy* to handle the exceptions and new situations that arise. As uncertainty grows, the volume of information from the points of action to the managers overload the hierarchy and the third strategy of *goal setting* is employed: the organization specifies targets to be achieved and allows the employees to select behaviours appropriate to the target. These three strategies of rules, hierarchical referral, and goal setting are characteristic of the basic, mechanistic, bureaucratic organization. As task uncertainty continues to rise, the number of exceptions increases until the hierarchy is unable to cope. At this stage, the organization has two choices. Either it can reduce the amount of information that needs to be processed, or it can increase its capacity to handle more information.

The organization can reduce information need by the creation of slack resources or the creation of self-contained tasks. In the *creation of slack resources* (increasing budget, delaying the completion schedule), the organization reduces the number of exceptions that occur by simply reducing the required performance level. In the *creation of self-contained tasks,* the number of exceptions is reduced by forming work groups that contain all the resources required to perform their designated tasks.

The other choice is for the organization to increase its information-processing capacity. It can do so by an *investment in vertical infor-*

mation systems. Vertical information systems, based on computers and information technologies, increase the capacity of existing channels of communication, create new channels, and introduce new decision mechanisms. Information is collected at the points of origin and directed at appropriate times to the appropriate places in the hierarchy for decision making. The organization can also increase its information-processing capacity by the *creation of lateral relations.* This strategy moves the level of decision making down to where the information exists rather than bringing it up to the points of decision. Galbraith lists seven forms of lateral relations in order of their increasing ability to handle more information, and in order of increasing cost to the organization. As task uncertainty grows, the organization will sequentially adopt these lateral mechanisms. The mechanisms are also cumulative: higher forms are added to, rather than substituted for, lower forms. The seven forms of lateral relations are:

1. Utilize *direct contact* between managers who share a problem.
2. Establish *liaison* roles to link two departments which have substantial contact.
3. Create temporary groups called *task forces* to solve problems affecting several departments.
4. Employ groups or *teams* on permanent basis for constantly recurring interdepartmental problems.
5. Create a new role, an *integrating role,* when leadership of lateral processes becomes a problem.
6. Shift from an integrating role to a *linking-managerial* role when faced with substantial differentiation.
7. Establish dual authority relations at critical points to create the *matrix design.* (Galbraith 1973, 48)

Galbraith's four information strategies (two for reducing information need, two for increasing information capacity) are meant to be exhaustive, so that the organization's information-processing capacity always balances out with the task information requirements. If the organization does not consciously match them, reduced performance through budget or schedule overruns will occur in order to bring about equality (Galbraith 1973, 19).

The Transaction Cost Model of Organizations

Williamson (1975, 1981) proposes that the unit of analysis in organizational study should be the transaction or the exchange of goods or services. An organization is seen as a pattern of transactions between individuals or groups of individuals, and it therefore adopts the structure that offers the lowest *transaction costs* for the exchanges it wishes to enter into. Market transactions of goods or services consist of contractual relationships. Williamson argues that the efficacy of the contracting mechanism depends on a pair of human factors interacting with a pair of environmental factors. The human factors are bounded rationality (Simon 1957) and opportunism. The latter implies that individuals are capable of "self-interest seeking with guile" (Williamson 1975, 26); they are not trustworthy and can seek ways to gain personal advantage. The environmental factors are the uncertainty/complexity that characterize the environment in which the transaction takes place, and the "small numbers" factor, which refers to a situation where there is only a small number of bidders or alternative partners. The pairwise interaction of these factors is then apparent: the limits of bounded rationality are reached or exceeded when the environment increases in uncertainty and complexity; and the hazards of opportunism are greater in small-numbers exchange situations. The interaction between uncertainty and opportunism produces a condition of "information impactedness," which "exists in circumstances in which one of the parties to an exchange is much better informed than is the other regarding underlying conditions germane to the trade, and the second party cannot achieve information parity except at great cost—because he cannot rely on the first party to disclose the information in a fully candid manner" (Williamson 1975, 14). Information impactedness can in turn give rise to a small-numbers exchange condition.

Williamson calls his model the *organizational failures framework:*[2] any interactive pairing of the four factors can lead to the breakdown of the governance structure that supports the exchange. Organizations move from the market to the hierarchical structure as transactions become more complex and uncertain. The hierarchy extends the bounds on rationality by allowing specialization in decision making and savings in communication expense; it curbs opportunism by allowing incentive and control techniques to be applied; it "absorbs" uncertainty and allows interdependent units to adapt to contingencies; it resolves small-numbers indeterminacies by fiat; and it reduces the information gap between exchange agents (in information impactedness) by being empowered to perform audits and other checks (Williamson 1975, 257).

Markets, Bureaucracies, and Clans

Ouchi (1980, 1981) extends the organizational failures framework with a third governance structure—the "clan." Just as hierarchies replace markets when transactions become moderately uncertain and complex, so clan structures replace hierarchies when transactions become very uncertain and complex. This happens because the costs of monitoring very complex exchanges by traditional or authority systems are prohibitive and will lead to the search for alternative control structures. A viable alternative is the clan structure in which members share common internalized goals and have strong feelings of solidarity. Ouchi (1981) suggests that a defining characteristic of the clan is that it offers long-term, if not lifelong, employment to its members. The clan structure operates in different ways from the hierarchy or bureaucracy:

> Although clans may employ a system of legitimate authority (often traditional rather than the rational-legal form), they differ fundamentally from bureaucracies in that they do not require explicit auditing and evaluation. Performance evaluation takes place instead through the kind of subtle reading of signals that is possible among intimate coworkers but which cannot be translated into explicit, verifiable measures. This means that there is sufficient information in a clan to promote learning and effective production, but that information cannot withstand the scrutiny of contractual relations. Thus, any tendency toward opportunism will be destructive, because the close auditing and hard contracting necessary to combat it are not possible in a clan. (Ouchi 1980, 137)

To summarize the transaction cost perspective, an organization adopts the governance structure that offers the lowest transaction costs for the exchanges in which it takes part. Bureaucratic organizations are most common because under specifiable conditions, the bureaucratic structure is the most efficient way of mediating transactions between parties. Under other conditions, market and clan structures exist because they reduce transaction costs.

Weick's Model of Organizing

In contrast to the Carnegie perspective of organizations as decision-making systems that guide the behaviours of members through decision premises and performance programs, Karl Weick (1969, 1979) proposes a model of organizations as "loosely coupled" systems in which individual participants have great latitude in interpreting and implementing directions. He stresses the autonomy of individuals and the looseness of the relations linking individuals in an organization. Although he also views organizations as information-processing systems, the purpose of processing information is not decision making or problem solving in the first instance. Instead, the focus is on reducing the *equivocality*[3] of information about the organization's external environment. Weick summarizes his organizing model as follows:

> The central argument is that any organization *is* the way it runs through the processes of organizing . . . This means that we must define organization in terms of organizing. Organizing consists of the resolving of equivocality in an enacted environment by means of interlocked behaviours embedded in conditionally related processes.
>
> To summarize these components in a less terse manner, organizing is directed toward information processing in general, and more specifically, toward removing equivocality from informational inputs. (Weick 1969, 90–91)

The actors of an organization *enact* the environment by creating the environment to which they then adapt; they separate out for closer attention selected portions of the environment based on their experience. In fact, the enacted environment is based on the retrospective interpretations of actions already completed. Enactment takes place through interlocked behaviours: repetitive, reciprocal, contingent behaviours that develop and are maintained between two or more organizational actors. These interlocked behavioural cycles are embedded in three processes that constitute the organizing activity: (1) the enactment process creates the information that the system adapts to; (2) the selection process sorts through the variety present in the equivocal information, and admits those portions that satisfy criteria established by past experience; and (3) the retention process basically stores the interpreted segments for future application.

In the *enactment* phase, managers as individual information processors receive information about the external environment and then create the environment to which they will attend. In creating the enacted environment, managers construct, rearrange, single out, or even demolish many "objective" features in their surroundings. The enacted environment is a sensible rendering of previous events stored in the form of causal assertions, and made binding on some current enactment and/or selection (Weick 1979, 166).

In the *selection* phase, the organizing process generates answers to the question "What is going on here?" The selection process acts as if it contains solutions in search of problems. Selection activity matches solutions with people, problems, and choices. The criteria for selection are typically lodged in the minds of decision makers in the organization. What the decision makers attend to and enact, the cues they use, why they use those cues, and their processes for scanning and monitoring, all become influential as sources of selection criteria.

In the *retention* phase, the organizing process determines what information is to be retained for future reference. Although the entire process operates to reduce equivocality, some equivocal features do and must remain if the organization is to be able to survive into a new and different future. Indeed, "organizations continue to exist only if they maintain a balance between flexibility and stability."

An interesting corollary of Weick's model is that organizational action often occurs first, and is then interpreted or given meaning. The connection between action and planning is thus topsy-turvy:

> Our view of planning is that it can best be understood as thinking in the future perfect tense. It isn't the plan that gives coherence to actions. . . It is the reflective glance, *not* the plan per se, that permits the act to be accomplished in an orderly way. A plan works because it can be referred *back* to analogous actions in the past, not because it accurately anticipates future contingencies. . . Actions never performed can hardly be made meaningful, since one has no idea what they are. They simply are performed and *then* made sensible; they *then* appear to be under the control of the plan. (Weick 1969, 102)

Organizations as Interpretation Systems

Weick, together with Daft, later introduced a model of organizations as interpretation systems.

> Organizations must make interpretations. Managers literally must wade into the swarm of events that constitute and surround the organization and actively try to impose some order on them. . . Interpretation is the process of translating these events, of developing models for understanding, of bringing out meaning, and of assembling conceptual schemes. (Weick and Daft 1983, 74)

What is being interpreted is the organization's external environment, and how the organization goes about its interpretation depends on how analysable it perceives the environment to be and how actively it intrudes into the environment to understand it. Whether the organization perceives that the environment is objective and that events and developments are analysable, or that the environment is subjective and essentially unanalysable, will affect its choice of interpretation mode. Furthermore, some organizations actively search the environment for answers and may also test or manipulate the environment, while others may just accept whatever information the environment gives them (Daft and Weick 1984, 287–88). The interpretation process itself varies according to the means for reducing equivocality, and the "assembly rules" that govern information-processing behaviour among managers. Equivocality is reduced by managers who extensively discuss ambiguous information cues and so arrive at a common interpretation of the external environment. Assembly rules are the procedures or guides that organizations use to process information into a collective interpretation.

Ambiguity and Choice in Organizations

James March, who collaborated with Simon in the early landmark work on decision making in organizations (March and Simon 1958), went on to develop theories that challenge the fundamental assumptions of the rational systems framework. March and his associates define their starting point as follows:

> We remain in the tradition of viewing organizational participants as problem-solvers and decision-makers. However, we assume that individuals find themselves in a more complex, less stable, and less understood world than that described by standard theories of organizational choice; they are placed in a world over which they often have only modest control. (March and Olsen 1976, 21)

They suggest viewing organizations as *organized anarchies* that are characterized by three features: the preferences used in making decisions are ill defined and inconsistent ("problematic preferences"); the processes by which the organization survives and produces are not understood by its members ("unclear technology"); and the involvement of participants changes from time to time ("fluid participation"). Under these conditions, the making of choices becomes especially ambiguous.

> Although organizations can often be viewed conveniently as vehicles for solving well-defined problems or structures within which conflict is resolved through bargaining, they also provide sets of procedures through which participants arrive at an interpretation of what they are doing and what they have done while in the process of doing it. From this point of view, an organization is a collection of choices looking for problems, issues and feelings looking for decision situations in which they might be aired, solutions looking for issues to which they might be the answer, and decision makers looking for work. (Cohen, March, and Olsen 1972, 2)

Furthermore, they model the decision-making situation or choice opportunity as a "garbage can into which various kinds of problems and solutions are dumped by participants as they are generated" (Cohen et al. 1972, 2–3). Which solutions are attached to which problems is a matter of chance, depending on which participants with what goals happen to be on the scene, when the solutions and problems are entered, and so on. A major feature of the garbage can process is the "partial decoupling" of problems and choices. Problems are worked upon in the context of some choice, but choices are made only when the shifting combinations of problems, solutions, and decision makers happen to make action possible. Although such a model of decision making may seem uncanny, it does produce decisions under highly uncertain conditions.[4] The garbage can process is not to be seen as an undesirable organizational dysfunction. By understanding the process, organizations can take account of its existence and, to some extent, manage it.

There is much that is in common between March's point of view and the organizing model of Weick. March agrees with Weick that actions often precede rather than follow goals, that human preferences are neither precise nor stable, and that these often have to be discovered. Weick argues that individuals enact the environment by a process in which they "construct, rearrange, single out, and demolish many 'objective' features of their surroundings" (Weick 1979, 164). March and his associates extend this concept with the notion of "attention structure" to describe the distribution of connections among individuals, the kinds of information they send and receive, the distribution of problems, and the rules about who is entitled to make choices about what is known (March and Olsen 1976, 40–41). Thus although individuals may enact their environment, they do this within an organizational structure that influences the types of information cues reaching them and sets constraints on their decisions and actions.

The Information Richness Model

Galbraith (1973, 1977) and Weick (1969, 1979) suggest respectively that an organization processes information in order to reduce task uncertainty and in order to reduce equivocality in the environmental information. Daft and Lengel (1984, 1986) propose an *information richness* model that integrates these two organizational information tasks. They extend Galbraith's model by stating that in processing information for internal coordination, the organization must both have sufficient information and reduce equivocality. These conditions are necessary because the departments of an organization are interdependent and at the same time differentiated. The amount of information needed between departments depends on their interdependence. The need to reduce equivocality arises because each department has developed its own functional specialization, goals, time horizons, language, and attitudes, the result being different frames of reference across the departments.[5] The way to reduce equivocality is for the organization to process rich information:

> Information richness is defined as the ability of information to change understanding within a time interval. Communication transactions that can overcome different frames of reference or clarify ambiguous issues to change understanding in a timely manner are considered rich. Communications that require a long time to enable understanding or that cannot overcome different perspectives are lower in richness. (Daft and Lengel 1986, 560)

The information media used in organizations determine the richness of information processed. Typical organizational information media may be arranged in order of decreasing information richness as follows: face-to-face meetings, telephone, written personal communications, written formal communications, and numeric formal reports. Face-to-face meetings are the richest information medium because they provide instant feedback, include multiple cues such as voice inflections and body gestures, add a personal touch, and use language variety. Numeric formal reports rank low in the scale because they lack all these qualities. Rich media enable people to interpret and reach agreement about difficult, unanalysable, emotional, and conflict-laden issues. Media of low richness are appropriate for the accurate and efficient transmission of unequivocal messages about the routine activities of the organization.

There are seven organizational structural mechanisms with varying capacities for reducing equivocality and for handling amounts of information to reduce task uncertainty. The least rich mechanism is the establishment of *rules and regulations*. They dictate a standard response to a known situation and play no part in reducing equivocality. *Formal information systems* include reports provided by computer-based information systems. They tend to report on defined and measurable aspects of the organization and do not help in reducing equivocality. *Special reports* or one-time studies and surveys are mainly used to obtain enough data to reduce uncertainty and are not important for reducing equivocality. *Planning* is at the middle of the scale because it involves both data processing and equivocality reduction: initial planning resolves ambiguity, while plans, schedules, and feedback provide data for uncertainty reduction. *Direct contact, integrators,* and *group meetings* provide increasing information richness, and they all use rich information media such as face-to-face meetings and personal means of communication.

Daft and Lengel also extend Weick's model of organizing as

processing information to reduce equivocality in the environmental information. They suggest that the information task of reducing equivocality is a function of hierarchical level. Top managers must confront ambiguous and conflicting cues about the environment, and then create and maintain a shared interpretation among themselves. They use rich media to discuss, analyse, and interpret the environment, and to develop goals and strategies for the organization. At the lower organizational levels, the activities of employees and first-line supervisors are governed by policies, rules and regulations, formal authority, and the physical requirements of the work technology. Because most of these are defined, interpretation is less equivocal, and information is processed through less rich media. The information richness model implies that the effective organization should balance its use of rich and less rich information mechanisms depending on the differentiation and interdependence of its subunits, and on the uncertainty and equivocality of its environment.

Summary

To summarize our survey of organization theories that view organizations as information-processing systems, we contrast the two perspectives that have framed our discussion—the decision-making view (Simon 1957, 1976), and the social enactment view (Weick 1969, 1979).

The decision-making perspective analyses organizations as rational decision-making systems. Unfortunately, the individual as decision maker is bounded by cognitive limitations. The task of organization design is thus to control the decision premises that guide the members' behaviours. Information is processed in order to reduce or avoid uncertainty. The organization sets its goals first then searches for alternatives, and selects courses of action which lead to goal attainment.

The enactment perspective analyses organizations as social, loosely coupled systems. Individual actors enact or create the environment to which the organization then adapts. The task of organizing is to develop a shared interpretation of the environment and then to act on the basis of this interpretation. Information is processed in order to reduce or resolve equivocality. Actions are often taken first and then interpreted retrospectively: in other words, action can precede goals.

Both perspectives offer valuable insights, and any attempt to understand and model the use of information in organizations will have to take into account the two points of view.

TOWARDS AN INFORMATION MODEL
OF THE ORGANIZATION

Although a unified theory of the organization as an information-processing system does not exist, the research that has been done suggests that the exploration of a number of issues would contribute towards an information model of the organization. In this section, we direct our attention at six such basic issues:

- The information processing requirements of organizations.
- The acquisition of information by organizations.
- Information processing behaviours of organizational participants.
- The nature of information in organizations.
- The use of information in organizations.
- The role of information technology in organizational information processing.

The Information-Processing Requirements of Organizations

Why do organizations process information? Our review of the organization theory provides two answers. Organizations process information to reduce uncertainty and to reduce equivocality. *Uncertainty* is the absence or lack of information: information that is needed to make decisions on the selection of an appropriate course of action, or information that is needed to perform tasks that involve coordination and problem solving. Organizations respond to uncertainty by searching for and acquiring a sufficient amount of information in order to make a choice or execute a task. *Equivocality* is the ambivalence in the information from the environment, information that is subject to multiple and conflicting interpretations. Organizations respond to equivocality by allowing their members to exchange information and opinions so as to collectively develop a common interpretation about environmental changes. Actions may then be taken based on the shared interpretation.

Galbraith (1973, 1977) discusses the need to process information in order to reduce uncertainty. Consider an organization that performs a fairly large and complex task that involves several interdependent subtasks, division of labour, and a high level of performance. A good deal of information must then be processed to coordinate the various interdependent activities. If the task itself is well understood, much of its execution can be preplanned. If the task is not understood, then during its execution more information and knowledge are acquired, which lead to changes in the task execution. In other words,

. . . the greater the task uncertainty, the greater the amount of information that must be processed among decision makers during task execution in order to achieve a given level of performance. (Galbraith 1973, 4)

Uncertainty is defined as the difference between the amount of information required to perform the task and the amount of information already possessed by the organization. The amount of information needed to perform a task is a function of the diversity of the outputs of the organization, the number of different input resources, and the level of goal or performance difficulty. A principal problem in organizing is therefore to design organization structures that would have the information-processing capability required to perform the task to the desired level of performance.

Daft and Lengel (1986) summarize three sources of uncertainty and equivocality that determine organizational information processing requirements: (task) technology; interdepartmental relations; and the environment. *Technology* comprises the knowledge, tools, and techniques used to transform inputs into organizational outputs. Following the typology of Perrow (1967), the technology is defined by two underlying task characteristics: task variety and task analysability. Task variety is the frequency of unexpected and novel events that occur in the conversion process. Task analysability is the extent to which the conversion process is analysable and can be controlled by set procedures or standard practices. Thus, in organizations that apply technology with high task variety and where the task is not analysable, large amounts of information are used to handle exceptions and rich information media are used to resolve unanalysable issues. In *interdepartmental relations*, it is the differentiation and interdependence of the departments that affect information requirements. Differentiation is the extent that each department has developed its own functional specialization, goals, frame of reference, time horizon, and language (Lawrence and Lorsch 1967). Interdependence is the extent to which departments depend on each other to accomplish their tasks (Thompson 1967). When the departments are highly differentiated and highly interdependent, large amounts of information would need to be processed and rich media would need to be used to resolve differences. In interpreting the *environment*, organizations assume the extent to which the cause-effect relationships in the external environment are analysable (Thompson 1967; Weick and Daft 1983), and then take up an active or passive policy in data collection (Weick and Daft 1983). When the environment is unanalysable and the organization is actively collecting data, large amounts of information are generated and rich media are needed to resolve equivocal cues.

At the individual level, the information-processing requirements of an organization's members are influenced by certain organizational properties. Structural and cultural features of the organizational setting can constrain the acquisition and processing of information by its participants. One of Simon's main arguments is that the organization influences its members' behaviours by controlling the *decision premises* upon which decisions are made (Simon 1976, 223). There are two categories of decision premises: one concerns establishing attitudes, habits, and a state of mind within the individual; and the other concerns imposing on the individual decisions reached elsewhere in the organization.

> The first type of influence operates by inculcating in the employee organizational loyalties and a concern with efficiency, and more generally by training him. The second type of influence depends primarily upon authority and upon advisory and informational services. (Simon 1976, 11)

The organizational properties that embody decision premises would include the organizational structure that defines authority positions, goals, and differentiation between departments; incentive systems that reward behaviours leading towards goal attainment; and group norms that become part of the individual's set of attitudes and values. This organizational context creates preferences and biases in the individual's acquisition of information: by influencing the availability or supply of information, the flow or distribution of information, the choice of information types and media, the setting of time constraints, and so on. It also creates preferences and biases in the individual's processing of information: by controlling the definition of goals, the formulation of rules and programs, the choice of preferred outcomes, the opportunities for sharing information, and so on. Both of these interactions are further discussed in the following subsections.

The Acquisition of Information by Organizations

In the study of organizational information processing, the topic of information acquisition has attracted much less attention, although its importance has been emphasized. For example, Nobel laureate Kenneth Arrow has pointed out that:

> Decisions, wherever taken, are a function of information received; then when information remains unchanged, no decision is made, or, to put

the matter in a slightly more precise way, the implicit decision is made not to change the values of certain variables. In turn, the acquisition of information must be analyzed, since it is itself the result of decisions. (Arrow 1974, 48)

Arrow goes on to make explicit the distinction between two kinds of decisions: decisions to act in some concrete sense, and decisions to collect information. Cyert and March (1963, 10) make a similar distinction between the need for a "theory of choice" and a "theory of search."

Decision makers in organizations are noticeably biased in their acquisition of information. They are biased by their own individual preferences as well as by the organizational contexts in which their information seeking takes place. For example, in the selection of information sources, a rational approach would be to use sources that are known to be of high quality. However, information user studies have found that it is the *accessibility* of the source that is the most important factor in source selection. Gertsberger and Allen (1968) found in their study of engineers that information channels that were considered more accessible were used first in the course of information search. When choosing among several information channels, the engineers seemed to apply a simplified form of the law of least effort: they picked channels that required the least average rate of probable work, but in so doing they did not consider future effort required in making decisions and the subsequent need to seek additional channels. O'Reilly (1982) in his study of welfare workers concluded that although decision makers recognized information sources of high quality, they used sources that provided lower-quality information but were more accessible. Similar findings have been reported in studies by Menzel and Katz (1955), Clausen (1973), and Culnan (1984). An explanation for the preference of accessible sources may be that significantly higher costs are involved in obtaining information from less accessible sources. Decision makers in organizations work under time constraints, have to divide their attention among several issues at a time, and are subject to frequent interruptions. Under these conditions, it may be that they are simply unable to seek out higher-quality information from less accessible sources.

Decision makers in organizations favour sources that they perceive as credible or *trustworthy*. Clausen (1973), for example, noted that congressmen frequently cast votes on legislation based more on the advice of a trusted colleague than on a personal understanding of the issue. In an organization, subunits may have conflicting interests and objectives, and they consequently become untrustworthy in terms of source credibility, even though a particular subunit may have the expertise and information required to make the decision.

Decision makers in organizations are also biased in their selection of information media. Many studies have shown that managers have a strong preference for oral, human sources of information rather than written or formal sources. Mintzberg found in his study of managers in five diverse corporations that verbal media (i.e., meetings, telephone calls, and tours) accounted for 78% of the managers' time and 67% of their activities (Mintzberg 1973, 38–39). Managers prefer face-to-face meetings and the telephone as information sources because they provide a high level of information *richness* the managers need to understand the social and hidden aspects of the problem, and to negotiate or persuade others with differing points of view (Daft and Lengel 1984, 1986).

Decision makers in organizations tend to prefer information sources that have a capacity to do what March and Simon call "uncertainty absorption":

> Uncertainty absorption takes place when inferences are drawn from a body of evidence and the inferences, instead of the evidence itself, are then communicated. The successive editing steps that transform data obtained from a set of questionnaires into printed statistical tables provide a simple example of uncertainty absorption. (March and Simon 1958, 165)

Unfortunately, through the process of uncertainty absorption, the recipient of such a communication is severely limited in the ability to judge its correctness; the decision maker relies on the confidence level in the source and the transformation process. Notwithstanding this, and mainly because of the heavy and competing demands on their time and attention, decision makers may choose sources that summarize voluminous detailed data, provide condensed treatments of complex issues, and supply the implications upon which courses of action may then be more speedily selected.

To recapitulate, when acquiring information, decision makers in organizations prefer sources which are accessible and trustworthy. They prefer sources that can provide rich information and absorb uncertainty. Rational selection criteria such as the quality of the source, or the expertise that the source has, are not important. Thus, the selection of information sources, channels, and media is strongly influenced by individual preferences as well as the biases that are formed as a result of the individual's participation in the organization.

Information-Processing Behaviours
of Organizational Participants

As our literature review suggests, this issue has been a recurrent motif
in the research on organizational information processing. The starting point is that individuals are subject to cognitive limitations so
that they behave with *bounded rationality* when making decisions:
they construct a simplified model of the complex real world based
on partial information, and they *satisfice* by looking for a course of
action that is "good enough" rather than the best possible (Simon
1957). Theories are then put forth on how these cognitive limits may
be overcome, largely through organizational structural mechanisms.

According to the "decision making" Carnegie school, the
information-processing model of organizational decision making is
characterized by these activities: sequential search ("one thing at
a time" approach), the activation of predefined action programs
(March and Simon 1958), the quasi resolution of conflict, and the
avoidance of uncertainty (Cyert and March 1963).

According to Weick's "enactment" model of organizing, organizational information processing takes place through three processes:
enactment, selection, and retention. During enactment, members create their own conceptual model of the environment. In selection,
members reduce equivocality by using past experience to make sense
of environmental changes. Finally, in retention, interpretations are
stored for future application (Weick 1969, 1979).

Mick, Lindsey, and Callahan (1980) adopt Weick's framework to
develop a model of information seeking in an organizational setting.
Using Weick's three stages of information processing, Mick et al. see
the *enactment* stage as establishing a context within which to view
information, which is then followed by the *selection* of information
inputs based on the enactment, and finally there is the *retention* of
those inputs that are judged as relevant to accomplishment of a specific task. They present a "generalized model of information seeking"
in which "a stimulus, generated within the context of a particular
situation which occurs within an environment and a set of attitudes,
generates an information need. A general plan of action is generated in response to this need, resulting in a specific action. Once the
specific action is performed, its results are evaluated and results of
the evaluation provide feedback to attitude and need (i.e., was the
need met?)" (Mick et al. 1980, 352).

Individual information processing may also be limited or biased
in other ways. Given that decision makers can cope with a relatively small amount of information, how are they to choose which in-

formation to process and use? The answer may be that organization members constrain their processing of information towards the attainment of preferred outcomes that are what they personally desire or what the organization has set as its goals. The organization provides clear signals about what these preferred outcomes are through its reward and incentive systems. In this scenario, organization members perform what O'Reilly (1983, 1987) calls "selective processing." Organization members may selectively process information that supports their preferred outcomes. They may process and present information in such a way as to bolster their own positions or put themselves in a favourable light. They may also process information so as to avoid undesirable consequences.

So far, we have seen how two sets of constraints can influence the use of information in organizations: the organization sets up goals, incentive systems, and norms; the individual exercises certain preferences for information sources and channels, and processes information in biased or limitedly rational ways.

The Nature of Information in Organizations

What is the nature of information used in organizations? To begin with, information is often partial, equivocal, and of variable richness. Organizational information is often partial or incomplete when it describes the real world for the purpose of problem solving. This brings the problem within the bounds of the decision maker's cognitive capacity to handle complexity. Organizational information is often equivocal: information stimuli come from several sources, and their interpretations are frequently ambiguous or conflicting. Organizational information varies substantially in richness and detail. Managers may prefer rich information media such as face-to-face communications, while shop-floor operators are given clear, concise instructions.

Land and Kennedy-McGregor (1981) propose a taxonomy of five organizational information types:

- Descriptive information describes the state and changes of the real world as well as the rules that govern or constrain the affairs of the real world.
- Probabilistic information constructs a model of the real world typically through a limited set of observations or measurements of the real world, and attempts to provide a model of the real world in the future on the basis of knowledge or statistical predictions.
- Explanatory and evaluative information explains why a real-world situation arose, and includes the norms, values, attitudes, and judgmental information used to explain and evaluate.

- Unexpected information is information that comes from an unanticipated source or information that was not at first seen to be relevant.
- Propaganda is information used to shape attitudes, beliefs, and behaviours.

Mintzberg (1979) proposes a functional view in which an organization consists of five groups of participants: workers at the operating core, middle-line managers, administrators at the strategic apex, analysts of the technostructure, and support staff. In the operatng core, the information resources used are simple and concrete, and relate directly to the task at hand. Middle managers are information transmitters and translators who collect and summarize raw data about the operating core to pass up to top administrators (cf., the "uncertainty absorption" process of March and Simon 1958). Top administrators need trend information from inside and outside the organization. Because they deal with broad, long-range problems, their information needs are fluid and their information resources are less predictable. The analysts of the technostructure (such as accountants and engineers) require specialized information in order to standardize outputs and work processes. Finally, the support staff engage in activities like research and development, public relations, and legal counsel, information-intensive activities that do not contribute directly to the attainment of task objectives.

Swanson (1978) proposes a "locus" for organizational information in which information is classified along three scales as being either inner- or other-directed; internally or externally produced; and self- or other-referencing. Information is inner-directed when it is employed for self-learning and internal management; it is other-directed when it is used for other influence and external propagation. Inner-directed information is "the stuff of decision making," while other-directed information is "the stuff of manipulation." Most organizational information is thought to be "two-faced"—that is, the product of inner- and other-directed needs taken together:

> But if decision making and manipulating are really the two sides of a single coin, i.e., two aspects of one organizational activity, then inner- and other-directed information must be similarly co-existent and non-separable. (Swanson 1978, 242)

In other words, organizational information exists in response to the organization's need to know and the organization's need to influence its environment.

Both the "decision making" school (Simon, March, Cyert) and the "enactment" school (Weick, Daft, March, Olsen) are concerned with the role of information in decision making and problem solving. From an information science perspective, MacMullin and Taylor (1984) identify a set of information traits that could be related directly to the dimensions of a problem. Information traits concern the need for information and refer to the processes and contexts for presenting information. Problem dimensions are those characteristics that go beyond specific subject matter, and set the criteria for assessing the relevance of information to specific problems. MacMullin and Taylor put forth two sets of eleven problem dimensions and nine information traits as follows:

Problem dimensions:
- design/discovery
- well-structured/ill-structured
- complex/simple
- specific/amorphous goals
- initial state understood/not understood
- assumptions agreed upon/not agreed upon
- assumptions explicit/not explicit
- familiar pattern/new pattern
- risk great/not great
- susceptible/not susceptible to empirical analysis
- internal/external imposition

Information traits:
- quantitative continuum
- data continuum (hard or soft data)
- temporal continuum (historical or forecasting
- solution continuum (single solution or options range)
- focus continuum (precision or diffusion)
- specificity of use continuum (applied or theoretical)
- substantive continuum (applied or descriptive
- aggregation continuum (clinical or census)
- causal or diagnostic continuum

The idea here is that by enumerating general sets of information traits and problem dimensions, it would then be possible to match particular information traits to particular problem types.

The Use of Information in Organizations

Organizations use information in order to make decisions, solve problems, or build up their knowledge base. Goldstein and Zack (1988) propose an information supply model that examines the effect of information supply and distribution on organizational information use, which in turn affects knowledge acquisition. *Information supply and distribution* here include the amount and type of data as well as the analytical tools that are made available. Thus, the dimensions of information supply would cover the availability of computer hardware (personal computers), software (databases, decision support tools), and the training and support needed to use them; the accessibility of data; the number and type of information sources; and the currency and reliability of the data. *Information use* is defined as the interpretation and analysis of information, which may be done with or without the help of analytical or decision support tools. The result of information use is *knowledge acquisition,* a process by which insights are gained into the relationship between the organization and its environment. Organizational information processing is driven by the organization's *information requirements.* These needs depend on their level of complexity and load, uncertainty, and equivocality. The model predicts that information use will increase with the supply and distribution of information, as well as its fit to the organization's information requirements. More information use will then lead to greater knowledge acquisition and a larger knowledge base.[6]

Organizations continually enact cycles of information gathering, interpretation, and learning or knowledge development. New information is both interpreted within the context of an existing *knowledge base,* and adds to that base. *Social factors* within the organization such as culture and power could also influence information-processing capabilities. Organizational culture as expressed through the values and attitudes of its members may affect the supply and use of information. Those in power could set decision-making agendas, control information resources, and impose meanings on ambiguous information. To sum up, the information supply model suggests that given some degree of fit between information supply and demand in the organization, the greater the amount of technology and resources allocated to information supply and distribution, the greater would be the level of information use and knowledge about the environment.

Although organization theory emphasizes the use of information for rational decision making, it is important to recognize that organizations also use information for reasons that do not make strict rational sense. Feldman and March (1981, 182) point out:

> Organizational participants seem to find value in information that has no great decision relevance. They gather information and do not use it. They ask for reports and do not read them. . . . information use symbolizes a commitment to rational choice. Displaying the symbol affirms the importance of this social value and signals personal and organizational competence.

Quite apart from actually using information to make rational decisions, the decision maker uses information as a *social symbol* of commitment to the principle of rational choice. The act of decision making is more important than the outcomes it produces. Decision making is an opportunity "for displaying authority, and for exhibiting proper behaviour and attitudes with respect to a central ideological construct of modern western civilization: the concept of intelligent choice" (Feldman and March 1981, 177).

Information may be used as a *political resource*. Since organizational goals and objectives are negotiated among groups of participants (Cyert and March 1963), it is unlikely that any allocation of resources will meet with general agreement. The divergence of goals and the contention for scarce resources make organizational decision making inherently a political process (Pfeffer and Salancik 1978), often marked by conflict and disagreement. The ability to use information to reduce the primary uncertainty that faces the organization can also be a source of organizational power. Hickson et al. (1971) suggest that such power may vary according to how critical the uncertainty is that the subunit can reduce, how effective the subunit is in reducing it, and how substitutable the function is that is served by the subunit. In general terms, when there is competition for resources, information may be used to support a position, to weaken an opposing one, or to justify decisions that have already been made. Pettigrew (1973) studied a large manufacturing organization and found a vivid example of how the ability to control information flow was used as a source of power. In the course of evaluating a large-scale capital investment decision, a senior manager who was positioned at the junction of the information flows between his subordinates, the vendors, and the company board "was able to exert biases in favour of his own demands and at the same time feed the board negative information about the demands of his opponents" (Pettigrew 1973, 232–40). Meltsner's study of policy analysts made the useful differentiation between two categories of information sought by decision makers: information used to *make* decisions and to *support* decisions that have already been made (1976, 72–79).

In an organization, information is not a homogeneous resource, but is exploited differently by the various participants. For some, it is the basis for decision making; for others it may be more a social symbol, a political resource, or a means to justify actions taken.

The Role of Information Technology in Organizational Information Processing

The possible interactions between information technology and organizational information processing are complex and multifarious, and we can only touch on a handful of issues that pertain to the present discussion.

1. Information technology may be used to reinforce and shape the decision premises of an organization. Simon (1976) argues that the organization influences its members not through the determination of individual decision outcomes, but through the determination of the decision premises upon which the decisions are based.[7] Information technology may be used to reinforce the decision premises in several ways. Information systems may be designed to function according to the steps and decision rules ensconced in standard operating procedures. For the system user, they may predefine a limited set of problem parameters or situation variables and constrain choice of action to a few alternatives. Information systems may also be used to regularly monitor, measure, and report on the performance of members in relation to objectives set by the organization. In addition, by controlling the collection, availability, and distribution of information, information systems can also shape what March and Olsen (1976, 40–41) call the "attention structure" of the organization. Pfeffer and Salancik (1978, 74) make a similar analysis:

> The information system is conceptualized as the reports, statistics, facts, or information that [is] regularly collected and their pattern of transmission through the organization. The fact that certain information is regularly collected focuses the organization's attention on it. The collection of certain information occupies the time and attention of the organization, which necessarily restricts the time and attention elsewhere.

2. Information technology may change the perception of information sources. Information technology may alter the information users' perception of sources available within the organization with regard to source accessibility, media richness, and the ability to absorb uncertainty. On source accessibility, information technology can blur the distinction between external and internal information sources. For example, CD-ROM drives will increasingly become standard fare with personal computers, and can be used to access very large amounts of data that are clearly supplied from "external" sources but that now appear to the user as a readily accessible "internal" information source. Similarly, the notion that information delivered by computers is by necessity low in information richness may have to be revised. Electronic mail has many characteristics similar to the telephone or written memos, because it provides for rapid feedback and can quickly reach a large, geographically dispersed audience. Rice and Love (1987) found that 30% of the total electronic message content in a cross-organizational study of medical professionals was used to express emotions. Video conferences have greater information capacity than the telephone, but are less rich than face-to-face contact. Undergoing trial use in a few organizations are various forms of computer-based support for meetings ("group decision support systems") that apply information technology in highly equivocal meeting situations. These systems seem to promise the best of both worlds: they support face-to-face discussion as well as provide access to hard information in databases. Information technology is also being used in systems that "absorb uncertainty" by automatically filtering and summarizing information from streams of incoming reports.

3. Information technology may be used to augment the information processing capacity of organizations. Information technology may be applied to enable an organization's members to cope with uncertainty, to process larger amounts of information, and in a more limited sense to help reduce equivocality in the information inputs. Information technology can help to manage complexity through the use of, for example, decision support systems that allow more variables to be analysed and related. Uncertainty may be reduced by using information technology to deliver data to where it is needed more efficiently and expeditiously. Information load can be lowered by using computer systems to filter, sort, route, or otherwise organize incoming information (Goldstein and Zack 1988). Equivocality can be reduced when managers use computer-based communication systems in conjunction with face-to-face interactions. An organization may set up elaborate procedures to give the appearance that information is processed in a highly traditional manner—Simon (1978) calls this "procedural rationality." Such procedures typically involve reporting, review, evaluation, and control activities in order to ensure, insofar as possible, that decision makers have complete information and are making their choices rationally. Information technology may again be used to support "procedural rationality": information systems may be implemented to supply the data and feedback required for planning and control.

4. Information technology may alter the organizational structures used to coordinate economic activity. According to Williamson (1975), organizations exist for the primary economic purpose of coordinating transactions, and they will adopt the organizational structure that lowers the costs of transactions. The two main structures are the market and the bureaucracy. The market structure coordinates the flow of goods and services through supply and demand forces. Transactions take place between many individuals and firms; buyers compare and choose from many sources; and market forces determine the design, price, quantity, and delivery schedules. In contrast, the hierarchy structure controls the flow of goods and services by directing it at a higher level in the managerial hierarchy: buyers buy from predetermined sources and managerial decisions determine design, price, and so on. Using this transaction cost framework, Malone et al. (1987) predict that information technology, by reducing the costs of coordination, will lead to an overall shift towards proportionately more use of markets rather than hierarchies to coordinate economic activity. Information technology enables three forces that drive this shift: a communication effect in which computers and telecommunications are used to transfer information, a brokerage effect in which many buyers and suppliers are connected through a central database that functions as a broker, and an integration effect in which information technology is used to tightly couple the processes that create and use information (as in, for example, "just in time" inventory systems). Already a number of examples of this shift toward electronic markets can be seen in the airline industry (ticketing systems), health care services (hospital supply systems), and financial services (home banking).

CONCLUSION

We may summarize our discussion as follows. An organization processes information in order to reduce uncertainty and to resolve equivocality in the informational inputs. Its information-processing requirements are determined by the task technology, environment, and organizational structure. Information is acquired and processed by the individual members. In acquiring information they exercise their own preferences as well as the biases that are formed as a result of their belonging in the organization. They selectively process information within the bounds of their cognitive limitations. The use of information in the organization pursues many purposes: information is used for decision making, as social symbol, and as power resource. Our discussion thus suggests a number of conceptual components that would need to be included in a theoretical model of information use in organizations, as shown in Figure 1.

Organizational research has to date employed the information-processing approach to analyse how an organization searches for alternatives and selects courses of action, to develop guiding principles for organization design, and to understand the processes by which an organization creates a shared interpretation of its environment. The emphasis of organization theory is on managerial decision making. There is rather less analysis on the nature and role of the information that sustains organizational activity: the various faces of organizational information, the seeking and acquisition of information, the modes and channels of information transformation, and the human and social purposes that information serves. There is insufficient knowledge about the behaviours of organizational members as information seekers and information users. This paper proposes that an information perspective that focuses on the use of information in organizations would enrich our understanding of organizational behaviour.

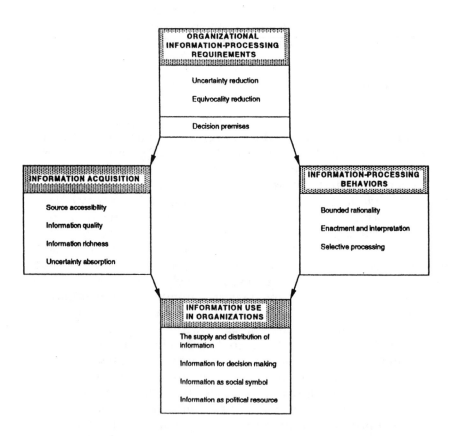

FIGURE 1.Elements of an information model of the organization

REFERENCES

Arrow, K. J. 1974. *The Limits of Organization.* New York: Norton.

Clausen, A. 1973. *How Congressmen Decide: A Policy Focus.* New York: St. Martin's Press.

Cohen, M. D., J. G. March, and J. P. Olsen. 1972. A garbage can model of organizational choice. *Administrative Science Quarterly* 17(March): 1–25.

Cyert, R. M., J. G. March, and J. P. Olsen. 1963. *A Behavioral Theory of the Firm.* Englewood Cliffs, NJ: Prentice Hall.

Daft, R. L., and R. H. Lengel. 1986. Organizational Information Requirements, Media Richness and Structural Design. *Management Science* 32(May): 554–571.

Daft, R. L., and R. H. Lengel. 1984. Information richness: A new approach to managerial information processing and organization design. In *Research in Organizational Behavior,* eds. B. M. Staw and L. L. Cummings. Greenwich, CT: JAI Press.

Daft, R. L., and K. E. Weick. 1984. Toward a model of organizations as interpretation systems. *Academy of Management Review* 9(2): 284–295.

Feldman, M., and J. G. March. 1981. Information in organizations as signal and symbol. *Administrative Science Quarterly* 26: 171–186.

Galbraith, J. 1973. *Designing Complex Organizations.* Reading, MA: Addison-Wesley.

Galbraith, J. 1977. *Organization Design.* Reading, MA: Addison-Wesley.

Gertsberger, P. G., and T. J. Allen. 1986. Criteria used by research and development engineers in the selection of an information source. *Journal of Applied Psychology* 52(4): 272–279.

Goldstein, D. K., and M. H. Zack. 1988. The Impact of Marketing Information Supply on Product Managers: An Organizational Information Processing Perspective. Proceedings of the 9th International Conference on Information Systems held in Minneapolis, Minnesota, November 30 to December 3, 1988.

Hickson, D., C. Hinings, C. Lee, R. Schneck, and J. Pennings. A strategic contingencies theory of intraorganizational power. *Administrative Science Quarterly* 16: 216–229.

Land, F. F., and M. Kennedy-McGregor. 1981. Effective Use of Internal Information. Proceedings of First European Workshop on Information Systems Teaching held at Aix-en-Provence, April 1981.

Larkey, P. D., and L. S. Sproull, eds. 1984. *Advances in Information Processing in Organizations.* Greenwich, CT: JAI Press.

Lawrence, P. R., and J. W. Lorsch. 1967. *Organization and Environment: Managing Differentiation and Integration.* Boston, MA: Graduate School of Business Administration, Harvard University.

MacMullin, S. E., and R. S. Taylor. 1984. Problem dimensions and information traits. *The Information Society* 3(1).

Malone, T. W., J. Yates, and R. I. Benjamin. 1987. Electronic markets and hierarchies. *Communications of the ACM* 30(6): 484–497.

March, J. G., and J. P. Olsen. 1976. *Ambiguity and Choice in Organizations*. Bergen, Norway: Universitetsforlaget.

March, J. G., and H. A. Simon. 1958. *Organizations*. New York: John Wiley.

Meltsner, A. J. 1976. *Policy Analysts in the Bureaucracy*. Berkeley, CA: University of California Press.

Menzel, H., and E. Katz. 1955. Social relations and innovation in the medical profession. *Public Opinion Quarterly* 19: 337–352.

Mick, C. K., G. N. Lindsey, and D. Callahan. 1980. Toward usable user studies. *Journal of the American Society of Information Science* 31(5): 347–356.

Mintzberg, H. 1979. *The Structuring of Organizations*. Englewood Cliffs, NJ: Prentice-Hall.

Mintzberg, H. 1973. *The Nature of Managerial Work*. New York: Harper & Row.

O'Reilly III, C.A. 1983. The use of information in organizational decision making: A model and some propositions. In *Research In Organizational Behavior*, vol. 5, eds. L.L. Cummings and B.M. Staw. Greenwich, CT: JAI Press.

O'Reilly III, C. A. 1982. Variations in decision makers' use of information sources: The impact of quality and accessibility of information. *Academy of Management Journal* 25(4): 756–771.

O'Reilly III, C. A., J. A. Chatman, and J. C. Anderson. 1987. Message flow and decision making. In *Handbook of Organizational Communication—An Interdisciplinary Perspective*, eds. F. M. Jablin et al. Newbury Park, CA: Sage.

Ouchi, W. G. 1981. *Theory Z*. Reading, MA: Addison-Wesley.

Ouchi, W. G. 1980. Markets, bureaucracies and clans. *Administrative Science Quarterly* 25(March): 129–141.

Perrow, C. 1967. A framework for comparative organizational analysis. *American Sociological Review* 32(2): 194–208.

Pettigrew, A. 1973. Information control as a power resource. *Sociology* 6: 172–204.

Pfeffer, J., and G. R. Salancik. 1978. *The External Control of Organizations*. New York: Harper & Row.

Pinfield, L. 1986. A field evaluation of perspectives on organizational decision making. *Administrative Science Quarterly* 31: 365–388.

Rice, R. E., and G. Love. 1987. Electronic emotion: Socio-emotional content in a computer-mediated network. *Communication Research* 15(1): 85–108.

Simon, H. A. 1978. Rationality as a process and as product of thought. *American Economic Review* 68: 1–16.

Simon, H. A. 1976. *Administrative Behavior*. 3rd ed. New York: Free Press.

Simon, H. A. 1957. *Models of Man—Social and Rational*. New York: John Wiley.

Swanson, E. B. 1987. Information channel disposition and use. *Decision Sciences* 18: 131–145.

Swanson, E. B. 1978. The two faces of organizational information. *Accounting Organizations and Society* 3(3/4): 237–246.

Thompson, J. D. 1967. *Organizations in Action—Social Science Bases of Administrative Theory*. New York: McGraw-Hill.

Weick, K. E. 1969. *The Social Psychology of Organizing*. Reading, MA: Addison-Wesley.

Weick, K. E., and R. L. Daft. 1983. The effectiveness of interpretation systems. In *Organization Effectiveness: A Comparison of Multiple Models*, eds. K. S. Cameron and D. A. Whetten. New York: Academic Press.

White, D. A. 1986. Information use and needs in manufacturing organizations: Organizational factors in information behavior. *International Journal of Information Management* 6(3): 157–170.

Williamson, O. E. 1981. The economics of organization: The transaction cost approach. *American Journal of Sociology* 87(Nov): 548–577.

Williamson, O. E. 1975. *Markets and Hierarchies: Analysis and Antitrust Implications*. New York: Free Press.

NOTES

1. March, who collaborated with Simon in their 1958 study of organizational behaviour, later went on to challenge the assumptions of the rational decision-making model.
2. Williamson uses "organizations" in a broader sense: organizations are any special arrangements within which transactions are conducted, and so include markets as well as firms and hierarchies.
3. The distinction between equivocality and uncertainty should be made clear. In a situation of uncertainty, managers are able to ask questions and obtain answers. Organizations respond to uncertainty by acquiring information and analysing data. In contrast, equivocality means ambiguity, the existence of multiple and conflicting interpretations about the organizational situation. Managers are not certain what questions to ask; and if questions are asked, there may be no data to answer them.
4. The garbage can model of decision making was based on seven studies of universities done in the early 1970s, mostly at the Copenhagen School of Economics and the University of Copenhagen. Cohen, March, and Olsen (1972, 11) observe that "University decision making frequently does not resolve problems. . . Active decision makers and problems track one another through a series of choice without appreciable progress in solving problems."
5. The concept of different frames of reference is similar to what Lawrence and Lorsch (1967) have described as "differentiation."
6. Empirical support for the model was provided by a comparative case study of product managers in two consumer goods companies that differed only in the dimension of interest, namely the approach to information supply and distribution. The company that had more data

and tools available for its product managers used more information and knew more about the factors affecting product marketing.

7. Pinfield's (1986) study of a decision process in the Canadian government bureaucracy showed that changes in the decision premises altered the nature of allocation decisions actually considered by the decision makers.

The Convergence of Management Attention upon Information: Lessons for Librarianship.

Marianne Broadbent and Michael Koenig

INTRODUCTION

An issue of some interest to librarianship, a field whose central interest is the handling of information, its storage, retrieval, and delivery, is the quite remarkable increase in attention in recent years paid to information and information technology by the general business literature.

It is important for the field of librarianship to be aware of this increased attention, and the reasons for it, for a number of reasons.

First, this increased attention, which is composed of a number of different threads, represents a large measure of very serious thinking some of it quite original, about information and information technology. Much of that analysis derives from a viewpoint quite orthogonal to traditional librarianship, and we have much to learn from it.

Second, library services are typically support services, and for us to perform effectively, it is crucial that we be conversant with the concepts, the thinking, and indeed the vocabulary of those who manage the institutions we support.

Third, much of that increased attention represents recognition of the importance of appropriate and intelligent use of information and information technology, a recognition of that is to a degree coextensive with the recognition of the utility and importance of librarianship.

Originally published in *IFLA Journal,* 15(3): 218–232, 1989 and also delivered as a paper during the 54th IFLA General Conference, Sydney, Australia, 30 August - 5 September 1988.

This article attempts to review and to analyze that literature, and to serve as a summary guide to it. [Note: a much more complete review by the same authors appears in the 1987 *Annual Review of Information Science and Technology.*]

The major components of this increased recognition of information technology are:

Strategic and Tactical Uses of Information Technology
- Competitive Advantage
- Markets Versus Hierarchies

Information and Strategic Decisions
- Evolution of MIS to DSS
- Recognition of the Importance of External Information
- Competitor Intelligence
- Decision Analysis

Design of Automated Information Systems
- Enterprise Information Analysis
- Data and Data Flow Driven Design

Information Resources Management

Information Operations Management
- Stage Hypotheses
- Convergence of the Archipelago

Information Technology and Organizational Structure

Information Technology and Productivity

The indentation in the list above suggests some quasi-hierarchical relationships. The list is also in effect a table of contents for this article.

STRATEGIC AND TACTICAL USES OF INFORMATION TECHNOLOGY

One major cluster of concerns is that which might be termed the use of information and information technology (frequently referred to as IT in the general business literature) for strategic and tactical operations. Early in the 1980s, Gerstein and Reisman (1982) identified the strategic potential of computer technology, but expressed some puzzlement at the under-utilization of data processing as a strategic resource. Shortly afterward the notion of using information technology for competitive advantage burst upon the business world.

Competitive Advantage

The concept of exploiting information technology to gain competitive advantage has been perhaps the single most emphasized topic in the general business and management literature concerning IT. To simplify greatly, literature may be said to have three central themes: 1) the securing of competitive advantage by reducing your own cost; 2) the creation of new value added services or capabilities; and 3) the creation of competitive advantage by reducing your suppliers' or customers' costs in a fashion that would increase their costs if they were to transfer their business to a competitor, that is by creating an efficiency based barrier to competition. The first and second points are relatively straightforward. The third point is more subtle. The now classic example of such use of information technology is that of a hospital supply company which provided microcomputers, modems, and inventory control software to its customers. Included was the capability, when triggered by the inventory control software, to reorder electronically (EDI) from that hospital supply company, but not of course from its competitors, for whom the customers would still have to spend time and money typing out orders by hand. Thus was created a customer efficiency based barrier to competition, an advantage entirely enabled by imaginative use of information technology (Parsons 1983).

The most frequently commented upon and the most visible articles have been those of Porter (1985, 1987), Porter and Millar (1985) and Parsons (1983). Good summaries and comments on this area can be found in works by Munro and Huff (1985), and Earl and Runge (1987).

Markets versus Hierarchies

At the same time that it is being recognized that information technology can be used to change the way organizations compete (McFarlan and McKenney 1983), it is also being recognized that a major long term consequence of the new information technology is decreased cost of information and of coordination. This it is increasingly being argued (Malone, Yates, Benjamin 1987) will tend to lead to proportionally more use of markets rather than of hierarchies for the coordination of economic activity.

Markets coordinate economic activity through the aggregated effect of individual transactions between individuals and firms. Hierarchies coordinate economic activity through higher level managerial decision making. In reality there are of course numerous variants and hybrids, and all economic operations are somewhere on the spectrum between pure market and pure hierarchy.

The central thesis then is that the increasing capability of information technology is driving economic activity toward the market end of the spectrum, and towards greater competition. The present international wave of demonopolization and privatization, which can in large measure be described as just such a shift in the balance between hierarchy and markets, coincides neatly with the growth of real time capability of electronic information systems.

INFORMATION AND STRATEGIC DECISIONS

Another cluster of concerns has in common the concern for the use of information and information technology in strategic decision making. The classic early work in this tradition was that of King and Cleland (1975, 1977), who were forerunners in recognizing the interrelationship of information systems, organizational structures, and strategic decision making. In the same tradition, Millar (1984) used case study material to emphasize the point that an information structure should be developed in accord with corporate management's selections and definition of strategic success factors. A key notion in contemporary business literature is that of "critical success factors" (Rockart 1982), the notion of identifying the key factors which an enterprise must do well to be successful, and then focusing management attention there. Much of the literature reviewed in this article assumes a knowledge of and builds upon that concept. Millar (1984) pointed out that one of the major difficulties in developing an appropriate information structure is that no one person is responsible for information and suggested the appointment of a chief information officer to oversee the merger of strategic planning and information processing.

The Evolution of MIS to DSS

Within the operational business information systems literature a major focus has been the transition from MIS, Management Information Systems, to DSS, Decision Support Systems. There have been charges that DSS is simply old wine in a new bottle, simply a response to the basic marketing precept that if one reintroduces a product that was a failure previously, one gives it a new name for its reintroduction; and there is probably some validity to that charge. In fact, DSS has not replaced MIS in operational terminology, and as a term, it is now rapidly disappearing in favor of AI (Artificial Intelligence).

Nevertheless, the DSS phenomenon did generate attention, and it did reflect some genuine changes in perspective. First, it recognized that the more strategic and truly managerial, the greater the reliance upon exogenous rather than endogenous information (Senn 1978; Synnott 1987; Hurtubise 1984; Holmes 1985; Koenig 1986a).

Second, it recognized that the system must conform to the culture and the expectations of the intended users, in particular the recognition that managers are not used to being told how to do their job, but rather what to accomplish. Third, it recognized the necessity that systems need to be used friendly, a somewhat belated recognition of Mooer's law (Mooers' 1959), that an information system will be used only if it is more trouble not to use it than it is to use it. There has been increasing recognition that MIS systems were not being used in the proactive fashion that their designers had in mind, but that the typical use of an MIS system by a manager is defensive rather than proactive (Alter 1976). A major part of the DSS philosophy was to design systems that would be sufficiently attractive for managers to use.

Recognition of External Information

At least as far back as Anthony's now classic taxonomy of managerial functions (1965) there has been a recognition of the importance of external or exogenous information to strategic decision making. Again, King and Cleland (1975, 1977) were in the lead in emphasizing the importance of external information.

The failure of MIS systems to meet expectations, and the consequent reexamination of the assumptions on which they were based has resulted in a greater awareness of the importance of external information. Holmes (1985) and Koenig (1986a) contend that in fact the principal cause of the disenchantment that arose with MIS systems in the late 1960s and 1970s was the failure to appreciate the role of external information in managerial decision making, and that many of the concerns and misgivings expressed about MIS systems (Ackhoff 1967; Dearden 1972) while not incorrect, were not focusing on the most appropriate target, the limitation of most MIS systems to data generated from internal operations and their accompanying failure to provide access to appropriate external data.

COMPETITOR INTELLIGENCE

Another thread in this cluster is that of competitor intelligence, which has produced a small flurry of recent publications, much of it stressing the necessity of good competitor and environmental intelligence for successful strategic decision making. Perelman (1983) saw business intelligence as the industrial equivalent of military intelligence and an essential input for strategic management. *Business Competitor Intelligence* (Sammon, Kurland, and Spitalnic, 1984) and *Com-*

petitor Intelligence: How to Get It, How to Use It? (Fuld 1985) both provide recent examples of rising interest in sources of external information of strategic concern to organizations.

Decision Analysis

Another development focusing attention on the relationship between access to information and strategic planning has been the development of decision analysis by the Rand Corporation (Milliken and Morrison 1973; Menke 1979). The basic notion of decision analysis is that one can estimate what the chance is that even though what has been selected is the alternative that is statistically the most likely to be the correct one, another alternative would in fact have turned out to be better. The expected value of that outcome times its probability is the EVPI, the expected value of perfect information, or less memorably but more descriptively, the expected cost of making a decision based on incomplete information.

From that concept follows the notion that at any decision point an alternative to be considered is to gather more information and then return to the decision point, and other factors being equal, that alternative should be pursued if the cost of gathering more information is less than the reduction of the EVPI which will be accomplished. In practice, EVPI calculations are not widely used, primarily because of their complexity. None the less, the argument that there is an EVPI and that an alternative that should always be explicitly examined is to recycle and gather more information, is an argument that has served to create a greater awareness not only of the information dependency of strategic decision, but of the importance of explicit attention to the information acquisition process.

DESIGN OF AUTOMATED INFORMATION SYSTEMS

The design of automated information systems represents another cluster of concerns. Concern for the effectiveness of the design process goes back to the classic Management Misinformation Systems article of Ackoff (1967), in which he pointed out a number of erroneous assumptions. The growing recognition that information systems must reflect the context of the organization which they are designed to support is best exemplified by the work of Keen and Scott Morton (1978).

Keen (1981) in another major contribution stresses the pluralistic nature of organizations, and highlights the political nature of information systems development. Keen's work is particularly useful because it articulates many of the reasons for resistance to information systems implementation. For example, it had long been recognized that clerical systems such as word processing provided better data for evaluation of personnel, and concern about that evaluation catalyzed resistance, but Keen was the first to stress that higher level information systems were inherently evaluative as well, and that also represented a major source of resistance. For librarians, now increasingly applying their skills to domains beyond traditional librarianship, and who come from a culture that assumes, generally correctly in that context, that more and better services will be welcomed, this is a rude but necessary shock which must be taken into account.

Enterprise Information Analysis

IBM has long been concerned with the successful planning of information systems, and in conveying that skill to its customers. IBM's interest is not entirely altruistic, if it can educate its customers as to how to anticipate and plan their information systems needs in a more effective and timely fashion, then those customers are likely to be able to purchase those system enhancements and up-grades from IBM sooner.

For some years, IBM has taught information systems planning as a package of techniques that they have labeled BSP, Business Systems Planning. Recently, IBM has extended their BSP package and relabelled it as "Enterprise Information Analysis," or sometimes simply "Enterprise Analysis." The concept of enterprise analysis is fundamentally simply the concatenation of Rockart's (1982) critical success factors with the BSP methodology (Parker 1982,1985). The result is that it takes a top down approach and implementation commences with senior management. The first three steps of enterprise information analysis as defined by IBM, are:

- Determine what your *Enterprise* is.
- Determine what *Decisions* must be made correctly to be successful in that enterprise.
- Determine what *Information* is needed to make those decisions correctly.

The fashion with which this places access to the right information as a fundamental concern for senior management is marvelously elegant, lucid, and almost unarguable. The result of course is a very much heightened management awareness of the importance of information, information technology, and information services.

Data and Data Flow Driven Design

A major recent development in systems development has been that of data driven systems design (Demarco 1979), also referred to as structured analysis (Gane and Sarson 1979), and as data flow analysis. The central notion of data design systems design is that the structuring of system development efforts is or should be based primarily on the flow of data within the system and only secondarily upon the logic of the functions performed (the basis of the traditional logical flowchart).

Programme reliability, programme maintainability, and the division of a programming effort into components that would allow a large system to be built rapidly are all major system development management concerns, and it was recognized early on that a key, perhaps the key, to addressing those concerns was program modularity. Collectively the systems design philosophy that arose from those concerns was known as structured programming (Djikstra 1968; Dahl et al., 1972; Whitehouse 1980). While much of structured programming focuses on the structure of the code itself, particularly the internal structure of the code and the avoidance of the "GO TO" statement, and upon adequate documentation (Jackson 1974), a principal thrust however remained modularity. The classic and the most accessible discussion of that concern remains Brookes (1975) *The Mythical Man Month.*

What increasingly came to be recognized is that the logical delimitation of modularity is the data that is passed between modules. Before two programmers can develop two modules in parallel, they must agree on what data will pass between them. From this realization there quickly developed structured analysis or data flow analysis methodology (Demarco 1979; Weinberg 1980).

Two different conventions for representing and analyzing data flow arose, known as Yourdon, or as Gane and Sarson after their principal proponents (Yourdon 1975; Yourdon and Constantine 1979; Gane and Sarson 1979; Martin and McClure 1985), but the conventions effectively differ only in their method of presentation. The basic philosophy is simply that the first major step in attacking a system design process is to analyze that data or information flow in a top down fashion. From this data flow analysis both the system programme modules and the required system data stores are derived directly. The consequence of this development has been a greatly increased awareness of the centrality of the information itself to the system design process, principally among MIS/DP staff, but that awareness has percolated up as well.

INFORMATION RESOURCES MANAGEMENT

Another thread that should be mentioned is that of Information Resources Management, though admittedly it has received relatively little attention in the general business and management literature.

In the 1970s and 1980s Horton (Horton 1974, 1979, 1981; Horton and Marchand 1982) developed the concept of Information Resources Management (IRM) to depict the notion of managing both the information resource (content) and information resources (tools) of an enterprise. The evolution of the IRM concept was an outcome to the United States Commission on Federal Paperwork, which ran from 1975 to 1977. As Director of the Commission's Information Management study, Horton articulated the need for "efficient, effective, and economical management of the organization's information and information resources" (Horton 1981). This approach sought to formalize the treatment of information and deal with data as a manageable and budgetable resource, in the same way that organizations must deal with human, physical, financial, and natural resources (Horton and Marchand 1982). During the 1970s and early 1980s there were some parallel developments in other countries including Canada and Australia (Broadbent and McIntyre 1983).

The other major contributor to IRM was Marchand (1983,1985) who identified Information Management in two dimensions: "management of data resources" and "management of the information processes". The latter has to do with the interaction of the organization with the data resources and supporting technology for decision making and analytical purposes. This emphasis in this dimension was on the *value* of resources that were used in the organization. Marchand also developed a stage hypothesis of information systems development which is discussed below.

INFORMATION OPERATIONS MANAGEMENT

As information management, in its various guises, becomes an increasingly larger part of an organization's questions, the management of those operations has correspondingly assured greater importance in the management literature. Strassman's (1985) work which focuses on the cost control of information operations is the most obvious example of that concern. A sub theme within that concern is that of the reduction of unallocated cost, which Koenig (1987) argues is a major, and often overlooked, force behind the increasing tendency to place libraries and information centres on a cost recovery basis. Within the larger theme, are a number of important sub-themes.

Stage Hypothesis

A major concern, driven in large part by the increasing proportions of organizational resources devoted to information systems, and some very genuine doubts as to whether value for money is being received, is that of how we can predict the future course and hopefully some of the consequences of the introduction of information systems. To that end, a number of stage hypotheses concerning information systems and information technology have arisen.

The first, and still the best known and arguably the most influential of these has been Nolan's stage hypothesis which attempts to describe the life cycle of systems and of individual technologies such as word processing or CD-ROM. The Nolan hypothesis was first set forth as four stages (Nolan 1973; Nolan and Gibson 1973) and later expanded to six stages (Nolan 1979). Those six stages are: Initiation, Contagion, Control, Integration, Data Administration, and Maturity. Perhaps the most commented upon ramification of the Nolan stage hypothesis is that ideally different stages should be met with different management strategies, looser in the initiation and contagion stages and tighter in the control and integration stages. That point has been expanded upon in particular by Lucas (1986) and by McFarlan (1983) who reshapes, relabels, and returns the Nolan stage hypothesis to four stages: 1) identification and initial investment, 2) experimentation and learning, 3) control, and 4) widespread technology transfer. Implicit in the Nolan and McFarlan cycles is a shift in emphasis from management of the technology to management of the data or information conveyed by that technology. There have been criticisms of the Nolan hypothesis to be sure, particularly as to the extent and generality of its applicability (King and Kraemer 1984; Sullivan 1985), but it has received wide recognition in the data processing community, and substantial recognition in the general management arena as well.

Subsequently, there have been several proposed stage hypotheses which address the growth and impact of information technology broadly over time, as opposed to the notion of repetitive and distinct life cycles for different technologies and different systems. The first of these, was that of Marchand (1983, 1985), who working primarily in the IRM, Information Resources Management, tradition, postulated a descriptive four stage development cycle of information management. The first stage (1900–1950) is Physical Control, the second (1960s–mid 1970s) Management of Automated Technology, the third (mid 1970s–1980s) Information Resources Management, and the fourth (late 1980s–1990s) Knowledge Management. Marchand's stages proceed from supporting lower concern with technology, the carrier, to concern with contents.

Shortly afterward, but apparently quite independently Rockart (1984) characterized three eras of information processing, the First Era—Clerical and Accounting, the Second Era—Operational, and the Third Era—Managerial. Rockart's characterization, which owes something to Anthony's taxonomy of managerial functions, is just that, a characterization. Gibson and Jackson (1987) however have taken the three eras, and fleshed them out into what they refer to as domains, derived from a benefit/beneficiary matrix (Figure 1 below).

Beneficiary Benefit	Individual	Functional Unit	Organization
Efficiency	Stage II	Stage I	Stage III
Effectiveness	Stage II	Stage I	Stage III
Transformation	Stage III	Stage III	Stage III

Figure 1. Gibson and Jackson Benefit/Beneficiary Matrix

Domain I they describe as the automation of traditional back office operations, yielding benefits to the functional unit, at first greater efficiency and then improved effectiveness. Domain II, which came about with the advent of the minicomputer, followed shortly by the microcomputer, resulted in greater efficiency and effectiveness particularly for end-user computing. Now, they maintain we are entering the third domain which will result in greater efficiency and effectiveness for the organization, and the transformation of jobs, functions, and roles at all levels—individual, functional unit, and organizational.

A third stage hypothesis has been posited by Koenig (1986a, 1986b). The origin of this stage hypothesis is quite orthogonal to those of Rockart, Gibson and Jackson, and Marchand. It derives from a pair of observations: 1) that the doubling periods of information technology tend to be very brief, on the order of a year or two, a phenomenon known as Moore's Law (Noyce 1977), and 2) that there are three fundamental components of information systems: computation, storage, and communication (Sullivan 1985). An analysis of those components in terms of their growth rates, argues Koenig, leads to three stages: Stage 1 (pre 1971) characterized by exponential Moore's Law growth of computational capability, and relative stasis in storage and communication, Stage II (1971–1989?) characterized by exponential growth of computation and storage and relative stasis in communication, and Stage III (post 1989?) characterized by exponential growth of all three components. These stages it is argued not only have predictive utility, but they also have important ramifications for the robustness of system design, system management, and system obsolescence. Like Nolan, Koenig has extended his stage hypothesis, in this case adding a fourth stage derived from Mooers' Law (Mooers 1959). This fourth stage will be ushered in by the achievement of continuous speech recognition (Koenig 1987a).

What is striking is the commonality of the three stage hypotheses Rockart/Gibson and Jackson, Marchand, and Koenig, particularly when they are graphically set out side by side, as in Figure 2 below.

All three hypotheses place us now at very much the same point of development, leaving the second stage of automated information systems development and entering the third stage. The commonality of that conclusion, the support that the stage hypothesis lend to each other, gives us rather more confidence that we really are in the process of moving from one stage to another, a new stage which really will be qualitatively different from what we have experienced in the last decade or so.

The Convergence and Integration of the Archipelago

Another major concern has been the management ramifications caused by the convergence of different information services, systems, and technologies in the organization. This is of course a logical subset of the larger convergence phenomenon, computers and telecommunications becoming for all intents and purposes one industry, which has received great attention in the press. What with the divestiture of AT & T, the privitization and opening to competition of hereto-fore single source PTT operations, and the steady stream of mergers and acquisitions across what were different industries, convergence is a buzz-word everywhere. Accompanying that awareness of the convergence phenomenon has come the recognition that as the various information technologies converge, so too do the managerial implications and requirements converge.

Marchand Stages (1983)	Rockart Eras (1984)	Gibson & Jackson Domains (1987)	Koenig Stages (1985)	
Stage 1 Management of Automated Technology	First Era Clerical & Accounting	First Domain Efficiency and Effectiveness of Unit Operations	Stage I Exponential Growth of Computation Stasis in Storage & Communication	T I M E
Stage 2 Information Resources Management	Second Era Operational	Second Domain Efficiency and Effectiveness of Individual Operations	Stage II Exponential Growth of Computation & Storage Stasis in Communication	
Stage 3 Knowledge Management	Third Era Managerial	Third Domain Efficiency and Effectiveness of the Organization & Transformation	Stage III Exponential Growth of Computation & Storage & Communcation	
			Stage IV Exponential Growth of Computation & Storage & Communication plus Continuous Speech Recognition	

Figure 2. Comparison of Development Stage Hypotheses for Information Management (◄──► = Roughly the Present Time)

Note: We have taken the liberty of excluding Marchand's first stage (Physical Control, 1900-1950s) as out of scope - pre-computer, and renumbering the other three stages.

The principal interpreters of this concern have been McFarlan and McKenney in their trilogy of articles in the *Harvard Business Review* about the "Archipelago of Information Services" (McKenney and McFarlan 1982; McFarlan 1983a, 1983b). Indeed the term "archipelago" has become standard shorthand for the issue. McFarlan and McKenney raise two principal points. The first derives from the circumstance that the different islands in the archipelago are typically spread across the organization, with, in a typical organization, data processing reporting to the chief financial office, telecommunications to the vice president for administration, the libraries (overlooked somehow by McFarlan and McKenney) to the vice president for R & D, etc. This great organizational dispersion of the islands of the information archipelago means that the accomplishment of convergence or coordination is a major managerial task, requiring either a substantial change in the organizational structure with many, including some very senior, toes stepped upon, or a complex and cumbersome cross organizational matrix-like arrangement, or some combination of both. The second point is that the islands of the information archipelago are almost certainly at different points along the Nolan life cycle discussed above and therefore need different managerial approaches, and this too adds to the difficulty of centralized and coordinated management.

INFORMATION TECHNOLOGY AND ORGANIZATIONAL STRUCTURE

Concern for the effect of information technology on organizational structure has been a topic of concern since the 1960s. The classic work in the field is that of Thomas Whisler who predicted that organizations would become more horizontal, with fewer layers of middle management and fewer professional jobs (Whisler 1970). Strassman (1985) makes the same point about information structures. Francis (1986) however, after analyzing a number of cases, argues that the effects upon corporate structure of the introduction of new information technology are primarily a function of what management intends to accomplish, and are only secondarily driven by the technology itself, and that there seems to be no consistent pattern toward flatter structures. Brophy (1985) has pointed out that in many cases, in particular the insurance industry, the typical consequence is to increase the ratio of professionals to non-professional staff, a result quite opposite in direction to that predicted by Whisler.

More recent work tends to eschew generalization and focus upon specific contexts, and centers around the realization that much "traditional" organizational structure derives from the requirement to structure job domain, functions, and even whole departments around the availability of information. Any central file operation is an example of that necessity. Information technology however is increasingly providing the capability to place the information where the user is, rather than require the user to go or to be where the information is (Keen 1981). The consequence of this is that information technology enables rather major changes in the structure of organizations, and this capability and its consequences demand management attention (Koenig 1986a).

The larger point that is increasingly being recognized is that whether predictable or not, and despite the fact that telecommunicating was over-hyped, information technology is changing management structures in major ways.

INFORMATION TECHNOLOGY AND PRODUCTIVITY

A major concern in business today is productivity, and one of the major, perhaps the major, component of that concern is the relationship between information technology and productivity. Most of what is written consists simply of anecdotal examples and hortatory charges to work smarter. It is difficult however to write more substantively because of the difficulties of measuring white collar productivity. There is also undeniable skepticism, expressed well by Schneider (1987) about the impact of information technology. To a degree of course that skepticism serves to enhance managerial concern for and attention to the appropriate implementation of information technology.

On the whole, the argument that there is a positive relationship between information technology and productivity and national competitiveness is taken for granted. In both the United Kingdom and France, major social changes have taken place as a result of that perception. In the United Kingdom, the Beesley report (1981) recommended the demonopolization of telecommunications primarily because of perceived enhanced international competitiveness. In France, the Minitel system which is having a profound effect upon French society (Delacy 1987) is a direct result of the Nora-Minc report (Nora and Minc 1978, 1980) which recommended increased government support of information technology to preserve and enhance France's economic position and its cultural identity. Japan has targeted information as essential to its continued economic growth. Both Europe and the United States have responded with programmes to support information technology.

In short, despite the lack of quantitative evidence about the nature of the relationship, there is a strong belief that the development of information technology is essential for increased productivity and competitiveness, and this belief, coupled with heightened concern for productivity and competitiveness in the world market has served to dramatically focus attention on information technology and the application of that technology.

SUMMARY

There are now many different issues and concerns merging in the area of management of information and information technology, all serving to focus management attention upon information and information technology. In this article, those components have been grouped together in a quasi-hierarchical fashion. If they were to be ordered by rank, in order of management attention, the order might be something like:

- Competitive advantage
- Managing the archipelago of information services
- Information enterprise analysis
- Information technology and productivity
- The remainder

The sum effect of all those components is substantial, and as a consequence management is paying attention to information and information technology as never before.

An old saying is "know your enemy" a more useful one with which we might hope to replace it is "know your potential allies," know their concerns, know their language, and we will be in a far better position to work cooperatively, to create services and systems that enhance our organizations, and to gain management support.

REFERENCES

Ackoff, R. L. 1967. Management misinformation sstems. *Management Science* 14(4): 147-156.

Alter, S. L. 1976. How effective managers use information systems. *Harvard Business Review* 54(6): 97-104.

Arthur, F. 1986. *New Technology at Work*. Oxford: Clarendon (Oxford University) Press.

Beesley, M. E. 1981. Liberalisation of the use of the British Telecommunication Network. Report to the Secretary of State, January 1, 1981. London: Her Majesty's Stationery Office.

Broadbent, M., and L. B. McIntyre. 1983. Information management: Promise and Reality. In *Automation Management: Proceedings of the Victoria Archives and Library Association VALA Second National Conference on Library Automation.* Melbourne, Australia: VALA.

Brophy, J. T. 1985. Presentation at the Conference Board's 3rd Annual Conference on New Opportunities in Management Information, New York, April 1985.

Brookes, Jr., F. P. 1975. *The Mythical Man Month: Essays on Software Engineering.* Reading, MA: Addison Wesley.

Dahl, O., E. Djikstra, and C. Hoare. 1972. *Structured Programming.* New York: Academic Press.

Dearden, J. 1972. MIS is a mirage. *Harvard Business Review* 50(1): 90-99.

Delacy, J. 1987. France: The sexy computer. *The Atlantic* 260(1): 18-26.

Demarco, T. 1979. *Structured Analysis and System Specification.* Englewood Cliffs, NJ: Prentice Hall.

Djikstra, E. W. 1968. Go to statement considered harmful. *Communications of the ACM* 11(3): 147-149.

Earl, M. J., and D. A. Runge. 1987. *Using Telecommunications-Based Information Systems for Competitive Advantage.* Oxford: Oxford Institute of Information Management.

Fuld, L. M. 1985. *Competitor Intelligence: How to Get It; How to Use It.* New York: Wiley.

Gane, C., and T. Sarson. 1979. *Structured Systems Analysis: Tools and Techniques.* Englewood Cliffs, NJ: Prentice Hall.

Gerstein, M., and H. Reisman. 1982. Creating competitive advantage with computer technology. *Journal of Business Strategy* 3(1): 53-60.

Gibson, C. F., and B. Bund Jackson. 1987. *The Information Imperative: Managing the Impact of Information Technology on Business and People.* Lexington, MA.: D.C. Heath.

Holmes, F. W. 1985. The information infrastructure and how to win with it. *Information Management Review* 1(2): 9-19.

Horton, F. W. 1981. *The Information Management Workbook: IRM Made Simple.* Washington, DC: Information Management Press.

Horton, F. W. 1979. *Information Resources Management: Concepts and Cases.* Cleveland, Ohio: Association for Systems Management.

Horton, F. W., and D. A. Marchand. 1982. *Information Management in Public Administration: An Introduction and Resource Guide to Government in the Information Age.* Arlington, VA: Information Resources Press.

Horton, F. W., and D. A. Marchand. 1974. *How to Harness Information Resources: A Systems Approach.* Cleveland, Ohio: Association for Systems Management.

Hurtubise, R. 1984. *Managing Information Systems, Concepts and Tools.* West Hartford, CT: Kumerian Press.

Keen, P. G. 1981. Information systems & organizational change. *Communications of the ACM* 24(1): 24-33.

Keen, P. G., and M. S. Scott Morton. 1978. *Decision Support Systems: An Organizational Perspective.* Reading, MA: Addison Wesley.

King, J. L., and K. L. Kraemer. 1984. Evolution and organizational information system: An assessment of Nolan's Stage Model. *Communications of the ACM* 27(5): 466–475.

King, W. R., and D. I. Cleland. 1977. Information for more effective strategic planning. *Long Range Planning* 10(1): 59–64.

King, W. R., and D. I. Cleland. 1975. The design of management information systems: An information analysis approach. *Management Science* 22(3): 286–297.

Koenig, M. E. 1987a. The convergence of Moore's/Mooers laws. *Information Processing and Management* 23(6): 583–592.

Koenig, M. E. 1987b. Fiscal accountability and the principle of minimum unspring weight. *The Bottom Line* 1(1): 18–22.

Koenig, M. E. 1986a. The Convergence of computers and telecommunications: Information management implications. *Information Management Review* 1(3): 23–30.

Koenig, M. E. 1986b. Stage III of information systems technology. In *Intelligent Information Systems For the Information Society*. A collection of papers presented at the Sixth International Research Forum on Information Science held at Frascati, Italy, September 1985, ed. B. C. Brookes. Amsterdam: Elsevier Science.

Lucas, Jr., H. C. 1986. Utilizing information technology, guidelines for managers. *Sloan Management Review* 28(1): 39–47.

Malone, T. W., J. Yates, and R. I. Benjamin. 1987. Electronic markets and electronic hierarchies. *Communications of the ACM* 30(6): 484–496.

Marchand, D. A. 1985. Information management: Strategies and tools in transition? *Information Management Review* 1(1): 27–34.

Marchand, D. A. 1983. Strategies and tools in transition. *Business and Economic Review* 29(5): 4–8.

Martin, J., and C. McClure. 1985. *Diagramming Techniques for Analysts and Programmers*. Englewood Cliffs, NJ: Prentice Hall.

McFarlan, F. W., and J. L. McKenney. 1983. The information archipelago—governing the New World. *Harvard Business Review* 61(4): 91–99.

McFarlan, F. W., J. L. McKenney, and P. Pyburn. 1983. The information archipelago—plotting a course. *Harvard Business Review* 61(1): 145–146.

McKenney, J. L., and F. W. McFarlan. 1982. The information archipelago—maps & bridges. *Harvard Business Review* 60(5): 109–119.

Menke, M. M. 1979. Strategic planning in an age of uncertainty. *Long Range Planning* 12(4): 27–34.

Milliken, J. G., and E. J. Morrison. 1973. Management methods from aerospace. *Harvard Business Review* 51(2): 6–12.

Millar, V. E. 1984. Decision-oriented information. *Datamation* (January): 159–162.

Mooers, C. N. 1959. Mooers' law; Or why some retrieval systems are used and others are not. *Zator Technical Bulletin* 136, and editorial (same title), *American Documentation* 11(3): i(1960).

Munro, M. C., and S. L. Huff. 1985. Information technology and corporate strategy. *Business Quarterly* 50(2): 18–24.

Nolan, R. L. 1979. Managing the crises in data processing. *Harvard Business Review* 57(2): 115–126.

Nolan, R. L. 1973. Managing the computer resources: A stage hypothesis. *Communications of the ACM* 16(7): 399–405.

Nolan, R. L., and C. Gibson. 1973. Managing the four stages of EDP growth. *Harvard Business Review* 57(2): 76–83.

Noyce, R. N. 1977. Microelectronics. *Scientific American* 237(3): 62–69.

Parker, M. M. 1985. *Enterprise-Wide Information Management: Emerging Information Requirements.* Los Angeles, CA: IBM Corporation.

Parker, M. M. 1982. Enterprise information analysis: Cost-benefit analysis and data-managed system. *IBM Systems Journal* 21(1): 108–123.

Parsons, G. L. 1983. Information technology: A new competitive weapon. *Sloan Management Review* 25(1): 3–14.

Perelman, L. L. 1983. The value of business intelligence. *New Management* 1: 30–35.

Porter, M. E. 1987. From competitive advantage to corporate strategy. *Harvard Business Review* 87(3): 43–59.

Porter, M. E. 1985. *Competitive Advantage: Creating and Sustaining Superior Performance.* New York: Macmillan.

Porter, M. E., and V. E. Millar. 1985. How information gives you competitive advantage. *Harvard Business Review* 63(4): 149–160.

Rockart, J. F. 1982. The changing role of the information systems executive: A critical success factors perspective. *Sloan Management Review* 24(1): 3–13.

Rockart, J. F., and M. S. Scott Morton. 1984. Implications of changes in information technology for corporate strategy. *Interfaces* 14(1): 84–95.

Sammon, W. L., M. A. Kurland, and R. Spitalnic. 1984. *Business Competitor Intelligence: Methods for Collecting, Organizing and Using Information.* New York: Ronald Press.

Schneider, K. Services hurt by technology. June 29, 1987, Section D:1&6 *New York Times.*

Senn, J. A. 1978. *Information Systems in Management.* Belmont, CA: Wadsworth.

Simon, N., and A. Minc. 1980. *The Computerization of Society.* Cambridge, MA: MIT Press.

Simon, N., and A. Minc. 1978. *Rapport sur L'Information de la Societé.* Paris: Republic of France.

Strassman, P. A. 1985. *Information Payoff: The Transformation of Work in the Electronic Age.* London: Collier.

Sullivan, Jr., C. H. 1985. Systems planning in the information age. *Sloan Business Review* 26(2): 3–12.

Synnott, W. R. 1987. *The Information Weapon: Winning Customers and Markets with Technology.* New York: Wiley.

Weinberg, V. 1980. *Structured Analysis.* Englewood Cliffs, NJ: Prentice Hall.

Whisler, T. L. 1970. *Information Technology and Organizational Change*. Belmont, CA: Wadsworth.

Whitehouse, G. E. 1980. *Systems Analysis and Design Using Structured Techniques*. Englewood Cliffs, NJ: Prentice Hall.

Yourdon, E. 1975. *Techniques of Program Structure and Design*. Englewood Cliffs, NJ: Prentice Hall.

Yourdon, E., and L. L. Constantine. 1979. *Structured Design*. Englewood Cliffs, NJ: Prentice Hall.

Additional Readings
Part I: Information Models
of Organizations

Aldrich, H. E. 1979. *Organizations and Environments.* Englewood Cliffs, NJ: Prentice Hall.

Beer, S. 1981. *Brain of the Firm.* 2nd ed. New York: John Wiley.

Brunsson, N. 1985. *The Irrational Organization: Irrationality as a Basis for Organizational Action and Change.* Chichester, UK: John Wiley.

Cohen, M. D., J. G. March, and J. P. Olsen. 1972. A garbage can model of organizational choice. *Administrative Science Quarterly* 17(1): 1–25.

Connolly, T. 1977. Information processing and decision making in organizations. In *New Directions in Organizational Behavior,* eds. B. M. Staw and G. R. Salancik, 205–234. Chicago, IL: St. Clair Press.

Cyert, R. M., and J. G. March. 1992. *A Behavioral Theory of the Firm.* 2nd ed. Oxford, UK: Blackwell.

Daft, R. L., and K. E. Weick. 1984. Toward a model of organizations as interpretation systems. *Academy of Management Review* 9(2): 284–295.

Drucker, P. F. 1993. *Post-Capitalist Society.* New York: HarperCollins.

Feldman, M. S., and J. G. March. 1981. Information in organizations as signal and symbol. *Administrative Science Quarterly* 26(2): 171–186.

Forester, J. 1984. Bounded rationality and the politics of muddling through. *Public Administration Review* 44(1): 23–31.

Fulk, J. 1991. Emerging theories of communication in organizations. *Journal of Management* 17: 407–446.

Galbraith, J. R. 1973. *Designing Complex Organizations.* Reading, MA: Addison-Wesley.

Grosser, K. 1991. Human networks in organizational information processing. In *Annual Review of Information Science and Technology,* ed. M. E. Williams, 349–402. Medford, NJ: Learned Information.

Handy, C. 1990. *The Age of Unreason.* London, UK: Business Books.

Hannan, M. T., and J. Freeman. 1989. *Organizational Ecology.* Cambridge, MA: Harvard University Press.

Hedberg, B. 1981. How organizations learn and unlearn. In *Handbook of Organizational Design: Adapting Organizations to Their Environments,* eds. P. C. Nystrom and W. H. Starbuck, 3–27. New York: Oxford University Press.

Huber, G. P. 1991. Organisational learning: The contributing processes and literatures. *Organization Science* 1: 88-115.

Huber, G. P., and R. L. Daft. 1987. The Information Environments of Organizations. In *Handbook of Organizational Communication*, eds. F. M. Jablin, L. L. Putnam, K. H. Roberts, and L. W. Porter, 130-164. Newbury Park, CA: Sage Publications.

Lawrence, P. R., and J. W. Lorsch. 1967. *Organization and Environment: Managing Differentiation and Integration*. Boston, MA: Graduate School of Business Administration, Harvard University.

March, J. G. 1994. *A Primer on Decision Making: How Decisions Happen*. New York: Free Press.

March, J. G. 1991. How decisions happen in oganizations. *Human-Computer Interaction* 6(2): 95-117.

March, J. G., and H. A. Simon. 1992. *Organizations*. 2nd ed. Oxford, UK: Blackwell.

Marchand, D. A., and J. F. Horton, Jr. 1986. *Info Trends: Profiting from Your Information Resources*. New York: John Wiley and Sons.

Morgan, G. 1986. *Images of Organization*. Newbury Park, CA: Sage.

O'Reilly, III, C. A. 1983. The use of information in organizational decision making: A model and some propositions. In *Research in Organizational Behavior*, eds. B. M. Staw, and L. L. Cummings, 103-139. Greenwich, CT: JAI Press.

O'Reilly, III, C. A., J. A. Chatman, and J. C. Anderson. 1987. Message Flow and Decision Making. In *Handbook of Organizational Communication*, eds. F. M. Jablin, L. L. Putnam, K. M. Roberts, and L. W. Porter, 600-623. Newbury Park, CA: Sage.

Perrow, C. 1986. *Complex Organizations: A Critical Essay*. 3rd ed. New York: McGraw-Hill.

Pettigrew, A. M. 1973. *The Politics of Organizational Decision Making*. London, UK: Tavistock Institute.

Roberts, N., and D. Clarke. 1987. *The Treatment of Information Issues and Concepts in Management and Organizational Literatures*. Sheffield, UK: Consultancy and Research Unit, Department of Information Studies, University of Sheffield.

Senge, P. M. 1990. *The Fifth Discipline: The Art & Practice of the Learning Organization*. New York: Doubleday Currency.

Simon, H. A. 1976. *Administrative Behavior: A Study of Decision-Making Processes in Administrative Organization*. 3rd ed. New York: The Free Press.

Sproull, L., and S. Kiesler. 1991. *Connections: New Ways of Working in the Networked Organization*. Cambridge, MA: MIT Press.

Starbuck, W. H. 1983. Organizations as action generators. *American Sociological Review* 48: 92-102.

Stinchcombe, A. L. 1990. *Information and Organizations*. Berkeley, CA: University of California Press.

Thompson, J. D. 1967. *Organizations in Action: Social Science Bases of Administrative Theory*. New York: McGraw-Hill.

Tushman, M. L., and D. A. Nadler. 1978. Information processing as an integrating concept in organizational design. *Academy of Management Review* 3(3): 613–624.

Weick, K. E. 1993. The collapse of sensemaking in organizations: The Mann Gulch disaster. *Administrative Science Quarterly* 38(4): 628–652.

Weick, K. E. 1979. *The Social Psychology of Organizing.* 2nd ed. New York: Random House.

Wilensky, H. 1967. *Organisational Intelligence: Knowledge and Policy in Government and Industry.* New York: Basic Books.

Zey, M. (ed.). 1992. *Decision Making: Alternatives to Rational Choice Models.* Thousand Oaks, CA: Sage.

II
Understanding the Information Requirements of Organizations

II
Understanding the Information Requirements of Organizations

INTRODUCTION

Almost every single activity in an organization is so tightly bound with information seeking and information processing that it seems futile to try to unravel an underlying structure beneath the unruly mess of organizational information needs. Yet without such a structure for understanding organizational information requirements, information cannot be managed. Researchers have approached the problem of organizational information needs at three levels: the systems level, the user-group level, and the cognitive level.

At a systems level, an organization is composed of activities and processes that transform raw materials (both tangible and intangible) into goods and services of economic or social worth. Each component process takes in a package of informational as well as physical inputs, works on it and brings it a few steps closer to its final form by adding more energy, information, or materials. In fact, more and more organizations today are creating economic value by including more and better information in both their processes and outputs—information applied in the form of efficient yet flexible procedures, accurate knowledge about customer wants, well executed product designs, ease of use, greater service responsiveness, and so on. An overarching goal of analyzing organizational information requirements is therefore to determine what and how information and intelligence may be introduced into the organization's processes and output in order to maximize learning and value-adding.

Strictly speaking, organizations do not seek information. Information is sought by the various groups of people that make up the organization—accountants, clerks, engineers, managers, operators, and many others. The second level of analysis is to study these groups of participants, separated by their professional, work or social boundaries, as distinct groups of information users, each with its each own information needs, information seeking habits, and information processing styles. Differences in information behaviors may be due to many reasons. For example, accountants may differ from engineers as information users because of their professional education and apprenticeship. Clerks may have a different attitude towards information from managers because of their work-related constraints or demands. The study of professionally or socially defined groups of users has always been actively pursued in library and information science, and will continue to supply insights into the information needs of particular organizational groups.

Beyond groups of users, information is obtained and made use of by individuals acting as cognitive, sentient persons. They begin their information search with information needs that may range from being impossible to articulate to the highly specific. As they encounter information, their behavior often appears erratic: they change direction frequently depending on what they find, they choose items that have no apparent relevance, and they gather information that they subsequently do not use. Yet recent research suggests that there is order beneath the apparent chaos. In seeking and using information, people are continuously constructing meaning out of the information they receive, and in doing so they appear to be employing certain basic strategies, depending on the kind of information-need situation they are in. Such research, which is ongoing, could lead to a fuller understanding of the information needs of organizational members.

In their article, "How information gives you competitive advantage," Michael Porter and Victor Millar describe the many ways in which information and information technology are transforming the products, processes, structures, and the very nature of competition. In order for organizations to gain an information advantage, they suggest that organizations start by assessing the *information intensity* of their products and services. A product has high information intensity when it mainly provides information, or requires substantial information processing or training to use. Today's firms are competing by increasing the information content of their products and services—appliance retailers set up customer hotlines, couriers maintain continuous tracking systems, database vendors offer free training, and so on. To assess the information intensity of a process, Porter partitions the work of the organization into a *value chain* of linked activities, each of which creates and uses physical and informational inputs and outputs. The value chain is information-intensive when the organization deals with a large number of suppliers or customers, requires many steps to produce its goods or services, or requires large quantities of information to sell its offerings. Assessing the information intensity of the organization's products and processes therefore provides a powerful way of understanding the strategic information requirements of the organization. Porter and Millar then go on to explain how information and information technology can alter the competitive structure of an industry, support cost and differentiation strategies, and spawn new businesses.

While Porter and Millar look at organizational processes and outputs at a systems level, Robert Taylor's focus is on the information needs of distinct groups of information users working in professional or social settings and using information to resolve typical problems. Taylor's starting premise is an important one—that there are factors in the users' information environment that go beyond information content and subject matter, factors by which users judge the value or usefulness of the information they receive. These factors are grouped into four categories: sets of people; structure of problems faced by these sets of people; work or social settings; and the resolution of problems. *Sets of people* are defined in terms of their information behaviors, and Taylor identifies four classifications: the professions (including managers), entrepreneurs, special interest groups, and special socioeconomic groups. Each set of people or information users has its own characteristics (e.g., education, media use, social networks, attitudes) that explain differences in information behavior. Each set of people is concerned with a distinct *class of problems*, created by the requirements of its profession, occupation, or life style. Problems change all the time as new information is obtained and as the user changes position and perception. Four attributes of the *work setting* influence information behavior: attitude towards information, task domain, information access, and past history and experience. Finally, each set of people has a different perception of what constitutes the *resolution of a problem*. Eight classes of information use are defined, as well as several information traits that can be related to problem dimensions to determine information usefulness. Taylor's framework suggests a systematic way of analyzing the information requirements of an organization: identify the groups of information users in the organization, recognize the kinds of problems they typically handle, examine their work and social settings, and understand the ways in which they consider a problem to have been resolved.

Taylor's approach is part of the user-centered movement in information science to understand information needs and design information services from the point of view of the user rather than from the perspective of the library or information system. The article by Ruth Morris provides a useful summary of the work of Brenda Dervin, Nicholas Belkin, Robert Taylor, and Carol Kuhlthau in this area. According to these researchers, information is something that is subjectively constructed by users, humans share common traits when seeking and using information, and information needs and use depend on the contexts in which these needs arise and information is sought. Being user-centered does not mean having to deal with the infinite variety of the needs and preferences of every individual user. Research has found that the ways in which people perceive their cognitive gaps or problem situations and the ways that they want information to help are good predictors of their information seeking and use behaviors. Furthermore, as people search for information, they move through stages that are characterized by different information-seeking behaviors and emotional states. The user-centered model of information and information needs provides a cognitive framework with which to analyze the information requirements of organizational members. Morris discusses the user-centered model, and draws practical implications for the provision of information services, including reference interviews, question negotiation, indexing and cataloguing, and knowledge transfer.

The list of additional readings at the end of this section contains selections from the business, information needs and uses, and information systems literatures. Many of the readings describe research that essentially adopts one of the three approaches we have discussed: the systems, user-group, or cognitive approach.

How Information Gives You Competitive Advantage

Michael E. Porter and Victor E. Millar

INTRODUCTION

The information revolution is sweeping through our economy. No company can escape its effects. Dramatic reductions in the cost of obtaining, processing, and transmitting information are changing the way we do business.

Most general managers know that the revolution is under way, and few dispute its importance. As more and more of their time and investment capital is absorbed in information technology and its effects, executives have a growing awareness that the technology can no longer be the exclusive territory of EDP or IS departments. As they see their rivals use information for competitive advantage, these executives recognize the need to become directly involved in the management of the new technology. In the face of rapid change, however, they don't know how.

This article aims to help general managers respond to the challenges of the information revolution. How will advances in information technology affect competition and the sources of competitive advantage? What strategies should a company pursue to exploit the technology? What are the implications of actions that competi-

Authors' note: We wish to thank Monitor Company and Arthur Andersen for their assistance in preparing this article. F. Warren McFarlan also provided valuable comments.

tors may already have taken? Of the many opportunities for investment in information technology, which are the most urgent?

To answer these questions, managers must first understand that information technology is more than just computers. Today, information technology must be conceived of broadly to encompass the information that businesses create and use as well as a wide spectrum of increasingly convergent and linked technologies that process the information. In addition to computers, then, data recognition equipment, communications technologies, factory automation, and other hardware and services are involved.

The information revolution is affecting competition in three vital ways:

It changes industry structure and, in so doing, alters the rules of competition.

It creates competitive advantage by giving companies new ways to outperform their rivals.

It spawns whole new businesses, often from within a company's existing operations.

We discuss the reasons why information technology has acquired strategic significance and how it is affecting all businesses. We then describe how the new technology changes the nature of competition and how astute companies have exploited this. Finally, we outline a procedure managers can use to assess the role of information technology in their business and to help define investment priorities to turn the technology to their competitive advantage.

STRATEGIC SIGNIFICANCE

Information technology is changing the way companies operate. It is affecting the entire process by which companies create their products. Furthermore, it is reshaping the product itself: the entire package of physical goods, services, and information companies provide to create value for their buyers.

An important concept that highlights the role of information technology in competition is the "value chain" (Porter 1985). This concept divides a company's activities into the technologically and economically distinct activities it performs to do business. We call these "value activities." The value a company creates is measured by the amount that buyers are willing to pay for a product or service. A business is profitable if the value it creates exceeds the cost of performing the value activities. To gain competitive advantage over its rivals, a company must either perform these activities at a lower cost or perform them in a way that leads to differentiation and a premium price (more value) (Porter 1980).

A company's value activities fall into nine generic categories (see *Exhibit I*). Primary activities are those involved in the physical creation of the product, its marketing and delivery to buyers, and its support and servicing after sale. Support activities provide the inputs and infrastructure that allow the primary activities to take place. Every activity employs purchased inputs, human resources, and a combination of technologies. Firm infrastructure, including such functions as general management, legal work, and accounting, supports the entire chain. Within each of these generic categories, a company will perform a number of discrete activities, depending on the particular business. Service, for example, frequently includes activities such as installation, repair, adjustment, upgrading, and parts inventory management.

A company's value chain is a system of interdependent activities, which are connected by linkages. Linkages exist when the way in which one activity is performed affects the cost or effectiveness of other activities. Linkages often create trade-offs in performing different activities that should be optimized. This optimization may require trade-offs. For example, a more costly product design and more expensive raw materials can reduce after-sale service costs. A company must resolve such trade-offs, in accordance with its strategy, to achieve competitive advantage.

Linkages also require activities to be coordinated. On-time delivery requires that operations, outbound logistics, and service activities (installation, for example) should function smoothly together. Good coordination allows on-time delivery without the need for costly inventory. Careful management of linkages is often a powerful source of competitive advantage because of the difficulty rivals have in perceiving them and in resolving trade-offs across organizational lines.

The value chain for a company in a particular industry is embedded in a larger stream of activities that we term the "value system" (see *Exhibit II*). The value system includes the value chains of suppliers, who provide inputs (such as raw materials, components, and purchased services) to the company's value chain. The company's product often passes through its channels' value chains on its way to the ultimate buyer. Finally, the product becomes a purchased input to the value chains of its buyers, who use it to perform one or more buyer activities.

Linkages not only connect value activities inside a company but also create interdependencies between its value chain and those of its suppliers and channels. A company can create competitive advantage by optimizing or coordinating these links to the outside. For example, a candy manufacturer may save processing steps by persuading its suppliers to deliver chocolate in liquid form rather than in molded bars. Just-in-time deliveries by the supplier may have the same effect. But the opportunities for savings through coordinating with suppliers and channels go far beyond logistics and order processing. The company, suppliers, and channels can all benefit through better recognition and exploitation of such linkages.

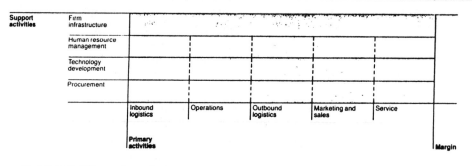

Support activities	Firm infrastructure					
	Human resource management					
	Technology development					
	Procurement					
		Inbound logistics	Operations	Outbound logistics	Marketing and sales	Service
		Primary activities				Margin

Exhibit I. The value chain

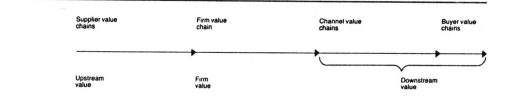

Supplier value chains	Firm value chain	Channel value chains	Buyer value chains
Upstream value	Firm value	Downstream value	

Exhibit II. The value system

Competitive advantage in either cost or differentiation is a function of a company's value chain. A company's cost position reflects the collective cost of performing all its value activities relative to rivals. Each value activity has cost drivers that determine the potential sources of a cost advantage. Similarly, a company's ability to differentiate itself reflects the contribution of each value activity toward fulfillment of buyer needs. Many of a company's activities—not just its physical product or service—contribute to differentiation. Buyer needs, in turn, depend not only on the impact of the company's product on the buyer but also on the company's other activities (for example, logistics or after-sale services).

In the search for competitive advantage, companies often differ in competitive scope—or the breadth of their activities. Competitive scope has four key dimensions: segment scope, vertical scope (degree of vertical integration), geographic scope, and industry scope (or the range of related industries in which the company competes).

Competitive scope is a powerful tool for creating competitive advantage. Broad scope can allow the company to exploit interrelationships between the value chains serving different industry segments, geographic areas, or related industries. For example, two business units may share one sales force to sell their products, or the units may coordinate the procurement of common components. Competing nationally or globally with a coordinated strategy can yield a competitive advantage over local or domestic rivals. By employing a broad vertical scope, a company can exploit the potential benefits of performing more activities internally rather than use outside suppliers.

By selecting a narrow scope, on the other hand, a company may be able to tailor the value chain to a particular target segment to achieve lower cost or differentiation. The competitive advantage of a narrow scope comes from customizing the value chain to best serve particular product varieties, buyers, or geographic regions. If the target segment has unusual needs, broad-scope competitors will not serve it well.

Transforming the Value Chain

Information technology is permeating the value chain at every point, transforming the way value activities are performed and the nature of the linkages among them. It also is affecting competitive scope and reshaping the way products meet buyer needs. These basic effects explain why information technology has acquired strategic significance and is different from the many other technologies businesses use.

Every value activity has both a physical and an information-processing component. The physical component includes all the physical tasks required to perform the activity. The information-processing component encompasses the steps required to capture, manipulate, and channel the data necessary to perform the activity.

Every value activity creates a formation of some kind. A logistics activity, for example, uses information like scheduling promises, transportation rates, and production plans to ensure timely and cost-effective delivery. A service activity uses information about service requests to schedule calls and order parts, and generates information on product failures that a company can use to revise product designs and manufacturing methods.

An activity's physical and information processing components may be simple or quite complex. Different activities require a different mix of the two components. For instance, metal stamping uses more physical processing than information processing; processing of insurance claims requires just the opposite balance.

For most of industrial history, technological progress principally affected the physical component of what businesses do. During the Industrial Revolution, companies achieved competitive advantage by substituting machines for human labor. Information processing at that time was mostly the result of human effort.

Now the pace of technological change is reversed. Information technology is advancing faster than technologies for physical processing. The costs of information storage, manipulation, and transmittal are falling rapidly and the boundaries of what is feasible in information processing are at the same time expanding. During the Industrial Revolution, the railroad cut the travel time from Boston, Massachusetts to Concord, New Hampshire from five days to four hours, a factor of 30 (Chandler 1977, 86). But the advances in information technology are even greater. The cost of computer power relative to the cost of manual information processing is at least 8,000 times less expensive than the cost 30 years ago. Between 1958 and 1980 the time for one electronic operation fell by a factor of 80 million. Department of Defense studies show that the error rate in recording data through bar coding is 1 in 3,000,000, compared to 1 error in 300 manual data entries (McKenney and McFarlan 1982, 109).

This technological transformation is expanding the limits of what companies can do faster than managers can explore the opportunities. The information revolution affects all nine categories of value activity, from allowing computer-aided design in technology development to incorporating automation in warehouses (see *Exhibit III*). The new technology substitutes machines for human effort in information processing. Paper ledgers and rules of thumb have given way to computers.

Initially, companies used information technology mainly for accounting and record-keeping functions. In these applications, the computers automated repetitive clerical functions such as order processing. Today information technology is spreading throughout the value chain and is performing optimization and control functions as well as more judgmental executive functions. General Electric, for instance, uses a data base that includes the accumulated experience and (often intuitive) knowledge of its appliance service engineers to provide support to customers by phone.

Information technology is generating more data as a company performs its activities and is permitting it to collect or capture information that was not available before. Such technology also makes room for a more comprehensive analysis and use of the expanded data. The number of variables that a company can analyze or control has grown dramatically. Hunt-Wesson, for example, developed a computer model to aid it in studying distribution-center expansion and relocation issues. The model enabled the company to evaluate many more different variables, scenarios, and alternative strategies than had been possible before. Similarly, information technology helped Sulzer Brothers' engineers improve the design of diesel engines in ways that manual calculations could not.

Information technology is also transforming the physical processing component of activities. Computer-controlled machine tools are faster, more accurate, and more flexible in manufacturing than the older, manually operated machines. Schlumberger has developed an electronic device permitting engineers to measure the angle of a drill bit, the temperature of a rock, and other variables while drilling oil wells. The result: drilling time is reduced and some well-logging steps are eliminated. On the West Coast, some fishermen now use weather satellite data on ocean temperatures to identify promising fishing grounds. This practice greatly reduces the fishermen's steaming time and fuel costs.

Information technology not only affects how individual activities are performed but, through new information flows, it is also greatly enhancing a company's ability to exploit linkages between activities, both within and outside the company. The technology is creating new linkages between activities, and companies can now coordinate their actions more closely with those of their buyers and suppliers. For example, McKesson, the nation's largest drug distributor, provides its drugstore customers with terminals. The company makes it so easy for clients to order, receive, and prepare invoices that the customers, in return, are willing to place larger orders. At the same time, McKesson has streamlined its order processing.

Finally, the new technology has a powerful effect on competitive scope. Information systems allow companies to coordinate value activities in farflung geographic locations. (For example, Boeing engineers work on designs on-line with foreign suppliers.) Information technology is also creating many new interrelationships among businesses, expanding the scope of industries in which a company must compete to achieve competitive advantage.

So pervasive is the impact of information technology that it confronts executives with a tough problem: too much information. This problem creates new uses of information technology to store and analyze the flood of information available to executives.

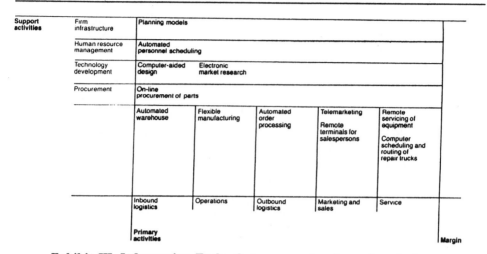

Support activities	Firm infrastructure	Planning models				
	Human resource management	Automated personnel scheduling				
	Technology development	Computer-aided design	Electronic market research			
	Procurement	On-line procurement of parts				
		Automated warehouse	Flexible manufacturing	Automated order processing	Telemarketing Remote terminals for salespersons	Remote servicing of equipment Computer scheduling and routing of repair trucks
		Inbound logistics	Operations	Outbound logistics	Marketing and sales	Service
		Primary activities				Margin

Exhibit III. Information Technology permeates the value chain

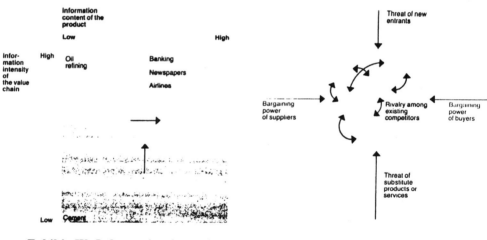

Exhibit IV. Information intensity matrix

Exhibit V. Determinants of industry attractiveness

Transforming the Product

Most products have always had both a physical and an information component. The latter, broadly defined, is everything that the buyer needs to know to obtain the product and use it to achieve the desired result. That is, a product includes information about its characteristics and how it should be used and supported. For example, convenient, accessible information on maintenance and service procedures is an important buyer criterion in consumer appliances.

Historically, a product's physical component has been more important than its information component. The new technology, however, makes it feasible to supply far more information along with the physical product. For example, General Electric's appliance service data base supports a consumer hotline that helps differentiate GE's service support from its rivals'. Similarly, some railroad and trucking companies offer up-to-the-minute information on the whereabouts of shippers' freight, which improves coordination between shippers and the railroad. The new technology is also making it increasingly possible to offer products with no physical component at all. Compustat's customers have access to corporate financial data filed with the Securities and Exchange Commission, and many companies have sprung up to perform energy use analyses of buildings.

Many products also process information in their normal functioning. A dishwasher, for example, requires a control system that directs the various components of the unit through the washing cycle and displays the process to the user. The new information technology is enhancing product performance and is making it easier to boost a product's information content. Electronic control of the automobile, for example, is becoming more visible in dashboard displays, talking dashboards, diagnostic messages, and the like.

There is an unmistakable trend toward expanding the information content in products. This component, combined with changes in companies' value chains, underscores the increasingly strategic role of information technology. There are no longer mature industries; rather, there are mature ways of doing business.

Direction and Pace of Change

Although a trend toward information intensity in companies and products is evident, the role and importance of the technology differs in each industry. Banking and insurance, for example, have always been information intensive. Such industries were naturally among the first and most enthusiastic users of data processing. On the other hand, physical processing will continue to dominate in industries that produce, say, cement, despite increased information processing in such businesses.

Exhibit IV, which relates information intensity in the value chain to information content in the product, illuminates the differences in the role and intensity of information among various industries. The banking and newspaper industries have a high information-technology content in both product and process. The oil-refining industry has a high use of information in the refining process but a relatively low information content in the product dimension.

Because of the falling cost and growing capacity of the new technology, many industries seem to be moving toward a higher information content in both product and process. It should be emphasized that technology will continue to improve rapidly. The cost of hardware will continue to drop, and managers will continue to distribute the technology among even the lower levels of the company. The cost of developing software, now a key constraint, will fall as more packages become available that are easily tailored to customers' circumstances. The applications of information technology that companies are using today are only a beginning.

Information technology is not only transforming products and processes but also the nature of competition itself. Despite the growing use of information technology, industries will always differ in their position in *Exhibit IV* and their pace of change.

CHANGING THE NATURE OF COMPETITION

After surveying a wide range of industries, we find that information technology is changing the rules of competition in three ways. First, advances in information technology are changing the industry structure. Second, information technology is an increasingly important lever that companies can use to create competitive advantage. A company's search for competitive advantage through information technology often also spreads to affect industry structure as competitors imitate the leader's strategic innovations. Finally, the information revolution is spawning completely new businesses. These three effects are critical for understanding the impact of information technology on a particular industry and for formulating effective strategic responses.

Changing Industry Structure

The structure of an industry is embodied in five competitive forces that collectively determine industry profitability: the power of buyers, the power of suppliers, the threat of new entrants, the threat of substitute products, and the rivalry among existing competitors (see *Exhibit V*). The collective strength of the five forces varies from industry to industry, as does average profitability. The strength of each of the five forces can also change, either improving or eroding the attractiveness of an industry (Porter 1979, 137).

Information technology can alter each of the five competitive forces and, hence, industry attractiveness as well. The technology is unfreezing the structure of many industries, creating the need and opportunity for change. For example:

- Information technology increases the power of buyers in industries assembling purchased components. Automated bills for materials and vendor quotation files make it easier for buyers to evaluate sources of materials and make-or-buy decisions.
- Information techologies requiring large investments in complex software have raised the barriers to entry. For example, banks competing in cash management services for corporate clients now need advanced software to give customers on-line account information. These banks may also need to invest in improved computer hardware and other facilities.
- Flexible computer-aided design and manufacturing systems have influenced the threat of substitution in many industries by making it quicker, easier, and cheaper to incorporate enhanced features into products.
- The automation of order processing and customer billing has increased rivalry in many distribution industries. The new technology raises fixed costs at the same time as it displaces people. As a result, distributors must often fight harder for incremental volume.

Industries such as airlines, financial services, distribution, and information suppliers (see the upper right-hand corner of *Exhibit IV*) have felt these effects so far (McFarlan, 1984, 98). (See the insert, "Information Technology and Industry Structure," for more examples.)

Information technology has had a particularly strong impact on bargaining relationships between suppliers and buyers since it affects the linkages between companies and their suppliers, channels, and buyers. Information systems that cross company lines are becoming common. In some cases, the boundaries of industries themselves have changed (Cash and Konsynski 1985, 134).

Systems that connect buyers and suppliers are spreading. Xerox gives manufacturing data to suppliers electronically to help them deliver materials. To speed up order entry, Westinghouse Electric Supply Company and American Hospital Supply have furnished their customers with terminals. Among other things, many systems raise the costs of switching to a new partner because of the disruption and retraining required. These systems tend to tie companies more closely to their buyers and suppliers.

Information technology is altering the relationship among scale, automation, and flexibility with potentially profound consequences. Large-scale production is no longer essential to achieve automation. As a result, entry barriers in a number of industries are falling.

Information technology and industry structure

Buyer power	Videotex home shopping services, such as Comp-U-Card, increase buyers' information. Buyers use their personal computers to browse through electronic catalogs and compare prices and product specifications. Customers can make purchases at any hour at prices typically 25% to 30% below suggested retail levels. Comp-U-Card is growing quickly: revenues have quintupled in two years to $9.5 million and membership is now 15,000. According to some projections, by the mid-1990s, 75% of U.S. households will have access to such services.
Buyer power	Shelternet, an electronic information exchange offered by First Boston Corporation, allows real estate brokers to determine quickly and easily what mortgage packages are available and whether the buyer will qualify for financing. This improves the position of both brokers and homebuyers in shopping for mortgages. The parties can make preliminary commitments within 30 minutes.
Substitution	Electronic data bases, such as NEXIS, are substituting for library research and consulting firms. NEXIS subscribers can quickly search the full text of any article in 225 periodicals. Users drastically reduce the time spent in literature searches. In addition, the buyer avoids the cost of journal subscriptions and pays only for the information required.

At the same time, automation no longer necessarily leads to inflexibility. For example, General Electric rebuilt its Erie locomotive facility as a large-scale yet flexible factory using computers to store all design and manufacturing data. Ten types of motor frames can be accommodated without manual adjustments to the machines. After installation of a "smart" manufacturing system, BMW can build customized cars (each with its own tailored gearbox, transmission system, interior, and other features) on the normal assembly line. Automation and flexibility are achieved simultaneously, a pairing that changes the pattern of rivalry among competitors.

The increasing flexibility in performing many value activities combined with the falling costs of designing products has triggered an avalanche of opportunities to customize and to serve small market niches. Computer-aided design capability not only reduces the cost of designing new products but also dramatically reduces the cost of modifying or adding features to existing products. The cost of tailoring products to market segments is falling, again affecting the pattern of industry rivalry.

While managers can use information technology to improve their industry structure, the technology also has the potential to destroy that structure. For example, information systems now permit the airline industry to alter fares frequently and to charge many different fares between any two points. At the same time, however, the technology makes the flight and fare schedules more readily available and allows travel agents and individuals to shop around quickly for the lowest fare. The result is a lower fare structure than might otherwise exist. Information technology has made a number of professional service industries less attractive by reducing personal interaction and making service more of a commodity. Managers must look carefully at the structural implications of the new technology to realize its advantages or to be prepared for its consequences.

Creating Competitive Advantage

In any company, information technology has a powerful effect on competitive advantage in either cost or differentiation. The technology affects value activities themselves or allows companies to gain competitive advantage by exploiting changes in competitive scope.

Lowering cost. As we have seen, information technology can alter a company's costs in any part of the value chain (Parsons 1983, 3). The technology's historical impact on cost was confined to activities in which repetitive information processing played a large part. These limits no longer exist, however. Even activities like assembly that mainly involve physical processing now have a large information-processing component.

Canon, for example, built a low-cost copier assembly process around an automated parts-selection and materials-handling system. Assembly workers have bins containing all the parts needed for the particular copier. Canon's success with this system derives from the software that controls parts inventory and selection. In insurance brokerage, a number of insurance companies usually participate in underwriting a contract. The costs of documenting each company's participation are high. Now a computer model can optimize (and often reduce) the number of insurers per contract, lowering the broker's total cost. In garment production, equipment such as automated pattern drawers, fabric cutters, and systems for delivering cloth to the final sewing station have reduced the labor time for manufacturing by up to 50%. (See the insert, "Aim: A Competitive Edge," for further examples.)

Aim:
a competitive edge

Lowering Cost	Casinos spend up to 20% of revenues on complimentary services for high rollers. One assignment for pit bosses has always been to keep an eye out for the big spenders. Now, however, many casinos have developed computer systems to analyze data on customers. Caesar's Palace lowered its complimentary budget more than 20% by developing a player-rating system for more accurate identification of big spenders.
Enhancing Differentiation	American Express has developed differentiated travel services for corporate customers through the use of information technology. The services include arranging travel and close monitoring of individual expenses. Computers search for the lowest airplane fares, track travel expenses for each cardholder, and issue monthly statements.

In addition to playing a direct role in cost, information technology often alters the cost drivers of activities in ways that can improve (or erode) a company's relative cost position. For example, Louisiana Oil & Tire has taken all ten of its salespeople off the road and made them into telemarketers. As a result, sales expenses have fallen by 10% and sales volume has doubled. However, the move has made the national scale of operations the key determinant of the cost of selling, rather than regional scale.

Enhancing differentiation. The impact of information technology on differentiation strategies is equally dramatic. As noted earlier, the role of a company and its product in the buyer's value chain is the key determinant of differentiation. The new information technology makes it possible to customize products. Using automation, for instance, Sulzer Brothers has increased from five to eight the number of cylinder bore sizes of new low-speed marinc diesel engines. Shipowners now choose an engine that is more precisely suited to their needs and thereby recoup significant fuel savings. Similarly, Digital Equipment's artificial intelligence system, XCON, uses decision rules to develop custom computer configurations. This dramatically reduces the time required to fill orders and increases accuracy—which enhances Digital's image as a quality provider.

By bundling more information with the physical product package sold to the buyer, the new technology affects a company's ability to differentiate itself. For example, a magazine distributor offers retailers processing credits for unsold items more efficiently than its competitors. Similarly, the embedding of information systems in the physical product itself is an increasingly powerful way to distinguish it from competing goods.

Changing competitive scope. Information technology can alter the relationship between competitive scope and competitive advantage. The technology increases a company's ability to coordinate its activities regionally, nationally, and globally. It can unlock the power of broader geographic scope to create competitive advantage. Consider the newspaper industry. Dow Jones, publisher of the *Wall Street Journal,* pioneered the page transmission technology that links its 17 U.S. printing plants to produce a truly national newspaper. Such advances in communication plants have also made it possible to move toward a global strategy. Dow Jones has started the *Asian Wall Street Journal* and the *Wall Street Journal-European Edition* and shares much of the editorial content while printing the papers in plants all over the world.

The information revolution is creating interrelationships among industries that were previously separate. The merging of computer and telecommunications technologies is an important example. This convergence has profound effects on the structure of both industries. For example, AT&T is using its position in telecommunications as a staging point for entry into the computer industry. IBM, which recently acquired Rolm, the telecommunications equipment manufacturer, is now joining the competition from the other direction. Information technology is also at the core of growing interrelationships in financial services, where the banking, insurance, and brokerage industries are merging, and in office equipment, where once distinct functions such as typing, photocopying, and data and voice communications can now be combined.

Broad-line companies are increasingly able to segment their offerings in ways that were previously feasible only for focused companies. In the trucking industry, Intermodal Transportation Services, Inc. of Cincinnati has completely changed its system for quoting prices. In the past, each local office set prices using manual procedures. Intermodal now uses microcomputers to link its offices to a center that calculates all prices. The new system gives thc company the capacity to introduce a new pricing policy to offer discounts to national accounts, which place their orders from all over the country. Intermodal is tailoring its value chain to large national customers in a way that was previously impossible.

As information technology becomes more widespread, the opportunities to take advantage of a new competitive scope will only increase. The benefits of scope (and the achievement of linkages), however, can accrue only when the information technology spread throughout the organization can communicate. Completely decentralized organizational design and application of information technology will thwart these possibilities, because the information technology introduced in various parts of a company will not be compatible.

Spawning New Businesses

The information revolution is giving birth to completely new industries in three distinct ways. First, it makes new businesses technologically feasible. For example, modern imaging and telecommunications technology blend to support new facsimile services such as Federal Express's Zapmail. Similarly, advances in microelectronics made personal computing possible. Services such as Merrill Lynch's Cash Management Account required new information technology to combine several financial products into one.

Second, information technology can also spawn new businesses by creating derived demand for new products. One example is Western Union's EasyLink service, a sophisticated, high-speed, data communications network that allows personal computers, word processors, and other electronic devices to send messages to each other and to telex machines throughout the world. This service was not needed before the spread of information technology caused a demand for it.

Third, information technology creates new businesses within old ones. A company with information processing embedded in its value chain may have excess capacity or skills that can be sold outside. Sears took advantage of its skills in processing credit card accounts and of its massive scale to provide similar services to others. It sells credit-authorization and transaction-processing services to Phillips Petroleum and retail remittance-processing services to Mellon Bank. Similarly, a manufacturer of automotive parts, A.O. Smith, developed data-communications expertise to meet the needs of its traditional businesses. When a bank consortium went looking for a contractor to run a network of automated teller machines, A.O. Smith got the job. Eastman Kodak recently began offering long-distance telephone and data-transmission services through its internal telecommunications system. Where the information techology used in a company's value chain is sensitive to scale, a company may improve its overall competitive advantage by increasing the scale of information processing and lowering costs. By selling extra capacity outside, it is at the same time generating new revenue.

Companies also are increasingly able to create and sell to others information that is a byproduct of their operations. National Benefit Life reportedly merged with American Can in part to gain access to data on the nine million customers of American Can's direct-mail retailing subsidiary. The use of bar-code scanners in supermarket retailing has turned grocery stores into market research labs. Retailers can run an ad in the morning newspaper and find out its effect by early afternoon. They can also sell this data to market research companies and to food processors.

COMPETING IN THE AGE OF INFORMATION

Senior executives can follow five steps to take advantage of opportunities that the information revolution has created.

1. *Assess information intensity.* A company's first task is to evaluate the existing and potential information intensity of the products and processes of its business units. To help managers accomplish this, we have developed some measures of the potential importance of information technology.

It is very likely that information technology will play a strategic role in an industry that is characterized by one or more of the following features:

- Potentially high information intensity in the value chain—a large number of suppliers or customers with whom the company deals directly, a product requiring a large quantity of information in selling, a product line with many distinct product varieties, a product composed of many parts, a large number of steps in a company's manufacturing process, a long cycle time from the initial order to the delivered product.
- Potentially high information intensity in the product—a product that mainly provides information, a product whose operation involves substantial information processing, a product whose use requires the buyer to process a lot of information, a product requiring especially high costs for buyer training, a product that has many alternative uses or is sold to a buyer with high information intensity in his or her own business.

These may help identify priority business units for investment in information technology. When selecting priority areas, remember the breadth of information technology—it involves more than simple computing.

2. *Determine the role of information technology in industry structure.* Managers should predict the likely impact of information technology on their industry's structure. They must examine how information technology might affect each of the five competitive forces. Not only is each force likely to change but industry boundaries may change as well. Chances are that a new definition of the industry may be necessary.

Many companies are partly in control of the nature and pace of change in the industry structure. Companies have permanently altered the bases of competition in their favor in many industries through aggressive investments in information technology and have forced other companies to follow. Citibank, with its automated teller machines and transaction processing; American Airlines, with its computerized reservations system; and *USA Today,* with its newspaper page transmission to decentralized printing plants, are pioneers that have used information technology to alter industry structure. A company should understand how structural change is forcing it to respond and look for ways to lead change in the industry.

3. *Identify and rank the ways in which information technology might create competitive advantage.* The starting assumption must be that the technology is likely to affect every activity in the value chain. Equally important is the possibility that new linkages among

activities are being made possible. By taking a careful look, managers can identify the value activities that are likely to be most affected in terms of cost and differentiation. Obviously, activities that represent a large proportion of cost or that are critical to differentiation bear closest scrutiny, particularly if they have a significant information-processing component. Activities with important links to other activities inside and outside the company are also critical. Executives must examine such activities for ways in which information technology can create sustainable competitive advantage.

In addition to taking a hard look at its value chain, a company should consider how information technology might allow a change in competitive scope. Can information technology help the company serve new segments? Will the flexibility of information technology allow broad-line competitors to invade areas that were once the province of niche competitors? Will information technology provide the leverage to expand the business globally? Can managers harness information technology to exploit interrelationships with other industries? Or, can the technology help a company create competitive advantage by narrowing its scope?

A fresh look at the company's product may also be in order:

Can the company bundle more information with the product?

Can the company embed information technology in it?

4. *Investigate how information technology might spawn new businesses.* Managers should consider opportunities to create new businesses from existing ones. Information technology is an increasingly important avenue for corporate diversification. Lockheed, for example, entered the database business by perceiving an opportunity to use its spare computer capacity.

Identifying opportunites to spawn new businesses requires answering questions such as:

What information generated (or potentially generated) in the business could the company sell?

What information-processing capacity exists internally to start a new business?

Does information technology make it feasible to produce new items related to the company's product?

5. *Develop a plan for taking advantage of information technology.* The first four steps should lead to an action plan to capitalize on the information revolution. This action plan should rank the stra-

tegic investments necessary in hardware and software, and in new product development activities that reflect the increasing information content in products. Organizational changes that reflect the role that the technology plays in linking activities inside and outside the company are likely to be necessary.

The management of information technology can no longer be the sole province of the EDP department. Increasingly, companies must employ information technology with a sophisticated understanding of the requirements for competitive advantage. Organizations need to distribute the responsibility for systems development more widely in the organization. At the same time, general managers must be involved to ensure that cross-functional linkages, more possible to achieve with information technology, are exploited.

These changes do not mean that a central information-technology function should play an insignificant role. Rather than control information technology, however, an IS manager should coordinate the architecture and standards of the many applications throughout the organization, as well as provide assistance and coaching in systems development. Unless the numerous applications of information technology inside a company are compatible with each other, many benefits may be lost.

Information technology can help in the strategy implementation process. Reporting systems can track progress toward milestones and success factors. By using information systems, companies can measure their activities more precisely and help motivate managers to implement strategies successfully (Millar 1984, 159).

The importance of the information revolution is not in dispute. The question is not whether information technology will have a significant impact on a company's competitive position; rather the question is when and how this impact will strike. Companies that anticipate the power of information technology will be in control of events. Companies that do not respond will be forced to accept changes that others initiate and will find themselves at a competitive disadvantage.

REFERENCES

Cash, Jr., J. I., and B. R. Konsynski. 1985. IS redraws competitive boundaries. *Harvard Business Review* (Mar/Apr). 64(2): 134–142.

Chandler, Jr., A. D. 1977. *The Visible Hand.* Cambridge, MA: Belknap Press of Harvard University Press.

McFarlan, E. W. 1984. Information technology changes the way you compete. *Harvard Business Review* (May/June): 62(3): 98–103.

McKenney, J. L., and E. W. McFarlan. 1982. The information archipelago—maps and bridges. *Harvard Business Review* (Sept/Oct): 109–119.
Millar, V. E. 1984. Decision-oriented information. *Datamation* (January): 159–162.
Parsons, G. L. 1983. Information technology: A new competitive weapon. Sl*oan Management Review* (Fall).
Porter, M. E. 1985. *Competitive Advantage*. New York: Free Press.
Porter, M. E. 1980. *Competitive Strategy*. New York: Free Press.
Porter, M. E. 1979. How competitive forces shape strategy. *Harvard Business Review* (Mar/Apr): 57(2): 137–145.

Information Use Environments

Robert S. Taylor

INTRODUCTION

In the information field there are essentially three approaches to the study of information transfer. First is the *technological* approach, which basically prescribes the size, shape, function, dynamism, and even the content of information systems. That is to say, what is and can be stored in a book (report, paper, or other formal retrievable message) or in a computer memory defines what is accepted as knowledge or information. In this context, information systems in Dervin's words, tend to protect whatever functional unit in which that system has a vested interest (Dervin 1975, 13). The second is the *content-driven* approach, which stems from the human concern with the subject classification and ordering of knowledge and information, especially as reflected in library classification schemes, indexing constructs, and such mechanisms as thesauri and data dictionaries. In the beginning such constructs are recognized as tentative and subjective; but they soon take on a life and validity of their own. They tend to become reality rather than human representations developed to provide ways of organizing, by subject matter, information about *reality.*

These conventional approaches need to be tempered and informed by a third approach that looks at the *user and the uses of information,* and the contexts within which those users make choices about what information is useful to them at particular times. These choices are based, not only on subject matter, but on other elements of the context within which a user lives and works. The explication of this statement is a major focus of this chapter.

These contexts are what the author has called *information use*

Reprinted with permission and originally published in *Progress in Communication Sciences* 10:217–255 *environments* (IUE): the set of those elements that (a) affect the flow and use of information messages into, within, and out of any definable entity; and (b) determine the criteria by which the value of information messages will be judged (Taylor 1986, 25–26). This chapter has been, in part, informed by Dervin's observation that "systems personnel and researchers have been looking at something they call information rather than at something users call information" (Dervin 1983a,158). Papers by Paisley (1980), Wilson (1981), Roberts (1982), and Wersig and Windel (1985) influenced a good deal of the underlying assumptions and direction of this chapter.

The intent in this chapter is not a complete survey of the literature. Rather it is concerned with the delineation of a structure and a description of a particular area of concern in the information sciences. The author comes from the operating and professional side of the information field. Hence the essay should be perceived as a bridge between (a) users and their environments, and (b) the world of the system designer, information manager, and those who really make the system work—from reference librarians to information analysts. The chapter has three objectives:

- to provide a structure for the study of IUEs, thereby defining what those environments are;
- to describe, using this structure, what it is we know about three specific IUEs; and
- to examine some of the problems of this approach.

There is, of course, an assumption underlying all of these concerns. That is that people, settings, and problems and their resolution can be described, at least in preliminary fashion, in information terms.

This chapter is in six parts. First is a discussion of some of the limits of the chapter: what it does and does not cover, and some terminological questions. Second, ways of structuring and organizing the data are described and discussed. This might be construed as a model, albeit tentative and descriptive. It provides a vehicle for illustrating different types of information users in context and a means of comparing one user class with another.

This chapter then is an early attempt to organize what we seem to know about the environments within which different types of users seek information and make choices about the utility of the information available to them. It is not graven in stone; indeed the author hopes that it will spur discussion and improvement as a means of organizing what it is we know, and that it will stimulate further research.

Limits

The area of concern is obviously vast. There are, consequently, two specific limitations. First, the *user population* is limited to those groups or classes of people who are active, experienced, and critical users of information. That is to say, they are aware of their problems; they know, at least in approximate terms, where they can find useful information; and they have a critical sensitivity to what constitutes a solution, or, better said, a resolution of a problem in their context. This population includes, for example, managers, scholars, scientists, teachers, social workers, engineers, farmers, physicians, small business people, etc. It might be more logical to discuss information users in terms of similar types of problems; we are, however, concerned with eventual input to systems design, and thus we will categorize users as managers, teachers, etc. That is to say, at this time, we believe that problems and their resolution in a management context are different from those in an engineering context, those in a teaching context from those in a physician's context, etc. The qualifier at this time in the last sentence implies that we may indeed find similarities useful to system design and operation among different professions and occupations in the process of defining specific IUEs. This is one of the intents of this chapter: to begin to isolate similarities and differences among varying populations in specific contexts.

We are also dealing with groups rather than with individuals. This says that, though individuals have specific idiosyncracies, there are real similarities among, for example, managers, whether they are in Seattle, Miami, or Boston. It is the argument of this chapter that each of these groups has different kinds of problems over varying time frames, different ways of resolving those problems, and consequently differing information seeking behaviors. The chapter excludes consideration of the general public, the elderly, consumers, the information-poor. It is not that these groups are not important but rather that they pose quite different sets of problems, experience, and information need which, in this brief essay, cannot be dealt with effectively. However, it is hoped that the structure presented here can also be used in organizing data about these groups.

It should also be noted that the chapter focuses especially on the American experience in the broader context of American culture. We suspect, without investigation, that there may be differences between European and American experience, education, and hence information behavior. There are, for example, certainly differences between the American practice of medicine and the Chinese practice (Eisenberg & Wright 1985).

The second limitation concerns use of the term *information*. Discussion here is limited to formal information—both oral and recorded—which is sought in the context of recognized problems or concerns. That is to say, information is defined as formal, *not* because of its physical format, e.g., book, image, computer print-out, but rather because it responds, and is perceived as—and is intended to be—relevant to a particular problem. A consultant's oral report to a client, for example, or a discussion among engineers concerned with a particular device or physicians concerned with a particular patient, is perceived here as formal information. In fact, because such activities are interactive, in information terms they may be far more relevant to a problem than a written report. An understanding of this is crucial to the user-driven approach. It is the recognition of problems and the processes of seeking resolution to these problems which defines the information process. This chapter is not necessarily concerned with nonverbal information, though we will see, in the case of practicing physicians, that nonverbal information may become important in a defined context.

Use(s) of Information

The term in the title phrase—*use*—requires mutual understanding and agreement. Generally—and somewhat cavalierly—we can say that use is whatever the particular population says it is. In a way, that is really what we mean: that is what the user-directed approach is all about. There are some caveats, however.

Use of an information store—library, management information system, consultant, analysis center, etc.—has widely differing interpretations (Bookstein 1982). It is the argument here, however, that such studies usually ask the wrong set of questions, start from the wrong end of the stick, from system-determined definitions rather than user's perceptions of information.

Dervin and Nilan (1986) argue that a paradigmatic shift is taking place in the study of information needs and uses. The "alternative" paradigm, in contrast to the "traditional,"

> posits information as something constructed by human beings. It sees users as beings who are constantly constructing, as beings who are free (within system constraints) to create from systems and situations whatever they choose. It focuses on how people construct sense, searching for universal dimensions of sense-making. It focuses on understanding information use in particular situations and is concerned with what leads up to and what follows intersections with systems. It focuses on the user. It examines the system only as seen by the user. It asks many 'how questions' e.g., how do people define needs in different situations,

how do they present these needs to the system, and how do they make use of what systems offer them (Dervin & Nilan 1986).

It is critical at this time to begin to provide some structure on the uses of information: what information does to or for the recipient *and for his or her problem or situation.*

STRUCTURING THE DATA

As a first pass, data about information use environments can be broken down into four categories: sets of people, typical structure and thrust of problems of those sets of people, typical settings, and what constitutes resolution of problems. This essay is about the *information behavior* of different sets of people. Information behavior is briefly defined here as the sum of activities through which information becomes useful. This essay is an attempt to put flesh on this bare-boned definition. We have already discussed what we mean by information. Two additional comments are necessary: (a) *activities* imply active search resulting from an area of doubt or more specifically a recognized problem; (b) *useful* implies ways of resolving a problem through clarification, alteration, or actual solution as a result of information gained. Following the pattern of the four categories noted above, information behavior is the product of the following elements of the information use environment.

- The assumptions, formally learned or not, made by a defined set of people concerning the nature of their work.
- The kinds and structure of the problems deemed important and typical by this set of people.
- The constraints and opportunities of typical environments within which any group or subgroup of this set of people operates and works.
- The conscious, and perhaps unconscious, assumptions made as to what constitutes a solution, or, better said, a resolution of problems, and what makes information useful and valuable in their contexts.

In these terms, the author believes that, generally speaking, the information behavior of engineers is different from that of practicing physicians, that of lawyers from that of farmers, etc. This essay is intended to explore and, it is hoped, to clarify some of these assertions.

Sets of People

What constitutes a *set of people* in terms of information behavior? What are the demographic and nondemographic characteristics of these sets of people? Are there differences within each set? Can those differences be seen in terms of information behavior?

In answering the question of what constitutes a set of people, there are two possibilities. First, is a set of people established on the basis of some set of variables and then labelled A, B, or C? Or is a set of people established a priori in a historical or social sense, i.e., doctors, engineers, farmers, etc., and then these groups examined to determine their information behavior? In a sense, society has already answered the question, and we already provide information services based on these societal distinctions. We call certain people physicians or engineers or managers because, in the first two cases, of their professional education, and because of their occupation in the case of managers. Their training, occupation, and usual activities are made up in part of sets of information behavior unique to the group under consideration.

For purposes of this essay, there seems to be a useful division into four classes of people. This division is based on an intuitive interpretation of information behavior, and will be argued in the chapter.

- *the professions:* engineers, lawyers, social workers, scientists, teachers, managers, physicians, etc.
- *the entrepreneur:* farmers, small business men, etc.
- *special interest groups:* consumers, citizen groups, hobbyists, political action groups, ethnic cultural groups, etc.
- *special socioeconomic groups:* information-poor, the disabled, minorities, the elderly, etc.

We are concerned principally with the first two classes. Each of us, of course, may be in several classes simultaneously. An engineer may also be a consumer activist, a teacher active in a political action group, a business person an amateur birdwatcher, a farmer active in a black minority group. Our concern, however, is only with the engineer acting as an engineer, the manager acting as a manager, etc.

In describing a set of people in *demographic terms* it is necessary to remember that, for this essay, we are concerned with those variables that help to define the information environment and behavior of a restricted population: professional and entrepreneurs. In general terms, *age, sex,* or *marital status* probably have little to do with the definition of the IUE, though they may have an effect on individual information behavior. Even with innovation and risk taking, age does not seem to play a role, though there is some inconsistency reported in the studies on the relationship of age to innovation (Rogers 1983, 251). It is the assumption here—though not proven—that education for a particular profession, including its reflection as information style, will be the same regardless of sex or marital status. An interesting question to examine may be to ask what the effect on information behavior is when a profession is principally female, e.g., teaching, nursing, etc. *Race* may make a difference in restricting the options, and hence, changing the nature of required information, for a black farmer or business person. These four demographic variables, however, do not really affect in significant ways the basic hypothesis that certain predefined categories of people have different information behaviors one from another. It also appears unlikely—although there is no evidence one way or another—that the *socioeconomic status* of a profession has any appreciable effect on information behavior, though it may influence the entrepreneur, affecting his or her access to information. These are factors which need further investigation. The author does not intend to pursue this here.

Of all the demographic variables, *education* appears to be the most significant. It is necessary to note two aspects of education here. On the one hand, there are those activities, called professions, that are significantly affected, indeed controlled, by their formal education: physicians, lawyers, teachers, social workers, scientists, engineers.[1] On the other hand, there are activities, sometimes called professions, that are less dependent on formal education, and are more defined by context and the kinds of problems faced: farmers, managers, legislators, small business persons. With business persons, however, level of education may have some bearing because of certain needed skills: accounting, marketing, specific technological know-how, etc. There is, however, no formal certifying process for practitioners of these activities. Hence, formal recognition of problems, and resultant information behaviors, are not necessarily learned through formal education, as in the formal professions. In all of these cases, it is the organization and conceptual structure that these different sets of people bring to a particular context that give value to information, makes it useful (Knott & Wildavsky 1980, 558).

Among the *nondemographic characteristics,* the more important in the context of this chapter seem to be *media use, social networks,* and *attitudes toward new technology, education, risk taking* and *innovation.*

Concerning *media use,* extensive and long-standing studies have been made of the use of different media and channels by the popu-

---

[1]   During the sixties, when the author was doing research on question negotiation, a law librarian in Washington made a most perceptive remark: "I can usually tell from which law school a person comes by the way he asks a question."

lations under consideration here (Fabisoff and Ely 1974; Lowry 1979; Dervin & Nilan, 1986). Such studies tell us, for example, that scientists are print-oriented (Price 1965; Allen 1977) and regular readers of their periodical literature (Garvey, Tomita, & Woolf 1979); that engineers use trade journals and textbooks much more than they use professional engineering journals (Allen 1977); that managers prefer face-to-face meetings or the telephone over any other channels for information seeking (Mintzberg 1975).

In *networks,* doctors find the social network of colleagues important for the confirmation of new drug information which they probably heard first from drug detailmen (Coleman, Katz, Menzel 1966). Productive scientists use the invisible college of colleagues throughout the world who are working on a particular research problem as the principle network for information transfer (Crane 1972). Engineers, on the other hand, are able "to communicate better with their organization colleagues than with outsiders because of shared knowledge" (Allen 1977, 139).

Attitudes toward education, new technology, risk taking, and *innovation* may be more individually idiosyncratic than collective, although the specific setting and attitudes toward rewards and penalties in that setting may well affect these attitudes, and hence their information behavior. Such a blanket statement, however, belies certain differences or gradations. Though in Section II-D below we will go into more detail in the context of problem resolution, generally knowledge is seen by a user as either enlightenment, *know-what,* or as instrumental, *know-how* (Boulding 1978). Scholars and policy makers who seek context and background, and those for whom curiosity and its satisfaction are primary drives, seek enlightenment. Those concerned with the design, development, and management of an operation find instrumental knowledge more useful.

Those concerned with the development and production of pharmaceutical drugs or space shuttles, or with renal biopsies, will have different attitudes toward *risk* than those concerned with the manufactures of diapers, steel ingots, or carburetors. Degree of perceived risk has an effect on the amount and quality of information required for decision (Slovic 1987).

Problems

What are the characteristics of typical problems that this particular set of people is concerned about? Do these problems change over time? If so, how? It should be noted here that our concern is not only with the subject matter as a definer of problems. It is rather with the nature of the problems themselves which are endemic or deemed important, and hence faced by a particular set of people.

Clients or users are perceived as a set of problems generated by a particular environment: problem types which can be described in information terms, and which have an effect on the kinds and nature of anticipated or appropriate response.

The term *problem* is used in a generic sense in this essay. Formalists tend to separate the concern into three parts: questions which specify, problems which connect, and sense making which orients (MacMullin & Taylor 1984). However, the user does not separate these into nice neat categories. There may indeed be gradations (Taylor 1962). The approach here, however, is that these differences may be more easily examined in the kinds of information sought and in the uses made of that information, than in a statement of the problem itself. What is conjectured here is that a problem and its resolution cannot readily be separated. We pose this as an interesting conjecture, one that needs further examination and analysis.

A user is concerned with establishing some degree of clarity in an area of doubt (a) by recalling previous experience for analogy; (b) through new knowledge or by confirming knowledge that illuminates, resolves, or alters the problem; or (c) with the discovery that there may be no resolution.

There are generally three concerns in discussing problems. The first is the tendency to think of them as static and immutable. Problems are not static. They change all the time in response to new information and in relation to the actor's position and perceptions. Frischmuth and Allen, in the context of engineering design, call this the 'concept of the variable problem,' which in large part goes unrecognized because engineering education focuses "almost exclusively on closed-form problems in which there is only one correct solution" (Frischmuth and Allen 1969, 63). This is not exclusive to engineering. Sometimes the change is partly formalized, as in the engineering design process, where recognizable steps are assumed each of which may require entirely different information responses. Related to this is that, in the beginning, problems are often not well articulated, and indeed may exist only as a vague dissatisfaction with things as they are (Taylor 1962, 1968). Responses, though that may be too formal a term, are apt at this stage to be highly informal and serendipitous.

A second concern is the recognition that each of the definable IUEs has a discrete class of problems, spawned by its particular setting and by the exigencies of its profession, occupation, or life style. Teachers in elementary or secondary school, for example, generally have problems that can be divided into five categories: subject matter and its organization, classroom control, discipline and aberrant behavior, presentation methods, and administration. It is from these contexts that a teacher's problems arise which define the shape of his or her information seeking and using. Because of the nature of the problems and the immediacy of the classroom, instrumental responses are apt to be most appropriate (Huberman 1983).

A third concern is with problem dimensions, a more formal set of characteristics each of which illuminates the criteria for judging relevance of response. MacMullin and Taylor (1984) discuss these dimensions at some length. Among the 11 dimensions noted, the more significant are:

- *Well structured/ill structured.* The former can be solved by the application of logical and algorithmic processes, and tend to require hard data. Ill-structured problems have variables that are not well understood and require more probabilistic information on how to proceed rather than hard data.
- *Complex/simple.* Complexity refers to the number and interaction of problem variables. Though they may be understood as single variables, their interactions with other variables are not known.
- *Assumptions agreed upon/not agreed upon.* In addition, assumptions may not be well understood or articulated. People tend to 'talk past each other' when they do not have some mutual understanding of assumptions which reflect their perceptions of the world or of that particular universe of discourse.
- *Familiar/new patterns.* Many problems are essentially procedural and rely on well-established method and techniques built up over centuries of practice. When this is not the case, trial and error become standard procedure.

Each of these dimensions would appear to have—though this has not been experimentally validated—an effect on the kinds of information deemed useful.

Setting

What is the nature and variety of settings these groups of people work in? What are the attributes of those settings? How does information generally move in those settings? What are the types and structures of information and means of dissemination in these settings?

We are concerned with physical context and with ways of describing the context in which a specific class of people usually works and lives, and which affects the way they seek and make use of information.

We tend to think of the bureaucratic organization as the only setting. Albeit important, the organization is but one setting. It has very little to do with, for example, practicing physicians, independent lawyers, farmers, or small business people, let alone consumers, the elderly, etc.

The rise of the service sector in the American economy is epitomized by the small organization (Fuchs 1969). In many cases these services, together with the farmer and the small businessperson, are closer to information—must be closer for survival—than are larger and more formal organizations. *Closer* means more dependent on current information of high quality.

Within limits, information behavior essentially transcends the bureaucratic organization. This goes beyond the usual distinction between those who are organizationally oriented and those who are professionally oriented (March & Simon 1958), which has to do with where one's loyalties are. Within a large corporation, the information behavior of, say, lawyers, when acting as lawyers, is significantly different from that of engineers, when acting as engineers. School teachers, with minor variations due to the local setting, will have basically the same set of problems and seek the same kinds of information whether they teach in Peoria or Portland.

Having said all this—principally to break our organizational bias—we need to ask, then, what are the elements of setting that influence information behavior? There seem to be four general influences.

1. *Importance of Organization.* Given different kinds of organizations, what effect does structure and style have upon the behavior of different classes of information users in the organization? Within a corporation management establishes, inadvertently or otherwise, an attitude toward information and consequently affects the information behavior of its employees. In research and development laboratories, for example, what executives emphasize and reward (useful products/processes *or* publishing a paper which adds significantly to the literature) has a great deal to say about the importance of different kinds of information services (Pelz and Andrew 1966, 297–299; Taylor 1986, 38). For the entrepreneurial farmer, however, this will have little meaning except as he may be a member of a cooperative or other kind of marketing association. These organizations do not impinge on or affect the farmer's activities in the same way a corporation affects the information behavior of a financial manager or production foreman.

2. *Domain of Interest.* Regardless of size or structure, what does the unit of concern do? (Unit of concern may be an organization of thou-

sands of people, a part of that larger organization, or it may be a single practicing physician.) It may manufacture aircraft parts, educate adolescents, heal the sick, design skyscrapers, formulate policy and pass laws, sell and service automobiles, raise catfish, or test materials. Each of these domains, like thousands of others, will have certain attributes peculiar to that domain: availability of information, patterns of dissemination, and to some extent the level of reliability. In certain cases, information in the usual sense may in fact be unavailable. This is true especially in farming and engineering. For example, if, several years ago, a farmer wanted to get into the production of fuel alcohol from crops, there was basically an information vacuum. The farmer had to break new ground. In such a situation trial and error—learning by doing—becomes the principal mode of information gathering. As a result, that particular farmer becomes an information source in the future (Consumer Dynamics, Inc. 1981, 17–20). Does the unit operate in the public or private sector? Research indicates that there are differing patterns of social science information use between public agency and private company. The major difference seems to be the high conceptual use (i.e., enlightenment) of research information in public organizations and high instrumental use of such information in private firms (Deshpande & Zaltman 1983; Caplan, Morrison, & Stambaugh 1975).

3. *Access to Information.* What effect does the setting have on perceived ease of access to information? Accessibility appears in many studies to be the single most important variable governing use of information (Gerstenberger & Allen 1968; O'Reilly 1979, 16). In almost all studies of information use among various populations, dependence on personal sources far exceeds impersonal sources (Aguilar 1967; Mintzberg 1975; Matthews & Stinson 1970, Chen & Hernon 1982). That is to say, personal memory and friends, relatives, colleagues, and peers are perceived to be more accessible than more formal sources. Accessibility in this sense means somewhat more than just physical access. It seems to have something to do with the perceived validity and utility of information and, perhaps above all, with a sense that personal dialogue will help to clarify both need and response, and hence to provide more useful information. Formal gatherers of information, e.g., libraries, information centers, management information systems, tend to be too far—both physically and psychologically—from the users of information (Feldman & March 1981; Taylor 1986). The information packages stored and transmitted by the more formal channels seldom match the way people want or use information (Dervin 1975).

This does not mean that formal text systems are not used. For scholars, scientists, policy report writers, decision formulators, and academicians generally such sources are important because these groups are paper centered, *papyrocentric* in the words of Derek Price (1965). Their output is paper, not devices, systems, decisions, or solutions.

4. *History and Experience.* In an organization, the passage of time and increased specialization will tend to bureaucratize, to make complex tasks routine, and thus reduce the effect of new information (Kimberley et al. 1980). An organization may absorb a great deal of information with very little effect. On the other hand, the change in traditional institutions and in the professions as a result of the knowledge explosion has directly affected specialization and compartmentalization of knowledge, and hence the relevance and transfer of information and knowledge (Schon 1983, 3-20).

Resolution of Problems

What constitutes, for a given set of people, resolution of a typical problem? What kinds of information (amount, degree of relevance, quality, format, etc.) do people in a particular set anticipate? What filtering mechanisms exist? What are the attitudes towards the benefits and costs of information use? What are the criteria of information choice? What does information do for people in specific settings?

General attitudes toward information unconsciously assume the more information the better. Such an attitude, of course, leads to overload of irrelevant information (Ackoff 1967). Despite the burden of overload to managers, there is still the feeling that "it is better from the decision maker's point of view to have information that is not needed than not to have information that might be needed" (Feldman & March 1981, 176). We really do not know much about information safety factors—so we tend to overload. People have developed a whole variety of means for deflecting unwanted information. One can (a) throw it away or (b) use colleagues, secretaries, assistants, or other staff to act as filters. Public and private bureaucracies—legal, marketing, public relations, research and development, strategic planning, budget departments—have grown during the past half century in good part to filter information for decision making (Taylor 1986, 136-140). We may well ask whether such methods lessen the burden of overload or cause it. One can use a social network of peers or relatives as a source for specific and reliable information.

More pertinent to our concerns, here, however, is the way a given set of people view their problems and what they anticipate as resolution. These perceptions and anticipations are, in a way, a built-in but unconscious means of controlling the amount of information used (Knott & Wildavsky 1980). Engineers, for example, in selecting among information channels,

> act in a manner which is intended not to maximize gain, but rather, to minimize loss. The loss to be minimized is the cost in terms of effort, either physical or psychological, which must be expended in order to gain access to an information channel. (Gerstenberger & Allen 1968, 277)

Business decision makers act on a good deal less than total information; 70% is considered high availability (Brinberg 1980, 6). That is to say, they satisfice, they "look for a course of action that is satisfactory or 'good enough' " (Simon 1976, xxviii). And that is reflected in their information behavior.

Problems, in the larger sense of this essay, are not usually resolved by a single question and answer. Rather they pose different requirements on the type of information perceived as necessary, and hence different uses to which information is put in the process of resolution. At the risk of premature classification, we will tentatively set up eight classes of information use, generated by the need perceived by users in particular situations. These are not mutually exclusive. Indeed, answers to one class may operate on the needs and questions in another class. These eight classes are listed with brief comment and a few typical questions and uses, which have been derived from a variety of sources and pertain to many different user types. The work of Dervin, Nilan, and colleagues (Dervin 1983b; Nilan & Dervin 1986) is highly relevant to this categorization, though there are differences in number and interpretation.

1. *Enlightenment:* the desire for context information or ideas in order to make sense of a situation. Dervin[2] calls this "Got pictures/ideas/ understandings." Are there similar situations? What are they? What is history and experience of Corporation X in making product Y, and how is this relevant to our intent to manufacture Y?
2. *Problem Understanding:* more specific than enlightenment; better comprehension of particular problems. This has to do with answerable questions. Blois (1984, 189–190) points out that a medical question such as "Why does this injured patient have fever?" may be unanswerable at present, but answers to other questions may shed

---

[2] In the eight categories, the statements preceded by "Dervin calls this ... " are from Dervin 1983b, 62.

light: "Does the patient have an infection?" "Did the patient receive a blood transfusion?" The *why* question requires interpretation of data and judgment as to their relevance. Dervin calls this "Able to plan: this category includes being able to decide, prepare, plan ahead."

3. *Instrumental:* finding out what to do and how to do something; instructions; under certain conditions, instrumental information needs will define the need for other types of information. Dervin calls this "Got skills." How do I read this device? How do I interpret the readings?

4. *Factual:* the need for and consequent provision of precise data. There are two constraints to factual data: (a) the actual quality of the data, how well do they represent reality; and (b) related to the above, user perception of quality. We tend to accept data and information without qualification as valid because they are printed, computer generated, or in numerical form (Taylor 1986, 64-65, 165). What is the thermal conductivity of copper? (Lide 1981, 1345-1346). What can cause upper abdominal pain and blisters on the skin? (Blois 1984, 152).

5. *Confirmational:* the need to verify a piece of information; in a medical context, to seek a second opinion. In Dervin's terms: "Got support, assurances, confirmation." Second opinions may not always confirm; indeed, they may confuse the situation. In such a case one may have to return to square one and reformulate the problem, or, in a very personal and intuitive way, decide which source to trust. Managers need to do this all the time (Kotter 1982).

6. *Projective:* future oriented, but not related to political or personal situation (see 8 below); concerned with estimates and probabilities. What will be the effect of flush riveting on air speed, wing design, and wing stresses in airplanes? (Vincenti 1984).

7. *Motivational:* has to do with personal involvement, of going on (or not going on). In Dervin's terms: "got started, got motivated"; "Kept going."

8. *Personal or Political:* has to do with relationships, status, reputation, personal fulfillment. In Dervin's terms: "Got control"; "Things got calmer, easier"; "Got out of a bad situation"; "Avoided a bad situation"; "Took mind off things"; "Relaxed, rested"; "Got pleasure"; "Got connected to others." How will this decision affect my position with my boss? What effect will my negative vote on this piece of legislation have on my constituents? What situation am I in? What can I challenge? What conditions must I adjust to?

There is a strong need for more studies of differing populations working in varying contexts, and how individuals in those populations describe, in their own words, how specific information is used and how its use (or nonuse) affects their concerns.

The other side of this coin of problem resolution is content oriented. It asks basically if there are identifiable traits inherent in information, beyond subject matter, that can be related to the dimensions of problems and to the needs of people. MacMullin and Taylor have made a start by isolating and describing several such information traits (MacMullin & Taylor 1984, 98-102). Eight are very briefly described here.

1. *Quantitative continuum:* from quantitative data (phenomena that can be measured and represented numerically) to qualitative (descriptive).
2. *Data continuum:* from hard data (empirically derived and replicable) to soft data (not directly observable, must be inferred).
3. *Temporal continuum:* ranging from historical or precedence to forecasting and future modeling.
4. *Solution continuum:* ranging from single solution which meets resolution criteria to a range of options among which the receiver can choose on the basis of some internal, possibly inarticulate criteria or intuitions.
5. *Focus continuum:* from factual information of well-understood problems to diffuse information of idea generation and brainstorming.
6. *Specificity of use continuum:* ranging from applied (instrumental, immediately useful) to substantive (descriptive, know-what) to theoretical (explains and predicts why something works as it does).
7. *Aggregation continuum:* ranging from clinical information (a population of one) to census or aggregated information derived from large populations.
8. *Causal/diagnostic continuum:* causal information discusses why something happens; diagnostic describes what is happening.

Summary

For ease of scanning, the main points of this tentative IUE model are outlined here.

1. *Sets of People*
   - the professions
     - defined by formal standards
     - defined by problems and contexts
   - the entrepreneurs
   - special interest groups
   - special socioeconomic groups
   - Demographic variables
     - age, sex, marital status, race
     - socioeconomic status
     - education

- Nondemographic variables
  - media use
  - social networks
  - attitudes toward new technology, education, risk-taking, and innovation
2. *Problems*
   - not static
   - each IUE has discrete classes of problems
   - problem dimensions (examples)
     - well structured/ill structured
     - complex/simple
     - assumptions agreed upon/not agreed upon
     - familiar/new patterns
3. *Settings*
   - importance of organization style and structure, if applicable
   - domain of interest
   - access to information
   - history and experience
4. *Resolution of problems*
   - information uses
     - enlightenment
     - problem understanding
     - instrumental
     - factual
     - confirmational
     - projective
     - motivational
     - personal or political
   - information traits
     - quantitative continuum
     - data continuum
     - temporal continuum
     - solution continuum
     - focus continuum
     - specificity of use continuum
     - aggregation continuum
     - causal/dianostic continuum

Three Information Environments

The following sections explore very briefly three information use environments in the context of the structure discussed above. The IUEs chosen illustrate different kinds of information needs and uses, varying types of problems, and significant differences between what each regards as information and accepts as problem resolution. All three are highly dependent on information, but the definition of *valid* information values. The discussion on each of these follows roughly the structure developed above.

In at least one case—*engineers*—the approach taken by the author is one not shared by those who insist that engineering is "the art or science of making practical application of the knowledge of the pure sciences" (Florman 1976, x). An all too brief explanation of the author's different point of view is argued below in "Engineers."

The second IUE—*legislators*—represent a setting in which what is called information wears many faces, its value frequently dependent on how it is to be used. As one member of the U.S. Congress put it: "Information? What's information? Congressmen don't deal with 'information'. That's talk for political scientists. What I need to know is what people think" (quoted in Maisel 1981, 264). Research concern with the legislature as an information-using organism is relatively recent.

The third IUE, that of the *practicing physician,* again poses a different set of information concerns. The emphasis, by the way, is on the practice of medicine, not on medical research. Medicine, over many centuries, has been a self-critical and self-aware profession. We know a good deal about clinical decision making. A fair amount of effort has gone into early prototypes of medical expert systems, even though they are not yet generally applicable for the practitioner. An indication of the interest may be seen in journals which have started in the past two decades, such as *Methods of Information in Medicine, Medical Decision Making,* and *Journal of Clinical Computing.*

ENGINEERS

Science, Applied Science, and Engineering

Since the Second World War we have linked science and technology (engineering) closely, with science, especially physics, assuming the dominant role and engineering merely applying the knowledge handed down to it. We have even coined the acronym STINFO to signify information for both. This has become part of our culture, with some unfortunate results, because it hides the fact that science and engineering are quite different intellectual systems. As Thomas Allen has pointed out, "empirical investigation has found little support for . . . the long held belief in a continuous progression from basic research through applied research to development." Allen further comments that "technology builds on itself and advances quite independently of any link with the scientific frontier, and often without any necessity for an understanding of the basic science which underlies it (Allen 1977, 48). This observation is borne out by the Department of Defense Project HINDSIGHT, which, in studying technological innovation in weapons research, found that basic science of the preceding 20 years did not play a significant role in the development of the innovation (Sherwin & Isensen 1967; Utterback 1971). Similar and partially supportive results were found in investigations on nonmilitary innovations (Mowery & Rosenberg, 1982). Indeed, as Rosenberg points out, "the normal situation in the past, and to a considerable degree in the present, is that technological knowledge has *preceded* scientific knowledge . . . workable technological knowledge is likely to be attained before the deeper level of scientific understanding" (Rosenberg 1982, 144). Technological advances then cannot be explained by prior advances in basic science (Layton 1978, 61).

Engineering has been thought of as applied science, which masks the long history of formal engineering thinking, know-how, technique. and design which preceded scientific thought by several millennia (Layton 1974, 1978; Rosenberg 1982; Vincenti 1984, 1986; Price 1965, 1984). There *is* an applied science, an intellectual product of the last century or so, but just where the borders are between it and engineering are hard to determine.

We have made these observations principally to emphasize the differences between the three modes (sciences, applied sciences, and engineering) of thinking, doing, learning, and, especially relevant to the concerns here, how each seeks and uses information.

Studies in Information Use

Much of the past work on the use of information by engineers is flawed for several reasons. First is the perceived linkage and its direction, already discussed, between science and engineering. Secondly, reflecting the biases of that linkage, is that most studies of possible relevance to the engineering IUE have been done within the research and development context, i.e., science and applied science. Such studies miss the production engineer, the manufacturing engineer, the highway engineer, the sanitary engineer, etc., who make up the bulk of the engineering profession (National Research Council 1985). In speaking on manufacturing and engineering, MIT President Paul Grey was recently quoted as saying that "The highest prestige has been reserved for advanced research and development, and only casual attention has been paid to manufacturing." To which Professor of Engineering Arnold Kerr added: "Then we are surprised our cars don't work" (Rowe 1987). A third reason why such work is flawed is that, in almost all cases, the studies have committed the sin that we have noted before: "Researchers have been looking at something

they call information rather that at something users call information"
(Dervin 1983a, 158). Some of the studies, however, have useful insight into the information process, but they are in researcher's or
system's terms, rather than in user's terms. We won't mention the
number of downright poorly designed studies, and there are many
of them.

The Engineering Process

Nonengineers tend to see engineering only as the process of developing new products/systems, of innovation derived from new information, when in reality most engineering work is "the steady accretion
of innumerable minor improvements and modifications with only very
infrequent major innovation" (Rosenberg 1982, 7; see also Vincenti
1984; Wolek 1969).
     Engineers not only learn by doing, but, perhaps more important,
by using. The inability to predict with any precision how a large and
complex system will operate under real conditions requires that very
large safety factors be built into the original design.

> In science, what you don't know about is unlikely to hurt you (except
> possibly in some unfamiliar experimental situations). In engineering,
> however, bridges fall and airplanes crash, and what you don't know
> about can hurt you very much. (Vincenti 1986, 751fn)

As engineers receive feedback from users and from related observation of actual operation, they are able to reduce the uncertainties
(lack of information) concerning performance, and can, with confidence, generate changes that improve efficiency and operation substantially (Rosenberg 1982, 120–140).

Information Storage and Transfer

Part of our problem in dealing with engineering is how information
is stored and transferred. It is not in the usual package of a paper,
report, or book. Engineering consumes information, transforms it,
and produces a product or a system which itself is information bearing. But it is not in verbal form. Thus, as Allen points out, the engineer obtains his or her information by analyzing and decoding
physically encoded information, i.e., through artifacts, or by direct
personal contact with other engineers (Allen 1977, 3–5). Very little
work has been done directly on this form of information transfer,
in part because it does not match the linguistic patterns of the
sciences, nor is the physical artifact something controlled by tradi-

tional information agencies. The process is illuminated especially by studies of specific engineering developments, such as flush riveting for aircraft (Vincenti 1984) and airfoil design (Vincenti 1986). For information people trained to think in terms of recorded knowledge and the transfer of information in formal linguistic packages, this description of engineering may seem strange and inconsequential. However, as we stated early in this essay, we wish to describe information use environments in terms that approximate the reality of that context, and not description dictated by the information service or system. It is true that such a description may have little to do with present formal information systems and services. That is something information professionals will have to face and resolve. As Shuchman points out: "For at least 15 years researchers have demonstrated that there is serious discontinuity between the system producing technical and scientific information and the engineers to whom the information would be most useful" (Shuchman 1981, 57).

Reliance on the written word appears to be useful only when the author is directly available to explain and to supplement the content (Allen 1977). In extreme cases, engineers may be penalized for using the literature. Rosenbloom and Wolek report that an engineering manager highly respected by his peers and subordinates remarked that "when I see one of my men reading a professional journal I know he is wasting his time" (Rosenbloom & Wolek 1970, 7). This may be partially the result of something Allen reports.

> Most professional engineering journals are utterly incomprehensible to the average engineer . . . rely heavily on mathematical presentation, which can be understood by only a limited audience. . . . Perhaps the most unfortunate circumstance that ever befell the engineering profession is that . . . it looked to the scientific societies . . . to determine their form and function [i.e., of engineering societies]. (Allen 1977, 73–76)

As a result, the engineer has turned to the trade journal as his principal source, rather than to the professional literature.

Engineering Problems

The definition of an engineering problem is often more important and more difficult than is idea generation, and it has a critical impact on the quality of the solution. During the idea generation stage, which may run 5%–10% of the total project time (Wolek 1969), it is usual to consider a large number of possible solutions. Of these types of messages, only a small percentage come through the literature (11%, according to Allen 1977, 63), the remainder through personal contacts. Engineers, in contrast to scientists, tend to talk to colleagues before consulting the literature, if they do so at all. Generally, as Shuchman points out, "most engineers regard their technical assignments as problems to be worked out at the 'bench' and consider research into published sources seldom worth the effort since most engineering problems require original solutions" (Shuchman 1981, 27-28). It is worth noting that engineering problems are not fixed; in a sense, their solutions are dictated by specifications that may need to be altered, depending on properties of materials and design and time constraints. As Schon points out, "Engineering design is understandable as a reflective conversation with the materials of a situation" (Schon 1983, 172). As a result the problem itself may be altered. One of the concerns of working engineers is that their professional education often fails to recognize the concept of the variable problem (Frischmuth & Allen 1969) and the need to break away from fixed solutions.

Setting

Most engineers are employed by a bureaucratic organization and see it as the controller of the only reward system of importance. Many engineers work on products and/or systems of a proprietary nature. Thus, external information exchange is not encouraged. Engineers tend to communicate principally with their organizational colleagues, not only for this reason, but also because of shared knowledge, in which each knows what the other is referring to (Allen 1977). This is especially true of those working on product and process development, in contrast to those working on research or technical services (Allen, Lee, & Tushman 1980; Tushman 1978; Allen 1986).

The size of the firm may affect the acquisition of nontraditional information, especially under contingency conditions. The small firm is at a disadvantage because of the lack of external contacts (Fischer 1979). In these studies of organizations most of the attention is focused on R & D operations, and, for reasons stated earlier, one is not sure if they pertain to engineers as we have described them in this chapter. This is one of the problems in the literature. A fair amount of work has been done on the 'gatekeeper' in R & D laboratories (Holland 1974; Allen 1977; Taylor & Utterback 1975; Pelz & Andrews 1966; Frost & Whiteley 1971). Holland calls gatekeepers persons with high information potential, i.e., the information source value placed on an individual by his colleagues.

Information Support Technology

In studies in which new information services were initiated and controlled, Rubenstein and his colleagues found that there is a significant difference between what a technologist actually does about information and what he or she thinks he or she would do if certain constraints were not there (Rubenstein et al. 1970). This observation, and that of Shuchman noted above, imply that superficial improvements in conventional information services will not have much impact on the use of engineering information nor on the quality of engineering work.

Modeling, simulation, and testing of small scale artifacts, e.g., airfoils in wind tunnels, has been a traditional way of deriving information for full scale design (Wolek 1969). One of the difficulties with this form of information derivation is that a model may not behave in quite the same manner when brought up to full scale and tested under actual conditions. Today computer modeling and simulation, computer-aided drafting, computer-aided design (CAD) and computer-aided manufacturing (CAM) may in fact be major ways information technology aids the process of information transfer. Estimates of improvement of engineering productivity as a result of these systems range from 35% to 100% (National Research Council 1985, 68).

Summary

- There appear to be fundamental differences between engineering and science which reflect on the processes of information transfer, relevance, and use.
- Engineering knowledge builds on the information carried in the device or system.
- Technical literature does not build on itself as does scientific literature: Published material in engineering will never be abreast of the state of the art.
- In searching for and using recorded information accessibility ranks first, and technical quality second (Goldhar, Bragaw, & Schwartz 1976; Dewhirst, Avery & Brown 1978; Gerstenberger & Allen 1968).
- Engineers rely almost wholly on personal contact for information (Allen 1977; Shuchman 1981).
- In selecting an information channel engineers act, not to maximize gain, but rather to minimize loss (Gerstenberger & Allen 1968).
- There appears to be no relation between the quality of a solution and the use of literature (Allen 1977).
- Such systems as computer-aided design and computer-aided manufacturing may be the major ways that information technology aids the process of information transfer.

LEGISLATORS

> I don't know if I have been eating magic mushrooms or wandering around Alice's Wonderland, but the more I learn about this field the bigger it gets. I'm always losing ground. I think I'm going to cry.
> —Congressman Al Swift (Frantzich 1982, 11)

The Setting

Legislatures in democratic societies are unique institutions in terms of information and its movement, power and influence, complexity and trade-offs, and problems and decision making. As Frantzich writes: "On the most basic level, the U.S. Congress . . . translates information on societal needs and desires into public policy by evaluating information on potential options" (Frantzich 1982, 9). It is the legislative setting and the problems associated with that setting that are the principle definers of the IUE. This is in contrast to the doctor or engineer whose education, background, personal predilections are what define the environment, as do the kinds of problems they are trained to see as important.

In speaking of the U.S. Senate, Abrams has described the context vividly:

> detail is politics, and politics is one subject on which senators keep a very tight grip. The staff member may listen to all sides, boil down arguments, gather data, and recommend a course of action, but the ultimate choice is almost always political—who gets what—and that choice a politician carefully keeps to himself. No amount of reorganization of the Senate's committees or expansion of its staff, no amount of computerization, can ever lift the Senate from the slough of detail. . . . The Senate's problems do not stem from mismanagement and cannot be cured by efficiency experts, for the Senate is not a bureaucracy and can never become one. Its political organization is more akin to that at Runnymede than that of a modern corporation, and this is a condition which not even McKinsey & Co. can ever remedy. (Abrams 1978)

This does not mean that we cannot describe a legislature. It means rather that such descriptions will be fuzzy and messy, because legislatures are indeed messy institutions where the same information can be both redundant and useful and where conventional objectivity may not be of particular value. What are some of the general observations that can be made about Congress and probably about most legislatures, that illuminate the description of context?

Congress is a verbal culture (Fox & Hammond 1977, 103). Legislatures are almost invariably nonhierarchical (Mackenzie 1981,

19–20). Party is a major centralizing force (Fox & Hammond 1977, 104). Time is one of the most valuable resources (O'Donnell 1981, 148). The collegial character of the Congress, especially of the House, distinguishes it markedly from the executive branch of the government (Kieffer 1981, 210) and, one might say, from traditional bureaucracies anywhere. The primary products are highly value-laden decisions. They constitute key outputs in the "decision-making processes of the state or political system and as such provide key determinations of the basic ends and means the society adopts when it acts as a collectivity" (Cooper & Mackenzie 1981, 239).

The nature of the American legislature, local, state, or national, has changed significantly during the past two decades, making it more complex. The process is still going on. This is due to several major societal trends:

- the complexity of legislation and its impact resulting from the growing interdependence of economic, technological, and environmental concerns
- the need by constituents for assistance in dealing with large federal and state bureaucracies
- the number and especially the variety of bills considered in each session
- the necessity to maintain oversight of implementation of legislation

In response to these pressures, information support services for the U.S. Congress literally exploded during the 1970s. Though on a smaller scale this is true also for state legislatures (Chartrand & Bortnick 1980). The figures below are from Malbin (1980, 252-258) except where noted, and pertain to the 1970s.

- Support agencies (General Accounting Office, Congressional Research Service, Congress Budget Office, Office of Technological Assessment) increased personnel by 35%, to 6,500
- Committee staffs increased from 1,337 to 3.300
- Personal staffs of Members grew from 7,000 to 11,700, split between Washington and home districts or states
- Constituent cases handled by an individual congressman's office in 1976–1977 ranged from a low of 20 to a high of 95,000, with an average of 12,000 cases (Johannes 1981, 79)
- Recorded votes increased from 1,110 to 2,700, though the number of public bills enacted declined from 695 to 634.

These figures are noted because they are a part of the information environment of the U.S. Congress, and are, to a lesser degree, reflected in state legislatures.

Problems

Basically, legislators have two concerns: (a) servicing of their individual constituencies, i.e., those who elect them; and (b) passing laws and, in some cases, overseeing their implementation. Because of the nature of the bicameral legislature, servicing the needs of individual constituents is more significant for the lower than for the upper house. Though we may depict these two concerns as separate, they are intertwined in a complex and intricate web which has a profound effect on the kinds of information needed and how that information may be used, and indeed on the structure of the legislatures themselves. Legislation must be considered a result of compromise among the competing interests, ideologies, constituencies, and personalities. Information, then, is needed in response to six basic questions.

1. WHO is to be benefited or burdened?
2. WHAT are to be the benefits or burdens?
3. WHEN are they likely to begin and terminate?
4. WHERE are they to be in effect?
5. HOW—organizationally and procedurally—are they to be effected?
6. WHY are these benefits or burdens and the methods for effecting them in the public interest? (Borchard, circa 1975, 13).

Types of Information

Careful reading of these concerns indicate the complex interplay of political and policy information. Indeed, there are four different kinds of information critical to the legislator (Sabatier & Whiteman 1985, 397; Maisel 1981, 249-251).

- *Political Information*—about the position of the other political actors on pending legislation, about the likely impact of the legislation on one's own constituency, and hence the effect on reelection or career prospects.
- *Policy Information*—on the actual content of proposed legislation, on alternatives and options, on the magnitude and causes of the problems they are designed to address, and on their probable effects on society.
- *Evaluative Information*—in their oversight function as evaluators of ongoing programs, legislators need to know how programs are functioning, how good the data are that they receive from the executive branch, and how they are to be interpreted.
- *Management Information*—procedural or operational information. Legislators, in order to manage their time, need to know what is happening on the floor, when bills are likely to come up for debate and

vote, what is going on in their committees and in other committees, under what procedures certain pieces of legislation will be considered, when the legislature will adjourn for the day, week, session. The lack of this information in the past has been a frustrating part of a legislator's job. Current computer systems in Congress have done much to alleviate these problems.

Information Transfer

In legislative decision making every legislator plays two roles (Zweir 1979). The first is as a *specialist,* a trusted colleague who is knowledgeable about a particular legislative issue, usually because of his or her experience on a specific committee, e.g., banking, science and technology, budget, defense, etc., and the knowledge built up over the years. The second is as a *nonspecialist*—and every legislator is a nonspecialist in some areas of concern. In each of these roles, they receive and process information in different ways. As specialists they are served by, and are dependent on, the considerable expertise of committee staffs who search for, listen to, filter, evaluate, and analyze information of concern. In their role as nonspecialists they are dependent on the party leadership, on input from specialist colleagues, and on voting cues from trusted colleagues who share their political outlook (Matthews & Stinson 1970).

From this brief review we can infer that any policy information which does not recognize the importance of constituent and electoral factors in shaping legislative choice will probably be neglected (Webber 1986, 287). In seeking scientific testimony, legislators and scientists tend to talk past each other. The scientist deals with probabilistic quantities and facts developed through consensus. The legislator, constrained by time and political pressures, cannot deal with probabilities, or with voluminous and detailed technical data, and hence must compromise (U.S. Congress 1971, 473–480). Research information is useful as enlightenment and context, but has little direct impact on legislation, because it is often seen as politically infeasible to base action on such research alone (Caplan et al. 1975; Mitchell 1980).

Staff as Filters

Staff have become key elements in the information flow of Congress. To a large extent they are gatekeepers. This appears also to be the case in state legislatures (Sabatier & Whiteman 1985; Bradley 1980; Wissell, O'Connor, & King 1976; Conniff 1982; Porter 1975).

In 1979, there were 17,275 staff in Congress itself to support 535 senators and representatives, or about 32 clerical and professional staff for every elected member of Congress. This does not include the separate support agencies, such as the General Accounting Office, Library of Congress, etc. (Malbin 1980, 252). These committee and personal staff members are important in the flow of information throughout the legislature. They not only perform constituent service activities, but also undertake investigations, oversight, planning, and program evaluation. Personal legislative aides are, in many ways, decision formulators (Taylor 1986, 173) for Congress, presenting options, alternatives, and, within the framework of their expertise, recommending decisions. They prepare testimony, write speeches, and coordinate legislative strategy (Fuerbringer 1984; Nash 1987; Fox & Hammond 1977, 1–2). In some cases committee staff mark up and design the final form of important bills for committee approval (Fox & Hammond 1977, 143).

Computer Information Systems

Except for the management information systems, staff are the primary beneficiaries of computer information systems. Through the variety of systems available, for example, staff can research federal assistance programs, review current and historical budget data, search the U.S. Code and federal court cases, retrieve complete text of issue briefs developed by the Congressional Research Service, and search bibliographic and economic data bases throughout the country. There are problems associated with this automation. One of the more significant for the information environment is "the increasing fiscalization of legislative analysis." That is to say, because computers can only deal with definable and quantifiable aspects of legislation, financial implications become much more important than they were before the advent of the computer. In a way, however, computers represent the culmination of earlier societal concerns with data, in which quantification became the only valid representation of reality. Instead, as Goldberg points out, "of concerning themselves with the physical, cultural, and sociological implications of national programs, members' principal attention often focuses on how programs will affect tax rates, inflation, the value of the dollar, or on the prospect of a balanced budget" (Goldberg 1981, 287–288). This note harks back to an observation at the beginning of this chapter that information technology, be it book or computer, tends to prescribe the size, shape, function, dynamism, and *even the content of information systems*. It defines what is acceptable as knowledge or information. This is indeed something to worry about.

Summary

We have presented perhaps a more chaotic picture of a legislature than is in fact the case. Legislatures do function: they do form policy, pass laws, and perform oversight responsibilities. They may not do these things in very rational fashion; they are not bureaucracies. In summary we can say the following:

- A legislature is a verbal culture.
- Legislatures need four different kinds of information: political, policy, oversight, and managerial.
- Committee and personal staff are primary gatekeepers and analyzers of information, which comes from legislative support agencies, executive departments, lobbyists, external sources, and constituents.
- Computer systems, at present, perform much needed management information functions; computers, however, may have a deep and restrictive effect on the types of information perceived to be utilizable, and hence on the basis upon which judgments are made.

THE PRACTICING PHYSICIAN

Types of Practitioners

Practicing physicians, and the settings in which they work, differ from the previous two contexts. The physician is generally not part of an organization, or, if he or she is affiliated with an organization such as a hospital, the relationships are not those to be found in the usual bureaucratic organization. In contrast to large engineering projects or to the setting of policy in legislatures, the physician's concern is directed toward the well-being of a single human being, a patient. The practitioner faces a tremendous variety of medical situations every day which demand judgment and decision, often without recourse to any external information source.

We need to distinguish first between the basic medical scientist and the practicing physician. The latter takes care of patients, and must know what he or she is trying to cure, and indeed what constitutes a cure. The basic scientist has no concern for these questions (King 1982, 136). In a sense these represent two contrasting views of disease. "One of these concepts views disease as an entity . . . as a thing existing by itself, whereas the other fixes attention upon a sick patient and contemplates the clinical attributes that are observed. . . . In the first a decision can be described completely in terms of attributes and without any reference to patients" (Blois 1984,

77–79). This dichotomy between a disease as (a) a thing described in texts, and (b) a set of dynamic symptoms which a physician observes in a patient poses some particular and peculiar (to medicine) problems in information and its utility.

Generally, students of medical information transfer have noted two types of practitioners. For the first, their patients are the only focus of their work: they are completely patient oriented. The second group "takes as their point of reference their professional colleagues, either those within the local community or those at the top of the profession" (Coleman et al. 1966, 185-186). This should not be misinterpreted; they are both patient oriented, the former exclusively so, the latter, who may be medical specialists, within the larger framework of their special branch of medicine. For example, the latter may write and publish; the former almost never will. These orientations affect information behavior. The Coleman study, for example, found there were sharp differences in time of introduction of the drug gammanym between the two types. The profession-oriented doctors "were considerably ahead of the patient-oriented group, both in date of introduction and in the proportion who had used it by the end of the 16-month survey period" (Coleman et al. 1966, 186). The authors further note that both the lack of information, and, when they did know of the drug, a sensitivity to their patient's economic situation, predisposed the patient-oriented doctor against the use of the drug. Since this study was done in the early 1960s, one may wonder today what affect medical insurance and medical malpractice suits might have on the acceptance and use of a new drug.

Problems

Basically, the problems, the questions, a physician faces have, historically speaking, remained the same over the centuries. The answers to those questions, and the means of deriving information useful in diagnosis have changed dramatically—but not the questions. King (1982, 9-10) suggests the following general questions as basic to the practitioner's frame of reference:

- What is the disease from which the patient suffers?
- How can we identify it?
- What can we do for it?
- How can we prevent it?
- What is the cause?
- How much confidence can we place in our assertions and our judgments?

King argues that these have been the fundamental questions of the medical profession for the past 2500 years.

Information Gathering

Several fundamental changes in 19th-century medicine had a profound effect on the gathering of information. First was a change in the approach to disease as something that always had to be treated to one in which "certain diseases were perceived to be self-limited, got better of themselves" (Thomas 1979, 160). The second was the invention of the stethoscope, a means whereby a doctor could derive data about a patient without depending only on the patient's own description (King 1982, 82–84). This, of course, was the beginning of a whole line of technological aids to help acquire diagnostic information, from the microscope to computed tomography, biopsies, and nuclear imaging.

In order to approach answers to these problems—and the answers still remain judgmental, even with today's diagnostic aids (King 1982 308)—the doctor gains information and knowledge from several sources. First of all is the particular patient. "Many distinguished physicians," Blois writes, "have taught that history-taking is the most critical step in the entire diagnostic process, and that performance in this is what separates the exceptional physician from the less able" (Blois 1984, 165). Even before a single word is spoken, however, a doctor will derive information from nonverbal clues: the gait, clothing, general appearance, handshake, age, gender (Cutler 1985, 12). As the interview proceeds, the doctor begins to formulate hypotheses about the patient's ailments (Elstein, Shulman, & Sprafke 1978, ix). In fact, as Cutler points out, "Two minutes of meaningful conversation directs you to the correct diagnosis nine times out of ten" (Cutler 1985, 186). The ability to derive useful information through interview and to interpret that information seems to be based, not unnaturally, on "the possession of relevant bodies of information and a sufficiently broad experience with related problems" (Elstein et al. 1978, x). The patient not only provides data through verbal means, the interview, but also through tests and other means such as x-rays, cardiograms, etc. The doctor must still interpret these varied data. Where there is high consensus in the profession that, when, for example, symptoms A, B, C, and D occur together in a certain type of patient, then that patient has x and can be treated accordingly. These are text book cases and the information problems are relatively trivial. It is when the symptomatic data do not match any easy or known pattern, when there is low consensus, or where there are honest differences in data interpretation or treatment, that information seeking becomes critical (Brittain 1985).

Transfer of Information

Mick's study of information behaviors in the Stanford Medical School indicates that, as one might expect, medical students generally were dependent on personal notes, plus colleagues (Mick 1972). As one moved to practitioners, there was far less dependence on notes and more on colleagues and other external sources. Stinson and Mueller (1980) studied the information habits of health professionals in staying abreast of current advances in medicine. Physicians made up about 75% of the sample; consequently, it is difficult to interpret the results in terms of practitioners alone. Their results do seem to indicate that health professionals in urban settings used journals more than those in urban or semiurban settings, and that those in solo practice made less use of local medical libraries than did those in group or institutional practice. On the interpersonal level, Weinberg and his colleagues studied physician networks in a single county (population 66,000, with 79 physicians, at least 100 miles away from a major medical center). The study centered on questions concerning suspected or confirmed heart disease. As one might surmise, there were a small number of clusters, six in this case, around medical opinion leaders in the cardiovascular field in the county, with some significant links outside (Weinberg, Ullian, Richards, & Cooper 1981).

The well-known work of Coleman and his colleagues in the early sixties concentrated on the introduction of the drug gammanym. One of the more frequently cited conclusions was that pharmaceutical representatives were the first source of information about the new drug (Coleman et al. 1966, 53). However, the study carefully distinguished between receiving the information and actual use of the drug, which was legitimated by professional colleagues and/or the professional literature (Coleman et al. 1966, 64). In contrast to the Coleman study, Manning and Denson (1980) found, in studying the introduction of cimetidine, that pharmaceutical representatives ranked considerably lower than medical journals, meetings, and colleague consultation as primary sources. Related to this, in the Scura study, several physicians responded that they had cut their use of representatives as sources, "since the representatives are now more likely to be trained in business and selling techniques than in the sciences, as had previously been the case " (Scura & Davidoff 1981, 141). These are obviously but a few of the many papers on the use of external medical information sources.

Effect of Information

In most studies of the physician's information behavior, little attention has been paid to the effect specific information has on physician behavior or on patient well-being. In most instances, such studies start from the service, for example, the library or continuing education unit, and hence tend to have the bias commented on before. In a study by Scura and Davidoff of the impact of clinical librarian service, they write that, "although we did not attempt measurement of the impact of clinical librarian services on outcome, we have obtained preliminary evidence that the services affected treatment in a substantial percentage, 20% of the cases" (Scura & Davidoff 1981, 51). Similar work has been done by D. N. King (1986) at the University of Illinois. Worth noting here is that there was no attempt, in either case, to obtain in the physician's own words exactly what the effect of the information was.

Information Support Systems

Recent work in support of the use of medical information has taken two forms. The first is the development of means of tapping the vast body of recorded medical knowledge through such traditional systems as MEDLINE. For the practitioner, however, they are too difficult to access and too undiscriminating, though clinical librarian intermediaries can be helpful. Recently we have seen the development of specific computer-based knowledge bases, e.g., the Hepatitis Knowledge Base, really dynamic equivalents of earlier handbooks and manuals on specific diseases. They are, however, costly forms of reorganizing, evaluating, and continually updating data on a specific medical subject matter (Siegel 1982). These, or something like them, are probably necessary in the long run, though just how practitioners will tap them is moot at this time—in terms of both physical and intellectual accessibility. The second direction is that of decision analysis, the development of computer programs for the management of common medical problems, e.g., "criteria for diagnosing chest pain" or "optimal timing of repeated medical tests." As one might expect, there is controversy over such programs, which require, because the computer requires, precise quantification in areas thought to be dependent on the powers of intuition, judgment, and hunch. In his review of the pros and cons of decision analysis, Cutler states that "there is room and need for all tactics. The good physician must learn to intertwine hard facts with soft intellect" (Cutler 1985, 45).

Both of these types of information support are attempts to provide easy access to external knowledge or to externally developed decision analysis. Blois points out that, in addition to specific patient information and the general corpus of medical knowledge, "the accumulation of the individual physician's own personal experience" is often overlooked in medical informatics. "We can thus visualize,"

Blois writes, "the physician's information environment as resulting from the merging of these [three] different information sources, and their flows converging at a single time and place" (Blois 1985, 49).

Kochen, in a very preliminary study, points out that "clinicians rely primarily on their internal memories of personal experiences" (Kochen 1983, 83). Physicians usually recall by patient's name. They also to a lesser extent rely on the recall of recent reading, meetings, and discussions with colleagues. Except for patient files there is little formal organization or linkage among remembered or physically stored information at present in the practitioner's office (Covell, Uman, & Manning 1985).

If this picture is approximately valid, then one of the primary needs for the practitioner is memory augmentation and data management, which would (a) organize and link his or her patient records with references and notes of reading, meetings, and discussion, and (b) provide easy access to a highly filtered recall of knowledge bases or decision trees when necessary. Such a data base management system is, of course, the dream of all professionals who work with a variety of information inputs. The physician, however, has particular pressures: Time, variety, recall of personal experience, and the magnitude of potentially useful external information.

Summary

- Practicing physicians have as their primary objective the well-being of patients.
- There are many patients every day with widely varying states and symptoms.
- The following questions are basic to the practitioner's frame of reference: What is the disease? How identified? What can be done? How can it be prevented? What is the cause? How much confidence do we have in our assertions and judgments?
- Information is derived from three sources: from the patient by interview and by tests, from personal experience, and from other external sources.
- In perhaps as many as 90% of cases, an experienced physician can make a correct diagnosis after a few minutes of interview.
- In the remainder of the cases, the physician may (a) require extensive tests; (b) scan personal files, including personal memory for analogous cases; (c) discuss with colleagues; and/or (d) try to retrieve relevant literature.
- The primary technological need for the practitioner is memory augmentation and highly personalized data management systems.

SUMMARY AND DISCUSSION

This chapter is an early attempt at structuring what it is we know about the information behavior of defined groups of people in their "natural settings." The author has covered a vast area. There are many points that need to be analyzed and hypotheses to be developed, and where possible, tested. The following comments are organized in three general areas.

Formalization of Listings

There are two specific areas where the author has abbreviated or listed without much discussion. Both occur in Resolution of Problems. The first is the list of information needs, or, better said, a list of uses to which information is put. In a way this difference in statement (needs and uses) signifies where one starts from: the problem which defines the need, or the resolution which defines the use. This needs clarification. The items in the list themselves require much fuller definition and possible expansion of categories, which can only come from more extensive studies of information use expressed in user terms.

The second is the listing of information traits and how these traits apply to or effect the resolution of problems. Not only does this relationship between information and problems need study, but, more fundamentally, the traits themselves need to be better explicated. Both analyses may need to be done in parallel, one informing the other.

Two New Categories

In the overall structure presented here—sets of people, problems, settings, resolutions—there may be a need for at least two additional categories of data which are important enough to be noted here. The first is how a given set of people perceive information. Because of the way they structure their universe, engineers, legislators, and physicians, for example, each see information differently. We hinted at this when we said that, for the engineer, the device or the system is a major carrier of information. In similar fashion, the physician must distinguish between what the patient describes or shows through testing as symptoms, and how he or she, the physician, interprets those symptoms. The former might be called raw information or *symptoms,* the latter interpreted information or *signs* (King 1982, 73–89). In this essay this concern was subsumed under *sets of people,* but it probably is critical and significant enough to be considered as a separate category.

The processes of decision represent a second possible new category. Generally, decision processes have been modelled on purely rational processes. Much financial support has gone into developing computer programs to make engineering or medical decisions or to assist the engineer or physician in making decisions. There has been a tendency in this work to perceive decision analysis as something formal, algorithmic, and thereby computable, excluding the importance of hunch and intuition based on experience and personal association. We need to have a better understanding of the nonrational (less rational?) environmental factors affecting these processes.

Requirements for Exploiting the Model

If the user-driven approach to information processes has promise, then there are several requirements beyond mere commitment to the user. In various ways these needs were threaded throughout the essay.

We need to free ourselves from the assumption that we can describe information behavior by starting from the system, the service, the knowledge base, or the information carrier. To use these as definers of useful information is misleading: only the recipient, the user, can define information in his or her context. This is not to say that this interface between information system/artifact and user is not complex and intellectually interesting, but the final determiner of information value is the user who sits in a particular context and develops criteria of information value from that context (Taylor 1986).

We need to examine very carefully certain assumptions, carried over from the scientific frame of reference, that such professions as engineering and medical practice can be assumed scientific in the same way that physics, chemistry, and biology are. We have argued that, especially in the case of engineering, it is precisely the processes of information storage, transfer, and use that make up many of the elements that distinguish engineering from the basic sciences *and their application*. The assumption of direct connectivity has in this case resulted in poor information support for engineering work.

We need an understanding of basic definitions, a sort of rigorous flexibility with such terms as *information, use, media, decision, memory, experience,* etc. Flexibility is argued because we need to realize that, for example, *information* may have varied interpretations according to context and in the processes by which it becomes useful. In medicine the work done on decision analysis has illuminated some of these processes, and concomitantly the types of information which play a role in these processes.

We need descriptions of information use and effect in words of the user. The recent work of Dervin and Nilan (1986) and of Nilan and Fletcher (1987) have pointed the way.

We need long-term and situation specific studies such as those done by Coleman et al. (1966), Allen (1977), Kotter (1982), and Blois (1984). We need studies of specific contexts, from which we can gradually build up a body of theories and testable hypotheses about particular IUEs. Such studies will of necessity be multidimensional, including such "unscientific" approaches as observation over long periods of time. Kotter, in his study of the general manager, discusses the necessity for and the difficulty of the multidimensional approach (Kotter 1982, 147-153).

If the presented structure is seen to be useful, then we need to ask if and how the results or insights of a particular study will contribute to the development of that structure. Perhaps more important, we need to ask if the structure as it develops can become a generalizable model, a fruitful means for organizing, describing, and predicting the information behavior of any given population in a variety of contexts.

REFERENCES

Abrams, E. 1978. The senate since yesterday. February 1978: 13 *The American Spectator*.

Ackoff, R. L. 1967. Management misinformation systems. *Management Science* 14(4): BB147–BB156.

Aguilar, F. J. 1967. *Scanning the Business Environment*. New York: MacMillan.

Allen, T. J. 1986. Organizational structure, information technology, and R & D productivity. *IEEE Transactions on Engineering Management* EM-33(May): 212–217.

Allen, T. J. 1977. *Managing the Flow of Technology*. Cambridge, MA: MIT Press.

Allen, T. J., D. M. Lee, and M. L. Tushman. 1980. R & D performance as a function of internal communication, project management, and the nature of the work. *IEEE Transactions on Engineering Management* EM-27(February): 2–12.

Blois, M. S. 1985. The physician's information environment. *Journal of Clinical Computing* 14(2): 48–51.

Blois, M. S. 1984. *Information and Medicine: The Nature of Medical Descriptions*. Berkeley, CA: University of California Press.

Bookstein, A. 1982. Sources of error in library questionnaires. *Library Research* 4(Spring): 85–94.

Borchard, K. 1975. Toward a Theory of Legislative Compromise. Paper presented at Faculty Seminar, Program on Information Technologies and Public Policy, Harvard University, Cambridge, MA.

Boulding, K. E. 1978. The future of the interaction of knowledge, energy, and materials. *Behavioral Science Research* 13(3): 169–183.

Bradley, R. B. 1980. Motivations in legislative information use. *Legislative Studies Quarterly* 3(August): 393–406.

Brinberg, H. R. 1980. The Contribution of Information to Economic Growth and Development. Paper presented at the 40th Congress of the International Federation for Documentation, Copenhagen, Denmark.

Brittain, J. M. 1985. *Consensus and Penalties for Ignorance in the Medical Sciences: Implications for Information Transfer.* British Library Research and Development Report No. 5842. London: Taylor Graham.

Caplan, N., A. Morrison, and R. J. Stambaugh. 1975. *The Use of Social Science Knowledge in Policy Decisions at the National Level.* Ann Arbor, MI: Institute for Social Research.

Chartrand, R. L., and J. Bortnick. 1980. An overview of state legislative information processing. In *Legal and Legislative Information Processing*, ed. B. Krevitt-Eres, 49–73. Westport, CT: Greenwood Press.

Chen, C. C., and P. Hernon. 1982. *Information Seeking: Assessing and Anticipating User Needs.* New York: Neal-Schuman.

Coleman, J. S., E. Katz, and H. Menzel. 1966. *Medical Innovation: A Diffusion Study.* New York: Bobbs-Merrill.

Conniff, W. P. 1982. Information Patterns of the New York State Assembly Staff. Syracuse University. Unpublished doctoral dissertation.

Consumer Dynamics Inc. 1981. Development of a Market Research Tool to Support the Design of Information and Education Programs. Final Report, Phase III, Contract No. USDA53-K06-9-76. Rockville, MD: Consumer Dynamics.

Cooper, J., and G. C. Mackenzie. 1981. *The House at Work.* Austin, TX: University of Texas Press.

Covell, D. C., G. C. Uman, and P. R. Manning. 1985. Information needs of office practice: Are they being met? *Annals of Internal Medicine* 103(October): 596–599.

Crane, D. 1972. *Invisible Colleges: Diffusion of Knowledge in Scientific Communities.* Chicago, IL: University of Chicago Press.

Cutler, P. 1985. *Problem Solving in Clinical Medicine.* 2nd ed. Baltimore, MD: Williams and Wilkins.

Dervin, B. 1983a. Information as a user construct: The relevance of perceived information needs to synthesis and interpretation. In *Knowledge Structure and Use: Implications for Synthesis and Interpretation*, eds. S. A. Ward, and L. J. Reed, 153–183. Philadephia, PA: University Press.

Dervin, B. 1983b. An Overview of Sense-Making Research: Concepts, Methods and Results to Date. Paper presented at Annual Meeting of the International Communication Association, Dallas, TX.

Dervin, B. 1975. Strategies for Dealing with the Information Needs of Urban Residents: Information or Communication. Paper presented at the International Communication Meeting, Chicago, IL.

Dervin, B., and M. Nilan. 1986. Information Needs and Uses. In *Annual Review of Information Science and Technology*, vol. 21, ed. M. E. Williams, 3–33. White Plains, NY: Knowledge Industry Publications.

Deshpande, R., and G. Zaltman. 1983. Patterns of research use in private and public sectors. *Knowledge: Creation, Diffusion, Utilization* 4(June): 561–575.

Dewhirst, H. D., R. D. Avery, and E. M. Brown. 1978. Satisfaction and performance in research and development tasks as related to information accessibility. *IEEE Transactions on Engineering Management* EM-25(August): 58–63.

Eisenberg, D., and T. L. Wright. 1985. *Encounters with QI: Exploring Chinese Medicine*. New York: W.W. Norton & Company.

Elstein, A. S., L. S. Shulman, and S. A. Sprafka. 1978. *Medical Problem Solving: An Analysis of Clinical Reasoning*. Cambridge, MA: Harvard University Press.

Fabisoff, S. G., and D. P. Ely. 1974. *Information and Information Needs*. Syracuse, NY: Syracuse University, Center for the Study of Information and Education.

Feldman, M. S., and J. G. March. 1981. Information in organizations as signal and symbol. *Administrative Science Quarterly* 26(June): 171–186.

Fischer, W. A. 1979. The acquisition of technical information by R&D managers for problem solving in nonroutine contingency situations. *IEEE Transactions on Engineering Management* EM-26(February): 8–14.

Florman, S. G. 1976. *The Existential Pleasures of Engineering*. New York: St. Martins.

Fox, Jr., H. W., and S. W. Hammond. 1977. *Congressional Staffs: The Invisible Force in American Lawmaking*. New York: Free Press.

Frantzich, S. E. 1982. *Computers in Congress: The Politics of Information*. Beverly Hills, CA: Sage.

Frischmuth, D. S., and T. J. Allen. 1969. A model for the description and evaluation of technical problem solving. *IEEE Transactions on Engineering Management* EM-16(May): 58–63.

Frost, P., and R. Whitely. 1971. Communication patterns in a research laboratory. *R & D Management* 1(April): 71–79.

Fuchs, V. R., ed. 1969. Production and Productivity in the Service Industries. *Studies in Income and Wealth* 34.

Fuerbringer, J. The men behind the men behind the budget. April 24, 1984. *New York Times*.

Garvey, W. D., K. Tomita, and P. Woolf. 1979. The dynamic scientific information user. In *Communication: The Essence of Science*, ed. W. D. Garvey, 256–279. Elmsford, NY: Pergamon Press.

Gerstenberger, P. G., and T. J. Allen. 1968. Criteria used in the selection of information channels by R & D engineers. *Journal of Applied Psychology* 52(4): 272–279.

Goldberg, J. A. 1981. Computer usage in the house. In *The House at Work*, eds. J. Cooper, and G. C. Mackenzie, 275–291. Austin, TX: University of Texas Press.

Goldhar, J. D., L. K. Bragaw, and J. J. Schwartz. 1976. Information flows, management style, and technological innovation. *IEEE Transactions on Engineering Management* EM-23(February): 51–62.

Holland, W. E. 1974. The special communicator and his behavior in research organizations. *IEEE Transaction on Professional Communication* PC-17(December): 48–53.

Huberman, M. 1983. Recipes for busy kitchens: A situational analysis of routine knowledge use in schools. *Knowledge: Creation, Diffusion, Utilization* 4(June): 478–510.

Johannes, J. R. 1981. Casework in the house. In *The House at Work*, eds. J. Cooper, and G. C. Mackenzie, 78-96. Austin, TX: The University of Texas.

Kieffer, J. A. 1981. Providing administrative support services to the house. In *The House at Work*, eds. J. Cooper, and G. C. Mackenzie, 210-236. Austin, TX: The University of Texas.

Kimberly, J. R., et al. 1980. *The Organizational Life Cycle.* San Francisco, CA: Jossey-Bass.

King, D. N. 1986. The Contribution of Hospital Library Information Services to Clinical Care: A Study in Eight Hospitals. Draft copy.

King, L. S. 1982. *Medical Thinking: A Historical Preface.* Princeton, NJ: Princeton University.

Knott, J., and A. Wildavsky. 1980. If dissemination is the solution, what is the problem? *Knowledge: Creation, Diffusion, Utilization* 1(June): 537–578.

Kochen, M. 1983. How clinicians recall experience. *Methods of Information in Medicine* 22(April): 83–86.

Kotter, J. P. 1982. *The General Managers.* New York: Free Press.

Layton, Jr., E. T. 1978. Millwrights and engineers, science, social roles, and the evolution of the turbine in America. In *The Dynamics of Science and Technology*, eds. W. Krohn, E. T. Layton, Jr., and P. Weingart, 61–87. Dordrecht, Holland: D. Reidel.

Layton, Jr., E. T. 1974. Technology as knowledge. *Technology and Culture* 15(January): 31–41.

Lide, Jr., D. R. 1981. Critical data for critical needs. *Science* 212(June 19): 1343–1349.

Lowry, G. B. 1979. *Information Use and Transfer Studies: An Appraisal.* Washington, DC: US Department of Education, Educational Resources Information Center (ERIC).

Mackenzie, G. C. 1981. Coping in a complex age: Challenge, response, and reform in the House of Representatives. In *The House at Work*, eds. J. Cooper, and G. C. Mackenzie, 3–22. Austin, TX: University of Texas Press.

MacMullin, S. E., and R. S. Taylor. 1984. Problem dimensions and information traits. *The Information Society* 3(1): 94–111.

Maisel, L. S. 1981. Congressional information sources. In *The House at Work*, eds. J. Cooper, and G. C. Mackenzie, 247–274. Austin, TX: University of Texas Press.

Malbin, M. J. 1980. *Unelected Representatives: Congressional Staff and the Future of Representative Government.* New York: Basic Books.

Manning, P. R., and T. A. Denson. 1981. How internists learned about Cimetidine. *Annals of Internal Medicine* 92: 690–692.

March, J. G., and H. A. Simon. 1958. *Organizations*. New York: John Wiley & Sons.

Matthews, D. R., and J. A. Stinson. 1970. Decision-making by US representatives: A preliminary mode. In *Political Decision-Making*, ed. S. Ulmer, 14–43. New York: Van Nostrand Reinhold.

Mick, C. K. 1972. Information Seeking Style in Medicine. Unpublished doctoral dissertation, Sanford University, Palo Alto, CA.

Mintzberg, H. 1975. The manager's job: Folklore and fact. *Harvard Business Review* 53(4): 49–61.

Mitchell, D. 1980. Social science impact on legislative decision making: Process and substance. *Educational Research* 9(10): 9–12; 17–19.

Mowery, D. C., and N. Rosenberg. 1982. The influence of market demand upon innovation: A critical review of some recent empirical studies. In *Inside the Black Box: Technology and Economics*, ed. N. Rosenberg, 193–241. New York: Cambridge University Press.

Nash, N. C. Power and the Congressional aide. February 22, 1987. *New York Times*.

National Research Council. 1985. *Engineering Education and Practice in the United States: Engineering Employment Characteristics*. Washington, DC: National Academy Press.

Nilan, M., and B. Dervin. 1986. Sense Making and Information Seeking: A Factor Analysis of Information Seeking Dimensions. Unpublished manuscript.

Nilan, M., and P. Fletcher. 1987. Information behaviors in the preparation of research proposals. In *Proceedings of the 50th ASIS Annual Meeting*, ed. C. C. Chen, 186–192. Medford, NJ: Learned Information.

O'Donnell, T. J. 1981. Controlling legislative time. In *The House at Work*, eds. J. Cooper, and G. C. Mackenzie, 127–150. Austin, TX: University of Texas Press.

O'Reilly III, C. A. 1979. *Variations in Decision Makers' Use of Information Sources: The Impact of Quality and Accessibility of Information*. Berkeley, CA: School of Business Administration.

Paisley, W. J. 1980. Information and work. In *Progress in Communication Sciences*, vol. 2, eds. B. Dervin, and M. J. Voigt, 113–165. Norwood, NJ: Ablex.

Pelz, D. C., and F. M. Andrews. 1966. *Scientists in Organizations: Productive Climates for Research and Development*. New York: Wiley.

Porter, H. O. 1975. Legislative information needs and staff resources in the American states. In *Legislative Staffing: A Comparative Perspective*, eds. J. J. Heaphey and A. P. Bulutis, 39–59. New York: Sage.

Price, D. 1984. Of sealing wax and string. *Natural History* 93(1): 49–56.

Price, D. 1965. Is technology historically independent of science? A study in statistical historiography. *Technology and Culture* 6 (Fall): 553–568.

Roberts, N. 1982. A search for information man. *Social Science Information Studies* 2(April): 93–104.

Rogers, E. M. 1983. *Diffusion of Innovations*. 3rd ed. New York: Free Press.

Rosenberg, N. 1982. *Inside the Black Box: Technology and Economics.* New York: Cambridge University Press.

Rosenbloom, R. S., and F. W. Wolek. 1970. *Technology and Information Transfer.* Boston, MA: Harvard University, Graduate School of Business Administration.

Rowe, J. 1987. More engineers for factory floors. *Christian Science Monitor* (March 9): 25.

Rubenstein, A. H., et al. 1970. Explorations in the information seeking style of researchers. In *Communication Among Scientists and Engineers,* eds. C. E. Nelson and D. K. Pollock, 209–231. Lexington, MA: DC Heath.

Sabatier, P., and D. Whiteman. 1985. Legislative decision making and substantive policy information: Models of information flow. *Legislative Studies Quarterly* 10(August): 395–421.

Schon, D. A. 1983. *The Reflective Practitioner: How Professionals Think in Action.* New York: Basic Books.

Scura, G., and F. Davidoff. 1981. Case-related use of the medical literature: Clinical librarian services for improving patient care. *Journal of the American Medical Association* 245(January 2): 50–52.

Sherwin, E. W., and R. S. Isenson. 1967. Project Hindsight. *Science* 156(June 23): 1571–1577.

Shuchman, H. L. 1981. Information Transfer in Engineering. Report No. 451-46-27, The Futures Group.

Siegel, E. R. 1982. Transfer of information to health professionals. In *Progress in Communication Sciences,* vol. 3, eds. B. Dervin and M. Voigt, 311–334. Norwood, NJ: Ablex.

Simon, H. A. 1976. *Administrative Behavior: A Study of Decision-Making Processes in Administrative Organization.* 3rd ed. New York: Free Press.

Slovic, P. 1987. Perception of risk. *Science* 236(April 17): 280–285.

Stinson, E. R., and D. A. Mueller. 1980. Survey of health professionals' information habits and needs. *Journal of the American Medical Association* 243(January 11): 140–143.

Taylor, R. L., and J. M. Utterback. 1975. A longitudinal study of communication in research: Technical and managerial influences. *IEEE Transactions on Engineering Management* EM-22(May): 80–87.

Taylor, R. S. 1968. Question negotiation and information seeking in libraries. *College & Research Libraries* 29: 178–194.

Taylor, R. S. 1962. The process of asking questions. *American Documentation* 13: 391–396.

Taylor, R. S. 1986. *Value-Added Processes in Information Systems.* Norwood, NJ: Ablex.

Thomas, L. 1979. *The Medusa and the Snail.* New York: Viking Press.

Tushman, M. 1978. Technical communication in research and development laboratories: Impact of project work characteristics. *Academy of Management Journal* 21(December): 624–645.

U.S. Congress. House of Representatives 92nd Committee on Science and Astronautics. 1971. *Technical Information for Congress.* 1969. Reprint. Washington, DC: Government Printing Office.

Utterback, J. M. 1971. The process of innovation: A study of the origination and development of ideas for new scientific instruments. *IEEE Transactions on Engineering Management* EM-18(November): 124–131.

Vincenti, W. G. 1986. The Davis wing and the problems of airfoil design: Uncertainty and growth in engineering knowledge. *Technology and Culture* 27(October): 717–758.

Vincenti, W. G. 1984. Technological knowledge without science: The innovation of flush riveting in American airplanes, ca. 1930 - ca. 1950. *Technology and Culture* 25(July): 540–576.

Webber, D. J. 1986. Explaining policymakers' use of policy information: The relative importance of the two-community theory versus decision-maker orientation. *Knowledge: Creation, Diffusion, Utilization* 7(December): 249–290.

Weinberg, A. D., L. Ullian, W. Richards, and P. Cooper. 1981. Informal advice and information-seeking between physicians. *Journal of Medical Education* 56: 174–180.

Wersig, G., and G. Windel. 1985. Information science needs a theory of "information actions." *Social Science Information Studies* 5(January): 11–32.

Wilson, T. D. 1981. On user studies and information needs. *Journal of Documentation* 37(March): 3–15.

Wissel, P., R. O'Connor, and M. King. 1976. The hunting of the legislative snark: Information searches and reforms in U.S. state legislatures. *Legislative Studies Quarterly* 1(May): 251–267.

Wolek, F. W. 1969. The engineer: His work and needs for information. *Proceedings of the Annual Meeting of the American Society for Information Science* 6: 471–476.

Zweir, R. 1979. The search for information: Specialists and nonspecialists in the U.S. House of Representatives. *Legislative Studies Quarterly* 4(February): 31–42.

Toward a User-Centered Information Service[1]

Ruth C. T. Morris

INTRODUCTION

Much of the dissatisfaction with current research and practice in information needs was captured in Dervin and Nilan's 1986 *ARIST* review. Frustration on the part of information professionals stemmed from, among other things, the proliferation of systems that puzzled or irritated users and from the nagging suspicion that the needs of users were not well understood. Researchers were concerned by the lack of a strong theoretical base from which to design systems and services and by the lack of replication and of building on existing research (Dervin & Nilan 1986). Not surprisingly, research had failed to inform practice.

If we are to bridge the gap, we need a persuasive theoretical underpinning to any changes in practice. We have that in the work of Brenda Dervin. Although Dervin's work is not free from problems, it is nonetheless a powerful theory-based, user-centered approach to information needs. What is missing—and very much needed—is a way of applying and extending Dervin's theory to the creation of a newly conceived information service in a traditional setting. Library services as we know them need to be reconceptualized in terms of a user-centered approach. This is by no means an easy task. There is not much to guide us, and the results are far from certain. But as many authors have pointed out, to remain content with the status quo is to risk obsolescence.

This study will focus on interpreting Dervin's theory in the practical context of library services. It will raise basic questions. "What does it mean to have a user-centered reference service?" "What would a user-centered approach to cataloging entail?" It will examine how we might apply the sense-making approach throughout the library or information center. A sense-making approach to understanding how users seek, acquire, understand, and use information will require us to rethink the traditional service categories, the ways in which we evaluate and measure our services, and the goals of our services. Ultimately, we will also need to reexamine the way in which information professionals are trained, as well as the ways in which users think about our services and about libraries in general.

The term "user-centered," of course, is less than sharply defined. It is normally associated with the idea of increased attention to the needs of users of systems. I employ it here to denote a focused approach to thinking about information services and systems: one that regards information as something in part constructed by users, that recognizes common traits which humans share in processing information, and that views the contexts in which information needs arise (and the contexts in which they are pursued) as significant factors in the design of user-centered information systems and services. I mean this article to be provocative and suggestive rather than prescriptive. It does not contain "the answer," nor does it ask all the questions. But it offers a start toward bridging the famous gap between research and practice.

THE TRADITIONAL INFORMATION PARADIGM

At the core of Dervin's approach is the rejection of the traditional paradigm of information and the substitution of a "constructivist"[2] paradigm. The traditional paradigm, based on Shannon and Weaver (1949), sees information as external, objective, as something that exists outside the individual. It is a message transmitted from sender to receiver through a channel, and the message is informational in that it reduces ambiguity by reducing the number of alternative messages that could have been sent. Information in this traditional sense exists in an ordered world that is discoverable, definable, and measurable. When we seek information through the traditional paradigm, our goal is to find the external "information reality" that corresponds to our internal need.

As Dervin (1976; Dervin, Jacobson, & Nilan, 1982) points out, we don't talk as if we hold this traditional view of information. On the contrary, we admit that knowledge isn't absolute, that what really matters are people, that people change, and that a message sent equal a message received. Yet the library world continues to make assumptions based directly on the traditional model of information. Information is seen as something objective to be ferreted out from systems and reference tools and presented to the user, preferably at the right time and in the right format. Whatever the user's need, there is information to satisfy it. If we don't have the information, we can get it. Information is acquired through formal information systems such as books, journals, and online databases. Information must be "objective" to be valuable. Our users want (and deserve) the best information available.

Such assumptions, based on the traditional model have dictated the kinds of services we supply and the kinds of libraries we have created. We have (until quite recently) concentrated primarily on acquiring and managing collections of materials. We have utilized extensive cataloging and indexing systems to provide access to these materials. We have provided access to numerous databases that produce citations and abstracts and even full-text. We retrieve and duplicate articles from our own materials and from sources outside of our institution. And we have not ignored the user. We ask users for feedback on our services; we survey them to find out what they want; we market our services to them; and we offer to train them in using our services and systems. Services based on the traditional model target the "middle range" of users, those, for example, neither totally naive nor fully expert.

In general, users often seem pleased with our services. Those who respond to our surveys frequently indicate that they like what we do. The complaints are usually the obvious ones: we don't process things fast enough, interlibrary loan procedures are cumbersome, cataloging seems arbitrary, we don't have the book they want. The response to such complaints is equally familiar: if we had more resources, we could add more staff, provide better and faster services, and all would be well.

The fundamental issue, however, is not whether additional staff and resources could make the traditional model function better. Improvement is certainly possible, although additional resources in the short term seem unlikely. The basic issue is whether we are seeking to improve the right model.

Indeed, the changing economic climate and the changing information climate indicate serious threats to our position as traditional information intermediaries. Particularly in special libraries, information brokers direct-market services to users. The electronic information explosion has increased access to information of all kinds from computers at home and at work. The integrated technologies first demonstrated in the 1980's will become a reality in the nineties. A cover story in *USA Today* (November 19, 1992) indicated that the traditional passively receptive television set is about to change into a "multimedia, interactive TV, on-demand video, a knowledge navigator or who knows what else." Such systems integrate hypertext and images, providing information on a multitude of topics and in all kinds of formats: transcripts, maps, graphs, photographs, texts. Customized, personalized information will become available to individuals directly. Libraries consequently will be forced to change if they want to continue to play a role in information provision. One option is to revamp libraries in ways that recognize the centrality of the individual and that understand the changing nature of information. This, I believe, requires a fundamental change in models: the shift to a contructivist concept of information linked to a "sense-making" model of information seeking.

THE CONSTRUCTIVIST MODEL

Dervin's constructivist model of information (1976, 1977, 1992; Waldron & Dervin 1992) views information not as something objective and external, but as something constructed by the user. Information does not exist in the abstract—it needs to be interpreted: a threatening shape in a dark alley turns out to be bags of discarded trash; an article on Ben and Jerry triggers an idea on how to market a drug. Further, Dervin sees individuals moving along a time-space continuum that is constantly shifting. Such a world requires that we strive to make sense of ourselves and our environment through continual adjustments. We construct cognitive maps of our environment that are constantly being altered and refined as we experience new information. We are changed by new information, which thus changes how we interpret information past and future. We do not just adapt to a static world but create a reality that changes with us. How many times have we reread an article only to find something new and unexpected in it?

The sense-making model which derives from this constructivist paradigm is basically a cognitive approach to information seeking, in that it recognizes information as something that involves internal cognitive processes. Sense-making is not, however, solely intellectual. Affect or emotion is intimately involved in the individual's cognitive response to information. It can be an important element in, for example, the evaluation of relevance.[3] It is clearly crucial in understanding the concept of *need*. While Dervin doesn't specifically focus on the affective dimension of cognitive processes, it can be inferred from her approach and developed in ways that complicate and enrich her model.[4]

The user of information becomes the focus in this sense-making model. Information becomes "whatever an individual finds 'informing'" (Dervin 1977, 22). The sense-making model sees information as subjective, situational, holistic, and cognitive (Dervin & Nilan 1986): in short as constructivist. It focuses on understanding information within specific contexts and on understanding how information needs develop and how they are satisfied. It regards the user not as a passive receiver of external information but as the center in an active, ongoing process of change: information triggers perceptual changes in the user, and changes in the user alter how the information is perceived.

This approach immediately raises questions. If the individual is to be the focus, how do we deal with the dizzying array of different, unique information needs that all these diverse individuals will have? How can we provide a coherent service if everyone needs something different? It is at this point that Dervin differs from others who also reject the traditional paradigm of information. Dervin's work has been directed at understanding information needs by finding a way to acknowledge the uniqueness of individuals and their circumstances, while identifying commonalities in the processes they go through. Such commonalities permit systems and services to be created that provide appropriate help.

Dervin's method for studying information needs employs the "situation-gap-use" metaphor. She argues that all information needs stem from a discontinuity or "gap" in one's knowledge. The gap develops out of a specific "situation," and individuals attempt to bridge the gap through employing various tactics. What gets them over the bridge are called "uses" or "helps." Dervin has identified (approximately) 13 categories of metaphoric "gaps" which describe the types of problems people experience: "I hit a blank wall"; "I came to a fork in the road"; "I lost my way."[5] After studying over 40 different groups of people from blood donors to librarians and cancer patients, Dervin concluded that sense-making assumes "there is something systematic about individual behavior to be found by pursuing process orientations" (Dervin 1992, 81). Individual needs are not chaotic but systematic, and the systematic quality of needs must be understood as a process rather than as a static state. In effect, Dervin (among others) believes that information needs can be addressed by understanding the *process* that each individual goes through in experiencing a gap, in trying to resolve it, and in gaining something (especially new knowledge) from the experience.

RELATED APPROACHES TO INFORMATION SEEKING AND HOW THEY DIFFER FROM DERVIN

Three researchers whose work seems most closely related to Dervin's cognitive sense-making approach to information seeking are Belkin, Taylor, and Kuhlthau.[6] Each of these researchers focuses on different facets of the user's information need. All three approaches reflect awareness of the constructivist approach and of the sense-making model. They vary considerably, however, in the extent to which such an understanding is reflected in their work. The order in which they are presented here is significant: Belkin is least representative of the constructivist approach, and Kuhlthau the most. A brief summary of their work will be useful in clarifying how it differs from Dervin's approach.

Belkin

Belkin's approach is based in the hypothesis that an information need arises from an anomaly in the individual's knowledge state (Belkin 1980, Belkin et al. 1982). Because individuals can't easily express what they don't know or what is missing, questions submitted to information systems based on the individual's request won't adequately represent what is needed. In order to get around this difficulty, Belkin focuses instead on a "problem statement" which the individual prepares describing how the information need developed. Here Belkin is taking account of context, of the situational elements of the information need, and at this point Belkin and Dervin are in agreement: exploring the user's situation (Belkin's problem statement) is key, and understanding the gap (Belkin's anomaly) is important. Belkin is taking a cognitive approach in trying to understand how the user has conceptualized his problem.

But here the similarity ends. Belkin's concern is representing the user's problem statement on an information retrieval system: to do so, he converts the words of the statement into a semantic network representing connections among the terms. The context or situation, as represented by the problem statement, has been converted to a series of words and stems. Thus, context is no longer relevant except as part of a semantic net, where the frequency of the words is what establishes proximity. In describing the problems out of which their anomalous state arose, for example, users might say "It was very difficult for me to understand why this particular problem occurred when it did." Such a statement, reduced to word proximities, loses its significance. It is finally difficult to see Belkin's approach as fully user centered.

Taylor

Taylor has been interested in the user for over 20 years. In his classic paper on question-negotiation (1968), Taylor describes four stages involved in the development of a need-related question, beginning with the inarticulate stirring of uneasiness and concluding with the negotiated system-ready question. His approach here is clearly cognitive. The process he describes, that of struggling to express a need and of seeking information to resolve it, is clearly that of sensemaking.

In his work on information use environments, Taylor (1991) has focused directly on the situational aspect of information needs. He believes it is critical to "provide some structure on the uses of information: what information does to or for the recipient *and for his or her problem or situation*" (Taylor 1991, 221). Users make choices about what information is useful to them at particular times. "These choices," he insists, "are based, not only on subject matter, but on other elements of the context within which a user lives and works" (Taylor 1991, 218). A major contextual emphasis for Taylor is the type of problem being researched (Macmullin & Taylor 1984); because scientists and teachers tend to research different types of problems, he approaches the study of information use through analyzing the specific professional context.

Taylor sees the information use environment as key to understanding similarities and differences in information seeking and in the information use behavior of specific groups. It is through studying the information seeking and information use of distinctive groups (in his case, engineers, legislators, and physicians) that Taylor sees differences in, for example, their definitions of information and in their conception of what constitutes resolution to a problem. This approach, in its emphasis on studying specific groups, is quite different from what Dervin is proposing.

Dervin is interested in the situation at the moment when an individual intersects with the library.[7] At this moment, demographics don't matter; scientists or activists, physicians or legislators all share the commonality of an information need. They have come because they feel that the library would be useful (Dervin 1977, 27). It is important to understand the situation that led the individual to seek information in the library and to understand what different kinds of situations lead to different uses of information. These same individuals, with the same demographics, may come to the library on another day for a vastly different purpose. While this is quite obvious in a public library situation, it is also relevant in a research environment. With the advent of increased interdisciplinary and team research a chemist is rarely involved solely in chemistry. Requests may range from the traditional substructure searches to information on disease states or cell biology. Systems which focus on demographics alone will not be responsive to situationally motivated needs. Dervin, for example, sees the situation of "being at a crossroads" as the critical issue. She directs her research at identifying the different kinds of problem situations and at clarifying the specific "helps" that would facilitate bridging the information gap. Taylor acknowledges that "it might be more logical to discuss information users in terms of similar type of problems," which is of course Dervin's approach, but he is most concerned with "eventual input into systems design" and therefore decides instead to categorize users by their professional context (Taylor 1991, 219).

Taylor's approach reflects findings from the studies on information needs of scientists during the 1970s and 1980s (e.g., Allen 1988; Garvey 1979; Paisley 1968). These studies, which focused on information-seeking behavior and on information flow patterns, found clear differences in the ways in which different scientific disciplines used information sources and communicated among themselves. There is, therefore, an obvious value in studying the use of information within a specific (group) context, particularly in a special library environment. Taylor's emphasis on context, however, need not be seen solely as an alternative to the more generic approach suggested by Dervin; it can serve as an effective and valuable supplement: *both* context and process matter in understanding information needs.

Kuhlthau

Of the three researchers, Kuhlthau's approach is closest to Dervin's. She is clearly constructivist in her understanding of information needs. In fact, she describes her theory as a "constructive process" approach (Kuhlthau 1993). It is obviously also a process approach, though the process she focuses on is different. Crucial to her theoretical position is the "uncertainty principle," a cognitive and affective state that accompanies the initial stages of the research process, when students are unclear about their topic and when they have a gap or lack of clarity in their understanding. She believes that individuals in their approach to information seek meaning rather than answers; that hypothesis formulation is the critical point in the research process; that affective states are influenced by redundancy or uniqueness of information encountered during research; that mood states can be linked to specific stages of the research process; and that personal involvement in the search process increases positive feelings (Kuhlthau 1993). As this summary suggests, a key for Kuhlthau is the affective state of the user during the research process.

In observing and studying students in several studies over many years, Kuhlthau defined a series of stages that describe the research process, and she has linked these stages with their accompanying emotional states and behaviors. (These stages she then links to "zones of intervention," which I discuss later.) This work shares with Dervin an emphasis on the importance of understanding the processes people go through in seeking information. Kuhlthau differs from Dervin, however, in her emphasis on the experience of students who are *assigned* research papers. As we have seen, Dervin's process stages (situation-gap-uses) are generic and apply regardless if whether the user is a blood donor or nuclear scientist and regardless of the specific need. Kuhlthau's approach is not generic, and I suspect that corporate research scientists, for example, have a different approach to research and experience somewhat different affective states during the process than students do. Kuhlthau, however, has done an extraordinary job of applying both theoretical constructs and the results of her multiple experiments to a practical system of library service that offers an alternative to the traditional tool and system-oriented approach.[8] In this, she stands alone.

Summary

Belkin, Taylor, and Kuhlthau are each working to expand our understanding of the user's information needs. Belkin actively seeks to model cognitive activity in individual users through exploring the problem state and matching it to retrieval systems; Taylor seeks to understand how specific environments (including the physical setting, the types of information sought, and the nature and characteristics of problems) affect information seeking in different groups; and Kuhlthau identifies stages of research where intervention on the part of information professionals can help users both identify and resolve their information needs.

There are several reasons for examining Belkin, Taylor, and Kuhlthau in relation to Dervin's model. First, their work lends strong support to the belief that we are presently engaged in putting together a constructivist model that marks a significant break with the past. Second, because this model is still in the process of development, individual theorists have significant differences of opinion, and they approach this alternative paradigm from different backgrounds. We must therefore pay careful attention to the ways in which their thinking differs. Third, and most important, Belkin, Taylor, and Kuhlthau offer an opportunity for supplementing Dervin's model. Kuhlthau in particular suggests ways in which a user-centered, constructivist approach to information can help transform the day-to-day practical operations of a library.

INTERPRETING THE SENSE-MAKING MODEL
IN AN INFORMATION SERVICE

If Dervin's theory is to be really useful, it needs to be interpreted for library settings. Dervin has been of some help in focusing on the application of her theory (e.g., Dervin 1977, 1983; Dervin & Dewdney 1986), and some selected instances exist of what seem to me truly user-centered approaches in specific library activities, but I have found no attempt to construct an information service based on the sense-making model. What follows is an initial (and incomplete) attempt to suggest some ways in which selected areas of the library might modify or change their approach to library services by incorporating ideas implicit in the sense-making model.

Changes in specific services will be clearer if we first look at the ways in which we now approach services in general. In a corporate research library, for example, we ask questions such as "What information needs do the scientists have?" "What services do they want?" "What kind of information resources do they need?" "How can we help them use our collection and online catalog more effectively?" Such questions center on information as an external commodity to be fitted to users. The general approach they reflect is basically system-oriented or what Dervin calls "information-oriented" rather than user-centered.

A sense-making framework for specific services generates a series of new questions: "What did the user come to understand or find out as a result of, for example, a literature search?" "How did the user construct a new sense of his problem?" "What library resource served as impetus?" "How did the user find the information useful?" Such questions focus on determining how information helped or why it did not. They will help us understand the basis on which the library is or is not helpful to the individual in various specific encounters, involving reference, literature searching, cataloging and the other main services of a library (Dervin 1976, 20-24).

Before information professionals look at specific services, they need to consider the purpose of the library and to develop a mission statement that reflects a user-centered perspective. In a pharmaceutical research library, for example, a mission statement based on a constructivist model could include *facilitating problem-solving*. Problem-solving is a large part of what corporate scientists do in a pharmaceutical company. As Taylor (1991) suggests, the professional work group of the user creates a large part of the environmental context in which information needs develop. The facilitation of problem solving, however, is definitely *not* the current mission in pharmaceutical libraries. Most information centers see their role as providing access to information. Providing access implies a mediating role between users and information sources. Facilitating problem solving, by contrast, implies a more direct involvement in a *process* of understanding that is occurring in users. And as Durrance points out.

> Well-focused services that require contact between a librarian and a client group within the context of a problem environment are likely to change the public's perception of the librarian as information specialist. Such services move the librarian beyond answering the isolated reference question and into the role of a professional visibly helping the client solve problems. . . (Durance 1988, 168).

Reference Interview

One of the most obvious places to begin to examine user needs is at the point where users approach information professionals: the information desk. According to Dervin,

> a major purpose of library research must be focused on the question of how libraries can intervene usefully in individual sense-making processes. Since the individual user of the library cannot be predicted in advance, the librarian cannot be expected to have a perfect system match ready and waiting for each unique user. The librarian can be aware, however, of alternative strategies for interacting with users . . . (Dervin 1977, 29).

Staff at the Information Desk know the difficulties of successfully negotiating an interview with a user who is seeking information. While some requests are simple and/or straightforward, others are not. It is important in a user-centered, constructivist model, as Kuhlthau points out (1993, 236), to distinguish between the two types of requests; using complex techniques to probe simple information requests is both annoying to the user and a waste of time. Yet some requests are very broad (articles on diabetes in children) when in fact something quite specific is desired (drug therapies); other requests are very specific (a textbook on entomology) when something entirely different is needed (termite control). Still other requests are vague, ambiguous, or incomplete. It is particularly important to understand a user's sense-making process in situations when an information need is ambiguous; the ambiguity indicates that an information need is poorly understood not just by the information professional but by the user.

A user-centered approach to reference, as well as to other information services, has at its core the assumption that it is the information need (rather than wants or demands) that should be addressed. This distinction between wants and needs has been argued in the literature for at least 20 years, without must progress.[9] In thinking about how to understand and create a user-centered information service, I find the following basic concepts to be most useful:

1. Information needs are not necessarily the same as information wants or demands (Green 1990). This has major implications for *how* we explore information needs with users in order to determine systems and services we should provide.
2. Information needs are often ambiguous and not easily articulated (Taylor 1968). We need to acknowledge that often the only way users can articulate what they need is after they see it; that is, they can *recognize* something that satisfies an information need even though they don't know what to ask for (Miller 1960, 170).
3. Ambiguous information needs—as a particular class of information need—are poorly understood by users and by information professionals alike. Understanding and clarifying ambiguous information needs should be a primary goal of information professionals.

Ambiguous Information Needs (AINs)

Ambiguity is not a state most people enjoy. Research scientists, faced with a problem they are not sure how to resolve, will try different approaches: focusing on the problem, avoiding the problem, working out possible approaches on paper, talking to a colleague, cleaning out files, and so on. What too rarely seems to happen, however, is a trip to the library or information center.[10]

Information centers are traditionally used most frequently either when specific information is required or when a broad introduction to a new area is desired. This is understandable: when an information need is ambiguous, it is also difficult to communicate. The thought of explaining something that you don't have a good grasp on—and explaining it to a near stranger (the information professional)—is an obvious deterrent. While no studies specifically address this point, the fact that users are unlikely to come to the information center is suggested by Taylor (1968) in his description of the first two stages of question-negotiation.

How would a user-centered information service deal with the problem of ambiguous information needs? There are several possible approaches.

In a pharmaceutical library, for example, where facilitating problem solving was an accepted goal, it would be valuable to provide scientists with assistance earlier in the development of their information need, at the stages when the need is not well-defined. If ambiguous information needs are not being presented to information professionals in formal settings, we will have to go to the scientists in their labs and in informal settings, encourage them to talk about research problems they may be encountering, and find opportunities to help them clarify their needs. Dervin and Dewdney (1986) have proposed "neutral questioning" as an effective way of identifying the user's information need during the reference interview; similar techniques can be used in less formal settings. Their approach involves using questions which are open-ended but also structured around the three parts of the sense-making model: questions about the *situation* (can you tell me a little about how this problem arose?); about the *gap* (what are you trying to understand about "x"?); about the *uses* (if you could have exactly the help you wanted, what would it be?). The approach is based on Dervin's theory and has been taught successfully in numerous workshops.

Kuhlthau offers yet another user-centered approach to the reference encounter, helpful regardless of whether the need is ambiguous or relatively clear. She identifies stages of research (selection, exploration, formulation, collection, and presentation) and suggests what type of intervention is appropriate at each level. She calls these levels "zones of intervention" and argues that a type of intervention appropriate for one zone will be inappropriate for another. The types of intervention are defined both for reference and for bibliographic instruction. By analyzing the questions received from users, the information professional aware of the constructivist model can "diagnose" what specific intervention activity is most appropriate.

Literature Searching

Relevance of literature searches have long been evaluated through measures of recall and precision. Relevance of this type has often been determined (by librarians or users themselves) primarily on the basis of the match with the topic being searched (Miller & Tegler 1986). In a user-centered service, the idea of "pertinence" rather than relevance would be paramount. As Harter distinguishes the two terms, pertinence

> is a subjective, private "creation of new knowledge" by the requester in the context of a personal information need. In this sense, relevance is not a property of a document and a request, but it is the property of a document and requester. (Harter 1984, 114).

This description of pertinence clearly epitomizes the constructivist information seeker that Dervin has described and suggests that pertinence should be reintroduced as a measure of search success.

Indexing/Cataloging

Classification schemes and thesauri are highly structure representations of knowledge. They are by no stretch of the imagination user-centered or individualistic. Library services in the traditional technical services area (usually described as cataloging, acquisitions, and serials) at first seem to offer little room for user-centered modifications short of completely reconceiving how knowledge is to be represented. The type of information that is indexed would need to be radically expanded. In archival document collections, for example, the subject of documents is not the only area of interest to researchers. Why the document was issued may be important; the context in which the document was created may matter; the author's motives, beliefs or values may be most significant. The creation of indexing categories that reflect the *context* of the document is an example of how indexing can be made more relevant to user needs (see Blair 1990, 1992; Dervin 1983). In fact, there are some obvious and effective changes possible that at least take account of the user even if they are not fully user-centered.

One such change might begin by considering when it is that technical services staff have contact with the user. Such contacts invariably involve tracking down items: missing issues, books still in cataloging, items not on the shelves, etc. Designing an easy way for users to check on and retrieve missing items would be a good step forward. The ability to indicate quickly that an item is missing and needed would at least minimize time spent hunting through the library. While this change may seem obvious, tracking systems for acquisitions and cataloging are usually designed for the staff in acquisitions and in cataloging. In some systems, such information is still not available to the users; in others, the tracking information may be accessible, but it is not presented to the user in an easily interpretable format.

Another user-centered approach is to look at the *results* of cataloging and indexing in order to expand the inherent limitations of these services. It is well-known that indexer consistency is low (e.g., Bates 1986). As Blair (1986) points out, indexer inconsistency is rivaled by the user's inconsistency in selection of search terms. This fact is lamented in the literature because (until quite recently) the primary goal of information systems was "to target the desired information through perfect pinpoint match on the one best term"

(Bates 1986, 361). The ideal of the perfect match, however, has little point in the context of sense-making, where the user is constantly constructing and reconstructing reality as information is being processed and created. Bates suggests that systems should instead be designed to

> show searchers a wide range of descriptive terms and thereby implicitly educate them on the need to produce variety. Do not worry about whether any one term is the best to search with; rather, get the searcher in the habit of using a number of terms . . . or at least exploring various terms until the most descriptive ones are found . . . (Bates 1986, 361).

This suggestion may sound as if we are still trying to get the user to match the system, but it is in fact based on the idea that associative patterns are the basis of human thinking: a stimulus triggers any number of potential connections, some more strongly, others less strongly. Bates's approach is an attempt to help users activate their brains when searching and to follow the natural patterns of human thought. By contrast, the user's most common approach under the traditional model is to guess what specific term(s) the system wants: in other words, to think like a machine—or, more accurately, to think like an indexer choosing preselected language to be manipulated by a machine.

Systems

Systems design is the most obvious place for pursuing a user-centered approach. The term "user-centered" may have come, in fact, from the work of Norman and Draper (1986) on systems design. Though the authors do not specifically define the phrase "user-centered system design,"[11] they pursue a pluralistic approach grounded in cognitive psychology to exploring what goals and needs users have, what tools they need, what kind of tasks they wish to perform, and what methods they prefer to use. The interpretation of these questions through the variety of approaches encompassed in their book provides a rich resource of system designs that can be considered "user-centered."

A clear understanding of the term *user-centered* is particularly necessary in systems design: without such a focus, it is difficult to know what kind of user to design a system for. Users may be painfully naive or highly skilled and sophisticated in their knowledge of systems. Which user do you design for? One approach in dealing with the issue of how "user" is defined is to focus less on the user and more on what the user is trying to accomplish. Blair (1990) places the central focus of system design on the activity that the users are engaged in. While his approach is certainly user-centered, it is focused on a single activity—the activity that the information-searching supports. Wilson (1973), in his discussion of situational relevance, suggests that the ideal system would decide for each item of information in its database (through a rigorous and logical process) whether or not it was significant and situationally relevant for the particular user.

User-defined feedback about the relevance of citations or of documents as they are retrieved offers a different approach to user-centered systems design. This approach acknowledges that while users may not be able to express the basis on which they make decisions, they nonetheless can recognize what is or is not relevant.[12] Tague (1989), for example, describes an interesting approach to incorporating the user's feedback into online public access catalogs (OPACs). She describes a system that takes words from user queries that succeed in retrieving relevant items and adds successful words to the bibliographic record for those items. A related approach is taken by experimental systems that employ profiles of users to act as a template in selecting appropriate articles. As the user's need changes, the profile can be altered to reflect new interests. Several systems (such as OKAPI) incorporate the user's relevance assessments into a reformulated search and retrieval.

Carroll and Rosson (1987) embrace the differences in users and focus directly on addressing the users' conflicting cognitive and motivational strategies in using systems. They see users as production-oriented, unwilling to spend a lot of time learning systems, and taking action even when they have little to go on. People try to apply what they already know when interpreting new situations, and unfortunately they often apply incorrect or inadequate knowledge. For example, many people who grew up with typewriters assume that the computer works like a typewriter except for a few new keys. Carroll and Rosson suggest designing systems that *assume* people will respond to new situations with preconceptions based on prior knowledge and then looking at methods to minimize the damage.

The approaches discussed here all attempt, in different ways, to place the user at the center of the system: the system is designed around what is known not so much about systems as about users.[13] A major advantage of the approach of Carroll and Rosson is that it incorporates into library and information studies some of the principles of human cognition and behavior that we can learn from the discipline of psychology.

THE USER

Ironically, one serious problem facing information professionals in implementing a user-centered information service is the mindset of the user. I do not refer to the often-discussed problems of user status, including users' misunderstanding about what information professionals can do and limited knowledge about libraries. I am talking about their attitudes toward information and information seeking. Users developed their attitudes toward information in the same way everyone else did—they attended school, were assigned papers, and went through the messy process of doing research. As a result, they often tend to view information as something external and objective: out there, somewhere. They, too, feel that there is a right answer for their information need—it's just a matter of finding it.

Dewdney (Dervin & Dewdney 1986, 508) points out that librarians, when sense-making theory is explained to them, see the constructivist sense-making model as "intuitively reasonable." But most information professionals don't see information and information seeking in this way *without* having it explained. Students in a public library or scientists in a corporate research library are even less likely to consciously adopt a constructivist approach to information seeking. Scientists especially have been trained in the highly ordered, linear scientific method, even though as Harter (1984) suggests, an orderly, linear process is not always rigidly followed. Objective, definitive, factual information is usually the goal.

Two points are useful to consider when thinking about the mindset of users: (1) users generally operate out of the traditional paradigm; and (2) their total behavior doesn't always reflect this limitation. That is, while users approach information in a highly ordered manner, their response to what they find indicates the presence of an intuitive, fluid, affective, nonlinear process of understanding. For example, when conducting a literature search, users frequently change direction based on what they find, select articles that have no apparent strong relevance, and generally reflect the real-estate maxim that buyers are liars.[14] They don't know exactly what they want, and users who *think* they know will often be very happy with something quite different. The shifting focus indicates that a constructivist process is taking place during which the information need is significantly refined. As the need alters, what constitutes appropriate information to resolve that need is also changing.

Over the past 15 years, the validity of measures of user satisfaction in regard to services and systems has been questioned (e.g., Bates 1977; Cochrane 1981; Whitlatch 1990). One reason why users seem to be generally satisfied with what they find is that, based on cumulative experience with research and with libraries, they have come to expect relatively little. If users saw information as something constructed, their criteria for satisfaction might be different. They would understand that the concept of a "right answer" is not the only way to approach information-seeking and that information often helps to define and clarify the need, not simply satisfy it. After all, most people were satisfied with black-and-white televisions before they were introduced to color. Typewriters satisfied a great many people before they learned about word processors. The change to a constructivist approach may well create satisfaction which users presently cannot imagine.

Decision Making and the Need for Clarity

Research in psychology can help us better understand the cognitive processes and associated behavior that might underlie a constructivist approach. For example, in libraries, as everywhere else, we move in an environment that is uncertain and ambiguous. Every day we face the need to make decisions based on incomplete, obscure, or inaccurate information. And we make them: we drive in fog or blinding rain, trusting that our sense of the road will not betray us; we begin essays, develop opinions, pursue a line of reasoning even when we are not sure where we are going. We do these things because we are driven to act, and the alternative to action feels worse. The need to make quick decisions based on the most likely interpretation of incomplete information is what William James (1892) described in emphasizing our attraction to "the probable and the definite." Sometimes we are wrong. The large, beige creature turns out to be a pile of dry leaves shifting slightly in the twilight breezes. When we act with incomplete information, even using our best guess as to what is most likely, what we gain in speed we sometimes lose in accuracy.

Few of the decisions we make in a library, of course, are matters of life and death. But some are, especially in medical or legal settings, and we are still governed by the need to make sense of our environment, and to do so quickly. The importance of quick, effective access to information thus highlights the need for a user-centered approach that takes account of the two fundamental cognitive-based processes indicated by the terms "question negotiation" and "knowledge transfer."

Question Negotiation

Unless it is verbalized or transmitted in signs, an information need is knowable only to the person who has it. Wherever it takes place, question negotiation is normally a verbal process crucial in clarifying information needs. It is likely that question negotiation takes place more than once: initially in the tentative, private struggle to clarify an ambiguous need and later in the public process of communicating the need to either a system or another individual.

Question negotiation has aroused considerable interest from many directions and in many disciplines. Fields such as philosophy, linguistics, semantics, sociology, psychology, information science, education, and computer science have attempted to analyze and understand the processes involved. To a large extent, these different fields have developed theories and approaches in isolation from each other (Graesser & Black 1985). One aspect of question negotiation especially relevant in a user-centered, constructivist approach involves understanding how questions are related to cognitive structure.

Questions are generated from existing cognitive structure: they have to come from somewhere. The act of asking a question appears to be very effective in "activating the relevant portions of this preexisting cognitive structure" (Kaplan & Kaplan 1983, 184). When we activate specific portions of our cognitive structure, the brain has a relevant place to put the new information that comes in the form of an answer. This is one reason why we remember answers to questions we ask more easily than we remember other kinds of information. Yet when we ask questions our preexisting cognitive structure must be in some way incomplete, and the dilemma created by our incomplete understanding is further complicated by the need to communicate publicly a sense of what it is we don't know. As LaFrance (1992, 23) puts it, questions occasion the telling of stories rather than the furnishing of answers.

The Process of Knowledge Transfer

One of the major stumbling blocks to successful communication is our frequent inability to present information in a way that can be understood and assimilated. Even under ideal circumstances, when two individuals *want* to understand each other, interest and enthusiasm are no guarantee of success. In a situation where a research scientist and an information professional attempt to reach a mutual understanding of the scientist's information need, additional complicating factors come into play. Some key features of this difficult interactive situation have already been touched on: the way in which new knowledge is integrated into existing cognitive maps; the desire for clarity; and the role of questions in activating cognitive structure. Now we must add two other concepts important in knowledge transfer: information capacity and expertise.

(a) Information Capacity. There is only so much information that we can absorb at one time. How much we can absorb is to some extent dependent on how much we already know about what is being presented. With a lot of preexisting cognitive structure for a topic, much of what we hear will be familiar and easily assimilated. We then easily pick out pieces of information that are new and place them within our existing knowledge. If we know little about a topic, we quickly begin to feel overwhelmed. We have little existing cognitive structure on which to append these new concepts or ideas.

The limit of our capacity to hold information in active memory is usually described as five, plus or minus two "chunks" or units of information (Mandler 1975).[15] As we become more expert in a field, the chunks can represent greater amounts of information. This limitation is not as frightening as it sounds: even novices find ways to remember additional things by grouping several concepts under a larger category (you then have to memorize only the larger category) and allowing vivid examples to stand for complex concepts.

(b) Expertise. Research scientists and information professionals are both experts. (Whether information professionals are *perceived* as experts is another issue.) Being an expert means possessing extensive knowledge and very sophisticated cognitive maps in specific subject areas. Being an expert, however, also seems to limit one's ability to transmit information to others. Part of the difficulty is that once experts understand an idea they seem to regard it as familiar and obvious. They assume that everyone else understands it. If experts often appear rigid and intractable in their ideas, it is because they see the "right answer" so clearly that there is no need for additional information. They tend to use specialized vocabularies and to consider individuals outside their specialty naive.

Three rather surprising aspects of expertise are discussed in a study by Kaplan et al. (1989). Their extensive review of the literature led them to conclude: (1) that experts are not expert by virtue of some generic problem-solving skill, but only in their knowledge of a particular content domain; (2) that the way in which experts initially *perceived* a problem is what distinguishes them from novices: how they proceed after the problem has been set up was not significant; and (3) that expert knowledge is "abstract, schematic and often inarticulate."

When experts attempt to explain the process by which they come to their conclusions, they frequently resort to logical or rule-based explanations even though the process they had actually gone through was clearly intuitive and not understood by them (Kaplan et al., 33-34). An expert, such findings suggest, is someone not intrinsically well-suited to communicating ambiguous needs.

The picture of the individual that emerges from these studies in psychology holds complex implications for a user-centered, constructivist model of information. Humans are, by their nature, contradictory; drawn to make quick decisions that reduce uncertainty but struggling to understand clearly enough to make a good decision; striving for order, but enjoying the intellectual challenge of disorderly facts and unconventional ideas; needing the familiar, but craving the risk of the unknown; unable to express what is needed, but nonetheless perpetually asking questions; highly knowledgeable but unable to transfer that knowledge. This is the user whom we wish to serve.

Obviously, developing a user-centered information service for such a complicated creature will not be easy. Nor will such a change solve all problems, revolutionize services, or eliminate unforeseen economic and social challenges to libraries. The full impact of a user-centered approach can only be imagined at this point. It will take time to understand and implement the changes required by the new paradigm. Meanwhile, one thing is certain. A truly user-centered service will require a new understanding—both by information professions and (ultimately) by users—of the very nature of information and of information seeking. A new understanding, however, is not impossible to achieve. Armed with a clear understanding of Dervin's sense-making theory, fortified by examples of how such theory could be applied in different areas of the library, and chastened by a cognitive psychology that takes a realistic view of the strengths and weaknesses of human beings in information-seeking situations, we can begin to reconceive how information services might become a far more powerful and effective tool for information seeking in a changing information environment.

REFERENCES

Allen, T. J. 1988. Distinguishing engineers from scientists. In *Managing Professionals in Innovative Organizations,* ed. R. Katz, 3–18. Cambridge, MA: Ballinger.

Bates, M. J. 1986. Subject access in online catalogs: A design model. *Journal of the American Society for Information Science* 37: 357–376.

Bates, M. J. 1977. System meets user: Problems in matching subject search terms. *Information Processing & Management* 13: 367–375.

Belkin, N. J. 1980. Anomalous states of knowledge as a basis for information retrieval. *Canadian Journal of Information Science* 5: 133–144.

Belkin, N. J., R. N. Oddy, and H. M. Brooks. 1982. ASK for information retrieval: Part 1, background and theory. *Journal of Documentation* 38(June): 61–71.

Belkin, N. R., R. N. Oddy, and H. M. Brooks. 1982. ASK for information retrieval: Part II, results of a design study. *Journal of Documentation* 38(September): 145–164.

Blair, D. C. 1992. Information retrieval and the philosophy of language. *Computer Journal* 35: 200–207.

Blair, D. C. 1990. *Language and Representation in Information Retrieval.* Amsterdam: Elsevier.

Blair, D. C. 1986. Indeterminacy in the subject access to documents. *Information Processing & Management* 22: 229–241.

Carroll, J. M., and M. B. Rosson. 1987. Paradox of the active user. In *Interfacing Thought: Cognitive Aspects of Human-Computer Interaction,* ed. J. M. Carroll, 80–111. Cambridge, MA: MIT Press.

Cochrane, P. 1981. Study of events and tasks in presearch interviews before online searching. In *Proceedings of the 2nd National Online Meeting,* 133–148. Medford, NJ: Learned Information.

Cooper, W. S. 1971. A definition of relevance for information retrieval. *Information Storage & Retrieval* 7: 19–37.

Dervin, B. 1992. From the mind's eye of the "user": The sense-making qualitative-quantitative methodology. In *Qualitative Research in Information Management,* eds. J. D. Glazier and R. R. Powell, 61–84. Englewood, CO: Libraries Unlimited.

Dervin, B. 1983. Information as a user construct: The relevance of perceived information needs to synthesis and interpretation. In *Knowledge Structure and Use: Implications for Synthesis and Interpretation,* eds. S. A. Ward, and L. J. Reed, 155–183. Philadelphia, PA: Temple University Press.

Dervin, B. 1980. Communication gaps and inequities: Moving toward a reconceptualization. *Progress in Communication* 2: 73–112.

Dervin, B. 1977. Useful theory for librarianship: Communication, not information. *Drexel Library Quarterly* 13(July): 16–32.

Dervin, B. 1976. Strategies for dealing with human information needs. *Journal of Broadcasting* 20: 324–333.

Dervin, B., and P. Dewdney. 1986. Neutral questioning: A new approach to the reference interview. *RQ* 25: 506–513.

Dervin, B., and M. S. Nilan. 1986. Information needs and uses. *Annual Review of Information Science and Technology* 21: 3–33.

Dervin, B., T. L. Jacobson, and M. S. Nilan. 1982. Measuring aspects of information seeking: A test of a quantitative/qualitative methodology. *Communication Yearbook* 6: 806–830.

Durrance, J. C. 1988. Information needs: Old song, new tune. In *Rethinking the Library in the Information Age: Issues in Library Research— Proposals for the 1900s,* vol. 2, 159–176. Washington, DC: Education Information Branch, Office of Educational Research and Improvement, U.S. Department of Education.

Faxon Institute for Advanced Studies. 1991. An Examination of Work-Related Information Acquisition and Usage Among Scientific, Technical and Medical Fields. Prepared and presented by Eric Almquist at the 1991 Faxon Institute Annual Conference, Reston, VA.

Garvey, W. D. 1979. *Communication: The Essence of Science.* Oxford: Pergamon Press.

Graesser, A. C., and J. B. Black. 1985. *The Psychology of Questions.* Hillsdale, NJ: Lawrence Erlbaum.

Green, A. 1990. What do we mean by user needs? *British Journal of Academic Librarianship* 5: 65–78.

Harter, S. P. 1984. Scientific enquiry: A model for online searching. *Journal of the American Society for Information Science* 35: 110–117.

James, W. 1892. *Psychology: The Briefer Course.* 1961. Reprint. New York: Harper & Row.

Kaplan, S., and R. Kaplan. 1983. *Cognition and Environment: Functioning in an Uncertain World.* Ann Arbor, MI: Ulrich's Books.

Kaplan, S., Gruppen, L. D., Leventhal, L. M., and Board, F. 1989. The Components of Expertise: A Cross-Disciplinary Review. Technical Report 89-NOV-01. Department of Computer Science, Bowling Green State University.

Kuhlthau, C. C. 1993. *Seeking Meaning: A Process Approach to Library and Information Services.* Norwood, NJ: Ablex.

LaFrance, M. 1992. Questioning knowledge acquisition. In *Questions and Information Systems,* eds. T. W. Lauer, E. Peacock, and A. Graesser, 11–28. Hillsdale, NJ: Lawrence Erlbaum.

MacMullin, S. E., and R. S. Taylor. 1986. Problem dimensions and information traits. *The Information Society* 3: 91–111.

Mandler, G. 1975. Memory storage and retrieval: Some limits on research of attention and consciousness. In *Attention and Performance* 5, eds. P. M. Rabbitt and S. Dornic. London: Academic.

Miller, C., and P. Tegler. 1986. Online searching and the research process. *College and Research Libraries* 47: 70–73.

Miller, G. A. 1960. Plans for searching and solving. In *Plans and the Structure of Behavior,* eds. G. A. Miller, E. Galanter, and K. H. Pribram, 159–175. New York: Holt, Rinehart and Winston.

Miller, G. A. 1956. The magical number seven, plus or minus two: Some limits on our capacity for processing information. *Psychological Review* 63: 81–97.

Nilan, M. S., R. P. Peek, and H. W. Snyder. 1990. A methodology for tapping user evaluation behaviors: An exploration of users' strategy, source and information evaluating. *ASIS Proceedings* 27: 152–159.

Norman, D. A., and S. W. Draper, eds. 1986. *User Centered System Design: New Perspectives on Human-Computer Interaction.* Hillsdale, NJ: Lawrence Erlbaum.

Oddy, R. N., E. D. Liddy, B. Balakrishnan, B. Bishop, J. Elewononi, and E. Martin. 1992. Towards the use of situational information in information retrieval. *Journal of Documentation* 48: 123–171.

Paisley, W. J. 1968. Information needs and uses. *Annual Review of Information Science and Technology* 3: 1–30.

Saracevic, T., P. Kantor, A. Y. Chamis, and D. Trivison. 1988. A study of information seeking and retrieving: Parts I-III. *Journal of the American Society for Information Science* 39: 161–216.

Schamber, L., M. B. Eisenberg, and M. S. Nilan. 1990. A reexamination of relevance: Toward a dynamic situational definition. *Information Processing & Management* 26: 755–776.

Shannon, C. E., and W. Weaver. 1949. *The Mathematical Theory of Communication.* Urbana, IL: University of Illinois Press.

Tague, J. M. 1989. Negotiation at the OPAC interface. In *The Online Catalogue,* ed. C. R. Hildreth, 47–60. London: Library Association.

Taylor, R. S. 1991. Information use environments. *Progress in Communication Sciences* 10: 217–255.

Taylor, R. S. 1986. *Value-Added Processes in Information Systems.* Norwood, NJ: Ablex.

Taylor, R. S. 1968. Question-negotiation and information seeking in libraries. *College and Research Libraries* 29: 178–194.

Waldron, V. R., and Dervin, B. 1988. Sense-Making as a Framework for Knowledge Acquisition. Paper presented at the American Society for Information Science Mid-Winter Meeting, Ann Arbor, MI.

Whitlatch, J. B. 1990. *The Role of the Academic Reference Librarian.* New York: Greenwood Press.

Wilson, P. 1973. Situational relevance. *Information Storage & Retrieval* 9: 457–471.

NOTES

1. I am using the term "information service" to cover all areas that serve users in a library or information center.
2. While Dervin describes "user constructs" (Dervin 1983) and contrasts traditional and "alternative" paradigms (Dervin & Nilan 1986), she does not apply the terms "traditional" and "constructivist" to the concepts of the old and new information paradigms. She generally refers instead to traditional and "sense-making" paradigms. The sense-making paradigm, however, is not an *information model,* but rather an *information-seeking* model. It is for this reason that I use the term "constructivist" when describing the new information model.
3. Both Cooper (1971) and Wilson (1973) compellingly describe "logical" theories of relevance that are pointedly nonemotive, and in Wilson's case, even the issue of "need" is entirely absent.
4. The distinction between cognition and affect is no longer as sharp as it once was. Cognition involves affect, particulary in information processing. But emotions have traditionally been studied as a separate area.
5. See Taylor (1991) for a helpful categorization of Dervin's "uses" of information.
6. There are other researchers whose work is related. For example, Saracevic and Kantor (1988), Oddy et al. (1992), and Nilan et al. (1990) are all exploring cognitive approaches to information retrieval and to the human-intermediary-computer interface in their latest work.

7. This aspect of Dervin's approach is troublesome: the days of waiting for users to appear in the library are over. However, this is an early article, and Dervin's work has demonstrated many times that nontraditional holistic approaches to users are valuable.

8. Kuhlthau concentrates exclusively on the areas of reference and bibliographic instruction, although she suggests that "process intervention depends upon the reflective practitioner who understands the dynamic process of learning from information and incorporates that awareness into all aspects of intervening with users" (1993, 269).

9. See, for example, Green (1990) for a recent summary of distinctions among wants, needs, and demands.

10. Although we have no figure on how many research scientists come to the information center with AINs, a recent study prepared for the 1991 Faxon Institute (1991) examining chemists, geneticists, and computer scientists reported that of 1,161 information encounters ("any use or acquisition of information, ideas, or data" relating to their work), 31% involved library use.

11. According to Norman and Draper (ix), *user-centered system design* was the name given to the human-machine interaction project at the University of California, San Diego to coincide with the University's acronym (UCSD).

12. For an early discussion of online retrieval relevance issues which cites classic articles, see Swanson, D. R. (1977). Information retrieval as a trial-and-error process, *Library Quarterly* 47:128-148. For a review of OPAC studies see, for example, Hildreth, J.C. ed. 1989. *The Online Catalogue: Developments and Directions.* London: Library Association.

13. Although this summary may sound as if designers are once again looking for the "common state" of users, Carroll and Rosson recognize that there are several ways to respond to a problem. They have identified a variety of ways in which the user erroneously approaches computer learning, and they incorporate strategies for dealing with each of these errors.

14. The apparent low relevance of some articles selected by users may be explained by the difference between topical (subject) relevance (which is clearly apparent to the searcher) and some other sense of relevance. But it is precisely those other understandings of relevance that are indicative of the "dynamic, situational" nature of the constructivist activity (Schamber, Eisenberg, & Nilan 1990).

15. The figure seven, plus or minus two (Miller 1956), is sometimes used. According to Kaplan (1989) the difference in capacity is due to differences in measurement. Mandler's figure represents the *mean* capacity (the average point before losses start to occur), while Miller's represents the *threshold* value (the point 50% above chance).

Additional Readings
Part II: Understanding the Information Requirements of Organizations

Allen, T. J. 1977. *Managing the Flow of Technology: Technology Transfer and the Dissemination of Technological Information within the R & D Organization.* Cambridge, MA: MIT Press.

Belkin, N. J. 1980. Anomalous states of knowledge as a basis for information retrieval. *The Canadian Journal of Information Science* 5: 133–143.

Belkin, N. J., R. N. Oddy, and H. M. Brooks. 1982. Ask for information retrieval: Part 1. Background and Theory. *Journal of Documentation* 38(2): 61–71.

Dervin, B., and M. Nilan. 1986. Information needs and uses. In *Annual Review of Information Science and Technology,* ed. M. E. Williams, 3–33. White Plains, NY: Knowledge Industry Publications.

Hewins, E. T. 1990. Information need and use studies. In *Annual Review of Information Science and Technology,* ed. M. E. Williams, 145–172. New York: Elsevier Science.

Katzer, J. 1987. User studies, information science, and communication. *Canadian Journal of Information Science* 12(3/4): 15–30.

Krikelas, J. 1983. Information-seeking behaviour: Patterns and concepts. *Drexel Library Quarterly* 19.

Kuhlthau, C. C. 1993. *Seeking Meaning: A Process Approach to Library and Information Services.* Norwood, NJ: Ablex.

Kuhlthau, C. C. 1991. Inside the search process: Information seeking from the user's perspective. *Journal of the American Society for Information Science* 42(5): 361–371.

Macmullin, S. E., and R. S. Taylor. 1984. Problem dimensions and information traits. *Information Society* 3(1): 91–111.

Marchand, D. A., and F. W. Horton Jr. 1986. *Info Trends: Profiting from Your Information Resources.* New York: John Wiley and Sons.

McKinnon, S. M., and W. J. Bruns Jr. 1992. *The Information Mosaic: How*

Managers Get the Information They Really Need. Boston, MA: Harvard Business School Press.

Mick, C. K., G. N. Lindsey, and D. Callahan. 1980. Toward usable user studies. *Journal of the American Society for Information Science* 31(5): 347–356.

O'Reilly, C. A. 1983. The use of information in organizational decision making: A model and some propositions. In *Research in Organizational Behavior*, eds. B. M. Staw and L. L. Cummings, 103–139. Greenwich, CT: JAI Press.

Paisley, W. 1980. Information and work. In *Progress in Communication Sciences*, eds. B. Dervin, and M. J. Voigt, 113-165. Norwood, NJ: Ablex.

Parker, M. M., and R. J. Benson. 1988. *Information Economics: Linking Business Performance to Information Technology*. Englewood Cliffs, NJ: Prentice Hall.

Porter, M. E. 1985. *Competitive Advantage: Creating and Sustaining Superior Performance*. New York: The Free Press.

Porter, M. E. 1980. *Competitive Strategy: Techniques for Analyzing Industries and Competitors*. New York: The Free Press.

Roberts, N., and D. Clarke. 1987. *The Treatment of Information Issues and Concepts in Management and Organizational Literatures*. University of Sheffield, UK: Consultancy and Research Unit, Department of Information Studies, University of Sheffield.

Rohde, N. F. 1986. Information needs. *Advances in Librarianship* 14: 49–73.

Saracevic, T., and P. Kantor. 1988. A study of information seeking and retrieving. Part II: Users, questions, and effectiveness. *Journal of the American Society for Information Science* 39(3): 177–196.

Saracevic, T., and P. Kantor 1988. A study of information seeking and retrieving. Part III: Searchers, searches, and overlap. *Journal of the American Society for Information Science* 39(3): 197–216.

Saracevic, T., P. Kantor, A. Y. Chamis, and D. Trivison. 1988. A study of information seeking and retrieving. Part I: Background and methodology. *Journal of the American Society for Information Science* 39(3): 161–216.

Taylor, R. S. 1986. *Value-Added Processes in Information Systems*. Norwood, NJ: Ablex.

White, D. A., and T. D. Wilson. 1988. *Information Needs in Industry: A Case Study Approach*. Sheffield, UK: Consultancy and Research Unit, Department of Information Studies, University of Sheffield.

Wilson, T. D. 1981. On user studies and information needs. *Journal of Documentation* 37(1): 3–15.

III
Information Behavior
of Managers

III
Information Behavior
of Managers

Managers are a distinct group of information users, whose information needs and information-seeking preferences are largely conditioned by the demands and context of their work. The work of managers is open-ended because managers have to grapple with a wide range of issues, but also in the sense that many of the problems have no apparent closure in the short-term, their resolution having to unfold over time. The tempo of managerial work is also unrelenting, situations pile up one after another, and managers, like the Red Queen of Alice in Wonderland, often have to run very hard just to keep in the same spot. As a result, managers break up their work into small and varied chunks, so much so that every manager is constantly thinking about how to divide up her or his limited time between various tasks and priorities. In performing their work, managers recognize that their attention and cognitive capabilities are not boundless, and whenever they can they use simplified mental models to capture the most salient features of a complex situation and apply problem-solving heuristics that they have learned from experience. All these work-related demands imply that managers operate in a rather unusual information-use environment. When seeking information, managers do not have the energy nor the cognitive need to be comprehensive in their information search. Time is of the essence, as managers are often required to act or respond swiftly. Because many of the problems they face involve uncertainty and ambiguity, managers typically prefer information sources and communication channels that can provide them with a sense of the hidden or informal dimensions of the situation. For these reasons, researchers have repeatedly found that managers prefer human information sources, and that they spend an overwhelming proportion of their time in meetings or on telephone calls. When searching for solutions, managers do not try to find the optimal answer—they search not for the sharpest needle in the haystack, but for a needle that is sharp enough to sew with. Managers are ready to make decisions when they are satisfied that the found alternatives are good enough choices.

The first article by Jeffrey Katzer and Patricia Fletcher reviews the literature on managerial information behavior. Their review suggests that managerial activities are dynamic, uncertain, and complex, often involving messy situations that are ill-defined. They take place in an environment that is "informationally overloaded, socially constrained, and politically laden." Partly as a result of this, managers prefer to communicate orally, with little time left over to read long documents. Managers gather information externally to learn what their directions should be and who can help them, and they sometimes make decisions based on intuition in which case information may be subsequently sought to justify these decisions. Overall, the authors conclude that the information behavior of managers is a dynamic *process* that unfolds over time, and that the process interacts actively with the information *environment* in which the managers work. The managers' information environment is defined by the organizational setting, the roles they perform, and the activities they undertake. With this as context, managers then seek and use information to deal with a series of "problematic situations" such as hiring staff, developing marketing plans, or preparing budgets. In handling each problematic situation, the manager determines what types of managerial roles and activities are most appropriate, and which dimensions of the situation are most salient. This set of roles, activities, and dimensions then shapes the manager's information behavior. As new information arrives, and as the manager reflects and acts on the problematic situation, the perception of the situation changes, creating new uncertainties and priorities. The problematic situation is redefined in terms of roles, activities, and dimensions, which in turn leads to revised information behaviors. The process iterates until the problematic situation is considered resolved in the manager's mind.

In their article, Richard Daft and Robert Lengel introduce the concept of *information richness* as a basis for understanding managerial information behavior. Managers essentially handle two sets of information tasks: processing sufficient amounts of information, and reducing information equivocality. They suggest that the accomplishment of these tasks and ultimately the success of the organization would require managers to balance the use of information richness in their organizations. Information richness is defined as the potential information-carrying capacity of the communication of some data; the communication is considered information-rich when it can change or provide substantial new understanding. The information media used in organizations offer different degrees of richness. Face-to-face communications are the richest because they allow feedback and the use of multiple cues and language variety. Conversely, numeric, formal reports such as computer printouts are the least rich because they lack these capabilities. Top managers need rich information when they are trying to interpret or reduce the equivocality of ambiguous messages about unclear situations, such as changes in the external environment. The interpreted information then moves down the organization through communications of progressively lower richness. Media of lower richness are used to define goals, policies and procedures at lower levels in order to provide the clarity and certainty for the organization to function efficiently. Overall, the balanced use of information richness enables the organization to learn about an uncertain environment, while providing direction for participants to do their work.

The article by Ethel Auster and Chun Wei Choo presents a study that attempted to apply some of the theoretical concepts introduced above. The objective of their research was to study how chief executive officers in two Canadian industries acquire and use information about the external business environment. Thirteen CEOs in the publishing and telecommunications industries supplied detailed accounts of 25 critical incidents of obtaining and using environmental information. The results suggest that CEOs do most of their information scanning in the competition, customer, regulatory and technological sectors of the environment. Economic and sociocultural sectors appeared to be less important. They acquire or receive information about the business environment from multiple, complementary sources, with personal sources being the most frequently used. Because they have limited time and attention, CEOs appear to use printed sources as an efficient way of doing a broad scan of the environment. On the other hand, personal sources have high information richness that allow the executives to interpret ambiguous situations. The CEOs used environmental information mainly in the entrepreneurial decisional role, in which they make decisions about new projects such as introducing new products and initiating market strategies.

The list of additional readings contains selections that elaborate and expand on our introduction and the articles in this part. Most of the readings focus on managerial functions and decision making in particular, but many contain discussions of the information seeking and information processing behaviors of managers.

Information Richness:
A New Approach
to Managerial Behavior
and Organization Design

Richard L. Daft and Robert H. Lengel

INTRODUCTION

Organizations face a dilemma. They must interpret the confusing, complicated swarm of external events that intrude upon the organization. Organizations must try to make sense of ill-defined, complex problems about which they have little or unclear information (Weick & Daft 1982). Inside the organization, more confusion arises. Departments pull against each other to attain diverse goals and to serve unique constituencies and technologies (Lawrence and Lorsch 1967). Divergent frames of reference, values, and goals generate disagreement, ambiguity and uncertainty. In response to the confusion arising from both the environment and internal differences, organizations must create an acceptable level of order and certainty. Managers must impose structure and clarity upon ambiguous events, and thereby provide direction, procedures, adequate coupling, clear data, and decision guidelines for participants. Organizations must confront uncertain, disorderly events from within and without, yet provide a clear, workable, well defined conceptual scheme for participants.

How do organizations perform this miracle? Through information processing. The design of organizations—even the very act of organizing—reflects ways to handle information (Galbraith 1977;

This article was first published in *Research in Organizational Behavior*, Vol. 6, 1984, pp. 191–233, and is reproduced here with the permission of JAI Press Inc., Greenwich, CT, USA.

Weick 1979). Managers spend the vast majority of their time exchanging information (Mintzberg 1973). Specific dimensions of organization structure, such as functional or product organizational forms, and the use of teams, task forces or vertical information systems, all reflect information processing needs within organizations (Galbraith 1973; Tushman & Nadler 1978). Several papers have appeared in recent years which focus on information processing requirements as the explanation for observed organizational performance (Arrow 1974; Porter & Roberts 1976; Weick 1979; Galbraith 1977; Tushman & Nadler 1978). Consider, for example, the following information processing activities.[1]

City Government. Late in the afternoon of March 13, 1980, a killer tornado bore down on the town of Elkhart, Oklahoma. The tornado cut a swath three blocks wide through the center of town. Everything in its path was destroyed. Several people were killed and scores were injured.

The city administration had prepared for the emergency. Four years earlier, the city council authorized development of an emergency plan. Working with a consultant, city department heads developed specific procedures to follow in the event of a tornado, flood, explosion, or noxious gas. The procedures were similar to procedures that had solved emergencies in other towns. A national guard armory had been turned over to the city. Medical supplies were stored in the armory, along with food, water, sanitary facilities, and beds for people left homeless. A communication center to coordinate police, firemen, and utility departments was in one room. Equipment necessary for a temporary morgue was in another room. Space and personnel were allocated for counseling bereaved family members or others in a state of psychological disorientation. The city fathers had thought of everything. . . almost.

The armory was in the path of the tornado. The armory was destroyed. Thirty minutes after the tornado struck, the Mayor realized a new plan would have to be developed from scratch. City councilmen, department heads and the firechief were all called to police headquarters. Individuals toured the community and reported back. The group stayed up all night listening to reports of damage, discussing needs, setting priorities, developing alternatives, and assigning tasks. The administrators were emotionally distraught but by morning the injured had been found and delivered to hospitals, the damaged areas were secure, and a plan for the next week's activities was in place. City officials, working together, carved an excellent plan of action from an unpredicted emergency. They received high marks from townspeople and visiting officials for their effective response to the crisis.

Business College. A new dean was hired to run a large school of business in a major university in the Southeast. The dean initiated a plan to hold aside a portion of the salary increase money to be allocated on top of normal raises—called super raises—for the ten best producers in the college. The department heads met with the dean to recommend top performers from each department and to discuss their relative merits. The purpose of this meeting was to establish a common criterion of performance across departments and to select top performers.

The dean quickly realized that assignment of super raises was going to be difficult. Each professor's record was unique. How did publication in a finance journal compare to publication in a marketing journal? What was the contribution to knowledge of an article, and how was journal quality to be weighted? What was the role of teaching and student learning in the evaluation? The dean simplified the problem by asking department heads to summarize in a single page the record of each individual they recommended for a raise. Seventeen names were submitted with a one page summary of activities. From these the dean had to select ten. He found the decision impossible so he returned the sheets to the department heads and asked them to rate all 17 people on a ten point scale. Professors with the highest average scores received the super raises, in essence, the complexity of each professor's record was first condensed onto a single page, and then into a single number. Several faculty members complained that the best performance in the college had not been rewarded. The following year, the dean and department heads devoted an entire day to discussion and analysis of performance records. Debate was lengthy and heated. Agreement was finally reached, and the outcome was acceptable to faculty members.

Retail Chain. Matthew B. was chief executive of a high fashion retail chain. The chain had 36 stores in 13 cities. Matthew B. hated formal reports. He preferred to discuss matters face-to-face and to reach decisions through consensus and discussion. Staying in touch required extensive travel. He visited stores to see what was selling and to get a feel for store design and layout. He had weekly breakfast meetings with top executives for discussion and planning. He also visited the company's plants and went to fashion shows to stay abreast of new trends.

Following a serious heart attack, Matthew B. retired and James N. became chief executive. He immediately acted on his belief in strong financial controls and precise analysis. He requested detailed reports and analyses for every decision. He relied on paper work and computer printouts for information. He canceled the breakfast meetings and trips to plants, stores, and fashion centers. Personal contact with others was limited to occasional telephone calls and quarterly meetings. James N. argued that managing a corporation was like flying an airplane. Watch the dials to see if the plane deviates from its course, and then nudge it back with financial controls. Within two years, a palace revolt led by a coalition of board members and vice-presidents ousted him as chief executive. They claimed that the chief executive had gotten hopelessly out of touch with the fast moving fashion environment.

The situations above illustrate ways organizations translate unexpected or complex problems into simpler, workable solutions. For the city of Elkhart, the ad hoc structure seemed to work well. Unclear events were interpreted and a workable course of action was developed. In the business college, the lengthy discussion used to evaluate faculty performance achieved a better outcome than the task of written descriptions or quantitative ratings. A similar thing happened in the retail chain. Management by discussion led to a more satisfactory outcome than managing by formal reports and paperwork.

Purpose of This Chapter

The purpose of this chapter is to propose new theoretical models that explain how organizations cope with the environment, coordinate activities, and solve problems through information processing, as illustrated in the above examples. The concept of information richness is introduced to explain how organizations meet the need for information amount and to reduce equivocality. *The premise of this chapter is that organizational success is based on the organization's ability to process information of appropriate richness to reduce uncertainty and clarify ambiguity.* The concept of information richness is combined with other information concepts to provide an integrated view of the organization as an information processing system. The chapter is divided into four parts.

1. The concept of information richness is presented in the next section and is used to integrate concepts from the information literature.
2. A model of manager behavior is then proposed, based upon the congruence between information richness and information needs.
3. Next, a model of organizations as information processing systems is proposed. Organizations have two information problems to solve: that of interpreting the environment and that of coordinating diverse internal activities. Models based on information richness explain how organizations such as the Elkhart city government and the business school described above resolve both interpretation and coordination needs.

4. Finally, traditional organization concepts, such as bureaucracy, politics, and organic structure are reinterpreted to show how they are associated with richness of information processing. Suggestions for future research are also explored.

DEFINITION OF INFORMATION RICHNESS

Daft and Wiginton (1979) proposed that human languages differ in their ability to convey information. The concept of language was used in the broadest sense to encompass various ways to transmit ideas, emotions, and concepts. High variety languages are those in which symbol use is not restricted and the language can communicate a wide range of ideas. Examples include art, music, and painting, which are subjective in interpretation. Low variety languages have symbols that are restrictive in their use, and the languages communicate a narrower range of ideas. Low variety languages include mathematics and statistics, which convey exact, unequivocal meaning to users. Daft and Wiginton argued that high variety languages were appropriate for communicating about difficult, ephemeral, social phenomena. Low variety languages communicate effectively about well understood, unambiguous topics.

The notion of language variety seems plausible, but it doesn't explain information processing in organizations. Managers typically don't use art, poetry, or mathematics to communicate about organizational phenomena. The range of language used within organizations is typically limited to natural language and simple numbers.

Lengel (1983) proposed a continuum of information richness to explain information processing behavior in organizations. Richness is defined as the potential information-carrying capacity of data. If the communication of an item of data, such as a wink, provides substantial new understanding, it would be considered rich. If the datum provides little understanding, it would be low in richness.

Lengel (1983), building upon the work of Bodensteiner (1970), argued that the communication media used in organizations determines the richness of information processed. He proposed that communication media vary in the richness of information processed. Moreover, communication media were proposed to fit along a 5-step continuum, as in Figure 1. Communication media include face-to-face discussion, phone calls, letters, written documents and numeric documents. The face-to-face medium conveys the richest information while formal numeric documents convey the least rich information.

The explanation for the hierarchy of media richness is contained in Figure 2. Each medium differs in (1) feedback capability, (2) com-

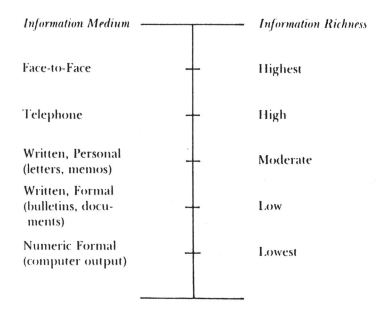

Figure 1. Communication Media and Information Richness.

munication channels utilized, (3) source and (4) language (Bodensteiner 1970; Holland, Stead, & Leibrock, 1976).

Face-to-face is the richest form of information processing because it provides immediate feedback. With feedback, understanding can be checked and interpretations corrected. The face-to-face medium also allows the simultaneous observation of multiple cues, including body language, facial expression and tone of voice, which convey information beyond the spoken message. Face-to-face information also is of a personal nature and utilizes natural language which is high in variety (Daft and Wiginton 1979).

The telephone medium is somewhat less rich than face-to-face. Feedback capability is fast, but visual cues are not available. Individuals have to rely on language content and audio cues to reach understanding.

Written communications are less rich still. Feedback is slow. Only the information that is written down is conveyed so visual cues are limited to that which is on paper. Audio cues are absent, although natural language can be utilized. Addressed documents are of a personal nature and are somewhat richer than standard flyers and bulletins, which are anonymous and impersonal.

Formal numeric documents are lowest in information richness. An example would be quantitative reports from the computer. Num-

Information Richness	Medium	Feedback	Channel	Source	Language
High	Face-to-Face	Immediate	Visual, Audio	Personal	Body, Natural
	Telephone	Fast	Audio	Personal	Natural
	Written, Personal	Slow	Limited Visual	Personal	Natural
	Written, Formal	Very Slow	Limited Visual	Impersonal	Natural
Low	Numeric, Formal	Very Slow	Limited Visual	Impersonal	Numeric

Figure 2. Characteristics of media that determine richness of information processed.

bers tend to be useful for communicating about simple, quantifiable aspects of organizations. Numbers do not have the information-carrying capacity of natural language. These reports provide no opportunity for visual observation, feedback, or personalization.

One value of the richness hierarchy in Figures 1 and 2 is that it organizes a diverse set of information concepts. For example, previous research has been concerned with information sources such as human versus documentary (Keegan 1974), personal versus impersonal (Aguilar 1967), and such things as files, formal reports, or group discussions (O'Reilly 1982; Kefalas 1975). The richness continuum makes sense of these differences, and may explain source utilization. Each medium is not just a source, but represents a difference in the act of information processing. Each medium utilizes differences in feedback, cues and language variety. Richness is a promising concept for understanding information behavior in organizations. In the next section, we show how information richness explains the information processing behavior of managers.

MODEL OF MANAGERIAL INFORMATION PROCESSING

Organizational phenomena confronting managers can vary from simple to complex. Simple phenomena tend to be mechanical, routine, predictable and well understood. Simple phenomena mean that managers typically can follow an objective, computational procedure to resolve problems. When phenomena are complex, however, no objective, computational procedure tells the manager how to respond. These issues are difficult, hard to analyze, perhaps emotion laden, and unpredictable. Managers have to spend time analyzing the situation and thinking about what to do. They will search for information and solutions outside normal procedures. Simple versus complex problems are similar to what Thompson (1967) called knowledge of cause-effect relationships and what Perrow (1967) called analyzability. Managers often experience difficulty seeing into complex tasks to analyze alternative courses of action, costs, benefits, and outcomes.

The proposed role of information media in managerial information processing is presented in the framework in Figure 3. Figure 3 illustrates that rich media are needed to process information about complex organizational topics. Media low in richness are suited to simple topics. The mechanical side of the organization is normally simple and measurable. Factors such as inventory control or employee attendance are not difficult to conceptualize. Managers can communicate about these phenomena through paperwork and quantitative reports. Other variables, such as organizational goals, strategies,

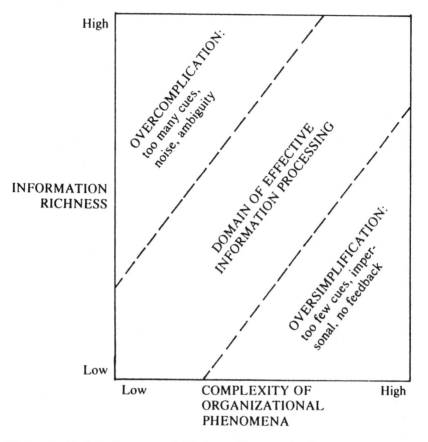

High

INFORMATION
RICHNESS

Low

Low   COMPLEXITY OF   High
                    ORGANIZATIONAL
                    PHENOMENA

Figure 3. Model of managerial information processing.

managerial intentions or employee motivation, are intangible. These
factors are not clear and discreet, and they can be difficult to interpret. Making sense of these factors requires a rich medium that provides multiple information cues, immediate feedback and a high
variety language. Rich information enables managers to arrive at a
more accurate interpretation in a short time.

The framework in Figure 3 hypothesizes a positive relationship
between information richness and the complexity of organizational
phenomena. Managers will turn to rich media when they deal with
the difficult, changing, unpredictable human dimensions of organizations. Rich media enable them to communicate about and make
sense of these processes. Face-to-face and telephone media enable
managers to quickly update their mental maps of the organization.
Rich media convey multiple cues and enable rapid feedback. Less

rich media might oversimplify complex topics and may not enable the exchange of sufficient information to alter a manager's understanding. For routine problems, which are already understood, media of lower richness would provide sufficient information.

The Figure 3 framework is a significant departure from the assumption that precise, clear information is best for managers. Memos, reports and other written media can oversimplify complex problems. They do not provide a means to convey personal feelings or feedback. These media do not transmit the subtleties associated with the unpredictable, messy, emotional aspect, of organizations. On the other hand, extensive face-to-face meetings for simple phenomena may also be inefficient. Face-to-face discussion sends a variety of cues, which may not always agree with one another. Facial expression may distract from spoken words. Multiple cues can distract the receiver's attention from the routine message.

This model, if correct, begins to explain why top managers make little use of formal information in organizations. Managers thrive on informal, personal communications (Mintzberg 1973). The retail chain chief executives described earlier in this chapter illustrate the role of information media. The executive who used rich media such as store and plant visits, breakfast meetings and phone calls kept well informed on myriad environmental and company issues. The executive who relied on formal reports and financial data got behind and out of synchronization with events. Face-to-face and telephone media, with multiple cues and rapid feedback, are needed to help top managers deal with the complex issues confronting them.

Management scientists, operational researchers, and other staff specialists are frustrated when managers ignore formal reports, systematic studies, and standard procedures. The model in Figure 3 explains why. Those media only work for certain tasks. The reason managers often ignore these sources of information is not personal ignorance, lack of training, or personality defects. Informal, personal media simply are capable of providing richer information to managers about certain problems. Managerial behavior reflects an intuitive understanding of how to learn about things. Many management problems are difficult and complex; hence formal information is not rich enough to convey adequate insight and understanding. Personal sources are more insightful. Thus managers' information processing behavior may make sense after all.

Research Evidence

Mintzberg's (1973) observation of top managers indicated that each manager is the nerve center for an information network. Managers have extensive contacts both within and outside the organization. They are plugged into channels for rumor and gossip, and are surrounded with formal information systems that provide periodic summaries and analyses of organizational activities. Managers spend over eighty percent of their time communicating. In this section we will review studies of information processing in organizations to determine whether previous research supports the Figure 3 relationship between media selection and problem complexity. This review is organized into three parts: (1) information sources, (2) mode of presentation, and (3) the use of management information systems.

Information Sources. Observations of managers indicate a strong preference for the verbal media. They prefer face-to-face meetings and the telephone. Mail and technical reports are used less frequently (Mintzberg 1972, 1973). Managers prefer current information and move away from formal reports and quantitative documents.

The information sources observed by Mintzberg represent differences in media richness. Face-to-face and telephone are rich and enable managers to process information about intangible activities. Mail and formal reports are less rich, and usually pertain to well understood aspects of the organization. The majority of manager information is processed through rich media because organizations are often fast changing, and many of the manager's responsibilities pertain to the social, emotional and poorly understood aspects of organization. Our model is consistent with and explains manager behavior such as observed by Mintzberg (1973).

A study by Holland, Stead, and Leibrock (1976) comes closest to evaluating the Figure 3 model of manager information processing. They proposed that individual working under high uncertainty would use richer media to transfer information than would individuals dealing with relative certainty. Holland, et al gathered questionnaire data from R&D units, and found that interpersonal channels of communication were important when perceived uncertainty was high. They also found a positive relationship between level of uncertainty and the reported usefulness of information sources. Holland, et al. concluded that managers experiencing uncertainty should be encouraged to use rich sources of information, even if it meant making long distance telephone calls or traveling. High rich media enabled participants to learn about complex topics in a short time. Written information sources, such as the professional literature and technical manuals, were preferred when task assignments were well understood.

A study by Blandin and Brown (1977) looked at the search behavior of managers. They examined external, formal, and informal information sources and related these to environmental uncertainty.

As the level of perceived uncertainty increased, managers relied more heavily on external and informal sources of information. The frequency and amount of time spent gathering information also increased. Thus, both the richness and amount of information increased with perceived uncertainty.

Although only a few studies have compared information source to topic complexity, the findings above do suggest that richer sources tend to be used when managers confront uncertain or complex topics. Less rich sources of information tend to be preferred when issues are well understood and routine. In general, the pattern of findings supports the positive relationship between media richness and task complexity proposed in the managerial information processing model.

Mode of Presentation. Research into the mode of presentation typically presents data in two or more forms to learn how it is perceived and acted on. Nisbett and associates found that case illustrations have stronger impact on people's judgment than hard data (Borgada & Nisbett 1977; McArthur 1972, 1976; Nisbett & Ross 1980). O'Reilly (1980) concluded that humans are more influenced by vivid, concrete examples than by dry statistics, even though statistics represent more systematic evidence from multiple observations. Other studies report that statistical data do have impact, but the case example gets more weight in decisions that appear to be objectively rational (Azien, 1977; Feldman, et al. 1976; Hansen and Donohue 1977; Feldman & March 1981; Manis et al. 1980). In a series of studies, Martin and Powers (1979, 1980, 1983) provided recipients with written statistical data and with a verbal story to assess which information swayed policy decisions. Stories tended to have more impact. They concluded that organizational reality is not objective, therefore statistical data pretends to report an objective reality which does not exist in the mental model of managers. Statistical data did tend to be influential when used to refute or overturn organizational policy. More precise evidence thus may be required to overturn a decision, while qualitative, story-based evidence is sufficient to support current policies.

Several studies show a strong preference for oral modes of information transfer. Mason and Mitroff (1973) argued that mode of presentation influences information preference. Landendorf (1970) found that interpersonal modes were preferred to written communication because interpersonal modes can be refined, adapted and evaluated to precisely fit the problem. Generally, oral information allows for rapid feedback and resolution of complex problems, and is often easier to gain access to. The importance of oral communication, especially face-to-face, is reflected in the impact of nonverbal signals. Eye contact, body movement, and facial expression communicate meaning beyond the verbal message. In one study of face-to-face communication, only seven percent of the content was transmitted by verbal language. The remaining ninety-three percent of information received was contained in the tone of voice and facial expression (Mehrabian 1971). A sarcastic versus enthusiastic tone of voice conveys as much meaning as the specific statements processed between managers.

Management Information Systems. Management information systems tend to be on the low end of the richness continuum presented in Figure 1. Most MIS's are formal and use quantitative or written reports.

Many studies designed to evaluate the usefulness of management information systems have attempted to operationalize economic value. Subjects purchase data and make simple decisions. These studies are not very helpful to understanding manager behavior because they employ naive assumptions about how managers use information. These studies are typically conducted in the laboratory, using sterile decision tasks and sterile information. The array of information cues typically available to managers are absent. The generality of these studies is extremely questionable (O'Reilly & Anderson 1979).

Perhaps the most widely accepted conclusion is that computer-based management information systems are not very useful to managers. The efforts to implement and use these systems have fallen short of providing maximum effectiveness and efficiency (Ackoff 1967; Dearden 1972; Larson 1974; Grayson 1973; Leavitt 1975). A number of factors have been cited to explain MIS failures. Management information systems provide data about stable, recurring, predictable events. MIS's provide data that skim over the nonquantifiable detail needed by managers. Management information systems supply quantifiable data. These data do not provide insight into the intangible, social dimensions of an organization.

Brown (1966) noted that information needs may depend upon level of decision. At the operational level in organizations, where decisions pertain to routine technical problems, decision support systems may have greater value. Several other studies support the conclusion that management information systems are most relevant to those managers who work with well defined operational and technical decisions (Dearden 1972; Dickson, Senn, Chervany, 1977).

A survey of fifty-six organizations in England by Higgins and Finn (1977) examined attitudes toward management information systems. While computer reports could be useful, they found intuitive judgment was used more often than computer analysis in management's strategic decisions. Executives typically drew on a variety of sources of information, weighing each for importance, and then making a final decision. Computer based data could play a role in these decisions, but a small one.

The small role of management information systems is not completely understood, but the primary reason seems to be that they do not convey information that meets managers' needs. MIS's work under the assumption that managers need large amounts of precise data. As managers receive more and more data, they should be able to solve their problems, which is not the case (Ackoff 1967).

Tushman and Nadler (1978) believe that information designers are more concerned with fitting data to their hardware than with understanding the overall information needs of managers. Information system designers lack a theory about manager needs and behavior. By limiting data to those things amenable to machine hardware, information designers miss the root causes of manager information processing. Most managerial tasks are too ill-defined for quantitative data, yet system designers assume that computer output is sufficient for management decisions. MIS systems are able to capture and communicate about the stable, predictable activities, but not about the important, subjective, ill-defined events relevant to decision making.

Summary. The pattern of findings about managerial information processing tends to support the notion that information richness is a useful explanation for information behavior. Only a few studies have examined managers' utilization of various media, or have related media to specific tasks (Lengel 1983). Available findings suggest that managerial behavior does reflect media choice based upon the uncertainty or complexity of management problems. When managers work in a highly uncertain context, they rely more heavily on rich media. These media provide a variety of information cues and immediate feedback to interpret and understand the situation. Managerial jobs are fast paced and fragmented, hence they often need to learn about a fuzzy situation quickly. Rich media serve this purpose.

Media of low richness, including formal information systems, seem best suited to well understood management issues. These media are used more often at the bottom of the organization and for problems that are considered objective and quantifiable. The evidence from the literature generally supports the theoretical model of managerial information processing presented in Figure 3. Managers use all media within the organization, and probably should be skilled with each one. Managers move toward rich media for information about difficult problems. They prefer rich media because it meets the information needs associated with the manager's job.

MODELS OF ORGANIZATIONAL INFORMATION PROCESSING

In this section we shift levels of analysis from the individual manager to the organization as a whole. Within organization theory, two theoretical perspectives have had significant impact on the conceptualization of information processing within organizations. These models pertain to what we call the vertical and horizontal information processing needs of organizations.

Two Perspectives

Vertical. The first theoretical view was developed by Karl Weick (1979). Weick focused on the concept of information equivocality. When managers observe or learn about an external event, the information cue is often ambiguous. Managers are unclear about what the event means or how to translate it into organizational action. Weick proposed that organizations are designed to reduce equivocality from the environment. Organizing is the construction of a consensually validated grammar for reducing equivocality (Weick 1979, 3). This means that when managers are confronted with equivocal cues, they must discuss the issue among themselves and gradually arrive at a common interpretation and frame of reference. The equivocality is reduced to an acceptable level, and the common interpretation is then used within the organization and becomes the basis for future action.

Weick's notion of equivocality is intriguing because it demonstrates that organizations must do more than process large amounts of information. Organizational environments can be confusing, impenetrable, and changing. Organizations cannot tolerate too much ambiguity and must cope with equivocal cues in a way that reduces equivocality to an acceptable level so the organization can take action and get things done. The equivocal stimulus triggers information processing within the organization that leads to greater certainty and clarity for participants. Organizations, then, must interpret ambiguous stimuli and reduce them to sufficient clarity for action within the organization. Weick identified this as an important problem that organizations must solve. By processing equivocal information into an agreed upon interpretation, participants can decide what to do. The organization can be reasonably clear about what it is doing and where it is heading.

Horizontal. The other view of information processing was developed by Jay Galbraith (1977, 1973). Galbraith proposed that as the level of uncertainty for managers increased, the amount of information processed should increase to reduce uncertainty. Galbraith argued that the uncertainty confronting an organization was influenced by factors such as diversity, task variability, and interdependence. Diverse products or goals means the organization must process a large amount of information to operationalize and monitor a number of activities. When task variability is high, managers confront unexpected events, so they must process additional information to learn about these events and thereby reduce uncertainty. Interdependence refers to the connectedness of departments. When the activities of one department influence other departments, information must be processed between them to provide the coordination needed for high performance.

The insight provided by Galbraith is that the amount of information processed within the organization explains why certain organizational forms are effective. By diagnosing points of uncertainty confronting the organization, a structure can be implemented that encourages appropriate information exchanges. When interdependence between departments is high, mechanisms can be designed to pass information between those departments. Likewise, when task variability is high, a structural design can be adopted to enable managers to acquire information in response to unexpected events. The selection of an overall structural form, such as product, function, or matrix, reflects the information processing needs of the organization. Each form directs the flow of information within the organization toward the points needed for effective performance. Galbraith provided a framework that explains the amount of information needed within an organization for effective performance. He also described how organizational design provides the correct amount of information where it is needed throughout the organization.

Interpretation vs. Coordination

Weick's theory of equivocality reduction pertains to the interpretation needs of organizations, which is the vertical dimension of information processing. Organizations interpret an ill-defined environment and define with some certainty a course of action for participants. Top managers are involved in the interpretation process. They read cues and then define goals, products, structure, strategy and technology. The vertical dimension of organizational information processing is top down. Upper level managers reduce equivocality to a level acceptable to others within the organization.

Galbraith's discussion of information amount pertains to information for internal coordination, the horizontal dimension of information processing. Horizontal information processing occurs within organizations to coordinate and execute organizational activities. Information is processed as needed for the organization to perform as a coordinated whole. Environmental interpretation is not the concern of people in the core of the organization. These people process large amounts of information when tasks are variable and activities are interdependent.

Figure 4 illustrates the two types of information requirements facing organizations. Organizations must both interpret the environment and coordinate tasks internally. As we will see, these two information needs are resolved in organizations through the use of rich information.

Information Tasks. Within the organization as a whole, a range of tasks are performed. Organizations use a technology to produce goods or services, and organizations work within an environment that is more or less uncertain. Organizational activities—in the broadest sense—impose specific information processing requirements associated with organizational technology, environment, and interdependencies (Poole, 1978). One information task is to reduce equivocality to the point where participants establish a shared view of events. The other task is to process sufficient amounts of information to enable internal coordination and task performance. These two information tasks represent the vertical and horizontal dimensions in Figure 4.

The importance of these two information processing tasks for human organizations can be seen in the comparison to other types of systems that also use information. Boulding (1956) proposed a hierarchy of system complexity that ranged from simple frameworks through control systems, cells, plants, animals, human beings and on to social systems (Pondy & Mitroff 1979; Daft & Wiginton 1979). Social systems are the most complex systems in the hierarchy. Figure 5 shows an abbreviated hierarchy of system complexity with 4 levels.

For machine systems at level one, the two information tasks are easy to resolve. Physical systems are usually closed off from the external environment, so little interpretation is necessary. Most knowledge required for performance is built into the physical structure of the system. In a machine system (e.g., clock, assembly line) internal elements are coordinated through physical linkages. In the case of the solar system, elements are linked by gravity, so that information processing is not required. For control type systems (e.g. thermostat), simple coordination data may be transmitted in response to predefined environmental stimuli (e.g. temperature). But this data is unequivocal and is processed in relatively small amounts compared to higher level systems.

Biological systems (level 2) require a greater amount of information processing than do physical systems. Biological organisms are differentiated, so data must be communicated among cells, organs

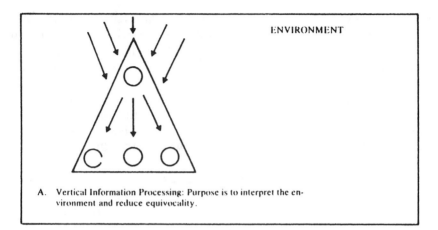

A. Vertical Information Processing: Purpose is to interpret the environment and reduce equivocality.

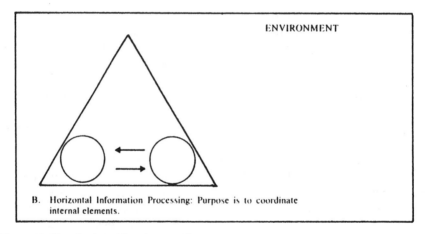

B. Horizontal Information Processing: Purpose is to coordinate internal elements.

Figure 4. Vertical and horizontal information processing in organizations.

and life sustaining subsystems. For an advanced species, a large amount of data would have to be processed on a continuous basis to enable physically differentiated subsystems to function congruently. Biological organisms also are open systems, so senses are used to interpret the environment. For the most part, however, environmental interpretation is unequivocal. Flowers sense and respond in a predictable way to sunlight. Birds and insects respond in an almost programmed way to environmental changes in weather, seasons, temperature, or location.

The internal information task for the human being (level 3) is similar to biological organisms at level 2. The human being is highly

| System Type | | INFORMATION TASK | |
		Amount Processed	Equivocality Reduction
Social System	Interpretation:	High	High
	Coordination:	High	High
Human Being	Interpretation:	High	High
	Coordination:	High	Low
Biological System	Interpretation:	Mod	Low
	Coordination:	Mod	Low
Machine System	Interpretation:	Low	Low
	Coordination:	Low	Low

Complex ↑ ... Simple

Figure 5. System complexity and information tasks.

differentiated, so large amounts of data are transmitted among internal systems, although these data are typically unequivocal. Interpretation of the environment, however, is equivocal. In only a few instances, such as putting one's hand on a stove, is the stimulus unequivocal and the response predictable. The majority of stimuli contain ambiguity. The external environment is alive with sounds, observed behavior, music, language, and symbols of all types. Most of these phenomena have multiple interpretations. Knowledge on any single topic is incomplete. People act on scraps of information and form these scraps into coherent wholes (Weick & Daft 1983). The ability to process and interpret equivocal stimuli from the environment is what distinguishes human beings from lower level systems.

The most complex system of all is the human social system (level 4). The human being is the building block of the social system. The information problem of interpreting the environment is similar to interpretation by individual human beings. Upper-level managers must respond to an uncertain, ill-defined environment, and define with some certainty a course of action for others with the organization.

Human organizations must also process information internally. Internal information must coordinate diverse activities as discussed by Galbraith, which may require enormous amounts of data, especially when the task is uncertain and the organization is complex. Internal coordination in a social system is also equivocal, a point not incorporated in Galbraith's framework. Organizational specialization and differentiation lead to autonomy among subgroups. Group participants have divergent frames of reference. They attend to their own tasks, use common jargon, and pursue group level goals. Information transmitted across departments often is not clear or easily understood. Ambiguities arise, especially when differences among departments is great. Disagreements will occur.

We propose in Figure 5 that critical information tasks in organizations are to meet the need for a large amount of information and to reduce equivocality. The need to process equivocal information both within the organization and from the environment is what distinguishes social systems from lower level systems. Unlike machine or biological systems, internal data can be fuzzy and ill-defined. Diverse goals and frames of reference influence information processing. The organization must be designed to reduce equivocality both from within and without. A model of organizational information processing that treats organizations as higher level social systems should explain the reduction of equivocality as well as the correct information amount. Concepts and models of organization design based on information richness that explain these two information tasks are developed in the remainder of this chapter.

VERTICAL INFORMATION MODEL

Hierarchical Level. The information task of reducing equivocality is a function of hierarchical level. At the top of the organization, the manager's world is subjective. Problems are fuzzy, complex, and poorly understood. Top managers shape reality for the rest of the organization. They decide goals and strategy, and influence internal culture (Pfeffer 1981). Top managers create and maintain a shared belief and interpretation system among themselves. They have few objective facts. They must confront uncertainty, make sense of it, and attempt to communicate order and meaning to the lower levels of the organization. Managers use symbols, metaphors, speeches, body language, and other forms of rich information to communicate values, goals and culture throughout the organization.

At lower organization levels, the need to reduce equivocality is minimal. The information task is objective. Employees and first-line supervisors can make use of policies, rules and regulations, formal authority, and the physical requirements of technology to govern their activities. The employees at lower levels work within the defined plans, goals, and technology of the organization. Interpretation is less equivocal. Information can be processed through less rich media and still convey relevant task information.

The equivocal information task along the hierarchy corresponds roughly to media usage, as illustrated in Figure 6. High rich media, such as face-to-face and telephone will dominate at the top management level. Issues here are complex and ill-defined, such as the relationship between the institution and the environment. Middle management works within a somewhat more well defined structure. High rich media will still be used, but paperwork, documentation and other forms of less rich data will also be processed. The lower levels are more objective. People within the technical core, for example, will make frequent use of numeric and written reports. To some extent, all media will be used at each level. But rich media will play a more prominent role in the interpretation of the environment and reduction of equivocality at the top level, while less rich media will play a more important role for lower level employees.

Richness Reduction. The information media used at each level is not random, but reflects the underlying process of organizing. Organizations must reduce subjectivity and equivocality (Weick 1979). Organizations move from high rich media at the interface with the environment to low rich media within the technical core. Top managers use rich media to discuss, analyze and interpret the external environment, and to develop goals and strategies. These interpretations can be translated into less rich policies, paperwork, rules and procedures for use at middle and lower organization levels. *Organizations reduce equivocality through the use of sequentially less rich media down through the hierarchy.* Reducing media richness is one way organizations reduce equivocality. Employees within the organization are thereby given a sense of specific roles, tasks, and purpose and are able to perform efficiently without having to inter-

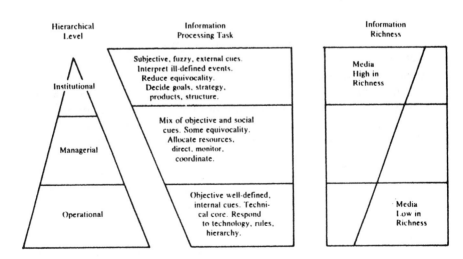

Figure 6. Hierarchical level and information richness.

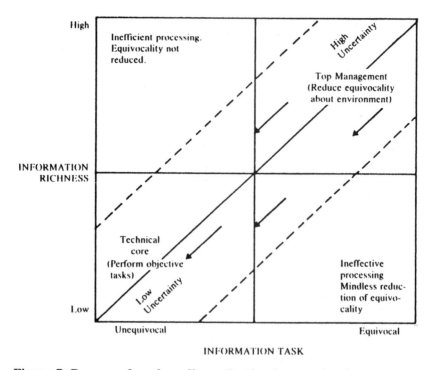

Figure 7. Process of equivocality reduction in organizations.

pret and define messy external issues. When organizations adapt to external changes, or when top managers develop new interpretations, the results work their way down through the organization in the form of new technologies, products, procedures, and reports.

The dynamic of richness reduction is illustrated in Figure 7. Media high in richness are used by top managers to cope with equivocal information processing tasks. Media low in richness are appropriate for the technical core. The diagonal in Figure 7 represents the extent to which the organizational context is objective or subjective. As top managers interpret the subjective environment and come to common definitions through the use of face-to-face discussions, they are able to reduce equivocality and provide greater objectivity for lower levels. Richness and equivocality are simultaneously reduced. Information processing inside the organization contains less equivocality and information tasks require less rich media.

The information processing that took place after the tornado in Elkhart, Oklahoma is a perfect example of the richness reduction process in Figure 7. City administrators were hit with an unexpected event that created a highly equivocal information task. They used rich media—continuous face-to-face discussion and personal observation—to interpret and define the environmental situation. As they began to understand and reach a common definition of the situation, administrators provided a more well defined course of action for volunteers who were assigned objective tasks as the act of organizing progressed. As Weick argued, uncertainty triggers the act of organizing. People cluster around the equivocal event and pool ideas and perceptions. This information should be processed through media of high richness until equivocality is reduced to an acceptable level so that less rich media can be used to communicate specific goals and tasks.

Information processing which takes place outside the diagonal in Figure 7 will not serve the organization well. In those cases where the organizations use rich media to resolve unequivocal issues, the organizing processes will be inefficient. Face-to-face discussions to process routine and well-understood events will confound rather than clarify. Participants will feel uninvolved because the equivocality that triggers discussion is not present. Face-to-face meetings will not serve a purpose or help resolve problems. On the other hand, when the organization inadvertently uses media low in richness to process equivocal information, the organization's interpretation will be ineffective. This would be the case when equivocal events are arbitrarily quantified and fed into computers for reports to top management. The equivocality reduction will not reflect the consensus among management, and will not be the outcome of diverse perspectives forged into a common grammar. This is analogous to what happened in the business school example at the beginning of this chapter. A number was assigned to the complex research record of professors. The numbers were assigned prematurely because department heads had not developed a common perspective and evaluation criteria through discussion. The richness reduction process was short circuited, and the resulting information was inaccurate.

The implication for organizing design is that information media should fit the vertical information task. Environments change. They can be hard to analyze. Organizations should stay open to the environment. They do that by using rich media at the top. Senior managers should maintain personal contacts in key external domains and use personal observation. Within the organization, top management should undertake informal discussions on unclear events. Executives can pool perspectives and build a common interpretation that will guide organizational activities.

As shared interpretations develop, the outcomes can be transmitted downward through less rich media. This creates certainty for lower level participants. Top management absorbs uncertainty through rich media, thereby enabling other employees to concentrate on production efficiency. To have everyone involved in equivocality reduction would be inefficient. Likewise, reliance on paper media by top management would close off the organization from the environment. Media of low richness do not transmit adequate cues to interpret the environment and do not permit managers to establish a common view and grammar.

HORIZONTAL INFORMATION MODEL

Galbraith's (1973, 1977) model of organization design specified structural devices to handle internal information processing. Computers, assistants-to, and information systems can be used to process data within organizations. Galbraith also specified structural devices for horizontal communications, including direct contact among managers, liaison roles, teams, task forces, and full time integrators. Any of these devices might be implemented depending upon amount of information needed within the organization.

We propose that one horizontal information task within organizations is to reduce equivocality, which Galbraith's model did not incorporate. A department in an organization is a system within a system. Each department develops its own functional specialization, time horizon, goals, (Lawrence & Lorsch 1967), language, and frame of reference. Bridging wide differences across departments is a complex and equivocal problem. The perspectives of marketing and R&D departments, for example, are more divergent than between industrial engineering and mechanical engineering. Coordination devices in the organization must not only match requirements for information amount, but must enable managers to overcome differences in values, goals, and frames of reference.

Information processing between departments has two purposes: reducing equivocality and providing a sufficient amount of information for task performance. Equivocality reduction is required by different frames of reference, which is similar to what Lawrence and Lorsch (1967) called differentiation. The amount of information needed between departments is determined by interdependence. The greater the interdependence between departments, the greater the coordination required. When frames of reference differ, coordination activities also involve equivocality reduction.

Rich information is needed when information is processed to overcome different frames of reference across departments. Managers must meet face-to-face, discuss their assumptions, goals, and needs, and develop a common language and framework with which to solve problems. In the initial stages of a new product, managers from research, marketing, and production would have to resolve their differences and reach agreement through task forces or committee meetings. Once these differences are resolved, less rich media can satisfy information requirements. Progress toward a common goal could be plotted on a pert chart, or data could be communicated with reports or other documents.

The decision process in the business college to give super raises across departments was an example of diverse frames of references. Each department had a different view on research quality. Rich media were needed to resolve these differences and achieve a common perspective for allocating raises. When the business college used face-to-face discussion to achieve a common grammar and perspective, the decision outcome was satisfactory to participants. However, when department heads used media low in richness (written description, numeric ratings) to resolve differences and make recommendations, coordination was not successful. Differences across departments were not integrated into a common grammar. Equivocality had not been resolved to the point where less rich media could be used. Only after a common perspective is established will paperwork and numerical ratings be accurate.

Interdependence determines the amount of information that must be processed between departments. As information amount increases, devices will be utilized that enable large amounts of data to be transmitted. An occasional telephone discussion between managers may be sufficient in the case of low interdependence. A daily meeting of a task force may be required when interdependence is great.

The ideas for horizontal information processing are summarized in Figure 8. Two problems must be faced—frames of reference and interdependence. The need to reduce equivocality is caused by divergent frames of reference that require rich media to resolve. Once a common language and perspective have been established between departments, less rich media such as memos, paperwork, and reports can be used for coordination. As the interdependence between departments increases, devices must be in place to allow sufficient volume of information to be processed, otherwise organizational performance may suffer.

Devices such as full-time integrators, integrating departments, and the matrix organization provide both rich media and large amounts of information (cell 2). These structural devices are required when organizational departments are highly interdependent, yet highly specialized with distinct technologies and frames of reference. When interdependence is high but differences are small (cell 4), information can be processed with less rich media. Written reports,

	INTERDEPENDENCE BETWEEN DEPARTMENTS	
DIFFERENCE BETWEEN DEPARTMENTS (frames of reference) — High	1. *High Difference, Low Interdependence* a. Media high in richness to reduce equivocality. b. Small amount of information. *Examples:* Occasional face-to-face or telephone meetings, personal memos, planning.	2. *High Difference, High Interdependence* a. Media high in richness to reduce equivocality. b. Large amount of information to handle interdependence. *Examples:* Full time integrators, task force, project team.
Low	3. *Low Difference, Low Interdependence* a. Media low in richnes. b. Small amount of information. *Examples:* Rules, standard operating procedures.	4. *Low Difference, High Interdependence* a. Media low in richness. b. Large amount of information to handle interdependence. *Examples:* Plans, reports, update data bases, MIS's, clerical help, pert charts, budgets.
	Low High	

Figure 8. Relationship between interdepartmental characteristics and coordination devices.

data bases, formal information systems, letters and memos will provide sufficient information for coordination. Clerical staff could be used to process more information through the paperwork system of the organization.

In the case of divergent frames of reference and low interdependence (cell 1), direct contact between departments can be used as needed. Face-to-face meetings would resolve differences, but would only be needed occasionally. Only a small amount of time and data would be processed in this situation. Finally, when differences and interdependence are both low (cell 3), coordination is a minor problem. Standing rules and procedures will be sufficient to accommodate any differences and information needs that exist.

The implication for organization design is that horizontal coordination devices should accommodate the dual needs of equivocality reduction and information amount. Different departmental frames of reference increase equivocality, hence the organization should design devices to process rich information and reduce equivocality in order to facilitate coordination. High interdependence between departments requires a large amount of information, so devices should be designed for sufficient volume of information to facilitate coordination. An organization design that achieves the correct amount of both equivocality reduction and information amount between departments will experience effective coordination, and hence high performance.

RESEARCH EVIDENCE ON VERTICAL AND HORIZONTAL INFORMATION MODELS

In this section we will briefly review research evidence on information processing by organizations. Research pertaining to interpretation of the environment (vertical model) is considered first, then evidence concerning internal coordination (horizontal model) will be discussed.

Vertical Model

One surprise in the literature on interpretation of the environment is that so few studies have been reported. Virtually all writers agree that organizations are open systems that must monitor the external environment. Yet studies of this process are notably sparse (Pfeffer & Salancik 1978). The specific evidence sought for this section is whether organizations use rich media to interpret the environment, and whether interpretations are then translated through less rich media to provide greater certainty at lower organization levels. The task of equivocality reduction is expected to diminish at lower hierarchical levels.

Hierarchical Level. Parsons (1960) proposed three levels of decision making in the organizational hierarchy: institutional, managerial and operational. These three levels were illustrated in Figure 6. The institutional level is the top of the organization, where the primary task is to set broad goals, and to decide the organization's products, technology, policy, strategy, and relationship with the external environment. The managerial level is the middle level in the organization. The requirement here is to plan and direct the activities of the organization and coordinate tasks laterally. This level is concerned with day-to-day management of organizational affairs. The technical level is at the bottom of the organizational hierarchy. At this level the operational work of the organization is accomplished.

Preliminary evidence indicates that the problems confronting the organization differ by level. Brightman (1978) argued that problems differ in uncertainty, complexity, and political nature. Problems at the top tend to be less programmed than decisions at the bottom. Stimuli at the top are less well structured (Leifer 1979; Brightman 1978). While there may be few routine elements, managers at the top have to deal with economic, legal, political, and social factors that are hard to analyze and define. They also must anticipate the impact of these factors on the organization and consider possible responses. Problems within the organization, although they are sometimes ill-structured, generally reflect a greater proportion of routine and well understood stimuli (Leifer 1979).

Is the difference in organizational levels associated with information richness? Leifer (1979) argued that inputs at the top of the organization tend to be informational while inputs used at the lower levels are data. Data tend to be more quantitative, objective, and less rich than the personal, subjective information used by top managers. Kefalas and Schoderbeck (1973) found that upper-level executives spent more time gathering information about the environment than those at the lower levels. Gorry and Scott (1971) also proposed that information characteristics at the upper level tend to be broad and less accurate. These data are richer than the detailed, well-defined, narrow data used at lower levels. Finally, the literature on management information systems reviewed earlier concerning manager information behavior (Dickson, Senn, Chervany 1977; Tushman and Nadler 1977; Higgins and Finn 1977) suggested that the formal systems were not used by top managers. MIS's are a low rich medium, and are more useful for well-defined activities at lower hierarchical levels.

Scanning. Scanning pertains to the organization's intelligence-gathering mechanisms. Most environmental scanning takes place at the upper levels of the organization (Aiken & Hage 1972). The few studies which have actually observed scanning behavior indicated that most scanning utilizes rich media. Aguilar (1967) compared personal to impersonal sources about the environment. He found that personal sources were of much greater importance to executives than impersonal material. Keegan (1974) compared human to documentary sources of information used by headquarters' executives in multinational companies. He found that two-thirds of information episodes were with human sources. The businessmen he studied used a network of human contacts in a variety of organizations to interpret the international environment. Documentary sources, such as the *Wall Street Journal* and the *New York Times,* were read regularly by the executives, but were less influential sources of information.

Bauer, Pool, and Dexter (1964) concluded that to a large degree American business communication is oral or by personal memorandum. Allen (1966) studied information sources for engineering decisions, and found that customers and vendors were the most used information source. Engineers had personal contact with these people to provide information on such things as new product needs. The formal literature, by contrast, was the least used source for this information.

The Keegan (1974) and Allen (1966) studies also indicated that information media reflect the nature of the underlying task. Keegan found that financial executives were more likely to use documentary sources, which is consistent with the well understood nature of accounting systems. General management and marketing, which experienced greater change and uncertainty, made greater use of human sources. Allen found that scientists who were working on well specified research problems made greater use of literature sources than did engineers who were involved in new product development.

Another source of information for top executives is personal observation. This is a very rich medium. It is not unusual for executives to take special tours, which involve face-to-face meetings with subordinates and the observation of facilities (Mintzberg 1973). Rich media provide greater insight into the organizational needs and problems than would be obtained by relying on letters or formal documentation (Keegan, 1974).

Kefalas (1975) reported a survey of scanning activities by managers in farm-equipment and meat packing companies. He found that upper-level executives devoted more time to scanning the external environment than did lower level managers. The source of scanning information was primarily face-to-face meetings with other people. Moreover, executives spent more time scanning the environment when it was dynamic rather than stable. The dynamic environment represented greater uncertainty and complexity, which was associated with greater use of rich media.

Conclusions reached independently by Keegan (1974) and Kefalas (1975) revealed the small role played by formal paperwork for senior managers. Keegan's study included fifty executives who each reported three communication incidents. Computer-based or quantitative reports were not reported in a single case as the source of external information. In much the same fashion, Kefalas found that formal surveillance received very little emphasis in organizations. Many businesses support organized technological and market research activities, but this data is not widely used within the organization. These systems are sometimes haphazardly designed so that information is not always available to the right people. These systems also fail to capture the novel and unstructured aspects of the external environment.

Summary. There has not been a great deal of research on the relationship between media richness and hierarchical level, but a reasonable inference is that the relationship proposed in Figure 6 receives modest support. Upper level management activities differ systematically from lower level activities, and upper level managers make extensive use of rich media to interpret and understand the external environment. Personal contacts appear to be essential for interpreting the external environment and reducing equivocality. Organizations undergo a process of richness reduction from the top to the lower levels of the organization. Rules, procedure, job descriptions, technical reports, and other forms of less rich media are more widely used at lower organizational levels. Rich information media are used for interpretation and decision making at the top, and sequentially less rich media are implemented at lower levels. Variation in media richness helps explain how equivocality reduction necessary for survival and efficient internal performance takes place.

Horizontal Model

A number of studies have examined communication and information processing inside organizations. Research relevant to the information richness models in Figures 7 and 8 are in the categories of technology, interdependence and internal culture.

Technology. Technology is a source of uncertainty for employees within the organization and thus, it influences information processing. Empirical studies have indicated that complex, nonroutine tasks require more information processing than simple, routine tasks. This relationship has been observed in small groups (Bavelas 1950), simulated organizations (Becker and Baloff 1969), research and development groups (Tushman 1978, 1979), and other organizational departments (Van de Ven and Ferry 1979; Randolph 1978; Daft and MacIntosh 1980).

Relevant to the theory presented in this chapter is evidence that media usage is associated with technological uncertainty. Woodward's (1965) seminal study of organizational technology found that communication media changed according to complexity of the task. People in highly routinized mass production organizations tended to rely on written communication and to have extensive formal procedures. Organizations that had less clear technology, such as continuous process or small batch, relied more on verbal media. The complexity of the task was associated with information media richness.

Studies by Van de Ven, et al. (1976) and Daft and MacIntosh (1980) support this general relationship. Van de Ven, et al. found that when task uncertainty was high, managers made more frequent use of unscheduled meetings and other forms of horizontal communications. When task uncertainty was low, rules, and plans were the primary means of communicating. Daft and MacIntosh reported that when tasks were less analyzable, participants preferred less precise information. Information had greater equivocality and required personal experience to interpret and actual use to solve the unanalyzable problems.

Meissner (1969) found that as technology varied from uncertain to certain, the media used by employees shifted from verbal to objective signs and written communications. Randolph (1978) observed that verbal media were used more frequently as technology increased in uncertainty. He also observed a shift from verbal to horizontal communication. Finally, Gaston (1972) found that nonstandardized tasks were associated with more face-to-face information transfer than were standardized tasks.

The communication patterns associated with technological uncertainty are consistent with our proposed models of information processing. The forms of communication observed by Woodward (1965), Van de Ven, et al. (1976), Daft and MacIntosh (1980), Meissner (1969), Randolph (1978) and Gaston (1972) can be interpreted to reflect differences in the continuum of information media. Media high in richness (face-to-face, personal contact) were used when tasks were complex and uncertain. Media low in richness (rules, regulations, written) were used when tasks were simple and certain.

Interdependence. There have been fewer studies of interdependence, but the general direction of findings seems to be similar (Tushman & Nadler 1978). As interdependence increases, the need for communication between groups increases, so the amount of information processed to achieve coordination increases (Van de Ven, Delbecq, & Koenig 1976).

Interdependence is also related to media richness. Thompson (1967) argued that when interdependence increased from pooled to sequential to reciprocal, techniques of coordination should change from rules to standardization to mutual adjustment. These coordination techniques are changes in media. Rules do not convey rich information, but mutual adjustment (face-to-face) is very rich. Van de Ven, et al. (1976) also found that communication shifted from rules to meetings as interdependence among employees increased. This finding also fits the richness model in Figure 8.

We theorized that differences in frames of reference across departments would require highly rich media to resolve. This idea receives modest support from the research of Lawrence and Lorsch (1967), who found that personal modes of coordination were used when differentiation within organizations was high. However, their study did not compare personal to impersonal media. The lateral information processing they found was face-to-face, which suggests the need for highly rich media to accommodate divergent frames of reference and perspectives.

Internal Culture. Organizational culture and climate may also be associated with information media. There is intriguing evidence to suggest that myths, stories, and metaphors are effective means of preserving social and emotional aspects of organization (Boje & Rowland 1977; Clark 1972; Meyer & Rowan 1977; Milroff & Kilman 1976). Myths, legends, sagas, and stories are prevalent in most organizations. These stories usually pertain to the socio-emotional side of the organization and provide employees with history, background, and meaning for their role within the organization.

Myths and sagas are not written down, and if they were, their usefulness might be lost, A similar finding is true for gossip and the use of the grapevine (Davis 1953). Information processed along the grapevine generally is of a personal nature and is communicated through rich media. The reason is that stories, myths and gossip pertain to the ill-defined, emotional aspects of organization that are best transferred through informal, personal media. Transmitting myths or gossip through informal, impersonal media would transform the stories into rational facts, and they would no longer pertain to the deeper, emotional needs of participants.

Summary. Once again, evidence from the research literature provides tentative support for the theoretical ideas expressed in this chapter. The findings suggest that rich media tend to be used when tasks are complex, and when differences between departments are great. Task complexity and interdependence are also related to information amount.

Taken together, these findings may mean there is a positive relationship between media richness and amount of information processed, since both seem to increase with task complexity and interdependence. The face-to-face medium, for example, enables managers to process rich information cues. Cues convey more insight, so managers actually acquire more information for understanding a complex issue or developing a new cognitive map. Amount of information may be increased by spending more time communicating or by shifting to richer media. The general conclusion is that requirements for horizontal information processing influence both richness and amount of information. Organizational design should enable the appropriate amount of information to be processed, and should provide managers with appropriate media richness depending on task uncertainty and interdependence.

DISCUSSION AND IMPLICATIONS

Early in this chapter, we proposed that organizational success is related to the organization's ability to manage information richness. Information richness was defined, and three models were proposed. The major points contained in this chapter are as follows.

1. Information is a core construct for understanding organizational form and process.
2. Human organizations, unlike lower level systems, must use information to reduce equivocality.
3. Organizations have two information related tasks, which are to interpret the external environment and to coordinate internal activities. Each of these tasks requires the reduction of equivocality and the processing of a sufficient amount of information.
4. Information richness is an important concept for explaining how organizations perform the task of reducing equivocality to an acceptable level for internal efficiency. Rich media utilize multiple cues, feedback, and high variety language. Rich media enable people to interpret and reach agreement about difficult, unanalyzable, emotional, and conflict-laden issues. Face-to-face discussions lead to a shared language and interpretation. Media of low richness are appropriate for communicating about routine activities within the organization. Paperwork, rules, and computer printouts are accurate and efficient for the transmission of unequivocal messages.
5. Media richness is the basis for the model of manager information processing behavior. For difficult, equivocal topics, managers use

face-to-face discussion for interpretation and equivocality reduction. Memos, bulletins, reports and other media of lower richness are used when the topic is specific and better understood. In a sense, there are two sides to managerial communication. Managers use informal, personal, direct contact when problems are ambiguous and unclear. They use formal, paperwork communications for routine matters. Effective managers should have skills with all media and be able to select among them depending on the nature of the problem.

6. Media richness also explains how organizations interpret the external environment, as described in the vertical information model. Media selection enables the organization to learn about an uncertain environment, yet provide a sense of certainty and direction for participants within. Face-to-face and other rich media are used to receive cues about the environment and to define a common grammar for use within the organization (Weick 1979). The organization reduces media richness as information moves down the organizational hierarchy. Media of low richness can he used to specify goals, policies, procedures, and technology at lower levels, thereby providing clarity and certainty for the efficient performance of routine activities. The key to vertical information processing is to incorporate a balance of media. When the environment is uncertain and equivocal, rich media are called for. Organization design should encourage face-to-face discussion to reduce equivocality and provide certainty within the organization. When activities are stable and analyzable, less rich media should be used.

7. Media richness is also the basis for the horizontal information model that explains how organizations coordinate internal activities. When departments are highly differentiated and interdependent, equivocality is high. When equivocality is high organizations will use rich information media to resolve departmental differences and to reach a common language and perspective. Once differences are resolved and agreement is reached, less rich forms of communication, such as memos and formal reports, will be sufficient for coordination. Media selection within the organization is related to the extent of differentiation and interdependence among departments.

Relationship To Other Frameworks

One outcome of the ideas described in this chapter is that they are consistent with other frameworks in the literature. Current perspectives can be reinterpreted in terms of media richness. Three frameworks—organic versus mechanistic organizations, bureaucracy, and politics—are considered here.

Organic Versus Mechanistic Organizations. The environment is a major source of uncertainty for organizations. Complexity, variability, and rate of change in the environment create additional uncertainty for managers in the organizations. Participants must spend more time finding out about the environment and adapting to changes in the environment.

Perhaps the most widely accepted relationship between organization and environment is that organic structures tend to evolve in uncertain environments, and mechanistic structures are suited to certain environments (Burns & Stalker 1961). In an organic organization, people are continually redefining and renegotiating tasks. There is widespread discussion about activities. Rules and responsibilities are ill-defined or nonexistent. In a mechanistic organization, activities are more rigidly defined. Rules, regulations and job descriptions are available to control behavior. Task redefinition is nonexistent. Communication tends to be vertical rather than lateral.

We suggest that the principle difference between organic and mechanistic organizations is media richness. The organic structure facilitates communication through rich media. The organization is constantly learning. Changes in the external environment are being interpreted and translated into new roles and internal tasks. Widespread face-to-face discussion enables continuous interpretation and adaptation to take place. The process of richness reduction is minimized in the organic structure because the entire organization is involved in interpretation, discussion and change.

The mechanistic structure makes greater use of media low in richness. Rules, procedures, and job descriptions contain the information necessary for successful task accomplishment within the organization. An extensive reduction in richness from the top to the bottom of the organization is accomplished. A small percentage of people are involved in environmental interpretation. Rules and regulations enable the organization to respond from habit and previous experience rather than through new interpretations. Formal media are appropriate in organizations that have well understood, predictable environments. Of course organic organizations would still utilize some low rich media and mechanistic organizations some high rich media. But rich media are used more extensively in organic organizations where the environment is changing and complex. Media low in richness are used more extensively in mechanistic organizations within stable environments.

Bureaucracy. Research on bureaucratic organizations has indicated that bureaucracy is similar to the mechanistic organizations studied by Burns and Stalker (1961). The literature suggests that as organizations increase in size, bureaucratic traits increase (Kimberly 1976). Weberian characteristics, such as division of labor, rules, and paperwork, are more extensive in large organizations (Blau and Schoenherr 1971; Dewar and Hage 1978).

These findings support the idea that richness reduction takes place. In a large organization, communication can be standardized, and relevant information is contained within the formal documentation of the organization. Large organizations develop a niche within the environment so that external conditions are relatively stable. Large organizations learn to take advantage of internal efficiences by responding through habit or by buffering the technical core when external changes do occur.

Studies that show increased formalization and large clerical ratios with organization size support the idea of reliance on information of lower richness (Daft 1978; Kasarda 1974). Formalization is a measure of the amount of documentary data in the organization. Large clerical ratios provide people to process large amounts of paperwork. Small administrative ratios in large organizations means the organization is run with less personal observation (rich media) and more by rules and regulations that act as substitutes for supervision. Media of low richness are substituted for media of high richness during bureaucratization. Even the increasing complexity in large organizations reflects information processing to some extent. An increasing number of departments and specialties is a way to divide the total information base needed for effective performance. Each department can develop a common language and frame of reference that will enable the use of less rich media for task accomplishment.

Politics. Politics is defined as those activities used to obtain one's preferred outcome in organizations when there is uncertainty or disagreement about choices (Pfeffer 1981). Recent surveys of organizational politics (Gantz & Murray 1980; Madison, Allen, Porter, Ranwick, & Mayes, 1980) indicate that political behavior occurs most often at the upper levels of organizations and for decisions high in uncertainty.

We propose that political behavior involves the utilization of rich media (face-to-face) to reach agreement when diverse goals and reference frames are brought to bear on uncertain problems. Disagreement is the result of diverse perspectives and goals across departments. Uncertainty is the result of the ill-defined nature of political issues. Politics is a device to encourage face-to-face discussion among a broad group of executives until a coalition is formed that reflects a common grammar and understanding. Media low in richness cannot be used to resolve political issues because paperwork and reports cannot convey the subtleties of power, obligations, and other intangibles. Politics is one vehicle through which rich media are used to reduce equivocality. Politics occurs both at upper levels and across departments when events are uncertain and reference frames diverge.

By contrast, rational models of decision making reflect the use of low rich media to process information and make decisions. The rational model is effective when factors are certain, and when participants agree on desired goals and cause-effect relationships (Pfeffer 1981). The rational model makes use of documentary sources of information, such as statistics and quantitative analysis. This approach to information and decision making is used more often for operational and technical decisions at lower levels in the organization.

Future Research Directions

The models in this chapter not only relate to the established frameworks above, they also can be the basis for a lengthy agenda of new empirical research. Very little research has been reported on topics such as the selection of media by managers, how organizations interpret the external environment, or the mechanisms used to process information horizontally between departments. A study by Lengel (1983) supports the underlying concept of a media richness and the relationship between media richness and the nature of communication topics. Additional studies based upon the models presented in this paper and beyond are suggested below.

Media Selection and Usage. The model of manager information processing in Figure 3 might be tested in a number of ways. A large sample of communications typically sent and received via each medium could be obtained and analyzed for systematic differences in content. Managers might be asked to describe critical communication incidents and to describe the medium used. Another approach would be to systematically test the relationship between task complexity and media selection. A sample of communication episodes could be developed according to complexity, ambiguity, conflict, emotional content, and accessibility. Then managers could be surveyed to determine their media choice for each episode. Analysis of these data would indicate the extent to which task complexity influences media selection. These data could also be analyzed by manager effectiveness and manager hierarchical level to see if media selection is associated with manager differences. A study could also test these relationships in the laboratory. Specific topics would be communicated through various media, such as telephone, face-to-face, and written. This research would indicate how media influence trust, understanding, and agreement among managers.

Boundary Spanning. Pfeffer and Salancik (1978) proposed that organizations face two problems in their relationship to the environment: (1) how to register needed information about the environment, and (2) how to act upon that information. The first problem is one of boundary spanning. Exploratory case type studies have been conducted by Aguilar (1967) and Keegan (1974), but systematic analyses of external information sources have not been published. An appropriate study would be to interview boundary spanning managers about information topics important to their functions. After two or three critical topics are identified, sources of information on these issues could be determined. External sources such as magazines, personal contacts, and opinion surveys can be identified. The transmission of information into the organizational decision center could also be traced. This study could begin with in-depth interviews of boundary spanning personnel, with a follow up questionnaire survey of information sources for specific topics. The outcome of this study would begin to shed new light on the intelligence gathering activities of formal organizations.

Interpretation and Effectiveness. Weick and Daft (1983) proposed that organizations systematically differ with respect to interpretation style. Interpretation style is an outgrowth of boundary spanning activity, and includes the development of shared perception, goals, and strategies among top managers. In a study of interpretation style, senior managers could be interviewed to identify how they learn about the environment. The role of organization design, such as the existence of a formal department to scan and analyze the environment, could also be examined. The effectiveness of interpretation systems could be evaluated by direct comparison of several organizations in a similar environment. Organizations in the same industry that have differing levels of profit, innovation, or other outcomes can be evaluated for interpretation differences.

Interdepartmental Coordination. Interdepartmental coordination pertains to horizontal information processing in organizations. Van de Ven, Delbecq and Koenig (1976) studied mechanisms used to coordinate members within a department. No studies have been conducted of coordination between departments or between major divisions of a large corporation. Galbraith's (1973, 1977) framework argues that coordination mechanisms reflect differences in information processing needs. A valuable study would examine these coordination processes in more detail. Specific coordination issues could be followed through the organization to learn how coordination was achieved. The model in Figure 7 could be tested by observing the extent to which media richness is related to frames of reference or to the amount of interdependence between departments.

Equivocality Reduction. The theme that underlies this entire chapter is equivocality reduction. Organizations must be able to translate uncertainty to certainty in order to achieve internal efficiency and stability (Skivington 1982). Equivocality may originate in the external environment or through internal disagreements. Despite the importance of equivocality reduction to organizational interpretation and coordination, we know virtually nothing about it from an empirical perspective. The process of perceiving an equivocal stimuli, evaluating it, discussing it, and coming to a resolution could be the focus of new research. This type of study might be conducted in either the laboratory or in the field. Groups or simulated organizations could be presented with an equivocal stimuli to observe how it is resolved. Specific environmental events might be traced into and through real organizations to learn how an acceptable level of understanding and certainty is reached. Almost any study of equivocality reduction, however exploratory and tentative, would discover significant new knowledge about organizations.

Symbolic Value of Media. Feldman and March (1981) proposed that information in organizations serves as signal and symbol. More information is gathered than organizations use, yet managers may request even more. Formal reports may not influence the rational decision process, but be used to support a course of action previously agreed upon. Feldman and March argued that the use of information is highly symbolic, and that information processing cannot be fully understood by considering only rational communication exchanges and decision making. The selection of media also may have strong symbolic overtones. Face-to-face discussion may be used when a manager wishes to communicate personal interest or to show others that he cares about them. Formal reports might be used to signal that extensive study lies behind a supposedly rational decision. Letters and memoranda convey a sense of the official and symbolize the legitimate role of the organization. The symbolic aspect of media could be assessed by identifying communication episodes and asking managers why they selected a specific medium. The deeper reasons for using media might be elicited through open-ended interviews. Similar interviews might be conducted with people who receive communications through various media. The deeper significance of media in the interpretation of messages could suggest new insights into the types of signals communicated within organizations.

CONCLUSION

This chapter has introduced the concept of information richness and proposed models of managerial information processing, organizational interpretation, and internal coordination processes. The models in this chapter have attempted to integrate ideas and topics from the literature on organizations. These topics include manager preference for personal contact and informal information, sources of information used by managers in various tasks, the observation that organizations must reduce equivocality about the environment (Weick 1979), and Galbraith's (1973) description of organization structure as a means of directing communication flows. The notion of information richness shed light on all these activities. When the task is complex and difficult, rich media enable successful information sharing. The information richness model provides a way to understand the behavior of individual managers as well as to integrate the notions of equivocality reduction and internal coordination.

Any model involves tradeoffs and unavoidable weaknesses. Probably the greatest weakness in the models presented in this chapter is reflected in Thorngate's (1976) postulate of commensurate complexity. Thorngate states that a theory of social behavior cannot be simultaneously general, accurate and simple. Two of the three are possible, but only at a loss to the third. The models in this paper are general and simple, and hence are not very precise at predicting details. The models represent frameworks that apply to organizations in general. More specific elaboration of the models can only be developed after additional study and research.

The major conclusion from the paper is the need for organizations to manage information richness. Richness has to reflect the organization's need to interpret an uncertain environment and to achieve coordination within. Organizations are complex social systems that have information needs unlike lower-level machine and biological systems. Rich information will have to be processed because environments will never be certain and internal conditions will never be characterized by complete agreement and understanding. Without some level of rich information, organizations would become rigid and brittle. They could not adapt to the environment or resolve internal disagreements in a satisfactory way. The process and outcomes of information processing are a good deal less tidy than would be the case in simpler, machine models of organizations. The ideas proposed in this chapter suggest a new view—perhaps a starting point of sorts—from which to interpret the richness of organizational activity.

REFERENCES

Ackoff, R. L. 1967. Management misinformation systems. *Management Science* 14: 147–156.

Aguilar, F. J. 1967. *Scanning the Business Environment.* New York: Macmillan.

Aiken, M., and J. Hage. 1972. Organizational Permeability, Boundaries

Spanners, and Organization Structure. Paper presented at the American Sociological Association, New Orleans, LA, 1972.

Allen, T. J. 1966. The differential performance of information channels in the transfer of technology. In *Factors in the Transfer of Technology*, eds. W. H. Gruber and D. G. Marquis. Cambridge, MA: MIT Press.

Arrow, K. J. 1974. *The Limits of Organization*. New York: Norton.

Azien, I. 1977. Intuitive theories of events and the effects of base-rated information on prediction. *Journal of Personality and Social Psychology* 35: 303–314.

Bauer, R. A., I. S. Pool, and L. A. Dexter. 1964. *American Business and Public Policy*. New York: Atherton Press.

Bavelas, A. 1950. Communication patterns in task-oriented groups. *Journal of Acoustical Society of America* 22: 725–730.

Becker, S. W., and N. Baloff. 1969. Organization structure and complex problem solving. *Administrative Science Quarterly* 14: 260–271.

Blandin, J. S., and W. B. Brown. 1977. Uncertainty and management's search for information. *IEEE Transactions on Engineering Management* 4(EM-24): 114–119.

Blau, P. M., and R. A. Schoenherr. 1971. *The Structure of Organizations*. New York: Basic Books.

Bodensteiner, W. D. 1970. Information Channel Utilization Under Varying Research and Development Project Conditions: An Aspect of Inter-Organization Communication Channel Usages. Ph.D. dissertation, The University of Texas, 1970.

Boje, D. M., and R. M. Rowland. 1977. A Dialectical Approach to Reification in Mythmaking and Other Social Reality Constructions: The P-A-C-E Model of OD. Unpublished manuscript, University of Illinois, 1977.

Borgada, E., and R. Nisbett. 1977. The differential impact of abstract versus concrete information. *Journal of Applied Social Psychology* 7: 258–271.

Boulding, K. E. 1956. General systems theory: The skeleton of a science. *Management Science* 2: 197–207.

Brightman, H. J. 1978. Differences in ill-structured problem solving along the organizational hierarchy. *Decision Sciences* 9: 1–18.

Brown, W. 1966. Systems, boundaries and information flows. *Academy of Management Journal* 9: 318–327.

Burns, T., and G. Stalker. 1961. *The Management of Innovation*. London: Tavistock Press.

Clark, B. R. 1972. The occupational saga in higher education. *Administrative Science Quarterly* 17: 178–184.

Daft, R. L. 1978. System influence on organizational decision making: The case of resource allocation. *Academy of Management Journal* 21: 6–22.

Daft, R. L., and N. B. MacIntosh. 1980. A tentative exploration into amount and equivocality of information processing in organizational work units. *Administrative Science Quarterly* 26: 207–224.

Daft, R. L., and J. C. Wiginton. 1979. Language and organization. *Academy of Management Review* 4: 179–191.

Davis, K. 1953. Management communication and the grapevine. *Harvard Business Review* (Sept/Oct): 43–49.

Dearden, J. 1972. MIS is a mirage. *Harvard Business Review* (Jan/Feb): 90–99.

Dewar, R., and J. Hage. 1978. Size, technology, complexity, and structural differentiation: Toward a theoretical synthesis. *Administrative Science Quarterly* 23: 111–136.

Dickson, G. W., J. A. Senn, and N. L. Chervany. 1977. Research in management information systems: The Minnesota experiments. *Management Science* 23: 913–923.

Feldman, N. S., and J. G. March. 1981. Information in organization as signal and symbol. *Administrative Science Quarterly* 26: 171–186.

Feldman, N. S., E. T. Higgins, M. Karlovac, and D. N. Ruble. 1976. Use of consensus information in casual attribution as a function of temporal presentation and availability of direct information. *Journal of Personality and Social Psychology* 34: 694–698.

Galbraith, J. 1977. *Organizational Design.* Reading, MA: Addison-Wesley.

Galbraith, J. 1973. *Strategies of Organization Design.* Reading, MA: Addison-Wesley.

Gaston, J. 1972. Communication and the reward system of science: A study of national invisible colleges. *The Sociological Review Monograph* 18: 25–41.

Gorry, G. A., and M. S. Scott Morton. 1971. A framework for management information systems. *Sloan Management Review* 13: 55–70.

Grayson, Jr., C. J. 1973. Management science and business practice. *Harvard Business Review* (Jul/Aug): 41–48.

Hansen, R. D., and J. Donoghue. 1977. The power of consensus: Information derived from one's and other's behaviour. *Journal of Personality and Social Psychology* 35: 294–302.

Higgins, J. C., and R. Finn. 1977. The chief executive and his information system. *Omega* 5: 557–566.

Holland, W. E., B. A. Stead, and R. C. Leibrock. 1976. Information channel/source selection as a correlate of technical uncertainty in a research and development organization. *IEEE Transactions on Engineering Management* 23: 163–167.

Kasarda, J. D. 1974. The structural implications of social system size: A three level analysis. *American Sociological Review* 39: 19–28.

Keegan, W. J. 1974. Multinational scanning: A study of the information sources utilized by headquarters executives in multinational companies. *Administrative Science Quarterly* 19: 411–421.

Kefalas, A. G. 1975. Environmental management information systems (ENVMIS): A reconceptualization. *Journal of Business Research* 3: 253–266.

Kefalas, A. G., and P. P. Schoderbeck. 1973. Scanning the business environment—some empirical results. *Decision Sciences* 4: 63–74.

Kimberly, J. R. 1976. Organizational size and the structuralist perspective. *Administrative Science Quarterly* 21: 571–597.

Ladendorf, J. M. 1970. Information flow in science, technology, and commerce. *Special Libraries* (May/June).

Larson, H. P. 1974. EDP—A twenty-year ripoff. *Infosystems* 21(November): 26–30.

Lawrence, P. R., and J. W. Lorsch. 1967. Differentiation and integration in complex organizations. *Administrative Science Quarterly* 12: 1–47.

Leavitt, H. J. 1975. Beyond the analytic manager: I. *California Management Review* 17(3): 5–12.

Leifer, R. 1979. Designing Organizations for Information/Data Processing Capability. Paper presented at the National Academy of Management Meetings, Atlanta, GA, 1979.

Lengel, R. H. 1983. Managerial Information Processing and Communication-Media Source Selection Behaviour. Unpublished Ph.D. dissertation, Texas A&M University, 1983.

Madison, D. L., R. W. Allen, L. W. Porter, P. A. Renwick, and B. T. Mayes. 1980. Organizational politics: An exploration of managers' perception. *Human Relations* 33: 79–100.

Manis, M., I. Dovalina, N. Avis, and S. Cardoze. 1980. Base rates can affect individual predictions. *Journal of Personality and Social Psychology* 38: 231–248.

Martin, J., and M. E. Powers. 1983. Truth or corporate propaganda: The value of a good war story. In *Organizational Symbolism,* eds. L. Pondy, P. Frost, G. Morgan, and T. Dandrige. Greenwich, CT: JAI Press.

Martin, J., and M. E. Powers. 1979. If Case Examples Provide No Proof, Why Underutilize Statistical Information. Paper presented at the American Psychological Association, New York, 1979.

Martin, J., and M. E. Powers. 1980. Skepticism and the True Believer: The Effects of Case and/or Baserate Information on Belief and Commitment. Paper presented at the Western Psychological Association Meetings, Honolulu, HI, 1980.

Mason, R. O., and I. A. Mitroff. 1973. A program for research on management information systems. *Management Science* 19: 475–485.

McArthur, L. C. 1976. The lesser influence of consensus than distinctiveness information on causal attributions: A test of the person-thing hypothesis. *Journal of Personality and Social Psychology* 33: 733–742.

McArthur, L. C. 1972. The how and what of why: Some determinants and consequences of casual attribution. *Journal of Personality and Social Psychology* 22: 171–193.

Mehrabian, A. 1971. *Silent Messages.* Belmont, CA: Wadsworth.

Meissner, M. 1969. *Technology and the Worker.* San Francisco: Chandler.

Meyer, J., and B. Rowan. 1977. Institutionalized organizations: Formal structure as myth and ceremony. *American Journal of Sociology* 30: 434–450.

Mintzberg, H. 1973. *The Nature of Managerial Work.* New York: Harper & Row.

Mintzberg, H. 1972. The myths of MIS. *California Management Review* 15(1): 92–97.

Mitroff, I. I., and R. H. Kilmann. 1975. Stories managers tell: A new tool for organizational problem solving. *Management Review* (July): 18–29.

Nisbett, R., and L. Ross. 1980. *Human Inference: Strategies and Short-Comings of Social Judgment.* Englewood Cliffs, NJ: Prentice Hall.

O'Reilly III, C. A. 1982. Variations in decisionmakers' use of information sources: The impact of quality and accessibility of information. *Academy of Management Journal* 25: 756–771.

O'Reilly III, C. A. 1980. Individual and information overload in organization: Is more necessarily better? *Academy of Management Journal* 23: 684–696.

O'Reilly III, C. A., and J. C. Anderson. 1979. Organizational communication and decision making: Laboratory results versus actual organizational settings. *Management Science.*

Parsons, T. 1960. *Structure and Process in Modern Societies.* New York: Free Press.

Perrow, C. 1967. A framework for the comparative analysis of organizations. *American Sociological Review* 32: 194–208.

Pfeffer, J. n.d. Management as symbolic action: The creation and maintenance of organizational paradigms. In *Research in Organizational Behavior,* vol. 3, eds. L. L. Cummings and B. M. Staw. Greenwich, CT: JAI Press.

Pfeffer, J. 1981. *Power in Organizations.* Marshfield, MA: Pitman.

Pfeffer, J., and G. R. Salancik. 1978. *The External Control of Organizations: A Resource Dependent Perspective.* New York: Harper and Row.

Pondy, L. R., and I. I. Mitroff. 1979. Beyond open systems models of organization. In *Research in Organizational Behavior,* vol. 1, ed. B. M. Staw. Greenwich, CT: JAI Press.

Poole, M. S. 1978. An information-task approach to organizational communication. *Academy of Management Review* 3: 493–504.

Porter, L. W., and K. H. Roberts. 1976. Communication in organizations. In *Handbook of Industrial and Organizational Psychology,* ed. M. P. Dunnette. Chicago: Rand-McNally.

Randolph, W. A. 1978. Organization technology and the media and purpose dimensions of organization communication. *Journal of Business Research* 6: 237–259.

Skivington, J. 1982. Strategic Planning and Organizational Stability. Unpublished manuscript, Texas A&M University, College Station, 1982.

Thompson, J. 1967. *Organizations in Action.* New York: McGraw-Hill.

Thorngate, W. 1976. "In general" vs. "It depends": Some comments on the Gergen-Schlenker debate. *Personality and Social Psychology Bulletin* 2: 404–410.

Tushman, M. L. 1979. Work characteristics and subunit communications structure: A contingency analysis. *Administrative Science Quarterly* 24: 82–98.

Tushman, M. L. 1978. Technical communication in research and development laboratory: The impact of task characteristics. *Academy of Management Journal* 21: 624–645.

Tushman, M. L., and D. A. Nadler. 1977. Information processing as an integrating concept in organizational design. *Academy of Management Review* 3: 613-624.

Van deVen, A. H., and D. L. Ferry. 1979. *Measuring and Assessing Organizations.* New York: Wiley-Interscience.

Van deVen, A. H., A. L. Delbecq, and R. Koenig, Jr. 1976. Determinants of coordination modes within organizations. *American Sociological Review* 41: 322–338.

Weick, K. E. 1979. *The Social Psychology of Organizing.* 2nd ed. Reading, MA: Addison-Wesley.

Weick, K. E., and R. L. Daft. 1983. The effectiveness of interpretation systems. In *Organizational Effectiveness: A Comparison of Multiple Models*, eds. K. S. Cameron and D. A. Whetten. New York: Academic Press.

Woodward, J. 1965. *Industrial Organization: Theory and Practice.* New York: Oxford University Press.

NOTE

1. The names in these examples are fictitious, but the examples are based on actual events.

The Information Environment of Managers

Jeffrey Katzer and Patricia Fletcher

INTRODUCTION

By virtue of their position, managers receive more information from more sources through more channels than almost anyone else in an organization. Whether one describes a manager's job in terms of overt behaviors (e.g., talking on the phone, reading a report, attending a meeting), functional responsibilities (e.g., planning, staffing, budgeting), or cognitive activities (e.g., decision making, problem solving, path finding), it is clear that management is an information-intensive profession (Huber 1980; McCall and Kaplan 1990; Whittemore and Yovits 1973). Organizations provide the setting in which managers act, and are being viewed more and more as information processing entities (Tushman and Nadler 1978).

In a world of diminishing resources, the key managerial resource—information—abounds. Unfortunately, managers find themselves bombarded with information—too much, too fast, too late. Interestingly, even with an oversupply of information, managers believe that they do not get all the information they need to do their jobs. The dilemma is clear: on the one hand, managers receive too much information, while, on the other hand, they don't get enough of the right information. A recent editorial in *Harvard Business Review* reinforces this point:

> Reports and data pile up faster and higher, but information is harder to get—and harder still to get meaning out of, even though colleagues and staff constantly suggest lots of meaning. From the outside, explosive

Reprinted from *Annual Review of Information Science and Technology*, 1992, vol. 27, pp. 227–263, with permission from the American Society for Information Science.

quantities of communications constantly bombard managers, promising big payoffs for their time and attention—heaps of magazines (trade, professional, technical, general, specialized), books, newspapers, TV and cable programs, radio reports, syndicated studies, newsletters, special mailings, special pleadings. Experts, consultants, speakers, tapes, seminars, and cassettes insist on and compete for attention. . . . With less and less time for managers to catch their breaths, to read, study and think, things submitted to them for attention are shrunk by others into skimpy summaries and threadbare conversations. Information and interpretations are delivered quickly via technicolor slides, easel presentations, and abbreviated conversations on the go (Levitt 1987, 4).

However, this problem cannot be easily solved by applying information systems and services as we commonly know them. One difficulty is that managers and organizations seem to use information in a way that appears illogical and unlike the way that many information professionals would expect them to act. March's description of organizational information behaviors reflects some of what is alluded to by "illogical." He says that organizations "gather information and don't use it. Ask for more and ignore it. Make decisions first and look for the relevant information afterwards. In fact, organizations seem to gather a great deal of information that has little or no decision relevance. . . ." (March 1982, 38). Nevertheless, the professional life of a manager is at least as information intensive as that of other user-community members, and the organization and the manager represent an increasingly important user population for *ARIST* readers. Thus, we believe that the ability of information professionals to function effectively in this environment requires some preliminary understanding of that environment. That belief forms the premise of this chapter.

We describe the information environment of managers by presenting a model of that environment and by reviewing selected writings that bear on the components of that model. The literature reviewed is bound by neither discipline nor time; it encompasses work from information and library science, business, management, public administration, psychology, organizational behavior, and related fields to provide a strong baseline for understanding the information behaviors of managers.

Because this is the first *ARIST* chapter on this topic and because the body of relevant literature is immense, we restrict our review to those writings—classical and contemporary—that support the model's structure or its components. The chapter also includes general studies that encompass the entire range of managers' information behaviors as well as those studies that focus primarily on the individual aspects of managerial information seeking and use. Toward the end of the chapter, we analyze what we think this literature means for information professionals. These implications focus on the challenges managers pose and the potential resolutions of these challenges in an applied setting.

To provide a focus that serves the aim of this chapter, the information behaviors of the individual manager are used as the thread to unite the literature review. It is at this level of the individual that we can begin to understand the information needs and uses of this group. To focus on the individual manager, the notion of problematic situations is developed and explicated to provide a basis for describing, understanding, and predicting the information behaviors.

To save space and to avoid unnecessary duplication, we do not include several related topics. Literature with an organizational perspective on information processing is included only if it directly sheds light on the information behaviors of the individual manager; for a broader review of the organizational perspective, see Choo (1991). Although environmental analysis and scanning as well as organizational climate and culture are all important to managers, they are ancillary to this review. Communication behaviors and information networks in organizations are also excluded because organizational communication is regularly covered in the field of communication and organizational behavior. A recent *ARIST* chapter (Grosser 1991) provides a broad and interdisciplinary review of the literature in this area.

This review is also limited to those problematic situations in which managers immerse themselves as individuals. When studied in the context of group activities, problematic situations interact with the manager differently from the way they would if they were dealt with by that same manager alone. Thus, group decision making, teamwork, and the like are not covered. Nor is there any systematic review of the relationship between managers and information systems, whether formal or informal. Although the literature reviewed here obviously has implications for system design, it would muddy the waters to review specific applications, such as decision-support systems (DSS), management information systems (MIS), executive information systems (EIS), and expert systems. Finally, unlike previous *ARIST* chapters on information behaviors, we do not include a separate consideration of methodology.

Even though there have been no previous *ARIST* chapters entitled "The Information Environment of Managers," this one is related to earlier *ARIST* writings. The most obvious connection is with the 11 chapters that covered information needs and uses. Of these, the two most recent (Dervin and Nilan 1986; Hewins 1990) also make a case for revising how one should think about the information behaviors of users; the model presented here is consonant with those revisions. As noted above, the chapter by Grosser (1991) includes many studies of organizational communication and informal networks that are directly connected with this one. In the same *ARIST* volume, Allen (1991) reviews a related area of cognitive research. Interested readers will find discussion of the present topic regularly included in the annual reviews of related fields, such as sociology (e.g., Hickson 1987), organizational communication (e.g., O'Reilly et al. 1987), and psychology (e.g., House and Singh 1987). Interestingly, the title of one such review (Huber and Daft 1987) is similar to ours, but the authors focus on the organization rather than the manager.

TOWARD A MODEL OF THE INFORMATION ENVIRONMENT OF MANAGERS

The model of the manager's information environment has its basis in the writings of Taylor. He defines "information use environments" as: "the set of those elements (a) that affect the flow of information messages into, within, and out of any definable entity or group of clients; and (b) that determine the criteria by which the value of information messages will be judged in these contexts" (Taylor 1986, 34-35). The major components of these environments are characteristics of people, the settings they are in, the problems they have, and the range of resolutions that are desirable or acceptable (Taylor 1990). These components, in a very real sense, provide clues about the information needs of any user group, and they provide the parameters that constrain how that group will seek and use information.

The structural components of the proposed model are also based on various descriptions of managerial behavior. The major variables in the model are related to the context in which the person functions, positing that context effectively constrains a person's information behaviors. As such, the model is part of a developing field of thought that argues that cognitive behaviors should be analyzed within the framework of the person's real-time situation. This approach has been advanced in several fields. In information service, Newby et al. (1991) argue this position for studying users' information behaviors in general, Schamber et al. (1990) apply it to the concept of relevance, Nelson (1990) uses it to study how people adjust to information technology, and Suchman (1987) advocates it in her examination of human-computer interaction (HCI). The same sort of viewpoint is evident in the presentation of managerial decision making by McCall and Kaplan (1990), in the analysis of organizational information use by O'Reilly (1983), and in the study of the behaviors of professionals in several fields by Schon (1983).

The model, as shown in Figure 1, portrays the components of a person's information environment as that person interacts over time. The dynamics of the model focus on the factors (including contextual ones) and processes that: (1) affect a person's subjective understanding of the situation he or she is facing and, (2) stimulate different information behaviors. Although the model as described here contains one-directional causal relationships, that is an oversimplification; most likely some of the links are bidirectional. The model's dynamics arise most immediately from the writings of Dervin, Nilan, Fletcher, their predecessors, colleagues, and students (see, e.g., Dervin 1983; Dervin and Nilan 1986; Fletcher 1991).

Components of the Model

The starting points for the model are two fairly fixed components: the context and the person. They exist in an objective, tangible sense, and they directly generate and significantly affect the other components. In the managerial realm, the person is instantiated most straightforwardly as the manager, and the setting as the organization.

A problematic situation is a personally defined subset of the endless and murky stream of events and meanings that continuously "flow through" a person's life. By identifying selected parts of that stream, by putting a fuzzy boundary around those parts, and by labeling those parts as a single entity that requires attention and possible action, the person creates a problematic situation. A problematic situation can be thought of as an "agenda item" that will require cognitive and perhaps behavioral action in order for it to be taken off that person's agenda and be considered resolved. Although a problematic situation is created and defined by a single individual, it is also shaped by features of the setting. Common problematic situations in the life of a manager include hiring new personnel, developing a marketing plan, and preparing the annual budget.

Settings differ in terms of their typical activities and roles. In the organizational setting, typical managerial activities include problem solving, decision making, and report writing while typical managerial roles include leader, negotiator, and communicator. In the laboratory setting, activities might include data collection and data analysis; typical roles might include statistician, interviewer, and communicator. Activities and roles are often defined or constrained by the legal requirements of a society, the standards of a profession, or the normative practices of a work group.

The model is concerned with how the activities and roles are relat-

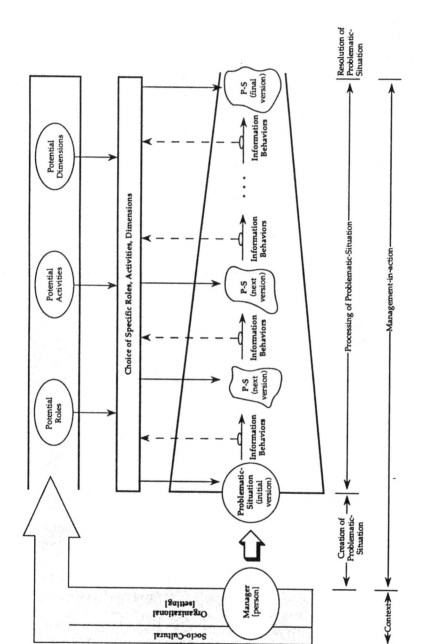

Figure 1. Model of the information environment of managers.

ed to the person's understanding of his or her current problematic situation and the person's information behaviors: managers who operate as leaders needing to make a decision are likely to have different information behaviors than managers who act as cost savers doing budgeting.

Problem dimensions are perceived characteristics of problematic situations and can, therefore, serve as criteria for determining the value of information. There are many potential dimensions, and they exist relatively independently of any particular user population or setting. In use with a given problematic situation, however, only a few dimensions would be treated as important. For example, among the many ways to think about a proposed merger, a manager might view it primarily as new, scary, and involving others. The salience of these dimensions (novelty, risk, interpersonalities) is affected by who the person is and what setting he or she is in. The dimension perceived as important will also affect what information is sought and how it is valued. Information, in turn, may also change the relative importance of different dimensions.

When acted on by the person, problematic situations generate information behaviors—i.e., the actions that contribute to the usefulness of information (Taylor 1990). The person needs to determine whether or not to seek information, what information to seek, where to seek it, how to seek it, how much to seek, how to interpret it, how to assess it, and how to use it. The person's responses to questions such as these produce information behaviors.

The Model in Action

The model is based on the belief that these problematic situations are the cognitive basis for the manager's uncertainties and concerns, which, in turn, may manifest themselves in overt information-seeking and -use behaviors. In making the problematic situation his or her own, the manager will determine (perhaps subconsciously) what type of managerial activity and role are called for and what dimensions of the situation are most salient. Over time, as the manager reflects and acts on the problematic situation, it changes; new uncertainties and concerns may emerge, different activities or roles become dominant, and other dimensions increase in importance. As long as the (revised) problematic situation remains unresolved, additional information behaviors will emerge. These, in turn, are influenced by the manager's current definition of the situation and current "choice" of activities, roles, and dimensions. This process continues until the problematic situation becomes resolved (but not necessarily "solved" in an objective sense) in the mind of the manager.

Conclusion

This model, like all models, provides a framework for identifying the variables that affect the information behaviors of any user population, although our focus is on managers. For *ARIST* readers, the model argues that it is not enough to study overt information behaviors. Instead, we believe that information scholars and professionals will gain a more useful understanding of these behaviors through knowledge of the information environment. In addition, we believe that this model can lead to practical applications. Dervin, Nilan, and their coworkers (e.g., Hert & Nilan 1992; Nilan et al. 1989) have shown that contextual factors limit the range of how problematic situations are perceived, the patterns of dimensions that are relevant for judging the usefulness of information, and the variety of information behaviors likely to occur. Results such as these can guide those who wish to develop information systems or provide services that better "understand" users as they work through their contextual-based, problematic situations.

STRUCTURAL COMPONENTS OF THE MODEL

Over the past 300 years, the United States has changed from a family-based social and work unit to one that is organizationally based (Zand 1981). We have become a society of organizations, with our main social tasks being carried out by large, managed organizations; in addition, for all organizations, management is the emerging function, task, and work that facilitates effectiveness (Drucker 1967). Drucker clearly defines this new and key role as follows:

> The emergence of management may be the pivotal event of our time, far more important than all the events that make the headlines. Rarely, if ever, has a new basic institution, a new leading group, a new central function, emerged as fast as has management since the turn of the century. Rarely in human history has a new institution proven so indispensable so quickly. Even less often has a new institution arrived with so little opposition, so little disturbance, so little controversy. . . . Today's developed society, sans aristocracy, sans large landowners, even sans capitalists and tycoons, depends for leadership on the managers of its major institutions. It depends on their knowledge, on their vision, and on their responsibility. (Drucker 1974, 10)

The attention given to managers in the literature has been considerable, too much to be thoroughly reviewed here. The early writings can be mostly ignored. The exception is not a specific body of writing as much as it is the flavor of that writing. Much of the early literature in this field (especially in the first half of this century) portrays management as a scientifically based profession whose members can and should act efficiently to maximize organizational objectives. Within this framework, managers are careful and deliberate planners, problem solvers, decision makers, and leaders who precisely assess the situation before them, acquire the relevant information, weigh it carefully, and reach the best solution.

Far fewer people today believe in this characterization of the manager than did so in the past. Nevertheless, it is a view that may be difficult to erase among information researchers and professionals because it is consonant with their view of how information ought to be sought and used (Katzer 1991; Roberts 1982). Thus, it affects how they design information systems for, and provide information services to, this population. In the current view of management, information also plays a crucial role (e.g., Drucker 1988; Etzioni 1989; McCall and Kaplan 1990), but it is a role based on a more realistic understanding of what managers actually do, in contrast with what they ought to do.

General Managerial Behaviors

A surprisingly consistent description of what managers do has emerged from a series of studies beginning in the 1960s that used structured observations and other methods to observe the manager in action. Of these, the results of Mintzberg's 1968 doctoral dissertation (Mintzberg 1973, 1975, 1980) and Kotter's study of the general manager (Kotter 1982a, 1982b) are the most significant. Other works (e.g., Allan 1981; Brewer and Tomlinson 1964; Kanter 1989; Lau et al. 1980; Luthans and Larsen 1986; Luthans et al. 1985; Stewart 1976) also contribute to the overall descriptions.

From these studies we see that in terms of overt information behaviors there is much similarity among managers in different organizations. First, managers work long hours. Kotter (1982b), for example, found that the average general manager he studies worked nearly 60 hours per week, and Brewer and Tomlinson (1964) report that the managers in their study had to take home some four to five hours of reading per week. Managers spend most of this time with others or communicating with others about a wide variety of topics. In their communication, it is clear that managers favor oral channels, preferably face-to-face conversation (Achleitner and Grover 1988; Brewer and Tomlinson 1964; Grover and Glazier 1984; Hale 1983; Kotter 1982a; Luthans and Larsen 1986; Mintzberg 1973). Also managers show a strong preference for quickly finding out what is or may be happening. If they had to choose, it seems that managers prefer speed of information over accuracy of information (Mintzberg 1973; O'Reilly 1982). Brewer and Tomlinson (1964) suggest that the greatest fear a manager has is being caught without information; consequently, managers spend most of their time accumulating information.

The literature also shows some important differences in the information behaviors of senior-level managers vs. lower-level managers. Because of their level, senior-level managers are expected to deal with strategic and ill-structured problems (Gorry and Scott Morton 1971). Thus, they have different needs for and sources of information (e.g., external vs. internal; soft vs. hard), and they exert more effort to make sense of that information (Mintzberg et al. 1976; O'Reilly and Pondy 1979; Perkins and Rao 1990).

Broad studies of managerial behavior also suggest that the manager-in-practice appears to be far less rational than generally believed. In a study of successful senior-level managers in the public and private sector, Isenberg (1984) found that managers' decision making didn't seem to follow any standard model (although their decisions could later by justified by data and logic). In terms of planning, these managers had no precise goals or objectives but rather a few "overriding concerns." Similarly, McCaskey (1979, 31) noted that "managers do face ambiguous situations and are sometimes forced to take action before goals or technology are clarified" Schon argues that managers cannot follow standard models of rationality because these models do not deal well with the situations that practitioners face: "uncertainty, instability, uniqueness, and conflict" (Schon 1983, 50).

From these general studies, it would be easy to conclude that managerial behavior is characterized by chaos, overload, and superficiality—i.e., too much to do about too many items involving too many people with too little time to resolve any of these items on any one occasion. However, there is a logic to these apparently frenetic managerial behaviors, and an understanding of that logic is a prerequisite for providing value-added information services to managers. We suggest that the logic has as its basis the structural components in the model of the manager's information environment. Our review of two of these components (the organization and the person) is somewhat abbreviated because these areas are vast and are reasonably well documented elsewhere (Choo 1991; Leavitt 1978; Paisley 1980; Pugh et al. 1985). Instead, our emphasis here is on managerial roles, managerial activities, and problem dimensions.

Managerial Roles

The landmark study by Mintzberg (1973) provides a framework for understanding managerial roles. Based on week-long structured observations and interviews of five upper-level managers, Mintzberg concludes that all managers' jobs are basically alike and can be described most usefully in terms of ten roles. Differences in managers are primarily differences in the relative importance of these roles. The ten roles were separated into three groups: interpersonal, informational, and decisional. All three rely on information as a key resource for the successful enactment of the roles. The interpersonal group includes the roles of the figurehead, leader, and liaison. The informational roles include monitor, disseminator, and spokesperson. The decisional roles are the entrepreneur, disturbance handler, resource allocator, and the negotiator. The specific information behaviors of managers are generally determined by the roles they "play." Although these ten roles are plausible, later studies have questioned whether other roles need to be included or whether these roles interact with managerial level and responsibility (see, e.g. Luthans & Larsen 1986).

Managerial Activities

Traditionally the manager's job is described in terms of functional responsibilities—i.e., planning, staffing, budgeting, coordinating. These responsibilities can be translated into managerial activities, which in turn may be linked to information behaviors. For example, planning may require different information from different sources than staffing would; budgeting may require more current and accurate information than coordinating. The problem with these traditional functional activities is that they rarely appear as discrete entities in observational studies of managerial behavior. Thus Mintzberg (1989) concludes that they "tell us little about what managers actually do. At best, they indicate some vague objectives managers have when they work" (p. 9). However, it must be remembered that the observational studies focused primarily on overt behaviors rather than the mental activities of their respondents. So while it is true that most managers had few occasions that could be labeled "planning" or "staffing," they do engage in these activities but probably in short bursts, spread out over long time periods, with frequent interruptions.

The in-depth study of 15 general managers by Kotter (1982a, 1982b) provides another class of managerial activities. According to

Kotter, general managers have to find ways to resolve two job-related dilemmas: (1) to figure out what to do despite uncertainty, diversity, and an enormous quantity of potentially relevant information; and (2) to get it done through a large and diverse group of people over whom they have little or no direct control (Kotter 1982a, 76).

As with Minztberg, Kotter described a set of behaviors that managers had in common and that relied heavily on information. The first set of behaviors come under the rubric of agenda setting. Agenda setting consists of information behaviors that are based on a loosely defined set of goals, strategies, and priorities. The managers develop, refine, and set their agendas through a vigorous search for information, gathered on a continuous basis, from a wide variety of sources. Kotter claims that better managers had longer time frames for their agendas and included more issues in their agendas. They also were more aggressive in seeking information.

The second set of behaviors is defined as network building. Here the managers "grow and feed" an interrelated network of cooperative relationships that could help further their agendas. These networks are created and maintained through interactions, often oral and face to face, in which both business and nonbusiness topics are discussed. The people in the networks can include individuals from inside and outside the organization in all relevant functional areas and at all levels, both formal and informal. Kotter reports that the better general managers were more successful at building these networks; they had broader networks containing more useful people.

More recent studies (Kanter 1989; Luthans 1988) reinforce the centrality of networks to successful management. Kanter states that "the ability of managers to get things done depends more on the number of networks in which they're centrally involved than on their height in a hierarchy" (Kanter 1989, 89). As managers increase their involvement in networks, they increase the number of channels available to them for strategic contacts. They can have more information available to them and greater opportunities to initiate action.

The description of managerial work has been developed further by Luthans and his colleagues (Luthans 1988; Luthans et al. 1985). These authors argue that the major activities of "real managers" come under the headings of communications, traditional management, networking, and human resource management. The exchange of information—i.e., communicating—by and large made the greatest contribution to managerial effectiveness. However, communicating may be too general a managerial activity to be helpful in constraining the range of the manager's information behaviors.

Decision Making

Although managerial activities can be analyzed in terms of communicating, agenda setting, network building, and various functional responsibilities, the largest body of "activity" literature focuses on decision making. In fact, an entire school of management thought proposes decision making as the defining element of management (see, e.g., Drucker 1974; Simon 1976, 1977). Of the many hundreds of studies in this area, which ones should be reported here? To answer this question we first expand the scope of what is included under decision making; then we focus on a few useful examples that illustrate how these activities affect the information behaviors of managers.

In the classical definition of decision making, a person must select from among several known alternatives; that is, decision making is concerned with choice. In contrast, problem solving involves only one alternative and some obstacle. That is, the task is to prevent, remove, or minimize a barrier. Decision making and problem solving can be thought of separately and have been studied separately, but "in the managerial world, these activities are so entangled that distinctions among them are only of semantic interest" (McCall and Kaplan 1990, 122). A third and related activity is "problem finding." Although this has been written about less frequently, the challenge of determining which events and situations deserve managerial attention should not be minimized. As commonly viewed, problem finding is a logical antecedent of problem solving, but, as Ackoff (1974) points out, problems don't always stay solved and problem finding can emerge from problem solving rather than vice versa. There are other intriguing variations on how these activities are defined, what roles they play, and what information they require and produce (see, e.g., Drucker 1974; Huber 1980; Mintzberg et al. 1976; Simon 1978). However, in terms of this chapter, the only distinctions that matter are those that affect managerial information behaviors.

A good example of the relationship between problem finding and managerial information behaviors is the work of Pounds (1969). He studied 50 executives in a large, technically based organization to determine how they knew when they had a problem. Pounds defined a problem in terms of a difference, perceived by the manager, between what exists and what is desired. When a difference existed, managers tended to question only one side of the gap. For example, if sales for the quarter failed to reach the goals for that quarter, managers would focus on what was wrong with the sales efforts; they never questioned whether the goal was realistic.

According to Pounds's argument, many problems in organizations may be a function of the information that is used to define the goal. If the information is out of date, irrelevant, or otherwise limited, the organization creates a needless "problem," which in turn will lead to information-intensive, problem-solving activities. Another intriguing information-related consequence of managerial problem finding was reported by Lyles and Mitroff (1980). In their study of 33 upper-level managers they found that almost 90% of their subjects learned of significant problems in their organizations through "informal sensing techniques"—that is, outside official reporting channels.

The fact that decision making is an information-intensive activity can be asserted without fear of challenge. The question of what information is related to decision making is far less certain. The classic model of decision making is based on a long history of Western rationalism. It assumes that the decision maker can and will engage in a thorough search for all relevant information (see Janis and Mann 1977, 11 for an example of what is meant by "thorough"). Huber (1980) identifies seven types of information that must be searched for: (1) possible alternatives, (2) criteria to evaluate the alternatives, (3) the relative importance of these criteria, (4) possible future conditions, (5) the probability that those futures will occur, (6) the possible payoffs, and (7) the constraints involved. Taken together, the totality of the information needed and the thoroughness of the search process make the classic model of decision making impossible in most realistic circumstances.

One method for coping within this impossible world is to restrict the information search. Simon (1976) suggests that people don't optimize their decisions but search for alternatives until they find the first one that meets their minimum requirements; they "satisfice." A related method is through what Tversky (1972) calls "elimination-by-aspect." Under this approach all the (remaining) alternatives are compared against one criterion or aspect. The number of alternatives are quickly reduced because only those that remain from a previous step are compared with the next criterion.

Another approach is to recognize the limits that exist in the classical model of decision making: limits of information, time, and the human decision maker. These limits define realistic bounds on an individual's rationality, and the task then is to determine what it means to work "optimally" within those bounds. In their classic work on "bounded rationality" March and Simon (1958) identified only the most basic limits on rationality. Forester (1984) extended this idea to include situations in which there are social (more than one person), oppositional (they are in conflict), and political (with unequal amounts of power) bounds as well.

To see how these different levels of boundedness can lead to different kinds of information behaviors, consider how organizational decision making would change according to which sets of bounds are explicitly recognized. Huber's analysis of organizational decision making and the design of decision-support systems offers some insight here (Huber 1981). He notes that under the classical model of decision making (relatively unbounded), organizational databases would need to include the seven kinds of information noted above. However, if the organization recognized that it make decisions in a competitive area (a higher level of boundedness), then the databases ought to include information that would be useful for bargaining, threatening, compromising and so forth. Huber's suggestions are attempts to incorporate alternative models of decision making in the design of decision-support systems. Each model postulates a different view of how organizations work, and each has different implications for information behaviors.

In addition to the standard (fully rational) model, other approaches to decision making deserve mention. For example, Lindblom (1959, 1979) describes organizational decision making as a series of successive, limited comparisons, commonly called "muddling through." He argues that in many organizations there usually is no ideal objective to maximize in decision making, but even if one did exist, it would be difficult if not impossible for key stakeholders to agree on. Thus, the organization moves incrementally through subobjectives toward a goal that remains unclear or is continually redefined as the process evolves. Muddling through is noncomprehensive in the sense that many outcomes are never examined, alternative courses of action are neglected, and many of the values affected by the decision are ignored—all of which decreases the information requirements of the decision maker.

Muddling through assumes that long-term objectives cannot and should not be identified prematurely; instead they emerge as a result of limited approximations. In those situations in which they can be specified, early Etzioni (1967, 1989) suggests that "mixed scanning" will enable the manager to work toward that goal without needing a complete information search. This model of decision making combines aspects of the fully rational model with some of the incrementalism found in muddling through. In information terms, the model begins with a broad (but perhaps shallow) scanning for agenda setting or problem finding, followed by a narrower but deeper analysis of those items or areas that are identified as important.

A completely different approach to organizational decision making is proposed by Cohen et al. (1972). Recognizing that few organizations make decisions in a fully rational and unbounded way, they suggest that organizations be viewed as "organized anarchies," and accordingly, a large component of chance should be imposed on their decision processes. In their model, a set of decision opportunities can be looked at as a garbage can that contains a mix of problems, participants, solutions, and choice opportunities. The problems that get addressed and "solved" depend on the chance encounter of a particular problem with a workable solution and the availability of the right people to see it through. "The central idea of garbage can models is the substitution of a temporal order for a consequential one" (March and Olsen 1986, 17). A related model is proposed by McCall and Kaplan (1990), who argue that organizations decide to act on problems when three conditions co-occur: (1) recognition of the problem, (2) resources needed to solve the problem, and (3) external pressure to motivate action. Isenberg (1984) adds to this perspective by noting that in his study, successful senior-level managers tended not to accept problems for consideration unless they thought they could be solved. Because these models of organizational choice contain a significant element of chance, managers in these environments must have the information needed to capitalize on that chance. For example, in Huber's models of decision-support systems, the database (or the manager's memory) for the garbage can model might include a list of problems and a list of unused resources (Huber 1981).

Problem Dimensions

The conceptual and actual study of situational dimensions has a considerable history, but it is fragmented. In a seminal article by Mac-Mullin and Taylor (1984), the notion of what they label problem dimensions is presented in terms of possible enhancements to the more traditional information system design criteria. Dimensions serve as supplements in that they offer criteria for assessing the usefulness of information to a user's situation. As defined by the authors, "problem dimensions are those characteristics that, beyond specific subject matter, establish the criteria for judging the relevance of information to a problem or to a class of problems" (MacMullin and Taylor 1984, 103). As such, problem dimensions can indicate what information would be useful to a manager working through a problematic situation. Because for MacMullin and Taylor these situations have multiple dimensions, they cannot always be categorized easily.

The problem dimensions proposed by MacMullin and Taylor are manifest in the subject and nonsubject components of the person's situation. Problem dimensions take into account characteristics of the information need that are idiosyncratic to the user group, to the individual in that group, and to that person's problematic situation. Acknowledging that problems are dynamic—i.e., they change as the information changes and as the person changes—Taylor (1986) suggests that the perceived salience of particular dimensions may also change.

MacMullin and Taylor proposed 22 dimensions, portrayed as 11 dichotomous categories (e.g., familiar-new, complex-simple), although they suggest that they are more likely to be continua. Their enumeration of dimensions was based on a conceptual analysis, not empirical data. The authors did not claim that their list was complete, that the dimensions were independent of each other, or that all dimensions would apply in all situations.

A review of the literature in information studies, management science, and public administration reveals that while many others have suggested similar approaches to problems, no one has defined such a range of dimensions or clarified the connection between dimensions and information behaviors as have MacMullin and Taylor. While given many other labels—e.g., "problem typologies" (Kochen 1980; Lyles and Mitroff 1980), "routines" (Mintzberg et al. 1976), "variables" (Thompson and Tuden 1964), and the like, the literature supports the fact that the concept of problem dimensions is well represented. There is considerable overlap between the dimensions noted by MacMullin and Taylor and those described by others (Cyert et al. 1956; Daft and Macintosh 1978; Einhorn and Hogarth 1987; March 1959; McCall and Kaplan 1990; Mintzberg et al. 1976; Radford 1981; Thompson and Tuden 1964; Zand 1981).

Empirical work by Fletcher further substantiates the existence of problem dimensions. In a study of 26 managers in the public and private sectors, Fletcher found support for 18 broad categories of problem dimensions. The managers related 52 problematic situations in which they were integrally involved and described the salient features of each event in these situations that could be interpreted as problem dimensions. Further analysis of the data indicated that ten of the 11 problem dimension categories proposed by McMullin and Taylor existed for managers.

Whether viewed as dimensions of the problem or criteria for assessing relevance, it is clear that many attributes of a situation may be salient at any one time and that these attributes may affect how information is valued and used as the person moves through his or her problematic situation.

The Person

Characteristics of the person are central to the description of the manager's information environment. These characteristics function separately and together to affect the other components of the model, including the manager's overt information behaviors. For the manager, the key factors include those cognitive, psychological, and physical attributes—whether innate or learned—that affect information-seeking and -use behaviors.

Much of the literature in previous *ARIST* chapters on information needs and uses might apply, including perhaps the survey of cognitive research in information science by Allen (1991). An early but more applicable review of how managers process information can be found in Ungson et al. (1981). Rather than repeat some of the same topics reported, we limit ourselves to introducing two research areas as examples of topics that link individual variables more directly with the information behaviors of managers.

The first research area focuses on how managers think. In a series of studies, Agor (1984, 1986) found that in comparison with other managers, those who were more senior were more intuitive and claimed that intuition helped them with their most important decisions. Isenberg (1984) also found support for the use of intuition among senior-level managers. Related to these studies are those that try to categorize managers according to how they think. A common tool here is the Myers-Briggs Type Indicator (MBTI). This personality test classifies individuals along four dimensions, two of which are directly related to information behaviors: the sensing-intuition dimension measures how information is acquired; the thinking-feeling dimension measures how that information is used. The working premise is that managers with different cognitive styles will prefer different kinds of information and will process information differently. Using the MBTI, Davis and Elnicki (1984) found that MBA students with different cognitive types differed significantly in their performance on certain tasks. Similar findings were reported by McKenney and Keen (1974), who studied about 200 MBA students and classified then (without using the MBTI) according to their cognitive styles for acquiring and using information. As predicted, they found that students who differed in their cognitive styles had different approaches to solving problems. There is some controversy about whether cognitive style should be a factor in implementing computerized information systems for managers (Huber 1983), but there is much less disagreement that these variables affect information behaviors of managers.

The other research area of interest is the application of cognitive biases to managerial information processing. Managers spend a lot of their time acting as what Nisbett and Ross (1980) call "intuitive scientists"—i.e., they engage in observation, categorization, prediction, inference, and so forth. These mental activities are difficult enough to do well in the scientist's laboratory; in a manger's daily life, the difficulties increase considerably. Because of the pressures of time, overload, complexity, or uncertainty, managers frequently use shortcuts in the information processing, which can lead to suboptimal decisions or judgments. Over the past decade or two, cognitive psychologists have learned a lot about how and when people tend to simplify their judgment processes (for general surveys see Hogarth 1980; Kahneman et al. 1982, and Nisbett and Ross 1980). More recently, researchers have tried to apply these learnings to the manager.

Hogarth and Makridakis (1981) listed about 30 potential biases, identified by cognitive scientists, that can affect judgment and choice behaviors. They analyzed these biases in the context of two important managerial activities—forecasting and planning—that require that information be accumulated to make useful predictions. Of particular relevance to forecasting and planning are the potential biases of "illusion of control" and "overconfidence in judgment." They also noted that the information-search component of planning and forecasting may be weakened through the manager's preference for redundancy in confirming information and avoiding disconfirming information. Similar results were found by Schwenk (1984, 1985, 1988) who studied strategic decision making in organizations. Schwenk classified potentially biasing heuristics according to the standard stages of decision making, such as goal formulation, problem identification, evaluation, and selection. With respect to seeking and use behaviors, a body of research shows that managers don't revise their judgments appropriately according to existing or new information (see, e.g., Moskowitz et al. 1976).

Many of the potential biases are related to inference. Managers live in an uncertain world and need to make plans for an even more uncertain future. They frequently need to incorporate information about probabilities and uncertainties in their decision making. A reasonable body of evidence indicates that as lay statisticians, managers may not be using this information appropriately. For example, the success of a plan is often based on conjunctive assumptions (A, B, and C must occur for the plans to succeed), whereas risk assessment often requires disjunctive assumptions (if A or B or C fails, then . . .). The basic rules of probability theory state that under plausible conditions, the conjunction of events ought to be smaller than the disjunction of the same events. In practice, however, when people make these calculations mentally, they seem to produce something like an average that falls between the conjunctive and disjunctive results. This average estimate is too high for success and too low for failure and leads the decision maker to be more confident of the future than the data justify (Tversky and Kahneman 1974).

Another bias related to uncertainty is the tendency to act as if conclusions based on small samples were as reliable as those based on larger samples. This so-called "law of small numbers" is another source of unjustified overconfidence (Tversky and Kahneman 1971) and is a problem of concern to most practicing professionals, including managers, who don't have access to large sample sizes or who may have to act before sufficient information can be obtained.

The Setting

Characteristics of the organization also play an important role in describing the manager's information environment. If we include: (1) the size of the organization, (2) its goals, product/service line, culture, and procedures, and (3) the external environment in which it functions, there would be too many organizational variables to be included in this chapter. Two interesting research areas are reviewed here to illustrate the relevance of setting variables to the information behavior of the individual manager: (1) the "rationality" of organizations, and (2) the structure of the organization.

As with managers, organizations often fail to follow completely the tenets of rationality (e.g., unboundedness, optimization) in terms of their information behaviors. Organizations also use shortcuts to escape or minimize the problems of overload, complexity, and ambiguity (Daft and Weick 1984; O'Reilly 1983; Sims and Gioia 1986).

One key to understanding the rationality of organizations is to view them differently—i.e., to recognize that they are social and political systems as well as technical and financial ones. Tichy (1983) identifies three dimensions of the organization: (1) the technical dimension, which is concerned with those factors related to the production of goods and services; (2) the cultural dimension, which includes the norms, expectations, and values of the organization; and (3) the political dimension, which addresses matters related to power. Diesing (1973) identifies five dimensions: (1) technical, (2) economic, (3) social, (4) legal, and (5) political. Multiple dimensions, combined with what Forester (1984) calls the social, political, and structural aspects of boundedness, contribute to a more complex but more realistic understanding of the organization. It is from this perspective that we can better appreciate the logic of alternative models of decision making such as the "muddling through" of Lindblom (1959) and the "garbage can" process of Cohen et al. (1972).

Organizational information behaviors also seem more reasonable when seen in the broader view of multiple dimensions and levels of boundedness. Organizations that gather information after the decision is made, that gather more information before processing what they already have, and that insist on having information regardless of its relevance do not conform to a traditional view of rationality. In an insightful analysis of these sorts of information behaviors, Feldman and March (1981) posit four reasons why organizations might behave like this. First, there are organizational incentives for acquiring too much information. Units that are responsible for gathering information are not always administratively linked to or evaluated by the users of that information. There is no punishment for those who acquire more and more information; in fact, they may be rewarded. Second, in order to anticipate opportunities and threats in their environment, organizations need to operate partly in a surveillance mode, which requires information across a broad range of sources and topics. Third, because decision making in organizations is political as well as technical, managers request additional information to protect themselves from others who may try to use that same information to advance their own objectives.

The fourth cause of "irrational" information use in organizations is related to the symbolic value of information. Organizations and the managers who work in them want to let others know that they are following a model of action (e.g., decision making, planning, problem solving) that conforms to society's beliefs about rationality. From this point of view, managers request information but don't necessarily use it because by merely requesting it or having it on their desks, they are letting others know that they are engaged in a thorough information search that will be used as part of a rational decision-making process. The symbolic role of information can be extended to information technology and may explain why some people have computers on their desks that they never use. The need to signal to others that the organization is acting rationally can also be used to understand the true role of many meetings, task forces, and the like that occupy so much of the manager's time and contribute so much to the manager's information load. O'Reilly (1983) suggests that "in order to achieve a semblance of rationality, if only to satisfy constituencies outside the organization, procedures may be established that give the appearance of comprehensive rationality but which, in fact, may be more symbolic than real" (O'Reilly 1983, 132).

The structure of the organization—whether it is tall or short, centralized or decentralized, flexible or rigid—ought to affect the kinds of information the manager needs or receives. Differences in structure are often associated with differences in processes and differences in culture, which also affect information flow and use.

Mintzberg (1981, 1983) presents one of the most intriguing analyses of organizational structure. He categorizes organizations in terms of how they effect coordination and control, which are information-intensive managerial activities. Mintzberg's "simple structure" usually describes a small, new organization; it has a manager and workers but no technocrats or staff. Communication and coordination are usually straightforward because there is little or no hierarchy or bureaucracy. Two other types of organizational form are: (1) the "machine bureaucracy," which fits the stereotypic view of the large, procedure-driven, formalized organization, and (2) the "divisionalized form," which covers organizations with separate operating divisions. Mintzberg's other two structures, the "adhocracy" and the "professional bureaucracy," are younger and consequently are still determining what information managers need and how that information should be obtained.

The organization of the future is expected to be leaner, have fewer levels, and be "boundaryless" (Drucker 1988; Hirschhorn and Gilmore 1992; Naisbitt and Aburdene 1985); the key managerial functions of coordination and control will be carried out to a greater degree through information technology. Responding to increased competition on a global scale, more organizations are moving toward Mintzberg's adhocracies, workteams, and "skunkworks" to obtain the flexibility and fast response time needed. Managers are urged to get out of their offices and "walk around," coach their subordinates, and be close to their customers (Peters and Waterman 1982). In these kinds of organizations, information needs to be shared widely, and more people from more areas both inside and outside the organization will participate in decision making. Clearly, managers in these organizations will need different kinds of information from different sources and may need to use that information in a different way (Schein 1989; Strassmann 1982; Zand 1981).

DYNAMICS OF THE MODEL

Although this chapter uses a model of the information environment of managers, the emphasis is not on the validity of that model. Rather the model's structural components have been used as a framework for organizing our review of the literature on managerial information behaviors. This short section contains some of the literature that relates to the dynamics of the model. Readers interested in the validity of this model or in other, perhaps related models in information science can start with the recent *ARIST* review by Burt and Kinnucan (1990) and the review of organizational information processing models by Choo (1991).

The dynamic nature of the model—i.e., problematic situations change over time—is an important concept in understanding information behaviors. As managers move through their problem situations, new information can shift their focus to a subproblem or to a different problematic situation, and in many instances it can redefine the problematic situation (Dill 1964; McCall and Kaplan 1990; Taylor 1986; Vickery 1965; Whittemore and Yovits 1973).

Wersig and Windel (1985) present a model for problematic situations that reflects this essential dynamism; a continuous redefining of the problem and the desired solution. The manager progresses through a number of phases and uses information in all the phases. The authors further propose that the information that may be useful will change from one phase to another, with each new iteration requiring very different information.

Probably the most comprehensive articulation of this dynamism is presented by Dervin (1983). She asserts that constantly changing situational conditions evoke the information behaviors. People go through their daily lives confronted by a wide array of problem situations that create uncertainties or "gaps." For some reason they become "stopped" and cannot move. They perceive this condition as troublesome and attempt, via information behaviors, to move either physically or cognitively. The notion of a journey down a road with detours is offered as a metaphor.

The important thing to remember is that problematic situations are not static. This fact has implications for the information provider in that information that is relevant at one point in the process may not be useful later on even though the problematic situation may have the same title or may be about the same topic.

SUMMARY AND IMPLICATIONS

What does this review of the literature tell us about managerial information behaviors? At a general level, the structure of the review argues for understanding the information behaviors of managers in terms of context-based dynamic cognitions. Specifically, we argue that the information environment of managers is defined by those factors that are related to managers as people who work in a setting, taking on various roles and carrying out various activities. Further, the model posits that the problematic situations that managers face are affected by these factors and the relative importance of different problem dimensions.

Since managers are people, the advice that information scientists give to those who deliver information services to other user populations applies to managers as well. Specifically, library and information science (LIS) professionals know that they must understand the user's information need in the context of the user's situation. For managers this means that information professionals need to refocus the query-negotiation process from that of answering questions to that of helping to resolve problematic situations (e.g., Dervin and Dewdney 1986; Taylor 1968), and they need to add value by filtering information to reduce overload. This view is not new. The literature in information science abounds with excoriations of technology-driven information systems and calls to develop user-driven models of these systems (Dervin and Nilan 1986; Mick et al. 1980; Nilan and Fletcher 1987; Rouse and Rouse 1984; Taylor 1986).

While such recommendations are known and are sensible, the information behaviors of managers present special challenges to information professionals. The literature review suggests that the following characteristics of managers are important and relevant:

- The activities that command their attention are dynamic, uncertain, complex, fast-paced, unstable, and unique;
- The situations they face are what Ackoff (1974) calls "messes"; they are not well defined, well articulated, unchanging, or independent;
- The environment in which these activities occur is informationally overloaded, socially constrained, and politically laden;
- The preferred mode of communication is oral, especially, face-to-face, and there is little time to read long documents;
- The gathering of information is often external, occurring outside their offices, to learn what ought to be on their agendas and who can help them; and
- The basis for decision making includes the use of intuition (especially for those at more senior levels), perhaps relegating formally requested information to legitimize those decisions after they are made.

We don't have an easy solution for meeting the unique and challenging demands of managers as users, but we can make a few suggestions. First, managers, as a population, can become an increasingly significant proportion of the users we serve. If we gain proficiency with managers, we can increase our value to other professionals (e.g., lawyers, politicians) because many user communities work in environments with similar characteristics.

Managers are becoming keenly aware that they need help in dealing with information overload. As key decision makers in organizations, they get most of their information (both formal and informal) from others. These people are instrumental to the manager and to the organization that enacts the manager's decisions. While information professionals with training in dealing with unstructured natural-language materials ought to have a competitive advantage over other information providers (e.g., system designers) when it comes to serving senior-level managers, it is necessary that they augment this skill with an understanding of how managers and organizations function. The immediate challenge, therefore, is for information scientists and information professionals to enhance their knowledge of this user environment.

The relationship between LIS professionals and managers-in-action is analogous to that between the manager and the management scientist, as described by Churchman and his colleagues (Churchman 1964; Churchman and Schainblatt 1965). They noted that these two different communities often acted as if they were two different cultures. They did not communicate, and there were differences in the values and norms of each community, which probably contributed to that lack of interaction. To surmount these differences, Churchman and Schainblatt argued for "mutual understanding," with both communities considered equally responsible for moving in that direction.

We also believe that information professionals would benefit by gaining more of an understanding of the multidimensional nature of organizations. LIS professionals have historically focused on information related to the technical dimension. However, in the world of the manager, the cultural, social, and political dimensions also matter—perhaps quite a bit. Within the framework of multiple dimensions, the information professional can gain a better appreciation of the alternative notions of "rationality," such as the advice of Forester (1989) that to be rational, one must be political.

Given an understanding of these broader, fundamental concerns, the LIS professional can specifically contribute in a useful way to the information activities of managers by:

- Supplying the manager with the information in the format appropriate to the problematic situation—i.e., not always relying on lengthy printed materials as solutions;
- Insulating the manager from the raw and often superfluous data that contribute to information overload;
- Acting as a filter by analyzing, grouping, and formatting the information for the manager;
- Generating a common organizational database for use on group-decision situations;
- Scanning the external environment to keep managers supplied with relevant information for their problematic situations;
- Generating an audit trail of information that can be linked to specific problematic situations;
- Alerting the manager to the existence of conflicting or contradictory data to provide a broader base for the solution; and

- Working with the manager to develop an organizational resource center that is timely, reliable, and relevant to the needs of both the manager and the organization.

The goal of the information professional is to provide information servces that treat the manager as a "clinician" who deals with unique circumstances in a time-compressed, complex setting. What the manager needs are the value-added services of screening, summarizing, synthesizing, highlighting, and presenting information in a useful and timely manner (Taylor 1986). Only then will the information professional be able to ameliorate the manager's dilemma, which is too much information, but not enough of the right information in the right format through the right channel at the right time.

REFERENCES

Achleitner, H.K., and R. Grover. 1988. Managing in an information-rich environment: Applying information transfer theory to information systems management. *Special Libraries* 79(2): 92–100.

Ackoff, R.L. 1974. Beyond problem solving. *General Systems* 19: 237–239.

Ackoff, R.L. 1967. Management misinformation systems. *Management Science* 14(4): B-147–B-156.

Agnew, N.M., and J.L. Brown. 1982. From skyhooks to walking sticks: On the road to nonrational decision making. *Organizational Dynamics* 11: 40–58.

Agor, W.H. 1986. How top executives use their intuition to make important decisions. *Business Horizons* 29(Jan/Feb): 49–53.

Agor, W.H. 1984. *Intuitive Management: Integrating Left and Right Brain Management Skills.* Englewood Cliffs, NJ: Prentice Hall.

Allan, P. 1981. Managers at work: A large-scale study of the managerial job in New York City government. *Academy of Management Journal* 24(3): 613–619.

Allen, B.L. 1991. Cognitive research in information science: Implications for design. In *Annual Review of Information Science and Technology*, Vol. 26, ed. M.E. Williams, 3–37. Medford, NJ: Learned Information, Inc. for the American Society for Information Science.

Alter, S.L. 1976. How effective managers use information systems. *Harvard Business Review* 54(6): 97–104.

Argyris, C. 1971. Management information systems: The challenge to rationality and emotionality. *Management Science* 17(6): B-275–B-292.

Behling, O., and N.I. Eckel. 1991. Making sense out of intuition. *Academy of Management Executive* 5(1): 46–54.

Belkin, N.J. 1984. Cognitive models and information transfer. *Social Science Information Studies* (UK) 4: 111–129.

Benbasat, I., R.N. Taylor. 1982. Behavioral aspects of information processing for the design of management information systems. *IEEE Transactions on Systems, Man and Cybernetics SMC* 12(4): 439–450.

Benbasat, I., R.N. Taylor. 1978. The impact of cognitive styles on information system design. *Management Information Systems Quarterly* 2(2): 43–54.

Blaylock, G.K., and L.P. Rees. 1984. Cognitive style and usefulness of information. *Decision Sciences* 15(6): 74–91.

Boynton, A.C., and R.W. Zmud. 1984. An assessment of critical success factors. *Sloan Management Review* 25(Summer): 17–24.

Brewer, E., J.W. Tomlinson. 1964. The manager's working day. *Journal of Industrial Economics (UK)* 12(3): 191–197.

Brittain, J.M. 1975. Information needs and application of the results of user studies. In *Perspectives in Information Science: Proceedings of the NATO Advanced Study Institute on Perspectives in Information Science; 1973 August 13#24, Aberystwyth, Wales*, eds. A. Debons and W.J. Cameron, 425–447. Leyden, The Netherlands: Noordhoff International.

Brunsson, N. 1985. *The Irrational Organization: Irrationality as a Basis for Organizational Action and Change*. New York: Wiley.

Burt, P.V., and M.T. Kinnucan. 1990. Information models and modelling techniques for information systems. In *Annual Review of Information Science and Technology*, vol. 25, ed. M.E. Williams, 175–208. Amsterdam, The Netherlands: Elsevier Science Publishers for the American Society for Information Science.

Carroll, S.J., and D.J. Gillen. 1987. Are the classical management functions useful in describing managerial work? *Academy of Management Review* 12: 38–51.

Chen, C.C., and P. Hernon. 1982. *Information Seeking: Assessing and Anticipating User Needs*. New York: Neal-Schuman.

Choo, C.W. 1991. Towards an information model of organizations. *Canadian Journal of Information Science* 16(3): 32–62.

Churchman, C.W. 1964. Managerial acceptance of scientific recommendations. *California Management Review* 7(1): 31–38.

Churchman, C.W., and A.H. Schainblatt. 1965. The researcher and the manager: A dialectic of implementation. *Management Science* 11(4): B-69–B-87.

Cleveland, H. 1985. *The Knowledge Executive: Leadership in an Information Society*. New York: Truman Talley Books.

Cohen, M.D., J.G. March, and J.P. Olsen. 1972. A garbage can model of organizational choice. *Administrative Science Quarterly*. 17(Mar): 1–25.

Compaine, B.M., and J.F. McLaughlin. 1987. Management information: Back to basics. *Information Management Review* 2(3): 15–24.

Connolly, T. 1977. Information processing and decision-making in organizations. In *New Directions in Organizational Behavior*, eds. B.M. Staw, and G.R. Salancik, 205–234. Chicago, IL: St. Clair Press.

Cotton, J.L. 1984. Why getting additional data often slows decision-making and what to do about it. *Management Review* 73(5): 56–61.

Craig, R. 1979. Information systems theory and research: An overview of individual information processing. *Communication Yearbook* 3: 99–121.

Cravens, D.W. 1970. An exploratory analysis of individual information processing. *Management Science* 16(10): B-656–B-670.

Curcuru, E.H., and J.H. Healey. 1972. The multiple roles of the manager. *Business Horizons* 15(4): 15-24.

Cyert, R.M., H.A. Simon, and D.B. Trow. 1956. Observations of a business decision. *The Journal of Business* 29(4): 237–248.

Daft, R.L., and R.H. Lengel. 1986. Organizational information requirements, media richness and structural design. *Management Science* 32(5): 554–571.

Daft, R.L., and R.H. Lengel. 1984. Information richness: A new approach to managerial information processing and organization design. In *Research in Organizational Behavior*, vol. 6, eds. B.M. Staw and L.L. Cummings, 191–233.

Daft, R.L., and N.B. MacIntosh. 1978. A new approach to design and use of management information. *California Management Review* 21(1): 820–892.

Daft, R.L., and K.E. Weick. 1984. Toward a model of organizations as interpretation systems. *Academy of Management Review* 9(2): 284–295.

Daniels, P.J. 1986. Cognitive models in information retrieval—An evaluative review. *Journal of Documentation* 42(4): 272–304.

Davis, D.L., and R.A. Elnicki. 1984. User cognitive types for decision support systems. *Omega (UK)* 12(6): 601–614.

Dervin, B. 1983. An Overview of Sense-Making Research: Concepts, Methods, and Results to Date. Paper presented at The International Communication Association Annual Meeting, May 26–30, 1983, Dallas, TX. Available from the author: Department of Communication, Ohio State University, Columbus, Ohio 43210.

Dervin, B., and P. Dewdney. 1986. Neutral questioning: A new approach to the reference interview. *RQ* 25(4): 506–512.

Dervin, B., and M.S. Nilan. 1986. Information needs and uses. In *Annual Review of Information Science and Technology*, vol. 21, ed. M.E. Williams, 3–33. White Plains, NY: Knowledge Industry Publications for the American Society for Information Science.

Dewhirst, H.D. 1971. Influence of perceived information sharing norms in communication channel utilization. *Academy of Management Journal* 14(3): 305–315.

Dickson, G.W., J.A. Senn, and N.L. Chervany. 1977. Research in management information systems: The Minnesota Experiments. *Management Science* 23(9): 913–923.

Diesing, P. 1973. *Reason in Society: Five Types of Decisions and Their Social Conditions*. Westport, CT: Greenwood Press.

Dill, W.R. 1964. Varieties of administrative decision. In *Readings in*

Managerial Psychology, eds. H.J. Leavitt, and L.R. Pondy, 457–473. Chicago, IL: University of Chicago Press.

Doktor, R.H., and Hamilton, W.F. 1973. Cognitive style and the acceptance of management science recommendations. *Management Science* 19(8): 884–894.

Downs, A. 1967. Search problems in bureaus. In *Inside Bureaucracy*, 175–190. Boston, MA: Little Brown. Also in: *Information Management in Public Administration*, eds. F.W. Horton, and D.A. Marchand, 103–119. Arlington, VA: Information Resource Press, 1982.

Downs, A. 1965. Nonmarket decision making: A theory of bureaucracy. *American Economic Review* 55: 439–446.

Dreyfus, S.E. 1983. How expert managers tend to let the gut lead the brain. *Management Review* 72(9): 56–61.

Drucker, P.F. 1988. The coming of the new organization. *Harvard Business Review* 66(1): 45–53.

Drucker, P.F. 1974. *Management: Tasks, Responsibilities, Practices.* New York: Harper & Row.

Drucker, P.F. 1967. *The Effective Executive.* New York: Harper & Row.

Einhorn, H.J., and R.M. Hogarth. 1987. Decision making: Going forward in reverse. *Harvard Business Review* 65(1): 66–70.

Etzioni, A. 1989. Humble decision making. *Harvard Business Review* 67(Jul/Aug): 122–126.

Etzioni, A. 1967. Mixed-scanning: A "third" approach to decision making. *Public Administration Review* 27(Dec): 385–392.

Feldman, M.S., and J.G. March. 1981. Information in organizations as signal and symbol. *Administrative Science Quarterly* 26(2): 171–186.

Ference, T.P. 1970. Organizational communications systems and the decision process. *Management Science* 17(2): B-83–B-96.

Fleischer, M., and J.A. Morrell. 1988. The use of office automation by managers: A survey. *Information Management Review* 4(1): 29–40.

Fletcher, P.T. 1991. An Examination of Situational Dimensions in the Information Behaviors of General Managers. Ph.D. dissertation. Syracuse University, Syracuse, New York. Available from University Microfilms, Ann Arbor, MI. (UMI order no. DA9204503).

Forester, J. 1989. *Planning in the Face of Power.* Berkeley, CA: University of California Press.

Forester, J. 1984. Bounded rationality and the politics of muddling through. *Public Administration Review* 44(Jan/Feb): 23–31.

Gorry, G.A., and M.S. Scott Morton. 1971. A framework for management information systems. *Sloan Management Review* 13: 55–70.

Grosser, K. 1991. Human networks in organizational information processing. In *Annual Review of Information Science and Technology*, vol. 26, ed. M.E. Williams, 349–402. Medford, NJ: Learned Information for the American Society for Information Science.

Grover, R., and J. Glazier. 1984. Information transfer in city government. *Public Library Quarterly* 5(4): 9–27.

Hale, M.L. 1983. A Structured Observation Study of the Nature of City Managers' Work. Ph.D. dissertation. University of Southern California, Los Angeles. Copies available from Micrographics Department, Doheny Library, University of Southern California, Los Angeles, CA 90089.

Hales, C.P. 1986. What do managers do? A critical review of the evidence. *Journal of Management Studies (UK)* 23: 88–115.

Hellriegel, D., and J.W. Slocum Jr. 1975. Managerial problem solving styles. *Business Horizons* 18(Dec): 29–37.

Henderson, J., and P.C. Nutt. 1980. The influence of decision style on decision making behavior. *Management Science* 26(4): 371–385.

Hernstein, R.J. 1990. Rational choice theory: Necessary but not sufficient. *American Psychologist* 45(3): 356–367.

Hert, C.A, and M.S. Nilan. 1992. Incorporating the user in system evaluation and design. In *Proceedings of the National Online Meeting* May 5–7, New York, 1992, 217–234. Medford, NJ: Learned Information.

Hewins, E.T. 1990. Information need and use studies. In *Annual Review of Information Science and Technology*, vol. 25, ed. M.E. Williams, 145–172. Amsterdam, The Netherlands: Elsevier Science for the American Society for Information Science.

Hickson, D.J. 1987. Decision-making at the top of organizations. *Annual Review of Sociology* 13: 165–192.

Hirschhorn, L., and T. Gilmore. 1992. The new boundaries of the "boundaryless" company. *Harvard Business Review* 70(3): 104–115.

Hogarth, R. 1980. *Judgment and Choice*. New York: Wiley & Sons.

Hogarth, R., and S. Makridakis. 1981. Forecasting and planning: An evaluation. *Management Science* 27(2): 115–138.

House, R.J., and J.V. Singh. 1987. Organizational behavior: Some new directions for I/O psychology. *Annual Review of Psychology* 38: 669–718.

Huber, G.P. 1983. Cognitive style as a basis for MIS and DSS Designs: Much ado about nothing? *Management Science* 29(5): 567–578.

Huber, G.P. 1981. The nature of organizational decision making and the design of decision support systems. *Management Information Systems Quarterly* 5(3): 1–10.

Huber, G.P. 1980. *Managerial Decision Making*. Glenview, IL: Scott, Foresman & Company.

Huber, G.P., and R.L. Daft. 1987. The information environment of organizations. In *Handbook of Organizational Communication: An Interdisciplinary Perspective*, eds. F.M. Jablin, L.L. Putnam, K.H. Roberts, and L.W. Porter, 130–164. Newbury Park, CA: Sage.

Isabella, L. 1990. Evolving interpretations as change unfolds: How managers construe key organizational events. *Academy of Management Journal* 33(1): 7–41.

Isenberg, D.J. 1986. Thinking and managing: A verbal protocol analysis of managerial problem solving. *Academy of Management Journal* 29(4): 775–788.

Isenberg, D.J. 1984. How senior managers think. *Harvard Business Review* 62(6): 81–90.

Janis, I.L., and L. Mann. 1977. *Decision Making: A Psychological An-*

alysis of Conflict, Choice, and Commitment. New York: The Free Press.

Kahneman, D., and A. Tversky. 1979. Intuitive prediction: Biases and corrective procedures. *TIMS: Studies in the Management Sciences (The Netherlands)* 12: 313–327.

Kahneman, D., P. Slovic, and A. Tversky, eds. 1982. *Judgment Under Uncertainty: Heuristics and Biases.* New York: Cambridge University Press.

Kanter, R.M. 1980. The new managerial work. *Harvard Business Review* 67(6): 85–92.

Katzer, J. 1991. Understanding How Information "Works" in Organizations: Plausible Assumptions and Confounding Realities. Paper presented at American Society for Information Science (ASIS) 54th Annual Meeting, 1991 October 27-31, Washington, DC. Available from the author, Syracuse University, School of Information Studies, Syracuse, NY 13244.

Kiesler, S., and L. Sproull. 1982. Managerial response to changing environments: Perspectives on problem sensing from social cognition. *Administrative Science Quarterly* 27(4): 548–570.

Kochen, M. 1980. Coping with complexity. *Omega (UK)* 8(1): 11–19.

Kotter, J.P. 1982a. *The General Managers.* New York: The Free Press.

Kotter, J.P. 1982b. What effective general managers really do. *Harvard Business Review* 60(Nov/Dec): 156–167.

Lau, A.W., A.R. Newman, and L.A. Broedling. 1980. The nature of managerial work in the public sector. *Public Administration Review* 40(Sept/Oct): 513–520.

Lau, A.W., and C.M. Pavett. 1983. Managerial work: The influence of hierarchical level and functional speciality. *Academy of Management Journal* 26(1): 170–177.

Leavitt, H.J. 1978. *Managerial Psychology.* 4th ed. Chicago, IL: University of Chicago Press.

Lengel, R.H., and R.L. Daft. 1988. The selection of communication media as an executive skill. *Academy of Management Executive* 2(3): 225–233.

Levitt, T. 1987. From the Editor. *Harvard Business Review* 87(1): 4–5.

Lindblom, C.G. 1979. Still muddling, not yet, through. *Public Administration Review* 39(Nov/Dec): 40–45.

Lindblom, C.G. 1959. The science of muddling through. *Public Administration Review* 19(Spring): 79–388.

Luthans, F. 1988. Successful vs. effective real managers. *Academy of Management Executive* 2(2): 127–132.

Luthans, F., and J.K. Larsen. 1986. How managers really communicate. *Human Relations* 39(2): 161–178.

Luthans, F., S.A. Rosenkrantz, and H.W. Hennessey. 1985. What do successful managers really do? An observation study of managerial activities. *Journal of Applied Behavioral Science* 21(3): 255–270.

Lyles, M.A., and I.I. Mitroff. 1980.Organizational problem formulation: An empirical study. *Administrative Science Quarterly* 25(March): 102–119.

MacMullin, S.E., and R.S. Taylor. 1984. Problem dimensions and information traits. *Information Society* 3(1): 91–111.

March, J.G. 1982. Theories of choice and making decisions. *Society* 20: 29–39.

March, J.G. 1978. Bounded rationality, ambiguity and the engineering of choice. *Bell Journal of Economics* 9: 587–608.

March, J.G. 1959. Business decision making. *Industrial Research* 1(Spring): 64–70.

March, J.G., and S.A. Herbert. 1958. *Organizations.* New York: Wiley & Sons.

March, J.G., and J.P. Olsen. 1986. Garbage can models of decision making in organizations. In *Ambiguity and Command: Organizational Perspectives on Military Decision Making,* eds. J.G. March and R.W. Weissenger-Baylon, 11–35. Boston, MA: Pitman.

McCall, Jr., M.W., and R.E. Kaplan. 1990. *Whatever it Takes: The Realities of Managerial Decision Making.* 2nd ed. Englewood Cliffs, NJ: Prentice Hall.

McCaskey, M.B. 1979. The management of ambiguity. *Organizational Dynamics* 7(4): 31–48.

McGowan, R.P. 1984. Organizational decision making and information systems. In *Decision Making in the Public Sector,* ed. L.G. Nigro, 261–288. New York: Marcel Dekker.

McKenney, J.L., and P.G. Keen. 1974. How managers' minds work. *Harvard Business Review* 52(3): 79–90.

Mick, C.K., G.N. Lindsey, and D. Callahan. 1980. Toward usable user studies. *Journal of the American Society for Information Science* 31(Sept): 347–356.

Mintzberg, H. 1973. *The Nature of Managerial Work.* New York: Harper & Row.

Mintzberg, H. 1989. *Mintzberg on Management: Inside Our Strange World of Organizations.* New York: The Free Press.

Mintzberg, H. 1980. *The Nature of Managerial Work.* Englewood Cliffs, NJ: Prentice Hall.

Mintzberg, H. 1973. *The Nature of Managerial Work.* New York: Harper & Row.

Mintzberg, H. 1981. Organization design: Fashion or Fit? *Harvard Business Review* 59(1): 103–116.

Mintzberg, H. 1976. Planning on the left side and managing on the right. *Harvard Business Review* 54(4): 49–58.

Mintzberg, H. 1983. *Structure in Fives: Designing Effective Organizations.* Englewood Cliffs, NJ: Prentice Hall.

Mintzberg, H., D. Raisinghani, and A. Theoret. 1976. The structure of "unstructured" decision processes. *Administrative Science Quarterly* 21(2): 246–275.

Moskowitz, H., R.E. Schaefer, and K. Borcherding. 1976. "Irrationality" of managerial judgements: Implications for information systems. *Omega (UK)* 4(2): 125–140.

Munro, M.C. 1978. Determining the manager's information needs. *Journal of Systems Management* 29(June): 34–39.

Munro, M.C., and B.R. Wheeler. 1980. Planning, critical success factors and management's information requirements. *Management Information Systems Quarterly* 4(Dec): 27–38.

Naisbitt, J., and P. Aburdene. 1985. *Re-inventing the Corporation: Transforming Your Job and Your Company for the New Information Society.* New York, Warner Books.

Nelson, D.L. 1990. Individual adjustment to information-driven technologies: A critical review. *MIS Quarterly* 14(1): 79–98.

Newby, G.B., M.S. Nilan, and L.M. Duvall. 1991. Toward a reassessment of individual differences for information systems: The power of user-based situational predicators. In *Proceedings of the American Society for Information Science (ASIS) 54th Annual Meeting: Vol 28, 1991 October 27#31, Washington, DC,* eds. J.M. Griffiths and N.J. Belkin, 73–81. Medford, NJ: Learned Information for ASIS.

Newman, M. 1985. Managerial access to information: Strategies for prevention and promotion. *Journal of Management Studies (UK)* 22(2): 193–221.

Nilan, M.S., and P.T. Fletcher. 1987. Information behaviors in the preparation of research proposals: A user study. In *ASIS '87: Proceedings of the American Society for Information Science (ASIS) 50th Annual Meeting: Vol 24, 1987 October 4-8, Boston, MA,* ed. C.C. Chen, 186–192. Medford, NJ: Learned Information for ASIS.

Nilan, M.S., G.B. Newby, W. Paik, and K. Lopatin. 1989. User-oriented interfaces for computer systems: A user-defined on-line help system for desktop publishing. In *ASIS'89: Proceedings of the American Society for Information Science (ASIS) 52nd Annual Meeting: Vol 26, 1989 October 30-November 2, Washington, DC,* 104–110. Medford, NJ: Learned Information for ASIS.

Nisbett, R., and L. Ross. 1980. *Human Inference: Strategies and Shortcomings of Social Judgment.* Englewood Cliffs, NJ: Prentice Hall.

Nutt, P.C. 1990. Strategic decisions made by top executives and middle managers with data and process dominant styles. *Journal of Management Studies (UK)* 27(March): 173–194.

O'Reilly, III, C.A. 1991. Organizational behavior: Where we've been, where we're going. *Annual Review of Psychology* 42: 427–458.

O'Reilly, III, C.A. 1983. The use of information in organizational decision making: A model and some propositions. In *Research in Organizational Behavior,* vol. 5, eds. L.L. Cummings and B.M. Staw, 103–140. Greenwich, CT: JAI.

O'Reilly, III, C.A. 1982. Variations in decision makers' use of information sources: The impact of quality and accessibility of information. *Academy of Management Journal* 25(4): 756–771.

O'Reilly, III, C.A., and L.R. Pondy. 1979. Organizational communication. In *Organizational Behavior,* ed. S.Kerr, 119–150. Columbus, OH: Grid.

O'Reilly, III, C.A., J.A. Chatman, and J.C. Anderson. 1987. Message flow and decision making. In *Handbook of Organizational Communication: An Interdisciplinary Perspective,* eds. F.M. Jablin, L. Putnam, K. Roberts, and L. Porter, 600–623. Newbury Park, CA: Sage.

Paisley, W.J. 1980. Information and work. In *Progress in Communication Sciences*, vol. 2, eds. B. Dervin and M.J. Voigt, 113–165. Norwood, NJ: Ablex Publishing.

Perkins, W.S., and R.C. Rao. 1990. The role of experience in information use and decision making by marketing managers. *Journal of Marketing Research* 27(1): 1–10.

Peters, T.J., and R.H. Waterman, Jr. 1982. In *Search of Excellence: Lessons from America's Best-Run Companies*. New York: Harper & Row.

Pounds, W.F. 1969. The process of problem finding. *Industrial Management Review* 11(1): 1–20.

Pugh, D.S., D.J. Hickson, and C.R. Hinings. 1985. *Writers On Organizations*. Beverly Hills, CA: Sage Publications.

Radford, K.J. 1981. *Modern Managerial Decision Making*. Reston, VA: Reston Publishing Company.

Roberts, N. 1982. A search for information man. *Social Science Information Studies (UK)* 2: 93–104.

Robey, D., and W. Taggart. 1982. Human information processing in information and decision support systems. *MIS Quarterly* 6(2): 61–73.

Robey, D., and W. Taggart. 1981. Measuring managers' minds: The assessment of style in human information processing. *Academy of Management Review* 6(3): 375–383.

Rockart, J.F. 1979. Chief executives define their own data needs. *Harvard Business Review* 57(Mar/Apr): 81–93.

Rouse, W.B., and S.H. Rouse. 1984. Human information seeking and design of information systems. *Information Processing and Management* 20(1): 129–138.

Rowan, R. 1986. *The Intuitive Manager*. Boston, MA: Little, Brown.

Schamber, L., M. Eisenberg, and M.S. Nilan. 1990. A re-examination of relevance: Toward a dynamic, situational definition. *Information Processing and Management* 26(6): 755–776.

Schein, E.H. 1989. Reassessing the divine rights of managers. *Sloan Management Review* 30(Winter): 63–68.

Schon, D.A. 1983. *The Reflective Practitioner: How Professionals Think in Action*. New York: Basic Books.

Schweiger, D.M. 1983. Measuring managers' minds: A critical reply to Robey and Taggart. *Academy of Management Review* 8(1): 143–150.

Schwenk, C.R. 1988. The cognitive perspective on strategic decision making. *Journal of Management Studies (UK)* 25(1): 41–55.

Schwenk, C.R. 1985. Management illusions and biases: Their impact on strategic decisions. *Long Range Planning* 18(5): 74–80.

Schwenk, C.R. 1984. Cognitive simplification processes in strategic decision-making. *Strategic Management Journal* 5(2): 111–128.

Simon, H.A. 1976. *Administrative Behavior: A Study of Decision-Making Processes in Administrative Organization*. 3rd ed. New York: Free Press.

Simon, H.A. 1981. Information-processing models of cognition. *Journal of the American Society for Information Science* 32(5): 364–377.

Simon, H.A. 1977. *The New Science of Management Decision*. Englewood Cliffs, NJ: Prentice Hall.

Simon, H.A. 1978. Rationality as a process and as a product of thought. *American Economic Review* 68: 1–16.

Sims, Jr., H.P., and D.A. Gioia. 1986. *The Thinking Organization: Dynamics of Organizational Social Cognition.* San Francisco, CA: Jossey-Bass.

Soelberg, P.O. 1967. Unprogrammed decision making. *Industrial Management Review* 8(2): 19–29.

Stewart. R. 1982. A model for understanding managerial jobs and behavior. *Academy of Management Review* 7(1): 7–13.

Stewart, R. 1976.To understand the manager's job: Consider demands, constraints, choices. *Organizational Dynamics* 4(4): 22–32.

Strassmann, P.A. 1982. Overview of strategic aspects of information management. *Office: Technology and People (UK)* 1: 71–89.

Suchman, L.A. 1987. *Plans and Situated Actions: The Problems of Human/Machine Communication.* Cambridge, England: Cambridge University Press.

Taggart, W., and D. Robey. 1981. Minds and managers: On the dual nature of human information processing and management. *Academy of Management Review* 6(2): 187–195.

Taggart, W., D. Robey, and K.G. Kroeck. 1985. Managerial decision styles and cerebral dominance: An empirical study. *Journal of Management Studies (UK)* 22(2): 175–192.

Taylor, R.S. 1990. Information use environments. In *Progress in Communication Sciences,* vol. 10, eds. B. Dervin and M.J. Voigt, 217–255. Norwood, NJ: Ablex Publishing.

Taylor, R.S. 1986. *Value-Added Precesses in Information Systems.* Norwood, NJ: Ablex Publishing.

Taylor, R.S. 1985. Information values in decision contexts. *Information Management Review* 1(1): 47–55.

Taylor, R.S. 1968. Question negotiation and information seeking in libraries. *College and Research Libraries* 29: 178–194.

Thompson, J.D., and A. Tuden. 1964. Strategies, structures, and processes of organizational decision. In *Readings in Managerial Psychology,* eds. J. Leavitt and L. Pondy, 496–515. Chicago, IL: University of Chicago Press.

Tichy, N.M. 1983. *Managing Strategic Change: Technical, Political, and Cultural Dynamics.* New York: Wiley.

Tushman, M., and D. Nadler. 1978. Information processing as an integrating concept in organizational design. *Academy of Management Review* 3(July): 613–624.

Tversky, A. 1972. Elimination by aspects: A theory of choice. *Psychological Review* 79: 281–299.

Tversky, A., and D. Kahneman. 1974. Judgement under uncertainty: Heuristics and biases. *Science* 185: 1124–1131.

Tversky, A., and D. Kahneman. 1971. Belief in the law of small numbers. *Psychological Bulletin* 76(2): 105–110.

Ungson, G.R., D.N. Braunstein, and P.D. Hall. 1981. Managerial information processing: A research review. *Administrative Science Quarterly* 26(March): 116–130.

Vickery, B.C. 1965. *On Retrieval System Theory.* 2nd ed. London, England: Butterworths.

Weick, K.E. 1983. Managerial thought in the context of action. In *The Executive Mind,* ed. S. Srivastva, 221–242. San Francisco, CA: Jossey-Bass. (Based on a symposium held at Case Western Reserve University in 1982.)

Weick, K.E. 1979. Cognitive processes in organizations. In *Research in Organizational Behavior,* vol. 1, ed. B.M. Staw, 41–74. Greenwich, CT: JAI Press.

Wersig, G., and G. Windel. 1985. Information science needs a theory of "information actions." *Social Science Information Studies (UK)* 5: 11–23.

Wetherbe, J.C. 1991. Executive information requirements: Getting it right. *MIS Quarterly* 15(1): 51–65.

Whittemore, B.J., and M.C. Yovits. 1973. A generalized conceptual development for the analysis and flow of information. *Journal of the American Society for Information Science* 24(3): 221–231.

Wildavsky, A. 1983. Information as an organizational problem. *Journal of Management Studies (UK)* 20(1): 29–40.

Wilson, T.D. 1984. The cognitive approach to information-seeking behavior and information use. *Social Science Information Studies (UK)* 4: 197–204.

Wright, W.F. 1980. Cognitive information processing biases: Implications for producers and users of financial information. *Decision Sciences* 11: 284–298.

Zand, D.E. 1981. *Information, Organization and Power: Effective Management in the Knowledge Society.* New York: McGraw-Hill.

How Senior Managers Acquire and Use Information in Environmental Scanning

Ethel Auster and Chun Wei Choo

INTRODUCTION

Information is the raw material of managerial work. A large part of
the manager's information comes from or concerns the environment
external to the organization. Customer preferences, competitor strategies, technological advancements, government regulations, and social and economic conditions are all in a constant state of flux.
Learning about developments in the environment thus becomes a critical activity of senior managers responsible for the survival and performance of their organizations. *Environmental scanning* is defined
as the acquisition and use of information about events and trends
in an organization's external environment, the knowledge of which
would assist management in planning the organization's future course
of action (Choo and Auster 1993; Aguilar 1967). Environmental scanning drives an organization's strategic planning process—the quality
of the planning depends on the quality of the scan. Yet the scanning
manager faces many challenges: The external environment is changing
rapidly in complex ways; information is available from numerous
sources; information about external developments is often ambiguous; and the information is to be used to make consequential decisions or long-term commitments by the organization. Although there
is general agreement that the acquisition and processing of informa-

Reprinted from *Information Processing & Management*, 30(5). E Auster and C.
W. Choo, How Senior managers acquire and use information in environmental
scanning, pp. 607–618. Copyright 1994, with kind permission from Elsevier
Science Ltd., The Boulevard, Langford Lane, Kidlington OX5 1GB, UK.

tion is central to managerial work, there is a relative lack of research in the information science literature on managers as a distinct group of information users. The present study focuses on senior managers' use of information about the external business environment. Specifically, our purpose is to understand how CEOs in two Canadian industries acquire information about the environment and then use this information in their decision making.

Scanning involves several modes of information seeking. Aguilar (1967) usefully differentiates between *searching* for information about a specific question, and *viewing* information or being exposed to information without a specific information need in mind. Scanning could range from a casual conversation at the lunch table or a chance observation of an angry customer dumping a product, to an extensive market research program to identify business opportunities. At a conceptual level then, environmental scanning may be seen as an extended case of information seeking, in that scanning not only includes searching for particular information, but also simply being *exposed* to information that *could* impact the firm.

CONCEPTUAL FRAMEWORK

Research on environmental scanning began in the 1960s with path-finding studies by Aguilar (1967) and Keegan (1968). Since then, most of the studies have revolved around a few research themes: the effect of perceived environmental uncertainty on scanning; the focus of scanning; information sources used; and scanning methods. In each of these areas, it is possible to discern a consistent picture of how managers scan. With regard to environmental uncertainty, most studies found that managers who perceive greater environmental uncertainty tend to do more scanning (see, for example, Nishi et al. 1982; Daft et al. 1988; Auster and Choo 1992, 1993). The focus of scanning is on market-related sectors of the external environment, with information on customers, competitors, and suppliers being the most important (Jain 1984; Ghoshal and Kim 1986; Lester and Waters 1989). The information sources most often used are personal sources, especially managers and staff within the organization, whereas sources such as the company library and online databases were less frequently used (O'Connell and Zimmerman 1979; Kobrin et al. 1980; Auster and Choo, 1992, 1993). Scanning methods can range from ad hoc, informal activities to systematic, formalized efforts, depending on the organization's size, experience, and perception of the environment (Thomas 1980; Klein and Linneman 1984; Preble et al. 1978). (A more detailed discussion of past research on environmental scanning is in Choo and Auster 1993). One of the gaps in the research is the relative lack of attention to how information gained from environmental scanning is actually used by the managers.

The present study examines environmental scanning by chief executive officers in two Canadian industries, and addresses three research questions:

1. What environmental sectors are scanned by the CEOs?
2. What information sources do they use in the environmental scanning?
3. How do they utilize the environmental information in decision making?

The study thus builds upon past research by investigating the focus of scanning, and the information sources used in scanning. At the same time, it extends past research by analyzing the ways that the environmental information is actually used in decision making.

External environment

Duncan (1972) defines the *environment* as ''the totality of physical and social factors that are taken directly into consideration in the decision-making behavior of individuals in the organization'' (p. 314). For the purpose of this study, the environment is viewed as a source of information, continually creating signals and messages that organizations should attend to (Dill 1962; Weick 1979).

The external business environment of a firm is divided into six environmental sectors, as defined by Daft et al. (1988) in their study of CEO scanning:

1. *Customer* sector refers to those companies or individuals that purchase the products made by the respondent's firm, and includes companies that acquire the products for resale, as well as final customers.
2. *Competition* sector includes the companies, products, and competitive tactics: companies that make substitute products; products that compete with the respondent firm's products; and competitive actions between the respondent's firm and other companies in the same industry.
3. *Technological* sector includes the development of new production techniques and methods, innovation in materials and products, and general trends in research and science relevant to the respondent's firm.
4. *Regulatory* sector includes federal and provincial legislation and regulations, city or community policies, and political developments at all levels of government.

5. *Economic* sector includes economic factors such as stock markets, rate of inflation, foreign trade balance, federal and provincial budgets, interest rates, unemployment, and economic growth rate.
6. *Sociocultural* sector comprises social values in the general population, the work ethic, and demographic trends such as an increasing number of women in the work force (Daft et al. 1988, 137-38).

This environmental typology is similar to those proposed in recent works on strategic management. For example, Jauch and Glueck (1988) identify six environmental sectors as follows: customers, suppliers, competition, socioeconomic, technological, and governmental. Fahey and Narayanan (1986) distinguish between a macroenvironment comprising social, economic, political, and technological sectors, and a task/industry environment comprising mainly the customer and competitor sectors.

Managerial decision roles

Mintzberg (1973) proposes a model of the managerial *use of information* that includes information acquired from the external environment. In his conceptualization of top managers as information processing systems, the manager's interpersonal roles provide access and exposure to information from a large number of external and internal information sources. The manager in the informational role of *Monitor* "continually seeks and receives information from a variety of sources in order to develop a thorough understanding of the organization and its environment" (Mintzberg 1973, 97). Access to information combines with positional authority to empower the manager to perform four decisional roles. As *Entrepreneur,* the manager initiates "improvement projects" such as new lines of business or joint ventures that exploit an opportunity or solve a problem. As *Resource Allocator,* the manager controls the distribution of all forms of organizational resources through, for example, budget allocations and setting of targets. As *Disturbance Handler,* the manager deals with unexpected but important events. Finally, as *Negotiator,* the manager engages in major negotiations with other organizations or individuals. In the present study, we investigate the use of environmental information within Mintzberg's decisional roles framework.

METHOD

Sample

The study is based on personal interviews with 13 CEOs in the Canadian publishing and telecommunications industries. Both industries are vital to the Canadian economy and thrive in volatile business environments characterised by technological advances, intense competition, new business structures, population growth, and changing social preferences. The industry sectors were defined by four-digit US Standard Industrial Classification Codes. Using these codes, online searches were done in the Canadian Dun's Market Identifiers and the Cancorp Canadian Corporations databases to identify 207 firms with annual sales equal to or greater than C$5 million. As part of an earlier questionnaire survey (Auster and Choo 1993), CEOs of these firms were asked if they were willing to be interviewed. Interviews were then requested with the 22 respondents in the province of Ontario who agreed to be interviewed. The decision to interview in Ontario is based on geographical proximity and on the fact that a large fraction of firms in both industries is located in the province. Eventually, 13 respondents were interviewed (most of the others were out of town during the three-month interviewing period).

Interview method

The interview format is based on the *focused interview* as described by Merton and Kendall (1956), and Judd et al. (1991). Originally, Merton and Kendall described two requirements for this type of interview: the persons interviewed have to be involved in a particular situation, and the interviewer has to theoretically analyze the situation beforehand. Judd et al., broaden the definition of a focused interview to include any interview in which interviewers know in advance what specific aspects of an experience they wish to have the respondent cover in their discussion, whether or not the investigator has observed and analyzed the specific situation. For this study, interview respondents are asked to recall their experiences and behaviours in specific incidents (situations) of receiving and using environmental information. The interviewer, on the other hand, knows what aspects of the incident are to be pursued, as well as what topics or what aspects of a question are to be addressed.

The interview design is also based on the principles of *Critical Incident Technique* (CIT). The CIT was developed by Flanagan at the American Institute for Research in 1947, where it was used in studies to determine critical requirements for the work of pilots, air force officers, scientists, air traffic controllers, and hourly wage employees (Flanagan 1954). The 'incident' to be studied should be a complete, recent incident that had clear consequences. The CIT seems well suited to studies of information-seeking behaviour, and has been applied in several information needs and uses studies (Martyn and Lancaster 1981). Because we wish to analyze complete sequences of acquiring and using environmental information, and to understand some of the cognitive processes that underlie this process, the CIT is selected as an appropriate data-collection strategy. Two classic scanning studies have also employed this method (Aguilar 1967; Keegan 1974).

In summary, the personal interviews are designed to *focus* discussion on *critical incidents* of acquiring and using environmental information. Specifically, each respondent related two 'critical incidents' of receiving information about the external environment in reply to the following question:

> Please try to recall a recent instance in which you received important information about a specific event or trend in the external environment—information that led you or your firm to a new initiative, a change of direction, or some significant action.
>
> Would you please describe that incident for me in enough detail so that I can visualize the situation?

Probes were used to prompt respondents to describe the substance of the information received, the issue or problem it addressed, the sources for the information, how the information was made use of, and what the end results were of acquiring and using the information.

FINDINGS

Profile of respondents

Thirteen CEOs in the publishing and telecommunications industries who were located in the province of Ontario were interviewed over a three-month period. A profile of the respondents is in Table 1.

Critical incidents

The 13 respondents related a total of 25 critical incidents of using environmental information to make significant decisions for the firm. These incidents are summarized in Table 2, which shows the content of the information acquired, the environmental sector it concerned, the decisional role the respondent was acting in, and the sources of the information. Interviewed respondents identified seven information sources in the incidents they recalled: Customers; Business Associates (suppliers, distributors, bankers, lawyers, etc.); Government Sources; Newspapers, Journals, and External Reports; Trade Associations; Internal Staff (including subordinate managers and staff); and Electronic Information.* (This grouping of informa-

Table 1. Profile of firms and CEOs interviewed

CEO name	Business	Sales/ employees	CEO age	Years as CEO	Previous function	Highest education
Albert	Supplier of real time financial information & communications networks	$21M/ 197 emp.	35–44	4 years as CEO, 8 years in firm	Operations	Others (technology)
Ben	One of Canada's largest cable television operators and the largest private paging company	$64M/ 450 emp.	35–44	5 years as CEO, 15 years in firm	Finance	Bachelor's degree, CA
Chris	Supplier of data communications equipment and services for LAN, WAN interconnection	$15M/ 65 emp.	35–44	1 year as CEO, 1 year in firm	Marketing & Sales	Bachelor Commerce (Hon.)
Dan	Manufacturer and distributor of network analysis products	$13M/ 40 emp.	45–54	Founded firm 15 years ago	Finance, marketing	High school diploma
Ed	Manufacturer of telecommunications components and devices	$5M/ 60 emp.	>65	Founded firm 20 years ago	Marketing	Bachelor's degree (Engineering)
Frank	Second largest reseller of long distance telecommunications services in Canada	$40M/ 47 emp.	35–44	1 year as CEO, 1 year in firm	Sales	Bachelor's degree
George	Manufacturer of multiplexing and switching equipment for common carriers, interexchange carriers	$29M/ 60 emp.	39	3 years as CEO, 4 years in firm	Marketing	Business administration certificate (community college)
Harry	Provider of packet switching data network services, providing access to cities across Canada and worldwide	$8M/ 10 emp.	35–44	2 years as CEO, 6 years in firm	Sales	Bachelor's degree (electronics engineering)
Peter	Developer and provider of online databases, document management services, and reference tools	$12M/ 120 emp.	45–54	Founded firm 20 years ago	—	Bachelor's degree
Quint	Wholesale distributor of books	$14M/ 135 emp.	55–64	3 years as CEO, 3 years in firm	'Supplier'	Bachelor's degree
Rob	Publishing firm involved with printing, publication, and wholesale of books	$45M/ 100 emp.	35–44	1 year as CEO, 1 year in firm	Marketing	Master's degree
Steve	Publisher and printer of a wide range of magazines and periodicals	$115M/ 1500 emp.	45–54	2 years as CEO, 2 years in firm	Marketing	Master's degree
Tom	Wholesale distributor of books	$17M/ 100 emp.	45–54	5 years as CEO, 5 years in firm	Marketing	Bachelor's degree

tion sources is consistent with that used in past research on scanning; see Aguilar 1967; Keegan 1974; Daft et al. 1988).

We do not have space to discuss each incident, but we select four to illustrate the use of environmental information in each of the four decisional roles.

Entrepreneur decisional role. Ben is CEO of one of Canada's lar-

---

*Electronic information sources include online databases, electronic mail, and office automation systems. Only one incident involved the use of Electronic Information, and this was related by a CEO whose firm is in the business of online financial information services.

Table 2. Summary of critical incidents

Sources of information

Incident	Information	Environmental sector	Decisional role	Customers	Business associates	Government sources	Newspapers, Journals, Reports	Trade associations	Internal staff	Electronic information
A1	Merger of 2 major customers, creating Canada's largest retail brokerage	Customer	Disturbance handler	•						•
A2	Deregulation of financial industry allowing banks to compete	Regulatory	Entrepreneur				•			
B1	Use of digital video compression to provide greater program flexibility	Technology	Entrepreneur	•	•	•	•	•		
B2	Assessment of competitors' strengths in the Canadian paging market	Competition	Entrepreneur	•	•			•	•	
C1	Identification of a market for smaller network routing systems	Customer	Entrepreneur	•						
C2	Firm's competitive position after entry to generic markets	Competition	Entrepreneur	•						
D1	News that a manufacturer wished to discontinue a product	Competition	Negotiator	•						
D2	Perception of an unfavourable political climate in Canada	Regulatory	Disturbance Handler				•			
E1	Identify component suppliers in Shanghai, after a visit to PRC	Competition	Negotiator	•					•	
E2	Customer expresses demand for a new coaxial cable switch	Technology	Entrepreneur	•						•
F1	Bell Canada's filing with CRTC to lower long-distance WATS rates	Regulatory	Disturbance Handler		•	•				
F2	New parliamentary bill on national telecommunications policy	Regulatory	Negotiator		•	•	•			
G1	Information on Process Management	Technology	Entrepreneur					•	•	
G2	News about economic downturn	Economic	Resource Allocator	•			•	•		
H2	Information about exhibition on video conferencing systems	Customer	Entrepreneur	•						
P1	News that a legal information service firm was selling its indexing service	Competitor	Entrepreneur	•				•		
P2	Joint venture offer by competitor to merge two databases	Competitor	Entrepreneur	•						
Q1	Customers buying from off-shore rather than domestic Canadian sources	Customer	Disturbance Handler	•	•	•		•		
Q2	Information on in-house desktop publishing	Technology	Entrepreneur					•		•
R1	Changes in consumer buying trend — consumers concerned with price	Customer	Resource Allocator	•	•			•	•	
S1	Re-acquiring printing business from publishing conglomerate	Competition	Negotiator	•		•				
S2	Assessing the sale of one of the firm's assets to a major customer	Competition	Negotiator	•						
T1	Opportunity for a joint venture with a US-based company	Competition	Entrepreneur				•	•		
T2	Market trends in different sectors of the publishing industry	Customer	Entrepreneur						•	•

gest cable television operators and the largest private paging company. The incident Ben described was a recent decision to participate in a joint experiment to use a new technology, Digital Video Compression (DVC), to transmit to pay-TV customers. According to Ben, this was the world's first commercial application of DVC technology. Ben identified the main sources of information as: his own reading of current engineering articles on DVC; his participation in the strategic planning committee of the Canadian Cable TV Association; suppliers; marketing staff; and government regulatory agencies. Ben recalled that

> information from these various sources had to come together for us to decide to go ahead with the project. The technology was first assessed to be ready and stabilized. Suppliers had to be prepared to experiment. Marketing people had to see the possibility of a viable market. Regulators must support the project. All these were integral to the decision-making process to go ahead with the experiment.

In this incident, Ben was making decisions in the Entrepreneur role, initiating a new project that applies recent advances in the Technology sector of the environment.

Resource Allocator decisional role. Rob is CEO of a publishing firm involved with the printing, publication, and wholesale of books. The incident that Rob described concerned declining book sales. Based on information from newspapers, business magazines, retail trade journals, as well as information from business surveys, conversations with retailers, and market analysts, Rob concluded that the main reason for falling sales was that customers had become very sensitive to price because of the prolonged economic recession, the introduction of a Goods and Services Tax that taxed book sales for the first time, and the Iraqi war. In order to lower book prices, Rob decided to close down the warehousing and distribution system in Canada, and to have the U.S.-based system undertake these functions. In this incident, Rob was making decisions in the Resource Allocator role, deciding to close the Canadian distribution system in order to respond to an increased price sensitivity in the Customer sector of the environment.

Disturbance Handler decisional role. Frank is CEO of the second largest long-distance telecommunications reseller in Canada. The incident Frank described concerned Bell Canada's response to the entry of telecommunications resellers in the Canadian market. Resellers buy leased lines from the carriers, and use their own multiplexing and switching equipment to create their own long-distance services. In 1991, Bell Canada filed for new, significantly lower tariffs for its own Wide Area Telecommunication Service (WATS) long-distance services. Frank's first source of information about Bell's rates filing was the regulator, with additional information from his contacts at a customer company. As a result of the filing, Frank decided to base his pricing structure on telephone Area Codes rather than WATS zones. This gave greater pricing flexibility, and customers could compute their savings more clearly. When the regulator finally approved Bell's new rates, Frank was able to adjust prices in less than a week to match the new rates. In this incident, Frank was making decisions in the Disturbance Handler role, responding to challenges in the Regulatory sector of the environment.

Negotiator decisional role. Steve is CEO of a large firm publishing and printing a wide range of magazines and periodicals. The incident Steve described concerned the reacquisition of the publishing business that was sold to a major Canadian newspaper publishing conglomerate. Steve recalled that during a meeting with banks involved in the transaction,

> I gave them my view of why the transaction from our own end wasn't as interesting as I hoped it would be and one of the bankers let slip, "Oh, we were afraid of that." Once I heard that, I knew that the presumption that I had just made was correct. That was a multi-million dollar bit of information—that slip of someone's lips. It was a perfectly normal reaction to what I had said, but what it served to do was confirm something that I was really speculating about.

Together with additional information from the national newspaper and asking other people, Steve was finally able to complete the purchase of the printing business at less than half of the original price. In this incident, Steve was making decisions in the Negotiator role, and was responding to information concerning the Competition sector of the environment.

ANALYSIS AND DISCUSSION

Scanning and use of environmental information

In Figure 1 below, each critical incident is represented by a circle placed within a matrix formed from the four decisional roles and six environmental sectors. Thus, each circle relates two aspects of each critical incident: the decisional role the respondent was acting in, and the environmental sector concerning which information was acquired and used.

Of the 25 critical incidents, 14 are associated with the Entrepreneur decisional role. This number is much larger than the num-

Role \ Sector	Customer	Competition	Technological	Regulatory	Economic	Sociocultural
Entrepreneur	C1, H2, T2	B2, P1, P2, C2	E2, B1, Q2, G1, T1	A2, H1		
Resource Allocator	R1				C2	
Disturbance Handler	A1, Q1			F1, D2		
Negotiator		E1, S1, S2, D1		F2		

Figure 1. Decisional role—Environmental sector matrix.

ber of incidents reported in the other decisional roles (5 in the Negotiator role, 4 in the Disturbance Handler role, and 2 in the Resource Allocator role). In other words, *respondents use environmental information mainly in the Entrepreneur decisional role*—they were deciding about 'improvement projects' such as introducing new products, and formulating market strategies (Mintzberg 1973). Seven of the thirteen respondents indicated that environmental information was used in ways strategic to the firm. This linkage between scanning activity and the Entrepreneur decisional role is predicted by Mintzberg (1973). In the Entrepreneur role, the manager initiates improvement projects to exploit opportunities or to solve problems. According to Mintzberg (1973, 78), "Entrepreneurial work begins with scanning activity," where the manager uses information from scanning the environment to identify opportunities or problems, and then to design and select improvement projects. The chief executive who scans a greater amount would therefore have more information about developments in the external environment, including information about opportunities or problems, as well as possible solutions or alternatives. As a result, the executive who scans more would have more environmental information to call upon and to use when deciding about improvement projects in the Entrepreneur role. The interview data are consistent with this interpretation. Two respondents (Ben and Dan) indicated that they regularly scan the environment for new business opportunities; one scans for new ideas about how technology is being applied in other countries, while the other reads accounts of how new products have been developed successfully elsewhere.

Twenty-four of the twenty-five incidents were spread over four environmental sectors: Competition, Customer, Technological, and Regulatory. No incident was recalled for the Sociocultural sector, and only one touched on the Economic sector. The distribution of incidents related suggests that the *respondents concentrate their environmental scanning on the competition, and customer sectors; followed by the technological and regulatory sectors.* This is in line with past research on scanning, which found that executives are most concerned about the market and competitor sectors of the environment when they scan (see earlier section and Choo and Auster 1993). Furthermore, CEOs in this study were also making use of environmental information on the technological and regulatory sectors. The fact that virtually no incidents were recalled concerning the Sociocultural and Economic sectors seems to suggest that the CEOs are more concerned with short-term developments that affect their business directly than with longer-term trends whose impact may be difficult to predict.

Use of information sources in decisional roles

In Figure 2 below, each critical incident is placed within a matrix formed from the six environmental sectors and seven information sources identified by interview respondents. Thus, each circle relates two aspects of each critical incident: the environmental sector concerning which information was acquired or received, and the source from which information was acquired or received. Where information came from a number of sources, an equivalent number of incident circles are drawn, linked by a dashed line.

The distribution of incidents in the matrix suggests that *respondents use personal sources frequently in their scanning and decision making.* The three most frequent sources of environmental information for decision making are Business Associates; Newspapers, Journals, External Reports; and Internal Staff. Two of these are personal sources, and the importance of personal sources may be interpreted as follows. Information about the external environment is often equivocal. Some of it may concern events or trends that are still evolving, some of it may be based on conjecture or opinion, some of it may be inaccurate or incomplete, and almost all of it may be

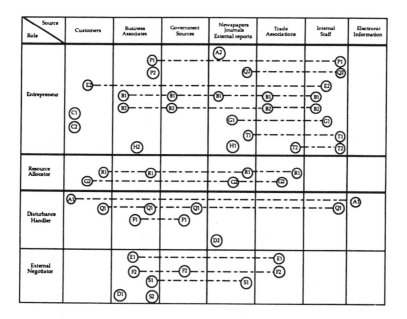

Figure 2. Decisional role—Information source matrix.

subject to multiple interpretations. The processing of environmental information must therefore aim at lowering its inherent equivocality (Weick 1979). Furthermore, the information task of reducing equivocality may depend on hierarchical level: top managers may need to confront and evaluate ambiguous environmental messages more often than middle-level managers. Equivocality is reduced by using sources of high *information richness* (Daft and Lengel 1986). Personal sources are considered rich because they transmit their information typically through rich media, such as face-to-face meetings and telephone conversations, that allow chief executives to seek instant feedback, observe additional cues, and receive personalized messages. It is the richness of information conveyed by personal sources, a richness needed to interpret equivocal environmental information, that accounts for the chief executive's reliance on personal sources in scanning and decision making. The finding that personal sources are important sources in scanning is consistent with past research.

Respondents acquire or receive environmental information from multiple, complementary sources. For 18 of the 25 incidents reported, information had been acquired or received from between two and as many as five sources. The sources used include both personal and impersonal sources, which may be internal or external to the firm. One respondent (Ben), when asked to identify his most critical sources, replied that it was difficult to say which sources are more important. Information from various sources, including the R&D staff, suppliers, marketing staff, industry association, and regulators, had to come together for decisions to be made. Another respondent (George) spoke of blending data from multiple sources, so as "to see or recognize a trend coming," and then solicit more information from additional sources. The interview data, therefore, suggest that the chief executives combined environmental information from several types of sources (personal/printed, internal/external). These sources complement each other. For example, personal sources provide rich information often about specific issues, whereas printed sources provide efficient ways of scanning broadly; external sources may be closer to the environmental news, but internal sources may better interpret their significance.

Use of information sources in relation to environmental sectors

In Figure 3 below, each critical incident is placed within a matrix formed from the six environmental sectors and seven information sources identified by interview respondents. Thus, each circle re-

Figure 3. Environmental sector—Information source matrix.

lates two aspects of each critical incident: the environmental sector concerning which information was acquired or received, and the source from which information was acquired or received. Where information came from a number of sources, an equivalent number of incident circles are drawn, linked by a dashed line.

For our discussion here, it is instructive to highlight two clusters in the distribution of incidents in the matrix. The first cluster, marked in Figure 3, indicates that *much of the information on the Technological and Regulatory sectors comes from the printed sources* of Newspapers, Journals, and External Reports. One respondent who heads one of Canada's largest cable television and paging firms said this about his firm:

> One of our key sources of information is the written word—we spend a lot of time accessing literature. There are several reasons for this. We are a technology-oriented company, the market is technology driven. The technology itself is changing at a great speed. Furthermore, we are a relatively small firm—we don't have the 9,000 engineers that [a Japanese multinational] hires for instance. Our response is therefore to use the printed word to keep up with the rapid rate of technical change. Every department head reads two to twelve journals. Interesting articles are selected and re-directed to other managers. These are accompanied by executive summaries which describe in two to three paragraphs why the content is important and should be read.

Six other interview respondents described critical incidents in which environmental information found in newspapers, business and management periodicals, and government documents was instrumental in their decision making.

We interpret this finding as follows. Because they have limited time and attention, chief executives use printed sources to carry out a general, wide-area viewing of the external environment in an efficient manner. Although printed sources lack information richness compared with face-to-face contact, they convey information using media that communicate accurately and efficiently unequivocal messages such as factual information, numerical data, rules and definitions, and so on. Ghoshal and Kim (1986) detected a differential use of personal and impersonal sources in their study of managers in South Korean firms. Whereas information about the immediate business environment (competitors, markets) is usually obtained from personal sources, information about the broader environment (general, social, political, and technological changes) is usually obtained from impersonal sources such as publications and reports. In the present study, 10 of the 25 incidents related involved information from printed sources; 7 of them concerned developments in the Technological and Regulatory sectors. Thus, the interview data appear consistent with Ghoshal and Kim's (1986) finding that impersonal sources are used more often when executives seek information on the broader environmental sectors for long-term planning.

The second cluster is centered on the Competition-Business Associates cell, and reveals how the respondents get their information about the Competition sector. None of the respondents related incidents in which they obtained information directly from their competitors. Figure 3 shows that *respondents obtain information on the competition sector most frequently through Business Associates.* The Business Associates mentioned by the respondents include suppliers, distributors, and bankers, but did not include any executives or competitor firms.

SUMMARY

In summary, our study of how chief executives use environmental information in decision making suggests several features of their scanning behavior. First of all, the chief executives seem to focus their scanning on the competition, customer, regulatory, and technological sectors of the environment. Much less importance seems to be given to the economic and sociocultural sectors. In most cases, the chief executives used environmental information in the Entrepreneur decisional role, initiating new products, projects, or policies. The chief executives acquire or receive environmental information from multiple, complementary sources. Among these sources, personal sources are used very frequently in their scanning and decision making. The most heavily used personal sources are Business Associates and Internal Staff. At the same time, printed sources such as Newspapers, Journals, and External Reports are also highly used, especially for information on the Technological and Regulatory sectors. There is some evidence to suggest a differential usage of information sources—information on the Customer and Competition sectors seems to be obtained mainly from personal sources, whereas information on Technological, Regulatory, and Economic sectors seems to come also from printed and formal sources.

ACKNOWLEDGMENT

This research was supported by a grant (File no. 410-91-0065) from the Social Sciences and Humanities Research Council of Canada.

REFERENCES

Aguilar, F.J. 1967. *Scanning the Business Environment.* New York: Macmillan.

Auster, E., and C.W. Choo. 1993. Environmental scanning by CEOs in two Canadian industries. *Journal of the American Society for Information Science* 44(4): 194-203.

Auster, E., and C.W. Choo. 1992. Environmental scanning: Preliminary findings of a survey of CEO information seeking behavior in two Canadian industries. In *Proceedings of the 55th Annual Meeting of the American Society for Information Science,* ed. D. Shaw, 48-54. Medford, NJ: Learned Information.

Choo, C.W., and E. Auster. 1993. Environmental scanning: Acquisition and use of information by managers. In *Annual Review of Information Science and Technology,* vol. 28, ed. M.E. Williams, 279-314. Medford, NJ: Learned Information.

Daft, R.L., and R.H. Lengel. 1986. Organizational information requirements: Media richness and structural design. *Management Science* 32(5): 554-571.

Daft, R.L., J. Sormunen, and D. Parks. 1988. Chief executive scanning, environmental characteristics, and company performance: An empirical study. *Strategic Management Journal* 9(2): 123-139.

Dill, W.R. 1962. The impact of environment on organizational development. In *Concepts and Issues in Administrative Behavior,* eds. S. Mailick and E.H. Ness, 94-109. Englewood Cliffs, NJ: Prentice Hall.

Duncan, R.B. 1972. Characteristics of organizational environments and perceived environmental uncertainty. *Administrative Science Quarterly* 17(3): 313-327.

Fahey, L., and V.K. Narayanan. 1986. *Macroenvironmental Analysis for Strategic Management.* St. Paul, MN: West Publishing.

Flanagan, J.C. 1954. The critical incident technique. *Psychological Bulletin* 51(4): 327-358.

Ghoshal, S., and S.K. Kim. 1986. Building effective intelligence systems for competitive advantage. *Sloan Management Review* 28(1): 49-58.

Jain, S.C. 1984. Environmental scanning in U.S. corporations. *Long Range Planning* 17(2): 117-128.

Jauch, L.R., and W.F. Glueck. 1988. *Business Policy and Strategic Management.* 5th ed. New York: McGraw-Hill Book Company.

Judd, C.M., E.R. Smith, and L.H. Kidder. 1991. *Research Methods in Social Relations.* 6th ed. Fort Worth, TX: Holt, Rinehart and Winston.

Keegan, W.J. 1974. Multinational scanning: A study of the information sources utilized by headquarters executives in multinational companies. *Administrative Science Quarterly* 19(3): 411-421.

Keegan, W.J. 1968. The acquisition of global information. *Information Management Review* 8(1): 54-56.

Klein, H.E., and R.E. Linneman. 1984. Environmental assessment: An international study of corporate practice. *Journal of Business Strategy* 5(1): 66-75.

Kobrin, S.J., J. Basek, S. Blank, and J.L. Palombara. 1980. The assessment and evaluation of noneconomic environments by American firms. *Journal of International Business Studies* 11(1): 32-47.

Lester, R., and J. Waters. 1989. *Environmental Scanning and Business Strategy.* London, UK: British Library, Research and Development Department.

Martyn, J., and F.W. Lancaster. 1981. *Investigative Methods in Library and Information Science: An Introduction.* Arlington, VA: Information Resources Press.

Merton, R.K., and P.L. Kendall. 1956. The focused interview. *American Journal of Sociology* 10(1): 541-557.

Mintzberg, H. 1973. *The Nature of Managerial Work.* New York: Harper & Row.

Nishi, K., C. Schoderbek, and P.P. Schoderbek. 1982. Scanning the organizational environment: Some empirical results. *Human Systems Management* 3(4): 233-245.

O'Connell, J.J., and J.W. Zimmerman. 1979. Scanning the international environment. *California Management Review* 22(2): 15-23.

Preble, J.F. 1978. Corporate use of environmental scanning. *University of Michigan Business Review* 30(5): 12-17.

Thomas, P.S. 1980. Environmental scanning: The state of the art. *Long Range Planning* 13(1): 20-25.

Weick, K.E. 1979. *The Social Psychology of Organizing.* 2nd ed. New York: Random House.

Additional Readings
Part III: Information Behavior
of Managers

Agor, W.H. 1986. How top executives use their intuition to make important decisions. *Business Horizons* 29: 49-53.

Aguilar, F.J. 1992. *General Managers in Action.* Revised ed. New York: Oxford University Press.

Anthony, R.N. 1965. *Planning Control Systems: A Framework for Analysis.* Boston, MA: Harvard University.

Blagden, J.F. 1980. *Do Managers Read?* Cranfield, UK: Cranfield Institute of Technology Press and British Institute of Management.

Browne, M. 1993. *Organizational Decision Making and Information.* Norwood, NJ: Ablex.

Choo, C.W., and E. Auster. 1993. Scanning the business environment: Acquisition and use of information by managers. In *Annual Review of Information Science and Technology,* ed. M.E. Williams. Medford, NJ: Learned Information, Inc. for the American Society for Information Science.

Daft, R.L., R.H. Lengel, and L.K. Trevino. 1987. Message equivocality, media selection, and manager performance: Implications for information systems. *MIS Quarterly* 11(3): 355-366.

Eisenhardt, K.M. 1990. Speed and strategic choice: How managers accelerate decision making. *California Management Review* 32(3): 39-54.

Grosser, K. 1991. Human networks in organizational information processing. In *Annual Review of Information Science and Technology,* ed. M.E. Williams, 349-402. Medford, NJ: Learned Information, Inc. for the American Society for Information Science.

Hales, C.P. 1986. What do managers do? A critical review of the evidence. *Journal of Management Studies* 23(1): 88-115.

Hickson, D. 1987. Decision-making at the top of organizations. *Annual Review of Sociology* 13: 165-192.

Hickson, D.J., R.J. Butler, D. Cray, G.R. Mallory, and D.C. Wilson. 1985. Comparing 150 decision processes. In *Organization Strategy and Change,* ed. J.M.P. Associates, 114-143. San Francisco, CA: Jossey-Bass.

Hill, M.W. 1985. Information for middle management decision making. *Information Services & Use* 5(1): 21-36.

Isenberg, D.J. 1986. Thinking and managing: A verbal protocol analysis of managerial problem solving. *Academy of Management Journal* 29(4): 775-788.

Isenberg, D.J. 1984. How senior managers think. *Harvard Business Review* 62(2): 81-90.

Jaques, E. 1976. *A General Theory of Bureaucracy.* London, UK: Heinemann Educational Books Ltd.

Kanter, R.M. 1989. The new managerial work. *Harvard Business Review* 67(6): 85-92.

Kotter, J.P. 1982. What effective general managers really do. *Harvard Business Review* 60(6): 156-167.

Lengel, R.H., and R.L. Daft. 1988. The selection of communication media as an executive skill. *The Academy of Management Executive* 11(3): 225-232.

Luthans, F., S.A. Rosenkrantz, and H.W. Hennessey. 1985. What do successful managers really do? An observation study of managerial activities. *The Journal of Applied Behavioral Science* 21(3): 225-270.

MacDonald, A.R. 1983. *Managers View Information.* New York: Special Libraries Association.

Markus, M.L. 1994. Electronic mail as the medium of managerial choice. *Organization Science* 5(4).

McCall, Jr., M.W., and R.E. Kaplan 1990. *Whatever It Takes: The Realities of Managerial Decision Making.* 2nd ed. Englewood Cliffs, NJ: Prentice Hall.

McKinnon, S.M., and Bruns Jr, W. J. B. 1992. *The Information Mosaic: How Managers Get the Information They Really Need.* Boston, MA: Harvard Business School Press.

Mintzberg, H. 1994. *The Rise and Fall of Strategic Planning: Reconceiving the Roles of Planning, Plans, and Planners.* New York: The Free Press.

Mintzberg, H. 1975. *Impediments to the Use of Management Information.* New York: National Association of Accountants.

Mintzberg, H. 1973. *The Nature of Managerial Work.* New York: Harper & Row.

O'Reilly, III, C.A. 1982. Variation in decision-makers' use of information sources: The impact of quality and accessibility of information. *Academy of Management Journal* 25(4): 756-771.

Rockart, J.F., and D.W. Long. 1988. *Executive Support Systems: The Emergence of Top Management Computer Use.* Homewood, Il: Dow Jones-Irwin.

Srivastva, S. 1983. *The Executive Mind.* San Francisco: Jossey-Bass.

Starbuck, W.H., and F.J. Milliken. 1988. Executives' perceptual filters: What they notice and how they make sense. In *The Executive Effect: Concepts and Methods for Studying Top Managers,* ed. D.C. Hambrick, 35-65. Greenwich, CT: JAI Press.

Stewart, R. 1989. Studies of managerial jobs and behaviour: The ways forward. *Journal of Management Studies* 26(1): 1-10.

Ungson, R.G., D.N. Braunstein, and P.D. Hall. 1981. Managerial information processing: A research review. *Administrative Science Quarterly* 26: 116-134.

Wilson, T.D. 1988. Information, managers, and information technology. *Argus* 17(2): 47-50.

IV
Strategies for Managing Information

IV
Strategies for Managing Information

INTRODUCTION

The recognition in organizations that information needs to be managed has been slow in coming. In the eighties it was common for firms to make massive investments in technology and consider their information problems solved. If difficulties arose, the standard response was to upgrade to the latest hardware with the newest bells and whistles. A patchwork of systems developed, each operating with its own systems and standards. Information handling was dispersed through the organization and among disparate professionals from data processors and systems designers to librarians and records managers. Separate departments became rivals for increasingly limited resources and instead of joining forces to devote their combined expertise and energies to achieving organizational goals, they turned inward as survival became ever more problematic.

As economic conditions worsened in the late eighties and early nineties, top managers awoke to the fact that their investments in technology had not necessarily translated into productivity and profits and that the massive amounts of data generated were often divorced from the strategic purposes of the firm. As competitive pressures increased, the need for accurate, timely, and relevant information about customers, competitors, technology, and markets intensified. Survival depended on the right person having the right information at the right time in the right format.

To achieve this goal, however, required a drastic new mindset. Information had to be accorded its rightful place as a valued organizational resource much like staff and materials. It needed to be properly managed. Organizational and managerial needs had to be identified and means to meet them planned, provided, coordinated, and evaluated. Information provision had to be directed toward furthering the goals, productivity, and competitiveness of the organization. Information structures, processes, and architectures had to be re-examined and systems, technologies, and skills marshalled to improve the internal as well as external performance of the firm. For such sweeping changes to succeed they had to become a top organizational priority allocated the level of support appropriate to their newly enhanced role.

Individuals and firms contemplating improvements to their information management strategies have much to choose from. On the one hand, the variety of strategies chronicled in the literature assures that at least a few will apply in any given situation. On the other, there is no one infallible method or technique that will guarantee results. Unlike the management of other major functional areas such as finance or personnel which have clearly defined practices and procedures from one organization to the next, information managers do not have strictly defined parameters within which they must operate; their relationships within the organization are not always clear; their processes are still evolving; and their contribution to the organization is not immediate or readily discernible. All the experts agree, however, that overlooking, neglecting, or mismanaging information will have dire consequences for the firm while properly managed information will result in improved competitiveness, productivity, and profits though it may take three to five years for these benefits to be realized.

A vigorous and prolific exponent of intelligent information management is Blaise Cronin, the author of the first article in this part of the book. Cronin asserts that to survive in an increasingly competitive marketplace, firms must recognize that their information assets are among their most valuable resources. He provides examples of British and U.S. organizations that have exploited these assets to solve business problems, survive, and thrive. For him, quality assurance and information management are inextricably linked in the intelligent corporation. Whereas Cronin provides us with a valuable introduction to the critical importance of information in the corporate sector, it is David Ellis and his co-authors who provide specific methods and techniques for identifying the types of information that actually exist in the organization.

Information audits generally identify the goals of the organization, determine its users' needs, inventory its information resources, describe how its systems function, and recommend improvements. Closely related to these operational advisory audits are communication audits which assess the state of communications in the organization as measured against a set of desired criteria. In the information-intensive organization, effective communication plays a crucial role in facilitating information flow. Hence an audit to determine interpersonal, management-employee, and organizational communication assumes renewed importance. Among the instruments used for examining communication channels are questionnaires, network analysis, interviews, and diaries. Among other things, analysis of communication patterns can reveal those individuals in an organization who are turned to most often by others in their search for information.

The information that exists in an organization may be graphically represented by a technique known as information mapping. Having evolved from the broader framework of information resource management (IRM), information mapping builds on the notion that information acquisition and use are directly linked to managerial effectiveness. The basic elements of this strategy are to establish goals and objectives, determine functional requirements, identify major tasks and milestones, identify software options, and evaluate the expertise through follow-up. Undertaking such a baseline inventory of the organization's information resources helps control costs, motivate employees, manage assets, and provide the foundation for an information infrastructure.

It is one thing to know where information exists in the organization, it is quite another to ensure that it reaches the desired level and function when it is needed. In jostling for corporate ascendency, departments have been known to hoard information for their own advantage. This results in duplication and hence wasted time, effort, and resources. Too much information may be generated resulting in overload. To resolve such problems as hoarding and "infoglut," Ruth Stanat proposes that organizations create shared information networks. She addresses such issues as the location of such a network within the corporation, the type, format and distribution of the information, methods of measuring the effectiveness of the network and the pitfalls that should be avoided. She concludes with suggestions for broaching and building support for the concept among one's corporate colleagues.

To gain the cooperation of information stakeholders in the organization a thorough understanding of information politics is advisable. From their extensive work studying the information management efforts of corporations to create information-based organizations, Davenport, Eccles, and Prusak conclude that many failed because they did not manage the politics of information. Some used initiatives that were inappropriate to the corporate culture. Others viewed politics as a peripheral not integral aspect of their organizational life. Based on their observations, the authors classify corporate information politics into five models: technocratic utopianism, anarchy, feudalism, monarchy, and federalism. Their suggested strategy for effective information management is to choose a model that most closely matches the culture of the organization, select a realistic technological platform, and elect an information politician who can build coalitions, acquire resources, and sway the electorate as well as opinion leaders. To bolster their arguments, they present experiences encountered in some of the leading U.S. corporations.

The selection of articles that has been included by no means exhausts the scope of strategies available to information managers. The readings that follow build on the topics presented and introduce others that space limitations preclude from inclusion.

Intelligence Management Systems for Intelligent Corporations

Blaise Cronin

INFORMATION AND DIFFERENTIATION

Organizational attitudes towards the management of information changed perceptibly during the 1980's. First came simplistic formulae (e.g. information technology + first mover advantage = competitive edge), followed by enlightenment (the trick is in sustaining, not just in gaining edge), disillusionment (competitive parity is easily attained) coupled with panic (the domino effect takes over), and finally *angst*, as information systems expenditures spiraled out of control. By the end of the decade lessons had been learned (Strassmann 1985, 1990), and the focus began to shift from cost-benefit to value analysis (Parker, Benson, and Trainor 1988), and from information systems engineering to the management of intellectual capital.

> "Every company depends increasingly on knowledge — patents, processes, management skills, technologies, information about customers and suppliers, and old-fashioned experience. Added together, this knowledge is intellectual capital... In other words, it's the sum of everything everybody in your company knows that gives you a competitive edge in the marketplace." (Stewart 1991, 42-43, 46, 50, 54, 58, 60)

Why this change in focus, from the tangible to the slippery? Organizations of all kinds survive by being different in certain key as-

---

This article was first published in *The Intelligent Corporation*, eds. J. Sigurdson and Y. Tagerud, 1992, pp. 143–159 and is reproduced here with the permission of Taylor Graham, London, UK.

281

pects. The bases for differentiation (which may also be the bases for competitive co-operation) include:

- Product range
- Innovativeness
- Reputation
- Proprietary know-how
- Customer care

- Time-to-market
- Quality
- Customization
- Scope and focus
- Cost

As a general rule, a successful product launch is something more than a matter of luck or unalloyed technical superiority. Information will have been gathered on competitor products and pricing strategies, possible substitutes, threats of new entrants, relevant manufacturing and process technologies, standards and regulatory requirements, demographic trends, market access mechanisms, advertising channels and the results of both quantitative and qualitative consumer research, etc. Cost-competitiveness will be achieved by systematically decomposing all parts of the value chain to identify opportunities for paring costs, increasing value linkages and achieving economies of scale and scope. Time-to-market will depend upon the ability to achieve time compression through the use of JIT (just-in-time) manufacturing techniques, the exploitation of a "company database" and the effective sharing of information between the R&D, design, manufacturing and marketing departments (such as via computer supported collaborative workgroups - CSCW). The product will have been contextualized through a more or less systematic process of intelligence gathering, analysis and sharing.

Take the case of an exporter of smoked bacon or kiwi fruit to the European Community who may have one or more kinds of comparative advantage (e.g. best of breed livestock; access to a high-technology food processing industry; climate; crop cycle) and for whose products there is known demand. However, the exporter is unaware of the minutiae of current packaging regulation, specifically EEC Directive 90/128 which relates to materials testing, migration and limitations of quality. The result could be disastrous, nullifying the product's intrinsic excellence: the perfect product needs to be located in an information framework. Excellence without conformance is not enough.

In a competitive marketplace, you need to know whether, how, where and when your rivals can compete. You need intelligence on their strengths, weaknesses and strategic intentions. For example, why in 1987 was Ferranti led into paying more than $700 million for ISC Technologies, apparently unaware of that company's tangled relationship with the US intelligence community? You have to distinguish between public posture and private purpose (there was recently intense speculation in the City as to whether or not Hanson would make a hostile bid for ICI, and analysts were interpreting the former's "body language" in an effort to second-guess the UK's most celebrated take-over artists). You also need to know the mood of the marketplace: what your customers need, want, and what they can afford. As an example, will the market for organic foodstuffs and wine grow sufficiently in the long-term to make it attractive to the major supermarket chains, or is it destined to remain outside the retailing mainstream?

To stay ahead of your competitors you need to know what is possible as well as what is: how real is the threat of a potential new entrant or of a substitute product or service? You need to know what might happen in addition to what is happening (i.e. issue management; and macro-environmental scanning; weak signal management). Intelligence, broadly defined, widely sourced and integratively managed, is the key: flexible information systems, which foster openness, connectivity and exchange, are the platforms for building heightened intelligence capability within organizations. But it is the quality, mix and timeliness of intelligence, as much as the trapping technologies themselves, which provide the edge. Current developments in the retail sector illustrate the point: the combination of point-of-sale information with customer profile data results in precision marketing which facilitates a totally new dialogue between vendor and consumer.

> "We believe the ultimate art form will be the market segment of one. We'll talk to every discrete customer in his or her own life-style terms. That is the way we are heading - and there are certainly no technological barriers. (Madden 1991)

REWRITING THE RULES

Innovation is the ability to do things differently, better or smarter. Not just once, but repeatedly. Business is a game. Games have players, and players have strategies and stratagems. There are informal and formal rules (e.g. established practice; tacit convention; company law; intellectual property rights; and standards); there are referees (including auditors; regulatory bodies; and trade agreements); and there are risks (such as political; financial; and entry/exit-level barriers) to be negotiated.

> The stakes have escalated in recent years: golden hellos and golden parachutes, stock option schemes and performance-related pay have inflated executive salaries. But as rewards have grown, so too have the

risks: hostile raids, greenmailing, LBOs (leveraged buy-outs), downsizing and restructuring have become daily features of corporate life and sharpened the competitive pressures on companies large and small. In the business jungle (to use a hackneyed metaphor) predators and prey need to be alert to all that is going on around them: the quality of an organization's intelligence gathering (the bush telegraph) and analysis capability are increasingly vital to survival (Cronin and Davenport 1991).

Clever players sometimes cause the rules to change. Adopting innovative approaches to the management of information is one way of rewriting the rules of the game: recognized examples include computerized customer reservation systems in the airline industry; tele-ordering in the drugs supply or bookselling business, and Automatic Teller Machines (ATMs) in banking. Quite simply, these kinds of developments change the way business is conducted.

However, the (soft) ways in which intelligence is gathered (using "liveware" rather than hardware) can also significantly change the rules of the game.

> "One Sunday morning in the summer of 1986, six Marriott employees on a secret intelligence mission checked into a cheap hotel outside the Atlanta airport. Once inside their $30-a-night rooms, decorated with red shag rugs and purple velour curtains, the team went into their routine. One called the front desk saying that his shoelace had broken - could someone get him a new one? Another carefully noted the brands of soap, shampoo and towels. A third took off his suit jacket, lay down on the bed and began moaning and writhing and knocking the headboard against the wall while a colleague in the next room listened for the muffled cries of feigned ecstasy and calmly jotted down that this type of wall wasn't at all soundproof. For six months this intelligence team travelled the country, gathering information on the players in the economy hotel business, a market Marriott strongly wished to enter. When Marriott finally decided to enter this fast-growth, but highly competitive, market it soon achieved an occupancy rate ten percentage points higher than the rest of the industry" (Dumaine 1988, 66-68, 70).

THE INFORMATION-INTENSIVE ORGANIZATION

Information is the primary source of added value in today's firm.

> "As labour, in the traditional sense, evaporates in most industries, and capital becomes a globally purchasable commodity, IT [information technology] will become the tool for building competitive organisational capability and stimulating competitive behaviour - along with investment in management. Indeed the computer industry already reflects

this with direct labour typically representing only 3% or so of sales.''
(Wilmot 1988)

Leverage is derived from the effective management of information assets (e.g. information technology and systems; information workers; locally created and bought-in information goods and services; intellectual capital). The role of the information manager is: to optimize the configuration and exploitation of those assets; and to create conditions which nurture creativity, promote social exchange and maximize delivered value to the greatest degree possible within the organization. This applies to both the public and the private sectors, although the goals, objectives and performance measures may well differ.

In standard accounting terms, an organization's assets are classified as tangible or intangible, current or fixed. For instance, stock-in-hand is a current tangible asset since it could be converted into cash, while a company's fixed tangible assets include its buildings and machinery. Goodwill (such as brand name value, cachet, and pedigree) is a an important intangible asset which can sometimes exceed a company's book value.

> "The importance of reputation, know-how etc., like the value of motherhood is readily acknowledged; but until recently there has been little attempt to identify, and give structure to, the nature and role of intellectual assets in the strategic management of a business. This is largely due to the fact that intellectual assets rarely have exchange value, either because property rights have not been, or cannot be, the subject of a transaction'' (Hall 1989, 53-67).

What, then, are an organization's information assets?

Under current tangible would be included, for example, competitor monitoring databases, customer files (ranging from ''prospects'' through to major accounts) and technology tracking databases, for example, would be included under current tangible assets. Fixed current assets would include such items as the telecommunications infrastructure (leased high-speed lines; switching gear, etc.) and the installed hardware and systems base (from local area networks to super-computing facilities). The collective know-how or intelligence of a business, sometimes called corporate or institutional memory, would be labelled as a current intangible asset.

> "The experience and heuristics of personnel, company lore and precedent have latent value which under certain conditions can be assigned a monetary equivalent, whether in terms of internal benefits (time and labor savings through not hiring external trainers/consultants) or ex-

ternal benefits where the company becomes a supplier of expertise to the outside world. However, these assets can depreciate in several ways; disaffection, obsolescence, senescence" (Cronin and Davenport 1991).

Copyrights, patents and registered designs also feature under the intangible heading, as they have a finite protected life and, though saleable, are of unpredictable and fluctuating value. For the sake of completeness, brand names and trademarks could be listed as fixed, intangible assets. These can sometimes have a massive impact on the balance sheet; much of the £1.6 billion paid by Ford for Jaguar in 1990 was for the Jaguar name and its resonant historical associations. An extreme statement of this position is provided by Oliviero Toscani, a design adviser to Benetton: "The only capital a company has is its image" (Time 1991, 38).

ASSET MANAGEMENT

The activities performed by an information centre, unit or service have traditionally been defined in terms of the management of a suite of functions, ranging from acquisition to retrieval. A consequence of this mind-set can be goal displacement: it may not be clear why a specific function is being performed, how it relates to other functions, or, indeed, to the organization's overall information strategy.

One way around this problem is to recognize that information work is basically concerned with the management of a portfolio of assets. Six generic assets (i.e., stock; property; installed IS (Information Systems) base; professional skills; goodwill; heritage items) in the context of information service have been identified (Cronin and Davenport 1991) but not all apply to every case. Property is only an asset if the information centre has control over use and disposal of its space, furnishings and fittings. Heritage items are more likely to turn up in the context of an archive or research library than, for example, in the technical information centre of an oil company.

The significance of the IT/IS (information technology/ information systems) asset base will also vary. Where there is a large sunk investment in computer and telecommunications systems, the scope for moving into facilities management, leasing, third party network management, information technology skills training and related areas is potentially high. A major but often undervalued asset is the mix of professional and technical skills possessed by the workforce. The information manager will want to ensure that such skills are fully developed, adequately capitalized and effectively deployed. A leading-edge information service/techno-economic intelligence unit may be strategically placed to offer advice, training and customized products to other sections of the parent organization or even to external markets.

A simple matrix (assets vs. options) can be used to identify different ways of managing the information base. The options (which are not mutually exclusive) range from outright disposal and lease-back through franchising, allowing a third party vendor to market government data sets, to contracting out or buying in a specialized information service from a commercial supplier.

TRANSPARENCY AND OPACITY

Assets can have latent value. One of the tasks of the information manager is to activate latent value; to put idle intellectual capital to work. What matters in most organizations is value-in-use. Value may go unrecognized for a variety of reasons: a connection may not be made between an event and a particular parcel of information (the final piece of the jigsaw); significant variables and relationships may be masked by the volume of data at hand (i.e., cognitive overload), or inappropriate packaging. In some cases, lack of structure may be the problem; in others fondness for structure may actually result in myopia or lost opportunity. More precisely, Swanson has detailed a number of cases of logically-related but non-interconnecting literature sets.

> "Suppose, for example, that one literature establishes that dietary factor A influences the structure of certain cell membranes and that a second literature establishes that the same changes in membrane structure influence the course of disease C. Presumably then anyone who reads both literatures could conclude that dietary factor A might influence disease C . . . two literatures that are both noninteractive and yet logically related may have the extraordinary property of harboring discovered causal connections." (Swanson 1990, 129-137)

How can value loss be reduced? Presumably by encouraging greater and more imaginative use of existing information systems, sources and services that is, by increasing rates of participation. Bar (1989, 69-78) for example, has described a simple, but effective, computer-based approach to multifile, multidisciplinary searching which can be used to generate new product ideas, while Myers (1991, 7-24) has demonstrated how patent databases and planning files can be used to refine high-grade intelligence upon which to base large-scale investment decisions.

Systems, whether social or technical, can be enchantingly simple or frustratingly complex to use. Information systems are no exception. Use is impaired by jargon (e.g. command languages), design complexity (e.g. classification schema), rites of passage (e.g. determination of an individual's eligibility for a password), bureaucracy (e.g. constraints to accessing governmnent archives or data sets), tariff structures (e.g. in the online database industry), and a lack of standards (e.g. in the codification and exchange of materials).

Open (transparent) systems should have clear structure, a paucity of rules and necessitate few media transformations. Does your system meet these criteria? How does it compare with similar systems? Opaque (closed) systems, on the other hand, are characterized by a lack of structural clarity (navigation is not easy), excessive regulation and multiple media transformations (the same piece of information is processed in different ways, formats or media).

TOTAL QUALITY ... TOTAL INFORMATION

The concept of total quality management (TQM) has been widely trumpeted in both manufacturing and service industries.

> "The company that focuses on quality grows closer to its customers and becomes aware of where it needs to improve. The outcome is that customers get what they really want and not what the supplier thinks they should have ... Total Quality is a means of achieving a cultural revolution that brings home to everyone that, ultimately, no errors will be accepted in supplying the specified product or service." (Price Waterhouse 1988).

There are signs that the information profession may be vaguely aware of the concept. Until recently, total quality had been noticeable by its absence from both the professional literature and the world of professional information practice. Budgetary pressures, demands for accountability and the rising costs of providing information systems/services have thrown quality issues into relief. Can quality be measured? What techiques and indicators are available? What does quality mean in the context of information and intelligence? How can customer satisfaction rates be monitored? Can the accuracy of intelligence predictions be tested and measured? Can the downstream benefits of information investments be quantified?

Numerous studies have demonstrated the inadequacy of public sector information and reference services. Online vendors have not yet succeeded in penetrating the lay market, and most online searches are still mediated by members of the information priesthood. The electronic information industry exhibits the classic features of an anti-service culture: systems lack conviviality, offering *table d'hote* menus rather than *a la carte* service. Obduracy and arrogance on the parts of designers and vendors combined with fiscal pressure and vested interests, have retarded the rate of innovation. The result? Disaffected users and sub-optimal exploitation of valuable information assets in organizations of all kinds.

Total quality depends on total information, i.e., information on risks, liabilities, limitations, behaviours and volatilities . . . of situations, physical and social structures, materials, services and people. It makes no difference if one is constructing an off-shore oil rig, conducting a laboratory experiment, offering a medical diagnosis or operating a current awareness service. Total relevant information is what clients require. Where and how it is sourced, selected, synthesized and sanitized need not be a matter of concern. What matters is that it should be timely, validated, pertinent and, of course, actionable.

INFORMATION MANAGEMENT AND QUALITY ASSURANCE

The health of a nation (reflected in morbidity and mortality rates) is a key quality of life indicator. Today, quality of health (and by extension, quality of life) increasingly depends on the quality of information management.

The National Health Service (NHS) in the UK is a multi-faceted, multibillion pound "business." It is also the largest employer in Western Europe. Health care is not simply about illnesses, drugs and hospital beds: it is about the management of information such as patient-related information, hospital activity analyses, epidemiological data, technical news, clinical trial data, expenditure patterns and remission rates.

With rising public demand and treatment costs, the need for effective, efficient and economic management is paramount. If this is true for the UK, it is even more so for the US where health expenditures as a proportion of GDP have reached absurd levels. The proposed restructuring of the NHS has resulted in formal recognition of the importance of information management at all levels of this complex organism (Hills 1989, 275-278). Consider the four domains below:

• Resource Management. Comparative information is necessary for clinicians who must decide about treatments that commit considerable sums of money. They must ask themselves: what is the best, most cost-effective treatment for a particular condition? Health Authorities will need aggregate information to identify priorities and trends, assess local health requirements, and compare hospital performance.

• Medical Audit. There is a need for better information about the outcomes of various treatments to enable clinicians to compare and evaluate their own decisions.

• General Medical Practices. General practitioners (community doctors) require faster and more accurate information to improve patient service. These might take the form of computerized medical records; out-patient booking systems; smart cards; laptop computers; online access to medical information services and so forth.

• Trading Information. In the proposed restructuring, Health authorities and larger general practices (groups of community doctors) become budget holders for satisfying the health needs of their local populations (typically 250,000 people) and for negotiating contracts with hospitals to provide such services. They will, therefore, need better budgeting, monitoring and forecasting tools. In other words, they will need better management information and decision support systems.

It is clear that the importance of information management has been firmly grasped.

"The NHS is an information intensive organisation, being dependent on patient and clinical information for treatment, and organisational and management information for organising its efficient running" (Scrivens 1985).

The recognition goes beyond rhetoric. The NHS Training Authority has launched an ambitious national programme in Information Management and Technology (IMT) to ensure that clinical, nursing, administrative and managerial staff are aware of current thinking and practice.

Information management awareness in the UK is not confined to the health sector. Since 1984, The Treasury has been spearheading an initiative to identify ways of getting better value for money from government information resources. Studies have since been conducted in a number of departments using the soft systems approach (Sangway 1989, 179-187). Information resources management (IRM) grew out of U.S. federal government policies that were initiated in the mid- 1970's and continuously fine-tuned throughout the following decade. The principles were also enthusiastically adopted by the corporate sector and by the academic community in the mid-1980s: witness the emergence of the Chief Information Officer (CIO) function in Fortune 500 corporations and the establishment of Integrated Academic Information Management Systems (IAIMS) across university campuses. But the focus of these initiatives has tended to be cost containment, paperwork reduction and expedited information flow - not the extraction and exploitation of intelligence.

THE INTELLIGENT CORPORATION

The use of metaphor in the information domain is pervasive. Information is routinely referred to as a "resource"; government reports talk of "tradeable information"; organizations husband their "information assets"; lawyers advise on "information property"; and the business press speaks of information as a "weapon" which confers competitive advantage. Architects design "smart buildings"; we shop with "smart cards"; and in the office we have replaced our "dumb" terminal with a workstation which offers an "intelligent front-end" and low-grade "artificial intelligence" capability. Books and journals appear with titles like *"The intelligent corporation"* or *"The intelligent enterprise"*; the BBC produces a documentary on Singapore entitled *"The intelligent island"*; and Toffler argues that organizations could be ranked (as if using a Wechsler-type scale) in terms of their collective intelligence quotients: high-brow, middle-brow or low-brow (Toffler 1990). The ascription of intelligence is now not only to individuals (the domain of psychometricians) or to machines (the cognitivist fallacy), but to groups of social actors (companies, nations). As Jequier and Dedijer observe: "In the same way that psychologists or neurologists speak of human intelligence one could speak of the intelligence of a society, or 'social intelligence' " (Jequier and Dedijer 1987, 1-23).

An intelligent corporation is one which can solve its business problems, survive and, ultimately, thrive. Characteristically, it will seek to anticipate micro and macro-environmental change, will recognize the value of institutional know-how, will promote social networking (within and outside the organization) and will be a keen exploiter of public domain and proprietary information. Information on customers will be linked with sales data and, in turn, correlated with lifestyle analyses to produce richer, multi-dimensional pictures of consumers' needs and preferences. This will enable marketers to spot shifts in public tastes, control inventory, adjust display and pricing strategies, and to finesse advertising campaigns.

Banks have moved from holding multiple accounts (mortgage, current, deposit, etc.) on their customers to developing integrated profiles. Hospitals have developed permanent (birth-to-death) patient records, which can be accessed immediately when a person is admitted to a hospital or visits a clinic as an outpatient. The concept of the diagnostic related group (DRG) is used by hospitals to divide patients into approximately 200 groups, in order to monitor and compare drug expenditure levels. In both cases, the quality of information (achieved through scaling and aggregation) results in more efficient allocation of resources and increased client satisfaction. Real-time data capture is also a feature of the GP's (general practitioner) surgery, with clinical data on drugs administered to patients being entered locally on PCs, and downloaded by a middleman for onward sale to pharmaceutical companies.

Salesforce automation is another means whereby intelligence can be harvested for relatively modest capital outlay. By providing a dispersed salesforce with lap/palmtop computers (Cronin and Davenport 1990, 278-287), companies are better able to monitor leads, sales and order flows than before, with resultant benefits to both supplier and buyer. The salesforce additionally has immediate access to key business indicators on both target and established customers, and can tap into the consolidated experience and know-how of their physically dispersed colleagues.

> "By finding ways to make knowledge move, an organization can create a value network - not just a value chain. It can link customers and suppliers to wipe out inventory, or put designers and production engineers at the same table (real or electronic) so that they can design products that are easy to build. Costs can be stripped out or value added to the total system, not just part" (Stewart 1991).

TECHNICAL PLATFORMS

Just as the military draws upon a variety of intelligence sources, ranging from human intelligence (humint) through signals intelligence (sigint) to radar intelligence (radint), so will businesses need to develop the ability to "broadcatch". The task of the business intelligence centre will be to develop comparable all-source intelligence capability by a variety of methods including: scanning widely, probing for echoes, identifying patterns or regularities in seemingly random events and data sets; constructing multiple, weighted scenarios; and massaging raw data and information into organized intelligence for use throughout the organization.

Enabling technologies and related software (e.g. expert systems, connectionist machines, powerful information retrieval packages, neural networks, object-oriented software, hypertext, natural language processing systems, multimedia platforms) are now in place which will allow organizations to increase their intelligence yields from both in-house and commercial databases. Major online hosts (of bibliographic and full-text databases) are introducing a variety of software enhancements (such as the ZOOM command offered by the on-line host, ESA-IRS) to rank and refine search output, and there is a growing range of concept searching software coming onto the market.

"It's a German company, and its name sounds like 'ground biscuits' ". No problem, says the software used by IDD Plus, a seamless combination of equities, corporate and M&A data designed for corporate finance or investment specialists. And in a few seconds it has come up with "Grundbesitz Invest' " (Owen 1991, 33)

The importance of synthesis and exchange in intelligence work has been clearly perceived by Dow Jones, whose International Network for News and Information (Djinni) allows you to:

" . . . follow topics of interest, compile historical backgrounds to important events, make your own connections between news stories, and share that information with co-workers worldwide . . . A unique feature of Djinni is its support of collaborative research. A user can construct an 'information package' on a subject which includes search results, documents, notes, upload material and, of course, the links that have been made between items, and send it to co-workers anywhere in the world" (Hoetker 1991, 27-31).

At the same time, advances in parallel programming techniques are making possible the development of what Gelernter (1989, 54-61) terms "information refineries". These are all powered by two kinds of machines: information filters which transform an incoming stream of data into higher-level knowledge, and smart databases which sort out interesting patterns from records of many similar objects or events. A prototype trellis machine which is used in an intensive-care unit to monitor and analyse patient data is described in the following passage.

The bottom-level software modules are designed to be connected to machines that monitor heart rate, temperature at various points, blood pressure at various points and so on; higher-level modules focus on increasingly more general questions about the patient's condition. Modules directly above the bottom rank look for trends or obvious noise (erroneous readings) in the data; the modules above them look for simple patterns, and still higher modules look for diagnoses that might involve the presence or absence of many simple symptoms. Modules in the upper reaches of the machine assess the likelihood that some complex pattern or condition holds true" (Gelernter 1989, 57).

This refinement of raw medical data into actionable information, what Myers calls just-in-time intelligence (Myers 1991, 21-23), could serve as a model for a variety of business applications, such as the dynamic analysis of sales, advertising and marketing data. With this kind of deep processing power, organizations will be able to develop superior intelligence on their customers and markets.

SOFT NETWORKS

Much potentially useful information is neither overt nor codified (e.g., gossip, leads, tips, opinions, speculation, insights) and is transmitted through a variety of informal exchange mechanisms. Tacit knowledge of this kind is an essential complement to the procedural and technical information which is stored in formal systems and manuals. Even in the most competitive industries, informal know-how trading is a fact of life (von Hippel 1987, 291-302). Invisible colleges, professional/trade associations and old boy networks are examples of highly tacit environments which are resistant to systematization. They are personal, direct, highly effective, and have low transaction costs. That is the basis of their appeal. The intelligent corporation recognizes this fact and nurtures its "gatekeepers", "boundary spanners", and "internal and external integrators". Even in the most computerized and market researched industry of all, the airline industry, a breakdown, or blindspot, in intelligence supply can be devastating. When United Airlines bought Pan Am's Asian routes in 1987 for $715 million, it was much to the chagrin of American Airlines' Chief Executive Officer, Robert Crandall.

> Not a whisper reached the industry bigwigs. Not even Crandall. That's painful to a guy who prides himself on knowing all, understanding all about the near Machiavellian nuances of life in the airline business. He was left completely in the dark . . . The failure to get those routes comes down to admitting that either his intelligence network or his interpretive powers failed him" (Business Traveller 1991, 65).

Much valuable know-how is stored sub-cranially, acquired osmotically and exchanged informally. Newcomers to any organization (from IBM to Phi Beta Kappa) have to learn the ropes. The experience may be straightforward or may entail complex rites of passage. Familiarization with a mass of historical, procedural, technical and policy documentation may be called for, in addition to divining the rules, norms, procedures, personalities, and structures which give the organization its special character. How can a tyro acquire this kind of institutional intelligence quickly and effectively; how can a virtual apprentice be fast tracked up the organization learning curve?

> "A virtual apprentice may serve years in the byzantine knowledge complex of the late twentieth century . . . Finding a mentor . . . is the traditional way to get under the skin of an organisation. In complex organisations this is beyond the scope of a single individual; we think, however, that a comprehensive hypertext might function as a social tutor, or cicerone . . . With a hyperbase which extends beyond navigation of a rule book (with memos, correspondence, inventories, bulletin boards, e-mail) you may be able to pick up correct cues more quickly, and read between the rules . . ." (Davenport and Cronin 1991, 65-70)

Robson Rhodes, for instance, is currently developing a prototype for a wide area networked hypertext-based training system which will allow students of accountancy, trainers and technical authors to access a company hyperbase via intelligent workstations.

> "The hypertext environment will contain an arbitrarily large number of richly interconnected documents comprising the firm's technical materials. These materials include our audit and tax manuals, professional guidelines, specialist articles generated by the firm's technical department and partners, and - importantly - case studies produced by the firm's technical trainers (Gregory 1991, 119-123)."

As those who work in the areas of government and military intelligence know, the great majority of what constitutes the "stuff" of intelligence is freely available in the public domain. Covert operations, surveillance and counter-espionage are only the visible tip of a much more mundane set of activities. Organizations, however, often fail to capitalize on their own internal information assets. Critical know-how is not trapped and shared; proprietary knowledge is undervalued; employees fail to leverage off one another's experience; connections are not made between discrete data sets; patterns are not perceived in events; weak signals are poorly monitored or misinterpreted; external sources of information are underutilized; or the significance of tacit knowledge and social exchange is not properly appreciated. These failings cannot be attributed to deficiencies in available information systems and technologies, but instead testify to a persistent intelligence myopia in the corporate sector.

REFERENCES

Bar, J. 1989. A systematic technique for new product idea generation: The external brain. *R&D Management* 19(1): 69-78.

Business Traveller. January 1991: 65.

Cronin, B., and E. Davenport. 1991. *Elements of Information Management.* Metuchen, NJ: Scarecrow.

Cronin, B., and E. Davenport. 1990. Laptops and the marketing information chain: The benefits of salesforce automation. *International Journal of Information Management* 10(4): 278-287.

Davenport, E., and B. Cronin. 1991. The virtual apprentice. *Journal of Information Science* 17(1): 65-70.

Dumaine, B. 1988. Corporate spies snoop to conquer. *Fortuen.* (November 7): 66-68, 70.

Gelernter, D. 1989. The metamorphosis of information management. *Scientific American* (August): 54-61.

Gregory, D. 1991. Corporate hypertext: A grand design. In *Advanced Information Systems: The New Technologies in Today's Business Environment,* 119-123. Oxford: Learned Information.

Hall, R. 1989. The management of intellectual assets: A new corporate perspective. *Journal of General Management* 15(1): 53-67.

Hills, P. 1989. The national strategic framework for NHS information management in England. *Aslib Proceedings* 41(19): 275-278.

Hoetker, G.P. 1991. DJINNI: Dow Jones International Network for News and Information. *Online Review* 15(1): 27-31.

Jequier, N., and S. Dedijer. 1987. Information, knowledge and intelligence: A general overview. In *Intelligence for Economic Development: An Inquiry into the Role of the Knowledge Industry,* 1-23. Oxford: Berg.

Madden, D. 1991. Shoppers' minds are on their cards. *Financial Times:* July 4.

Myers, J. 1991. The 'brain gain': JIT and data warehouses. *The Intelligent Enterprise* 1(4): 21-23.

Myers, J.M. 1991. Social intelligence in real estate planning. *Social Intelligence* 1(1): 7-24.

Owen, T. 1991. It's lonely at the top. *The Intelligent Enterprise* 1(4): 33.

Parker, M.M., R.J. Benson, with H.E. Trainor. 1988. *Information Economics: Linking Business Performance to Information Technology.* Englewood Cliffs, NJ: Prentice Hall.

Sangway, D. 1989. Government approach to information management. *Aslib Proceedings* 41(5): 179-187.

Scrivens, E. 1985. *Policy, Power and Information Technology in the National Health Service.* England: Centre for the Analysis of Social Policy, Bath University.

Stewart, T.A. Brainpower. *Fortune* June 3 1991: 42-43.

Strassmann, P.A. 1990. *The Business Value of Computers: An Executive's Guide.* New Canaan: Information Economics Press.

Strassmann, P.A. 1985. *Information Payoff: The Transformation of Work in the Electronic Age.* New York: Free Press.

Swanson, D.R. 1990. The absence of co-citation as a clue to undiscovered causal connections. In *Scholarly Communication and Bibliometrics,* ed. C.L. Borgman, 129-137. Newbury Park: Sage.

Toffler, A. 1990. *Powershift: Knowledge, Wealth, and Violence at the Edge of the 21st Century.* New York: Bantam.
Toscani, O. 1991. Quoted in *Time,* March 18: 38.
Total Quality: Achieving Competitive Advantage. 1988. Middlesbrough: Price Waterhouse.
von Hippel, E. 1987. Cooperation between rivals: Informal know-how trading. *Research Policy* 16: 291-302.
Wilmot, R.W. 1988. Organisational Issues and I.T. A management briefing prepared from a presentation to IBM CUA conference 21 April 1988. London: Oasis.

Information Audits, Communication Audits and Information Mapping: A Review and Survey

David Ellis, R. Barker, Susan Potter
and Cheryl Pridgeon

INFORMATION AUDITS

The idea that information represents a resource which needs effective management has led to the development of interest in the use of information audits. Information audits extend the concept of auditing from the traditional concern with evaluating an organization's accounting and financial procedures to that of the organization's overall information system. There are two main types of auditing, compliance audits and advisory audits (Chambers 1978). The compliance audit refers to the traditional idea of an audit of an organization's accounts or finances. There the audit is employed as a check that procedures are being followed correctly and that fiscal and legal standards are being adhered to. In contrast, the advisory audit is more concerned with informing users of existing systems and practices and with problems with those systems and practices and with assessing the appropriateness of existing systems, standards and practices to the organization's goals or objectives. The compliance audit is more concerned with financial systems, the advisory audit with strategic planning. Information audits tend to follow the advisory rather than the compliance model but sometimes elements of a compliance audit

This article was first published in *International Journal of Information Management*, Vol 13, No 2, April 1993, pp. 134-151, and is reproduced here with the permission of Butterworth-Heinemann, Oxford, UK.

may be present, which can lead to the auditor having to fulfill two roles of adviser and inspector — with the possibility of role conflict between the two.

A number of different approaches to information auditing have been proposed each leading to different recommendations as to how the audit should be undertaken. However, to fulfill its functions any information audit should:

- Establish what the major goals of the organization/operation are and what kind of organizational constraints acts upon the operational information systems.
- Determine the needs of the users.
- Inventory the resources available.
- Build up a coherent picture of how the system functions from the information gathered in the first three stages.

The techniques involved in achieving these objectives may involve:

- Gathering information.
- System analysis and representation.
- System evaluation.
- Testing.

The different approaches to information auditing have been characterized by Barker (1990) as constituting:

1. Cost-benefit methodologies.
2. The geographical approach.
3. Hybrid approaches.
4. Management information audits.
5. Operational advisory audits.

Examples of these approaches are considered below.

Cost-benefit methodologies

The objective of a cost-benefit analysis is a list of options compared to each other on the basis of their cost and perceived benefit. Cost-benefit methodologies have been proposed by Riley (1976) and separately by Henderson (1980). Henderson's approach is much more system-oriented, and as such, analyses the value of information in the current system, but the methodology reverts to cost-benefit criteria. The result of the analysis is a list of options balanced against each other on the basis of their cost and perceived benefit to the organization. Henderson noted that frequently the costs of acquiring, manipulating and storing information are overlooked and that far more consideration is given to the management of resources such as manpower and supplies, perhaps because they are more visible to managers.

One of the first occurrences of the expression information audit occurs in Riley's paper (1976). He defines it as a means of evaluating different information products on a cost-benefit basis. These costs and benefits are, he contends, to be measured in terms of the coverage currency and timeliness of the product, requirements for space and the redesign efforts or duplication of work which will be eliminated as a result of its installation and use. However, this is a restricted view of the information audit, and what is designed to be achieved, as it assumes an already existing plan for the management of information which is never reviewed. It can also only be used as pre-event audit in the sense that it requires a pre-defined problem and set of solutions in order to be of use. All other audit methodologies seek first to review the existing system of information management, identify problems and recommend solutions for those problems.

A more comprehensive and rather less crude approach is given by Henderson (1980). The approach to information auditing suggested by Henderson consisted of six steps:

- Define the objectives to be achieved by the system.
- Assess alternative methods for meeting the objectives.
- Determine the costs of the alternatives.
- Establish models relating the costs of each alternative to an assessment of the extent to which each assists in the attainment of the objectives.
- Establish criteria weighing estimated costs against estimated effectiveness to rank alternatives in order of desirability and to identify the most promising.
- Study pay-offs, trade-offs, break even points, and diminishing returns.

This is a much more system-oriented approach than that proposed by Riley. It does, however, retain much of the emphasis on the cost-benefit analysis of alternative solutions which characterizes Riley's version of the information audit.

The geographical approach

An approach to carrying out an information audit which is referred to as the geographical approach because the intention is to identify the major components of the system and map them in relation to each other was put forward by Gillman (1985). Gillman's approach has less emphasis on cost-benefit analysis and more on systems analysis. The stages involved were:

- Education — to make users and information providers alike aware of actual and potential use of information services.
- Analysis of needs — through a series of iterative unstructured interviews with users.
- Analysis of resources — this is a purely inventory rather than a costing approach.
- Analysis of existing services — mainly of those which might be provided by an information centre or library and an evaluation of the appropriateness of these to the needs of the users.
- Matching needs to resources — employing systems analysis techniques a mapping exercise is undertaken.

Unlike many other information auditing techniques this approach does not attempt to generate alternative methods of satisfying a given objective but aims to meet identified needs within the system as it stands. The approach has some interesting parallels with information mapping. Its essential concern is with discovering what the major components of the system are and mapping out their relation to one another.

Hybrid approaches

A hybrid approach to the information audit was outlined by Quinn (1979, 18-19). The approach has some similarities to the geographical approach adopted by Gillman (1985) but with greater emphasis on the costs and values of the components of the information system — which is similar to the cost benefit analysis approach. In this approach seven steps are outlined:

- Profile the current set-up — essentially an enumeration of the major resources which supply the company with information, usually in terms of information centres or libraries.
- Identify the purposes for which information resources were initially provided in relation to corporate goals.
- Identify whether the information centres provide generalized or specialized information services and what the major areas of concentration are.
- Identify the types of service provided (e.g. maintenance of document collections, provision of SDI services, data summaries etc.).
- Identify the position of the information centre in relation to the company as a whole.
- Costs and values of information.
- Recommendations for improvement of the information and information management system.

In many respects, this is essentially a geographical approach, the emphasis being on the identification of what the information resources are and where they reside in relation to the rest of the information system. Like Gillman's (1985) description of the Aslib methodology there is no stage at which alternative solutions to problems are generated but there is some concern for the costs and values of services and products, although these are not part of a formalized cost-benefit analysis as in the Riley (1976) and Henderson (1980) versions of the audit. There is also an apparently greater emphasis on specific control and management procedures, such as the budgeting of information costs and the congruence of information provision with organizational policies.

Worlock (1987) outlined a less structured approach to the information audit which represents a hybrid between the cost-benefit and the geographical approaches. In Worlock's approach there is a concern with the mapping of needs and resources and their relation to one another but there is also room for a consideration of solutions which arise from outside the system. For exampte, if a resource is not being utilized a market may be actively sought either inside or outside the organization, while needs may be met by changing the system of information provision quite radically. To some extent, therefore, there is a stage at which alternative solutions to problems will be generated, although this is not formalized in any way. There is also a concern for the relative costs and values of information and resources, these being assessed on the basis of the utility of the information, its quality in terms of timeliness, currency etc., and its contribution to the productivity of the organization.

Management information audits

Apart from the contributions of the information profession to the literature on information audits, there has also been a certain amount of interest from those in the auditing, accounting and management consultancy professions. This has mainly been in the audit of management information systems (MIS), but has a potential for broader application. The audit of MIS is, apparently, a fairly widespread practice, though still relatively new, a survey by Chambers and Selim (1983) showing that, of a sample of 55 companies, 89 per cent claimed to perform an internal audit of MIS, 49 per cent indirectly as part of an audit of another function or department and 40 per cent as a specific task. It should be noted however that the expression 'MIS' is a slightly ambiguous one and is sometimes used to refer only to computerized information systems.

This perhaps explains why Reynolds (1980, 66-69) refers to his approach simply as an audit of management information rather than of a management information system. Reynolds confined the scope of his audit to formal information and, in particular, to reports. Reynolds' management information audit was largely concerned with identifying reports circulated and their purpose and use to each recipient. The audit's principal objective was to identify weaknesses in the reporting system.

The steps involved in carrying out the audit were:

- Inventory the distribution of formal information by obtaining lists of reports produced/used and their circulation lists.
- Consider the stated purpose of the report in relation to the hierarchical position and responsibilities of each recipient.
- Identify weaknesses in the reporting system — in the first instance by comparing reports received by similar individuals and then via discussion with the auditees.
- Identify priority areas for improvement in consultation with management.
- Prototype proposed design changes and test them.
- Implement changes which prove to be useful.

This approach is most similar to the geographical and hybrid approaches as there is again no specific generation of alternative solutions, nor a formal cost-benefit approach to choices for implementation. It has, however, a much shallower conception of the information system than the methodologies proposed by Gillman (1985) and Quinn (1979).

Operational advisory audits

The scope of an operational advisory audit has been detailed by Gruber (1983) who considered that the objectives should be:

- To define the purpose of the audited system and to establish how effectively it is being accomplished.
- To establish whether the purpose is in congruence with the purpose and philosophy of the organization.
- To check on the efficiency and effectiveness with which the resources are used, accounted for and safeguarded.
- To find out how useful and reliable the information system supporting the organization is.
- To ensure compliance with obligations, regulations and standards.

The first or operational objective is central to all information audit methodologies with the exception of that of Riley (1976). The system objective for an information audit is the fulfillment of users' information requirements. The auditor must, therefore, have some means of determining how effectively those requirements are being met.

Gruber's second objective is that the purpose of the operation should be in accordance with the philosophy of the organization of which it is part and that the information provided by the system should be congruent with the operational goals and help towards their fulfillment. This means that the information auditor needs to understand not only the functioning of the information system but that of the operational system which it supports. Quinn (1979) specifically urges the auditor to do this and Reynolds (1980) recommends that the auditor consider the stated purpose of the report in relation to the position in the hierarchy and responsibilities of the recipient.

The third objective is to check on the efficiency and effectiveness with which resources are used, accounted for and safeguarded. This is an area in which many information audit methodologies are lacking. While there is usually a great concern for the effective use of resources there is generally a lack of concern for the costs and budgeting of resources. Only Quinn (1979) appears to be specifically interested in accounting procedures, recommending that the audit should check that budgets are properly imposed on the information system. The audit itself does provide a means of accounting for resources, but alone it is rather inadequate, and there should be consideration of the provision and checking of additional accounting controls. In terms of the safeguarding of resources, there appears to be hardly any concern at all in some approaches. This aspect, it seems, is more a focus of records management programmes than of information audits. The safeguarding of resources can be accomplished, however, if the appropriate standards and procedures for storage and distribution are in force — which should be the auditor's responsibility to check.

Perhaps the most difficult objective for the information audit is the fourth one, as it is the supporting information system itself which is being audited. However, any system of management needs to gather data to control and monitor the system properly. This is, in fact, an area which is largely ignored by information audit methodologies, partly because it is a rather marginal consideration, while the very fact that an information audit is being carried out should in itself be an indication that the system is being monitored with some degree of care and effectiveness.

Gruber's final objective — that the auditor should ensure compliance with obligations, regulations and standards — occupies the lowest priority in the information audit, perhaps because it may prove incompatible with the more advisory aspects. Nonetheless, it is a valid objective, and, if it cannot be accomplished as part of the advisory audit — a separate audit programme should be established.

To achieve these objectives Barker (1990) devised a 10-stage model for an information audit based on work by Chambers (1978), Diamond (1983) and Taylor (1982). The steps involved were:

- Establish the operational objectives and define the organizational environment.
- Determine the information requirements for the users.
- Inventory the information resources.
- Identify system failures and key control points.
- Evaluate system failures.
- Test key control points.
- Generate alternative solutions for system failures.
- Evaluate the alternatives.
- Check conformity of the system with existing regulations and standards.
- Propose recommendations.

These steps are described in more detail below.

The first step in Barker's approach is to establish what the major goals of the organization/operation are and what kind of organizational constraints act upon the operational and information systems. Taylor (1982) calls this defining the organizational environment and poses a number of questions which this stage of the audit should seek to answer. For example: What are the goals of the organization? Is it decentralized or centralized? What is its managerial style? What are its reward systems? How are systems, processes and people evaluated? Who are the organization's clientele or customers?

In addition the following questions might be added: Are there any specific policies relating to the information system (for example, retention times for certain forms of material, active promotion of information awareness of users, etc.)? What are they? Are information costs budgeted for and, if so, how? Who are the user set and what is their position in the organization? The purpose of this first stage of the audit is primarily to establish what effect these elements have on the flow and the effective, productive use of information.

The second step is to determine the needs of the user set. This is probably the most crucial stage of the audit, it is the primary means for determining the relevance of the information supplied to users. A number of considerations should be kept in mind when carrying out this phase of the audit. These include the type of problem for which the information is an input, its complexity and structure, the complexity and structure of the information, the need for metadata (e.g., knowing that information is available on a given problem or topic and where and how to get hold of it), the need for instruction (including on how to make the best use of the information system), and the various attributes of the information such as its currency, timeliness, accuracy, reliability and presentation both physical and logical (Taylor 1982).

The next stage is to inventory the information resources available. When doing this it may be useful to differentiate between two types of resources — those products and services which are designed to be used as they are and which do not undergo further processing and those resources and raw materials which are used to create these finished products. In both cases the key question is whether the resources actually meet requirements and how effectively and efficiently they are utilized. The auditor may also consider whether a greater or lesser degree of processing is required to create an adequate finished product.

The auditor should then attempt to build up a coherent picture of how the system functions from the information gathered in the first three stages. This involves consideration of such issues as: Which resources fulfill which needs? How are resources stored and safeguarded? How does the organizational environment affect information flow and use? The weaknesses and strengths of the system should begin to become apparent at this stage in the form of unmet or poorly met needs, resources which are underutilized, inefficient processing and policies and other environmental factors which adversely affect the flow of information within the organization.

At this stage key control points in the system should also become apparent. For instance there may be areas in which the provision of information with particular attributes is vital for the operation to function successfully. Likewise there may also be key areas of control which owe their existence less to the needs of the operation than to the prevailing organizational environment. If, for example, there are tight constraints on money or manpower there may be a strong requirement for management information to coordinate operational programmes to make the most economical use of these resources.

The next step is to evaluate the weaknesses discovered in the system. The auditor should have some idea of the potential seriousness of system failures and the extent to which they have affected operations. In an ideal world all system deficiencies would be able to be eliminated, but the auditor is likely to find himself in the position of having to determine priorities for improvement. In doing this he should consider the system failure in the light of both the extent to which it is damaging operations and the costs of repair or improvement, the latter being measured in terms of finance, manpower, disruption to the organization and any other factors deemed relevant by management.

The question of why the weakness has occurred is also important here as this may have a bearing on the feasibility and method of improvement. The auditor should be aware of the temptation of stating the obvious in establishing this. Suppose, for example, that the audit reveals that a database to which a subscription has been newly purchased is not being used. On asking this the auditor is told that this is because it is not relevant to the needs of the organization. If the auditor leaves the matter there, the conclusion may well be simply that the subscription should not be renewed. However, further investigation may show up deeper weaknesses in the system. For example, pursuit of the question of why the subscription was made in the first place may reveal inadequate evaluation and vetting procedures for purchases of this kind. Thus the cause of the system failure may be more deep-seated than is initially apparent.

The auditor should test the key control points in the system to ensure that they are functioning properly. This should be done whether or not system failures have been detected. The auditor should also generate alternative methods for solving the problems which have come to light. This is not strictly a necessary part of the audit methodology by operational audit definitions, though neither is it excluded on those grounds. It is used here as a means of preventing only incremental improvements being recommended and is simply a formal statement of a process which will probably take place anyway. Ideas from operational personnel and from managers may be welcome at this stage, in addition to those of the audit team, as they will have a greater familiarity with the system from a user's point of view and may have a clearer idea of what the constraints on it are. This should also increase the likelihood of changes being accepted by users. The auditor should then evaluate the alternatives suggested and make recommendations for change accordingly. This process is likely to take place in tandem with an assessment of the seriousness of system failure and the benefits, costs and feasibility of improvements.

The auditor should check that existing standards and regulations are adhered to. An example of this kind of procedure is the files audit described by Diamond (1983) which would normally require conformity with the following standards — legible, accurate labels on all file drawers or folders in an open shelf system; no overcrowding (drawers and shelves should have at least three inches of free space); use of out cards, a tickler file or other follow-up system for records that are checked out; conformity with rules for alphabetic filing; existence of up-to-date indexes where appropriate (e.g., for numeric files); and conformity with records disposition or retention schedule.

Finally the auditor should make recommendations in accordance with the audit findings. The final audit report should be a full documentation of recommendations, reasons for them and supporting evidence from tests, etc. The auditor should take care that records of the audit are complete and accurate in order that they might form a good basis from which management can make and implement decisions and perhaps provide a foundation for future audits.

Barker's model is not strictly chronological, and although it does follow a sequential pattern and some attempt has been made to impose a rough time framework on it, many of the processes will form iterative cycles. The approach also has a stronger orientation towards aspects of control — of budgeting, monitoring, checking and testing — than many of the others considered previously. This reflects the concerns of the operational audit which — while it has undoubtedly developed considerably in matters of assessing effectiveness and efficiency from the financial audit — still retains a focus on traditional aspects such as reliability, accuracy and control. However, this seems a perfectly valid stance even for an audit which is intended to have an advisory role, as it seems somewhat doubtful that effective and efficient operations, once installed, can be properly maintained without adequate control and monitoring procedures.

THE COMMUNICATION AUDIT

A related concept to the information audit is that of the communication audit. The communication audit is intended to provide a means of assessing the state of communications in an organization against a set of desirable criteria. Despite the importance of communication being emphasized in management theory (Mintzberg 1973), there has been relatively little documented attempt to measure the effectiveness of this communication. In practice, managers tend to rely on their instincts as to whether problems exist. Booth (1986, 1988a, 1988b) however, identified a resurgence of interest in communications in the 1970s and 1980s caused by two factors which might lead the modern manager to take a more critical look at communications in his organization. First, increased economic turbulence in these decades has called for much organic restructuring so as to avoid corporate collapse. Maintenance of effective communication during this restructuring is vital to the existence and competitive stance of the organization. Second, a reassessment of the organization's needs in relation to telecommunications and other electronic media is essential in making planned, informed decisions in this rapidly moving area of comunications media. Cost efficient communications again help to maintain the organization in a competitive environment.

At a functional level another reason why a manager might wish to audit communications is that effective communication is recognized as a motivator of the workforce. If people receive adequate information to do their jobs, are informed about their role in the organization's overall mission and where the organization stands in the outside environment, their contribution to that mission is likely to be more effective. It is the manager's responsibility to ensure that such information is communicated to employees. Whilst not being the reason for the existence of the organization, communication supports its purpose and achievement of its goals.

For the research community the study of organizational communication has emerged as a science in its own right (see, for example, Goldhaber (1974) and Rogers (1986)) rather than purely as a skill required by management. Adoption of the systems approach in this research has placed communication as the dependent variable rather than the independent variable that can affect other forms of behavior (Rogers 1986). The system's view acknowledges conflict of purpose and function in communication and tries to identify patterns such as operational and informal communication networks in existing communications. An audit such as the ICA (Goldhaber and Rogers 1979) attempts to increase knowledge about communications so as to aid in neutralizing problematic communication in individual organizations. Rogers (1986) has advocated a new approach to the study of communications based on the arrival and continuing development of telecommunications and computers. Through these new channels records of communications events are available for study. What once was a matter of relying on people's memories and written materials can now be backed up by these recorded events.

However, while the potential of the communication audit as a means of measuring the effectiveness of communications has been recognized by both the business and research communities, the literature on communication auditing is sparse. Reviewing the literature is also made difficult because the expression ''communication audit'' has been used as an umbrella description for a range of objectives and instruments of analysis which have been put to use in a number of situations. Generally, however, the communication audit implies a scrutiny, against some criteria, of communications, or evaluation of the extent of mutual understanding achieved between the parties involved.

Booth (1986) attempted to classify the communications audit according to whether it covered 'hard' projects which scrutinize technological hardware or the 'softer' people-oriented activities which he refers to as motivation audits. The 'hard' audits are concerned less with people than the mechanics and systems of computer and telecommunications. The people oriented audits tend to aim to analyse the way employers are communicating with employees and thereby seek to motivate the workforce.

The communication audit thus embraces a broad spectrum of activities which have been characterized by Potter (1990) as representing:

1. A means of assessing the effectiveness of introduction of information technology in an organization.
2. A measure of interpersonal communication.
3. A measure of management/employee communications.
4. A means of assessing the effectiveness of organizational communications.
5. A measure of public relations activity.

These different approaches are described in more detail below.

The communication audit as a means of assessing the effectiveness of introduction of IT in an organization

The communication audit can have a role to play in the introduction of IT as part of a larger project or as an end in itself to assess effects of technological change. The rapid pace of office automation and the introduction of computing and telecommunications systems into organizations may have a significant effect on the structure of the organization and the logistics of work operations. Control over the introduction of such systems is required so that decisions can be made about how they can best serve work and human requirements. Meyer and Boone (1987) explain how the effective and efficient use of IT can give competitive advantage to an organization.

Booth (1986) provides examples of the 'harder' IT-oriented approach to communication audits conducted in government departments in the UK. The 'hard' audit approach is also commended by Jagger (1984) of Deloitte Haskin and Sells, the management consultants. Communications are cast in the mould of a supportive role to the business of the organization. The human motivation aspect is treated as being merely one part of the whole system. The Deloitte's audit is divided into six mini-audits, the main concern being the cost effectiveness and efficiency of the communication system. The overall rationale is that of a 'slimming down' exercise. IT and staff are streamlined and reassessed in terms of reducing costs and improving communications services. However, much activity that might come under this label is probably being carried out without being referred to specifically as a communication audit.

Planning the IT strategy needs to be meshed with company goals to avoid long-term costly mistakes. In order to do this the human communication system operating with the technological system needs to be understood and perhaps reorganized prior to the implementation of a new IT system (Otway and Peltu 1984). The 'soft' approach to communication auditing dealing with the human aspect of IT implementation cannot be ignored when considering communication in this light and a user-oriented approach is essential to its success. The audit can be applied to assess various aspects of IT communications. For example, to assess business objectives involving IT such as the study of a particular communication system for its effectiveness in terms of efficiency, operational load, traffic, cost-effectiveness and configuration in the light of communication needs. A communication audit may be undertaken as part of a systems analysis and design project to gain a picture of who communicates with whom in the organization in terms of operations and functions, or as an exercise after the implementation of a system to check whether communications have benefited or otherwise from the change, how people react to the change, and the overall impact on organizational communications.

Much research has be conducted on the effects of IT after its introduction, but Rogers (1986) advocates proactive research during the design and introduction of the new technology so that it can better serve human needs and work capabilities. Rogers also points out that — while communications research constitutes one approach by which to study IT implementation — IT has a potential role to play in the study of communications.

The communication audit as a measure
of interpersonal communication

Machin and Tai (1979) and Machan and Woolley (1981) developed an approach to communications audit at Durham University Business School in the late 1970s. They used a tool they have called the 'expectations approach' to have senior managers audit their own communications. This technique appeared to be the only one employing self-analysis of communication procedures, and, as such it resembles Checkland's soft systems approach (1981) used to identify problem situations by the actors in the situations themselves. The 'expectations approach' was developed to identify where poor communication existed and to use the results of the audit to focus on and attempt to improve unsatisfactory inter-personal communication.

A case-study report by Machin and Tai (1979) outlines the following reasons for implementing the audit in a company. A change in company ownership had brought a change in personnei. Changes in technology had brought changes in machinery and methods of manufacture. The changes in methods had called for different skills at all levels in the company. Therefore, the communications audit was seen as a starting point for corporate planning, representing a kind of check-up and initial diagnosis of problem areas. As with Checkland's exploration of the problem situation the technique was employed to highlight areas for further investigation rather than to provide instant solutions to problems identified.

Valentine (1981) at the University of Missouri also employed an audit approach to study interpersonal communications. This audit aimed to assess the skills of a particular professional group — educational administrators. After explaining that communication is an essential tool for the educational administrator, Valentine described how he based the design of his single instrument technique on five basic theoretical constructs of communication. These five constructs placed the administrator as:

- affector;
- encourager;
- involver;
- provider; and
- promoter.

The teacher was asked to rate the administrator in those terms and the audit of administrator communications (AAC) generated data about the administrator's communicative ability in relation to demographic groups of teachers. These data have been used both for the researcher and the administrator as Valentine collected and stored data about the individual's ability to communicate over time.

The communication audit as a measure
of management-employee communications

Rockey (1977) describes communication as a management skill and tool. He outlines a set of goals for good communication which are then supported by his interpretation of communication, not as a linear process, but as a mutual understanding model. Rockey's work supports Rogers' (1986) concept of covergence in communication where adequacy in communication channels and skills is what is required since total understanding between two parties is unobtainable.

Bland (1980) reflects the work of many authors on communication in holding that communication is not a function of the organization, but rather that the organization exists to produce something and communication supports this goal. Literature specifically referring to an audit of communications of this sort includes an early article by Odiorne (1954) in the USA. The audit was carried out in a company that had experienced rapid growth from a handful of employees to over 300. A questionnaire was constructed for employees to answer and then management answered the same questions in terms of how they thought the employees felt. Odiorne's criteria for good communication between management and employees included principles such as feedback and reliability of information being transmitted through the company.

A similar exercise was carried out more recently at Rolls Royce in the UK (Stanton 1981). Stanton viewed the point of the exercise as being to help motivate the workforce and improving the communication in such a large organization was seen as one way of assisting this process. The audit attempted to form a clear current picture of communications in this organization. By interviewing managers and questioning the workforce they sought to assess how much information managers were passing to employees about the company and the work done against how much employees thought they should receive. The results of the audit did provoke action in the company. A full-time employee communication manager was appointed at the head office to coordinate internal communications.

Gildea and Rosenberg, working as consultants for Towers, Perrin, Forster and Crosby in New York, saw the communication audit as a means of checking on the motivation given to employees. The audit was likened to an annual physical; a periodic review of communications can be employed as a diagnostic procedure which can be used both to highlight functions and dysfunctions in organizational communication (1979). The scope of their audit can vary from the whole organization to a specific employee group. It might be narrowed down to particular medium in use or, as in the case of Rolls Royce, the audit might test the attitudes of employees to information they receive and what they would prefer to receive from top management. As a 'how to' document the authors give examples of the tools they use, questionnaires, interviews, both group and individual, and a technique developed by them called the 'Communicard'. However, they emphasize that the statistical comparisons generated by the exercise have to be interpreted in terms of the realities of the everyday working life of the organization.

They also advocate regular check-ups on communications as valuable contributions to the 'body and soul' of the organization. Although such activity would clearly be a luxury for many organizations there is logic in their suggestion that the occasional audit provides only a snapshot of what is an ongoing process. Longitudinal research of the same organization with the same techniques would provide more valid data to assess this process.

The communication audit as a means of assessing the effectiveness of organizational communications

This is probably the most common approach to the communication audit. Emanuel (1985) indicates that it can be employed to reveal:

- information blockages;
- organizational hindrances to effective communication;
- lost opportunities in terms of communications;
- expose misunderstandings in communications;
- help gauge media effectiveness;
- provide evaluation of ongoing programmes.

He also adds a list of what a communication audit is not — which for him includes readership surveys and opinion polls two tools which other authors are not averse to using (see, for example, Strenski 1978).

By identifying organizational goals and philosophy and the nature and information needs of the audience, communication can be located and designed so as best to meet these needs. The tools Emanuel uses are interviews of top management, surveying staff by various means followed by a critique of all the media in use, both formal and informal. Emanuel sees the communication audit as a diagnostic tool and as a means of periodically checking on ongoing communication programmes — two ideas which permeate nearly all the literature on the topic.

Kopec (1982) also views communication as a management function which supports organizational goals. Kopec was a consultant with Hay communications; the flowchart approach he provides offers detailed steps to be undertaken in the audit to cover external and internal communications and an inventory of communication media in use. The inventory of media in use is a technique common to many of the audits mentioned. Campbell (1982) refers exclusively to this aspect under the heading communication audit. Their approach to the communications audit concentrates wholly on written media generated by the organization. The readability of an organization's messages, their format, syntax and usage need to be assessed to establish if they succeed in conveying 'goodwill' not only internally but also externally with customers.

The notion of periodic check-ups on communications is taken one step further by Greenbaum and White (1976). They use the analogy of biofeedback which places the audit as a sensory instrument for developing a level of internal sensitivity and adaptiveness. The periodic communication audit is highly recommended as a means of obtaining some feel as to whether an organization's efforts to improve communications are being effective. They also provide the broadest definition of organizational communication as a process which encompasses any event, process or behaviour from which a member of the organization may perceive a meaning. Their reasons for auditing are based very much on their theory of communication. Like Rogers (1986) they feel that communication, by its very nature, can never be perfected and that the communication audit fulfills a moderating function in relation to communication problems in organizations. Another aspect of their work reflects the American trend of recognizing a need for communication departments in organizations, arguing that communication is a major function which should be planned, organized and controlled.

In contrast, Cortez and Bunge (1987) consider the applications of the communication audit as a library management tool. The aim of the audit is to ensure, primarily, that communication channels and their information flows are supporting the process of decision making. The reasons they give for the need for a communications audit in a library are that:

- The current emphasis on planning requires an accurate, timely and smooth flow of information.
- The increased recognition of the impact of the importance of management information systems for decision making, which calls for a perception of communication patterns, information needs and media in use.
- Library staff stress and burnout call for motivation and valuation of employees.

The most comprehensive of the audits detailed in the literature is the ICA audit (Goldhaber and Rogers 1979) set up to research organizational communication in 1971. The audit is used to collect computed normative data to contribute to long-range research problems as well as the immediate problems in hand. The use of a single instrument approach in the audit is criticized by the authors who recommend a five instrument audit consisting of:

- a questionnaire;
- network analysis;
- interviews;
- communication experiences;
- and diaries.

Among other advantages this approach allows for cross-checking of results gained via each instrument.

The authors provide detailed information about how to use each tool, and give examples of the structure and content of each in the ICA. The tools are designed to produce attitudinal, perceptional and behavioural data from respondents in the organization about the current system and their preferred system. The precise objectives of the audit are broad and encapsulate a holistic view of the organization. The reasons for commissioning such a comprehensive audit are expressed with the comparison of the financial audit and the analogy of the medical check-up. The authors also emphasize the importance of the manager's use of the information received via communication channels for effective decision making.

The communciation audit as a measurement of public relations activity

This interpretation of the terms appears to be exclusive to the USA. Strenski (1978) for example, does not exclude internal communication but the emphasis is on communications with relevant publics outside the organization. The audit is seen as a means of finding out what messages are getting through to which audiences and with what success. Strenski casts the audit as a marketing exercise the end-result of which would be a marketing position. The audit has the following steps:

- identification of target audiences to investigate;
- identification and classification of current communication techniques;
- application of the techniques of auditing as they relate to the specific audiences.

Strenski also points out the value of periodic audits as a means of assessing the effectiveness of a marketing communication programme. This in turn can contribute to the business development of the organization.

Wirtz, an employee of Dix and Eaton corporate communication consultants in 1981, also saw the communication audit as having a similar function to PR activity, internally and externally, and argued that the communication audit can contribute to organizational planning and that the communication department should, therefore, compete for managerial attention, especially at budget time (1981). As a means of measuring the effectiveness of communications, Wirtz considered the audit should assess:

- the degree of management credibility;
- employee attitudes and knowledge of the company;
- how well feedback programmes are functioning;
- how effective employee publications are;
- how effective first line managers are.

Wirtz, like Greenbaum and White (1976), is clearly referring to organizations which have communication departments, seeing their role as public relations and advertising both internally and externally. The sort of audit he has in mind is set in the context of a large corporation where management and employees need to be informed about the organization and their roles in it.

In the UK Booth has produced three works as a result of research into communications audits. His work brings together the different strands evident in the USA and the UK (1986) and he has provided a guide to the communications audit for managers as a result of the research (1988a). He has also considered the question of the qualitative evaluation of IT in communication systems (1988b), an area that has received inconsistent attention in the research field. The effectiveness of systems can be measured by three techniques, the hard methodology, the 'soft systems' approach or the communication audit. This approach to the design and evaluation of IT in terms of the principles of 'good' communication was the sort advocated by Rogers (1986) but has yet to receive much attention in the research field.

Finally, the work undertaken by Allen (1977) in the context of information flows in and between technological laboratories still serves as a model for what can be achieved by systematic mapping of organizational communication flows. Allen studied a large number of factors which affected both intraorganizational communication and interorganizational communication including:

- the communication system in technology;
- communication in the laboratory;
- communication among organizations;
- the influence of formal and informal organizational structures on the structure of communication networks;
- the influence of architecture on communication networks.

Allen found that different organizational structures were reflected in different communication patterns and that office design affected communication patterns so that changing the layout of a laboratory led to changes in communication patterns within the laboratory. From analysis of the communication patterns he was also able to identify communication stars — those who communicated frequently with a large number of other people — and gatekeepers — those who exhibited a high degree of contact outside their organizations and were frequently turned to by others in the organization for information.

INFORMATION MAPPING

Information mapping is an approach to information systems evaluation which is relatively new to the information world and information professionals alike. It is an approach which explores information use and needs with a view to graphically representing part or parts of the information system under study. The expression 'information mapping' has evolved from the general area of information resource management which links managerial effectiveness with information acquisition and use (Roberts and Wilson 1987).

However, information mapping is, again, a concept which means different things to different people, and the literature on information mapping, although relatively sparse, varies from systems analysis techniques (for example, see Best 1985) to techniques identifying individual resource entities with a view to highlighting and, therefore, effectively exploiting the strategic information resources of an organization (Burk and Horton 1988; Horton 1988, 1989). The common theme throughout is the idea of discovering the information resources of an organization, although the means of doing so may vary according to the technique adopted, and 'mapping' these out by displaying them graphically is not always done.

An approach to information mapping has been outlined by Best (1985) where it is deployed as a technique to assist in IT implementation in an organization. Best's method takes a control and command oriented view of management and was developed in a production environment. It is one of the few published methods claiming to be an 'information mapping' technique. It highlights the ambiguity of the concept while embodying the idea of information evaluation linked to graphical display. Best's approach is top-down in arriving at the formulation of IT strategy and bottom-up in its implementation of changes. The method consists of eight steps:

- Define corporate mission — in a similar way to the Checkland approach to environment, clients, activities, etc. are examined in order to identify discrepancies between this definition and actual structure.
- Examine the actual organizational structure.
- Define and examine problem areas.
- Produce the first information map — this is a set of working papers and maps of information flows, function and purpose in the areas selected for examination.

- Examine technology options.
- Compare the first information map and technology options to produce a 'creative' map which specifies interfaces, processing devices, etc. Costs/benefits can then be derived.
- Produce recommendations.
- Implement.

The limitations of Best's method are the restriction of the information mapping technique to computer systems and a lack of attention being focused on the systems users. Best's method, therefore is a form of systems analysis which pays scant attention to the user.

An approach to information mapping which is not restricted to computer systems and IT options but which aims to study every aspect of information systems — including the use of such systems has been devised by Pridgeon (1990). Pridgeon has put forward the following information mapping methodology:

- Identify the need for an information map.
- Choose the information mapping project.
- Planning — define and agree to the purpose and scope of the project, agree to the methodology and discuss the final presentation form.
- Preparation — team preparation and preparation with the group.
- Information gathering — through interviewing, study of documentation and sample forms and systems, and observation.
- Collate and evaluate information in parallel with further information gathering.
- Map format — alternatives include entity relations/diagrams, object-oriented representation, process oriented maps, the use of colour to represent processes/entities, or an 'Infomap' display (where information resource entities are plotted on a two grid map).
- Feedback to the group.
- Produce and release report.

Infomapping — an information mapping technique

This approach to information mapping is described in Burk and Horton's 'Infomap: a complete guide to discovering corporate information resources' (1988) and in a series of articles by Horton (1988, 1989). It claims to be a rigorous methodology which aims to manage information for maximum corporate gain. It is an approach to information systems evaluation which relies heavily on the concept of 'cost justification', working on the premise that the value and benefits derived from information should equal, if not exceed their costs and expenses. 'Infomapping' is a term which refers specifically to the Burk and Horton technique — rather than to the general concept of 'information mapping'.

Infomapping objectives are achieved by 'mapping' information resource entities (IREs), and placing tliem at appropriate points on a two matrix grid system in relation to spectra of information resource characteristics (Burk and Horton 1988). The idea behind infomapping is to take an individual information resource and analyse to what degree it is composed of Functions attributes (e.g. 'service') as opposed to Holdings (e.g. 'products'), and Media/Conduit (e.g. its container), as opposed to Content (e.g. its meaning). Subsequent examination of the 'infomap' and the creation of boundaries around clusters of resources may reveal the duplication of certain information resources or areas within the organization where information resources are particularly lacking. The map display enables all IREs to be seen together on a single page and so facilitates analysis.

There are four stages involved in the methodology, although its creators emphasize that it is not necessary to follow all through completely to derive benefit:

- surveying;
- cost and valuing;
- analysis;
- synthesis.

Stage one involves the surveying (identifying and categorizing) of IREs into service, source or system categories, largely by collecting summary data by interview, and recording these findings on a simple one page form. The output from this stage will be a preliminary inventory of all IREs, both internal and external, listed alphabetically and given a unique identification number. The cost/value analysis of each IRE forms stage two, with analysis and creation of the map as stage three. Stage four is a synthesis of findings which enables 'corporate', and therefore vital, IREs to be separated from the less important. A software package 'Infomapper' is available to assist in the infomapping process.

REFERENCS

Allen, T. J. 1977. *Managing the Flow of Technology.* Cambridge, MA: MIT Press.

Barker, R. 1990. Information Audits: Designing a Methodology With Reference to the R and D Division of a Pharmaceutical Company. Department of Information Studies, Occasional Publications Series No. 8, University of Sheffield.

Best, D. 1985. Information mapping: A technique to assist the introduction of information technology in organizations. In *Information Management: From Strategies to Action,* ed. B. Cronin. London: Aslib.

Bland, M. 1980. *Employee Communications in the 1980s.* London: Kogan Page.

Booth, A. 1988a. *The Communication Audit: A Guide For Managers.* Cambridge: Gower.

Booth, A. 1988b. The Qualitative Evaluation of IT in Communication Systems. British Library R and D report number 5968. London: Taylor Graham.

Booth, A. 1986. *Communication Audits: A UK Survey.* London: Taylor Graham.

Burk, C. F., and F. W. Horton. 1988. *Infomap: A Complete Guide to Discovering Corporate Information Resources.* Englewood Cliffs, NJ: Prentice Hall.

Campbell, M. E. 1982. The business communication audit: Evaluating and improving business communication. *Montana Business Quarterly* 20: 15-18.

Chambers, A. D. 1978. The internal audit of research and development. *R and D Management* 8: 95-99.

Chambers, A. D., and G. M. Selim. 1983. The Audit of Management Information Systems: The State of the Art. City University Business School working paper no. 53., City University Business School, London.

Checkland, P. 1981. *Systems Thinking, Systems Practice.* Chichester: Wiley.

Cortez, E. M., and C. A. Bunge. 1987. The communication audit as a library management tool. *Journal of Library Administration* 8: 41-64.

Diamond, S. Z. 1983. *Records Management.* New York: AMACOM.

Emanuel, M. 1985. *Inside Organizational Communication.* New York: Longman.

Gildea, J. A., and K. Rosenberg. 1979. Auditing organizational communications: Is there life beyond print-outs? *University of Michigan Business Review* 31: 7-12.

Gillman, P. L. 1985. An analytical approach to information management. *The Electronic Library* 3: 56-60.

Goldhaber, G. M. 1974. *Organizational Communication.* New York: Brown.

Goldhaber, G. M., and D. P. Rogers. 1979. *Auditing Organizational Communication Systems: The ICA Communications Audit.* Dubuque, Iowa: Kendall-Hunt.

Greenbaum, H. H., and N. D. White. 1976. Biofeedback at the organizational level: The communication audit. *Journal of Business Communication* 13: 3-15.

Gruber, T. 1983. The operational audit - an integrated approach. *Internal Auditor* 40: 39-41.

Henderson, H. L. 1980. Cost effective information provision and the role for the information audit. *Information Management* 1: 7-9.

Horton, F. W. 1989. Mapping corporate information resources. *International Journal of Information Management* 9: 19-24, 91-95.

Horton, F. W. 1988. Mapping corporate information resources. *International Journal of Information Management* 8: 249-254.

Jagger, H. 1984. The communication audit. In *Telecoms Today: Tools, Tactics and Strategies*, 215-225. London: Online (Proceedings of the 1984 International Conference).

Kopec, J. A. 1982. The communication audit. *Public Relations Journal* 39: 24- 27.

Machin, J. L., and C. H. Tai. 1979. Senior managers audit their own communications. *Journal of Enterprise Management* 2: 75-86.

Machin, J. L., and A. Wooley. 1981. Inter-manager communications: Matching up to expectations? *Personal Management* 13: 26-29.

Meyer, N. D., and M. E. Boone. 1987. *The Information Edge*. New York: McGraw Hill.

Mintzberg, H. 1973. *The Nature of Managerial Work*. New York: Harper & Row.

Odiorne, G. S. 1954. An application of the communication audit. *Personnel Psychology* 7: 235-245.

Otway, H. J., and M. Peltu, eds. 1984. *The Managerial Challenge of New Office Technology*. London: Butterworths.

Potter, S. 1990. The Communications Audit: A Small Scale Pilot Study Exploring Communications Between an Information Service and Its Customers in a Pharmaceutical Company. Department of Information Studies, MSc dissertation, Sheffield: University of Sheffield.

Pridgeon, C. A. 1990. Techniques For Information Mapping in a Pharmaceutical Research Organization. MSc dissertation, Department of Information, University of Sheffield.

Quinn, A. V. 1979. The information audit: A new tool for the information manager. *Information Manager* 1: 18-19.

Reynolds, P. D. 1980. Management information audit. *Accountants Magazine* 84: 66-69.

Riley, R. H. 1976. The information audit. *Bulletin of the American Society For Information Science* 2: 24-25.

Roberts, N., and T. D. Wilson. 1987. Information resource management. *International Journal of Information Management* 7: 67-75.

Rockey, E. H. 1977. *Communication in Organizations*. Cambridge, MA: Winthrop.

Rogers, E. M. 1986. *Communication Technology: The New Media in Society*. New York: Free Press.

Stanton, M. 1981. How to audit communications. *Management Today* (November): 68-74.

Strenski, J. B. 1978. The communication audit: Primary PR measurement tool. *Public Relations Quarterly* 23: 17-18.

Taylor, R. S. 1982. Organizational information environments. In *Information and Transformation of Society*, ed. G. P. Sweeney. Amsterdam: North Holland.

Valentine, J. 1981. Audit of administrator communication. *Peabody Journal of Education* 59: 1-10.

Wirtz, J. R. 1981. The communication audit - your road map to success. *Journal of Organizational Communication* 10: 15-17.

Worlock, D. R. 1987. Implementing the information audit. *Aslib Proceedings* 39: 255-260.

The Shared
Information Network

Ruth Stanat

INTRODUCTION

How many times have you been in a meeting or in a discussion with
your boss and tried to remember an article you read on a key competitor or event within your industry or marketplace? You may have
clipped the article, filed it in a folder, or just made a mental note of
its content. You need supporting documentaion, however, to make
your point. What do you do?

At the bare minimum, it is necessary for you to locate the magazine, find the article, reread the article, and perhaps find other articles to support your case. Similarly, within your organization someone
may have published a study on a certain topic and may have subsequently left the company. You will quickly realize that when the
author of the report leaves the company, so does the author's intelligence. You are now faced with the task of retrieving information
generated internally within the organization in addition to staying
abreast of all the information published by sources external to your
company. How can a human being absorb and digest all this information and still do an effective job?

Organizations need a way to obtain information that affects their
business and are searching for an effective mechanism that will enable
them to integrate their internal intelligence networks with vital external information. They need a shared information network.

In developing such a network, an organization must follow a series of steps. These steps can prove difficult to implement, however,

because of various issues. This article examines the issues involved in developing a corporate intelligence network to provide a framework for such a network and to avoid stumbling blocks to implementing the steps needed to develop the network.

THE BASIC ISSUE

Let's take the case of the small business. The president of the company has perhaps a handful of people who represent his or her management team. The information flows freely on a daily basis in this "flat" organization. If someone in this small company picks up the paper and notices a new promotional program initiated by a competitor and posts the ad on the bulletin board, nearly everyone in the firm is notified of the event by midmorning. As a company grows in size and as layers of management are added, achieving this "instant competitive intelligence" becomes more and more of a task. This problem is exemplified by a company with multiple field locations, both domestic and abroad. In short, large and midsize corporations are faced with the challenge of achieving the goal of rapid access to intelligence.

WHY SHARE INFORMATION?

Most organizations experience the "hoarding of intelligence." No matter what size the company, corporate executives have begun to realize that information is power. Nowadays, as the size of organizations fluctuates, less and less information is documented or catalogued. Yet the hoarding of information is inherent to the management system in both large and small companies because managers are rewarded for innovative ideas and original thinking.

The hoarding of intelligence is exacerbated with increased size and complexity of an organization. Large corporations that are decentralized and have numerous operating divisions are faced with a tremendous amount of duplication of effort. In one company, more than six different departments generate studies on the same topic area at the same time. How many times have you just finished looking up some information to discover that a report in another department already contains the information? This hoarding of intelligence puts companies at a competitive disadvantage. Companies that can quickly retrieve internal information and efficiently synthesize and disseminate external information have an advantage over those organizations that cannot. Furthermore, each manager or executive is a database of information, with years of functional and industry expertise making him or her a resident expert on certain topics. Getting access to your coworkers' or subordinates' areas of expertise requires that you tap into their data bank of information, which is stored in their brain. Thus, the "infoglut" factor has led to the increased emphasis and importance of information sharing within organizations. Consider the following actual story.

Reducing the Information Glut

A major consumer products firm prided itself on the dissemination of marketing information on a worldwide basis. Much of the internal documentation, however, included 40-page memos that summarized worldwide marketing meetings. Additionally, more than 100 staff members were copied on these memos worldwide. Calculations showed that at least two months of an administrator's time were required just to copy and disseminate this correspondence. In this case, it was recommended that the firm condense this semiannual paper into a two- to three-page summary and put the document into their electronic mail package, which could be accessed by all their affiliates in the United States and abroad. This system significantly reduced the duplication of effort within the organization, thus reducing their infoglut factor.

Thus, an effective shared information network can work to resolve infoglut and information hoarding, two factors that can negatively affect the efficiency with which organizations manage the universe of information. When companies recognize the need for a shared information network, they are faced with the following issues:

- What is system architecture, and what components of this make up a shared information network?
- Who or what functional area is responsible for gathering, selecting, and disseminating information?
- What type of information should be "shared"?
- What format can be used to distribute the information, and what should it look like?
- How is this type of information effectively distributed?
- What resource requirements are necessary to effectively implement this process?
- How does the company measure the effectiveness of the process?
- What are the pitfalls of these programs?

The following sections address each of these issues.

SYSTEM ARCHITECTURE

From a broad perspective, "system architecture" can be defined as *the visual representation of a system through which information provided by source documents is changed into final documents.* Clearly, the purpose of systematizing information is to maintain the basic elements of input-process-output. This allows an organization with a large infrastructure to sustain itself. The author has found no single system architecture appropriate for the development of a shared information network. The flow and circulation of information are largely based on the structure of the organization, as well as the corporate culture. Figure 1 depicts a simple system architecture in which a database and other forms of information are derived from source documents.

In this simple example, internal and external information sources are pulled together to create a database. Such a database, which increases in value over time, can become part of a corporatewide intelligence network and the center for distribution of information in various forms (for example, company newsletters and quarterly reports).

Consider the history of system architecture. During the 1950s and 1960s, the concept of system architecture was confined to accounting or transaction systems. Such systems were data processing systems run on behalf of accountants. Transactions systems, which were used by various professionals, not just accountants, began to evolve in the late 1960s and early 1970s. Their distinguishing characteristic is that they capture data as the transaction occurs, in "real time"—not after the fact—through a variety of input methods,including scanning, user entry on-line, and electronic coding (credit cards). Data are transformed upon entry into readily accessible, usable information by the sophisticated software used in these systems. Thus, in their most evolved form, these systems are called "strategic information systems": The transaction information is shared with the customer, supplier, or distributor of the product

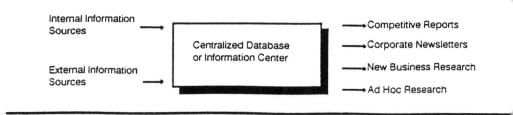

Figure 1. Simply system architecture.

or service, creating competitive advantage for each with timely, accurate information. For instance, strategic planners and market research professionals can now access textual and analytical information that provides them with timely information about their competitive environment.

Brenda Lewis, president of Transactions Marketing, Inc., describes the change as follows:

> The economic upheavals of the mid-1970s—quadrupled energy prices, deregulation of financial markets, advances in global communications and transportation, the rise of foreign competition as the dollar inflated—fostered dramatic changes in the need for competitive intelligence. Fortunately, the advent of the personal computer broke the accounting function's hammerlock on corporate data processing systems, with their emphasis on past performance data, and permitted the development of proactive marketing information systems, including competitive intelligence (Lewis 1989).

Today, the amount of information in textual form continues to increase. As a result, some organizations have become buried in information. Executives are searching for effective ways to capture, store, disseminate, and, most important, share timely information that is relevant to their business; in other words, they are seeking a systematized shared information network. When applied to a shared information network, system architecture refers to the following components:

- the "flow" of information;
- the technology-based components involved in developing these systems; and
- the end-user commnunity.

Information flow

Within an organization, information flow refers to any number of formal or informal processes that circulate information. In many organizations, this flow can be very simple and involve numerous forms. It may involve such informal processes as information obtained from telephone conversations, interoffice or routing memos, and internally published newsletters and bulletins. Thus, much of this information involves voice and hard copy. Information flow can also be quite sophisticated. Clearly, the larger and more diversified an organization is, the more sophisticated is its informational flow.

Typically, the information coordinators and corporate library gather mounds of information from the external environment (for instance, published sources) and from the operating divisions of the organization (for example, field sales information). In addition, they gather, filter, and disseminate competitive and strategic information and distribute key findings to top-level decision makers, in most cases senior executives.

A database is a vehicle to store either textual or numeric information. Most of the information used in middle- to senior-level decision making is from textual sources (newspapers, periodicals, internal analyses, and reports). A database, however, does not have to be a sophisticated computerized system. It can simply be a file folder of papers on your desk. The file folder, however, is organized according to a specific purpose and may contain papers on financial performance of a product line or competitive advertisements on your business. In short, you would look for specific information on a certain topic within a specific folder.

A growing amount of information is in textual form, not just numeric. The development of a system architecture involves putting both textual and numeric information into computers and making the information accessible through software programs. This has prompted many software publishers to develop sophisticated packages for computers that are designed to integrate market and financial data for the business analyst. Some software packages are marketed as the solution to all information needs (transaction processing, data analysis, graphics, and data management). As a result, new software products such as database management systems and executive information systems often emerge.

The technology

The technological components of a shared information network may be as simple as a single computer or workstation. Such a system works best when one or a few people are responsible for accessing information that is then distributed as hard copy on an ad hoc basis or as requested by management. Thus, the technological components are very centralized and may serve the needs of a division or functional department of an organization. At the other extreme, the components may comprise a sophisticated electronic system in which information is continually accessed by many users throughout an organization. Some firms maintain large-scale information networks that use mainframe computers and sophisticated programming languages.

The application of technology and its architectural integration into intelligence networks will increase in the future. According to Jim Onalfo, systems manager for the desserts division of General

Foods, "Companies in the nineties are going to survive because the executives in those companies know how to employ high-tech technology to improve their infrastructure. Those that do not have executives with these skills will fail and their companies will suffer" (Onalfo 1989).

For the development of a shared network, the technological components are constantly evolving as advancements in information management are made. Artificial intelligence or expert systems are now performing functions usually associated with human intelligence, including reasoning, learning, and self-improvement. However, corporations must first develop their own internal intelligence network prior to the successful application of artificial intelligence systems. By the year 2000, those corporations that have successfully developed a corporate intelligence network probably will be able to apply artificial intelligence to the systems architecture. In essence, these will be "intelligent databases" able to emulate human intelligence to make projections into the future.

This communications component of systems architecture provides a means to tie together a corporate intelligence network. As with hardware and software, a communications network may employ a high level of technology, for example, an interactive information system such as a local area network or an electronic mail system. A sophisticated intelligence network usually involves the use of telecommunications devices (telephones, modems, PBXs, and so forth).

The technological components of a shared information network can be the driving force behind the network. Prior to the 1980s, all information was gathered and distributed manually and there did not exist a means to "pull it all together." Since the advent of the personal computer in the early 1980s, technology has affected how information is stored. Clearly, the technological components of a shared information network vary with the information needs of an organization, its size, and its business and competitive environments. They also determine the effectiveness of a shared information network.

End-User Community

Probably the most important aspect of the system architecture of a network is its end-user community, because the end users of a network are responsible for turning information into intelligence. In addition to acting as the "voice" of the network, the end users must provide feedback about the network. Such feedback provides a necessary interactive and human element to the network and a "loop" to the overall system architecture. Thus, the architecture of the network will incorporate intelligence from such areas as field sales.

It is necessary to keep in mind five points about the system architecture of a shared information network:

1. Corporate intelligence networks do not have a single system architecture. They are based on the structure of an organization and its corporate culture.
2. Because a corporate intelligence network is designed to be efficient, the architecture exploits state-of-the-art technology.
3. The system architecture of the network has a continual feedback process and is constantly evolving and changing with the needs of the organization. Thus, the system must be interactive and involve people.
4. The system architecture is not volume-driven. The network should not become a source for archival information or information that is outdated. Rather, it should be a source for timely, high-value information that could affect the organization.
5. As more and more organizations expand their international presence, the architecture of a corporate intelligence network should be global in scope.

RESPONSIBILITY FOR DEVELOPING THE INTELLIGENCE NETWORK

In many instances, one department may assume responsibility for developing the network to minimize duplication of effort and maximize productivity of information dissemination. Unfortunately, there is no clear-cut guideline as to what department or functional area should be responsible for this task. Clearly, the organization of the company will dictate which departments are well positioned to execute the network. The decision involved in delegating this responsibility can be based on various factors. Among them are the actual size of the organization, whether the organization is centralized or decentralized, the actual job responsibilities or job descriptions of each functional department within the organization, the type of information that the intelligence network will provide, and the strategic objectives of the network.

In most companies, corporate staff departments from the following functional areas have the capabilities to develop the network:

- corporate/division marketing,
- information systems,
- strategic planning, and
- corporate library.

Corporate/division marketing

To meet the internal information needs of corporations, corporate marketing or strategic intelligence centers have been formed. In the past, this function was met by the traditional corporate library. However, as strategic planning and the concept of strategic marketing received greater emphasis from senior management, the corporate marketing departments became the most viable setting for a corporate intelligence network.

In today's business environment, many organizations have organized a corporate marketing information center. Compared with many other functions within an organization, marketing departments are most closely associated with the success or failure of the company's products or services. Thus, the development of an information center within the marketing department has become one of the most viable ways of gathering market and competitive information that is timely, accurate, and actionable.

As part of a centralized corporate intelligence network, the marketing department performs the functions of data gathering and data screening and analysis. That is, the department gathers information that is relevant to the organization's scope of business and disregards information that is not. Oftentimes, the department may even have its own in-house news clipping service or may hire an external source for this chore.

When the corporate marketing function develops an intelligence network, the network acts as a support unit for the entire organization. It provides the organization with information from a wide variety of published sources (for instance, industry trade publications) and from other information providers (such as on-line commercial databases). In addition, it honors quick information requests from other functional areas of the organization. On a small scale, when the marketing department of a division or business unit develops an intelligence network, it acts as a test site or model for other departments of the organization to emulate.

Of course, there can be problems when a marketing division sets up an intelligence network. Although some marketing divisions take on a very proactive role, others are more reactive and do not respond favorably. Or, there may be a split among sections within the division. The author developed a corporate intelligence network for one of the marketing divisions for a large packaged-food company. The division was organized into groups by type of product (for example, frozen, dry, or refrigerated). Because some of these groups were more successful than others, the responses to the idea of an intelligence network varied among the groups. The key to resolving this problem was to identify an internal champion who could help convince the negative factions that the network would be advantageous.

The members of marketing departments at the divisional level should realize the benefits they can reap from a shared intelligence network. They are much closer to the sales function than the members of other departments are, both at the divisional and corporate levels. By being so close to the sales force, the marketing department of a division can use the salespeople as an information source and can use the intelligence network to keep the salespeople abreast of competitive, business, and environmental activity that may affect their role within the organization.

Information systems

By 1990, the information services sector is expected to account for 6 percent of the nation's gross national product. This estimate, combined with continued advances in techology, has led to the development of information systems (IS) departments in many corporations. A growing number of IS departments have actively become involved in developing corporate intelligence networks, especially because many have become more closely associated with the sales and marketing functions of organizations. In addition, the IS departments as a whole are increasing in personnel, corporate backing, and budgets to finance a shared information network. At the divisional level, also, IS departments usuallv respond very favorably to corporate intelligence networks.

The overall role of IS professionals will become much clearer in the future with regard to the corporate intelligence network. With the newly created title "chief information officer" (CIO) in many organizations, the IS function will gain a stronger presence in the corporate intelligence network, primarily because most CIOs have information systems or data processing backgrounds.

Strategic planning

As the word "strategic" began to infiltrate corporations during the 1970s, so too did strategic planning departments. Because "strategic" underscores the notion of competitive, business, and environmental intelligence for many organizations, the strategic planning department has become an information center and the basis for a corporate intelligence network in some organizations.

Within a corporate intelligence network, strategic planning departments serve some of the same functions as the corporate marketing department. Recognizing this duplication of effort, senior management in some corporations has centralized the corporate intelligence network in one department. This has become one of the major upheavals leading to the corporate downsizing trend that is now so prevalent. As a result, strategic planning departments are much smaller now than they were in the past.

Because of this downsizing, the strategic planning function often relies more heavily on external firms for research. In addition to developing intelligence networks, these departments request ad hoc research and analysis on such topics as internal business matters and competitor profiles. Whether the research is supplied on a one-shot or ongoing basis, the key to this type of research is that it is future oriented. That is, the information is to be used as a planning tool and distributed to senior management.

Although the strategic planning department may not be the centralized setting for a corporate intelligence network, it does play a vital role in the evolution of the network. The strategic planning role can be part of a coordinated effort with other functions to develop an intelligence network.

Corporate library

In many organizations, a corporate library provides the same type of services that public libraries provide for the general public. The corporate library is usually the department senior executives turn to when they need published information on an ad hoc basis. Yet, in some instances the corporate library acts as the functional area responsible for a corporate intelligence network. Corporate libraries are effective information centers for organizations and, more and more, are becoming the centralized setting for a corporate intelligence network.

As have most other functions within corporations, the corporate library has been negatively affected by the downsizing trend. Many corporate libraries have one or two persons with library science backgrounds who are solely responsible for maintaining a library, retrieving information requests, and keeping senior management abreast of competitive, business, and environmental events that affect the organization. In addition to these vital tasks, corporate librarians may play a very proactive role in the development of a corporate intelligence network.

Sometimes, it may take a coordinated effort between the corporate library department and another function to develop a corporate intelligence network, as in the following example.

Interdepartmental Intelligence Network

For a major consumer products/technology firm, developing a corporate intelligence network entailed pooling resources between the corporate marketing department and the corporate library. In this particular case, there were two internal champions: a corporate librarian with a strong library science background and extensive database searching skills and a manager in corporate marketing with the organizational clout and budget necessary to finance and implement an intelligence network. The company benefited from the fact that the library was already the setting for many information sources and department personnel were already finely attuned to information management skills and database searching.

Upper management favored this coordinated effort between corporate marketing and the library for four reasons:

1. Such a coordinated effort would promote the notion of inter-departmental teamwork, which benefits the organization as a whole.
2. The involvement of both departments would increase the level of user input and feedback to the network.
3. The project would be an enhancement of an existing department, rather than the creation of a new department or function.
4. Pooled resources would reduce duplication of effort and the number of staff hours needed to implement the system.

Additional criteria for choosing a department

Although there is no clear-cut guideline as to which department or functional area should be responsible for developing and maintaining a shared information network, there are some important criteria to consider. These guidelines follow:

1. Pick a department that is already a viable source of business and competitive information for either all or a significant part of the organization. Thus, the department should have a strong knowledge of the organization and the competitive and business events that affect the company. Although the corporate library or information center represents an ideal setting in many organizations, both large and small, it may take a coordinated effort between this function and another department that has more ready access to the current activities of the organization.

2. Choose a department that can work well with other deparments and whose personnel have excellent communication skills. This becomes very important when the department is trying to "sell" a shared information network to other departments and senior management. These skills are also important if you are part of a small division of a large organization or if you are the only person responsible for gathering information in a small organization.

3. If there are various departments that could be the setting for a shared information network, choose one that is very forward thinking, results oriented, and respected throughout the organization. Thus, department personnel should be willing to withstand the potential risk and pitfalls associated with a companywide information network.

Other responsibilities of the intelligence network department

The department or functional area responsible for a corporate intelligence network may serve a number of other functions. The department may act as a liaison to external information suppliers, consulting firms, and research firms. In some instances, the department may even establish a competitive or business information hotline. This allows personnel from other departments to tap the resources of the department by telephone computer. The department may even publish a monthly or weekly internal newsletter that highlights key business and competitive events.

WHAT TYPE OF INFORMATION SHOULD BE PART OF A SHARED INFORMATION NETWORK?

Most corporations are interested in keeping their employees informed of the key competitive or business events that affect their products or services. In today's business environment, most executives are finding an increased need for actionable information and global information. This information can be readily available or new information that is not yet available. The key notion here is to centralize the key topics that are important to the organization. The following are broad topic areas needed by almost every type of business:

- Industry trends: Industry trends are general tendencies or consistent directions in a given market or industry. For instance, a trend in the food industry is the tremendous amount of consolidation and reorganization among supermarket chains.
- Environmental trends: Demographic and socioeconomic factors strongly affect the business environment. Examples of such trends are the growing elderly segment, the influx of dual income families, and the convenience-oriented society of today.
- Legislative and regulatory events: Government regulations have become an increasing concern of corporations. Now more than ever, businesses are affected by local, state, and federal governments, as well as regulatory agencies such as the Food and Drug Administration and the Securities and Exchange Commission.
- Competitor activity: More and more organizations are systematically monitoring the activities of their competitors.

- Product development: Whether it be a new type of ready-to-eat cereal or a new patented process for the development of a fat substitute, organizations are demanding real-time information on new products.
- Mergers and acquisitions: With merger mania still rampant, organizations have become financial prey to their peer organizations, leveraged buyout concerns, and stock brokerage houses. Acquisitions have sensitized some organizations to a point where their strategic objective is to remain independent.
- International events: In today's global business environment, many multinational organizations have beefed up their overseas operations and are looking to new areas for growth. International events will affect many businesses, especially as trade barriers continue to fall in Europe and parts of Asia.

The challenge facing executives is to organize the universe of external information along with their internal information within these broad topic areas in relation to their line of business. In many organizations, file folders serve this purpose quite well. However, a growing number of corporations are designing systems that effectively integrate internal and external information.

FORMAT OF THE INFORMATION

An electronic database or computerized system containing copy file folders allows users to search several topic areas or file folders. Commercial database publishers generate information on a wide variety of topics and use sophisticated software to enable the user to retrieve the information through keyword search techniques and other methods. Many managers need some type of customized corporate filing system or intelligence database with which to access information. Such a database should provide synthesized information from a wide variety of textual sources that are relevant to the operations of the organization.

Hard copy

If you are employed in a small company that does not have access to a personal or mainframe computer, you can construct your own intelligence database in hard copy. Many companies have a library that catalogs internal information and keeps relevant records for the company. Although file folders help a company keep hard copy files for its records, access or retrieval of the information can become difficult as these files grow in size. A hard copy database design may suffice under any of the following scenarios:

- the organization is small and the decision makers are few;
- the products and services offered are few and very specialized;
- the competitors are few and well defined; and
- the business, competitive, and environmental factors that affect the organization are very stable and do not change much over time.

Electronic format

With the advent of the personal computer and the increasing storage capabilities in desk-top equipment, many companies are looking toward a corporate intelligence database customized to their needs. Electronic format of the information enables users to pull up the information on a computer screen, and sophisticated text retrieval software enables end users to search the database in an efficient manner.

In many cases, an organization develops an information network in which a hard copy format parallels the information in electronic format. Such a design works well for several reasons. It gives the network consistency and continuity. Also, incorporating hard copy and electronic forms satisfies the information needs of a wider audience. For instance, many middle- to senior-level executives do not have the time or even the desire to read important information on a computer screen, so a hard copy approach works well, On the other hand, many managers who have data processing or library science backgrounds prefer to read information from computer screens.

Design of the database

The design of a corporate intelligence database is the most important element of the system. Some companies spend millions of dollars on elaborate corporate intelligence databases only to find out that it is easier to use file drawers to retrieve the information than it is to navigate the database. The database, however, should reflect how the management of the organization views the business. Key variables such as the lines of business, competitors, markets, and products should be well thought out.

If a company has an objective to keep hundreds of its employees informed of key business events on a daily, weekly, or monthly basis, electronic information networks most efficiently store and disseminate this type of information. On the other hand, if the company is a moderate-size firm, the circulation of a daily news sheet or weekly or monthly newsletter may be more effective.

In a growing number of corporate settings, senior managers are becoming the most viable end users of intelligence networks that are derived from a variety of internal and external sources. To meet the need of the executive to pull information from diverse sources, the notion of executive information systems (EIS) evolved. These systems, which are networked using personal computers, allow senior managers to monitor and control large, geographically dispersed, and complex organizations. Although such systems are effective, the utility of EIS needs to be distributed to the departments or functional areas of an organization.

In a certain respect, many corporate departments or functional areas of an organization serve as information brokers with the operating divisions or field operations. Because their function dictates that they gather information from and feed information back to the business units, they are the best end users of a corporate intelligence network.

DISTRIBUTION OF THE INFORMATION

Clearly, shared information networks increase in complexity with the increase in information stored and the increase in dissemination to diverse and multiple departments. The most effective shared information networks encompass extensive organization, synthesis, and digestion of the information prior to distribution to select departments. The following story from one company describes such a situation.

Designing an Effective Shared Information Network

A large parent company was faced with the task of gathering and disseminating timely and relevant information to diverse operating divisions. This objective was complicated by the fact that the parent company and operating companies had considerably diverse product lines, on a domestic and worldwide basis.

To accomplish the task, the corporate marketing department assumed the role of internal champion, and, with the assistance of an outside consultant, conducted an extensive strategic information audit. The audit revealed that both managers and executives had a need for a shared information network that contained the following information categories:

- general business environmental information,
- specific competitor information, organized by line of business,
- international competitive information, and
- internal documents relevant to the aforementioned categories.

Moreover, the information had to be scanned, digested, and put into the system on a daily basis, for access the next morning. How did the firm accomplish this objective? One of the first steps taken by corporate marketing was to schematically design the optimum shared information network from the results of their strategic information audit (see Figure 2).

Following development of the schematic, corporate marketing, with the assistance of corporate information systems and an outside consulting firm, developed a prototype and installed the data on a flexible, mainframe text retrieval package. A systematic schedule was then developed for users to log into the system. One of the keys to success of the system was an extensive feedback process that corporate marketing built into the system. The system included the installation of an electronic mail function that allowed end users to provide feedback on the system, give comments or highlight information that was on the system, and communicate with the outside consulting firm. This process was conducted on a continuous basis and had support from the operating units.

Bottom Line Impact

The operating divisions in newly developed markets gained rapid access to business and technical information that enabled them to accelerate their product development cycle. The mature operating divisions now had an organized process by which to monitor their competition on an ongoing basis. The greatest value was derived from information on competitors in the Far East. Reduced duplication of effort was cited in areas of new business or market development projects.

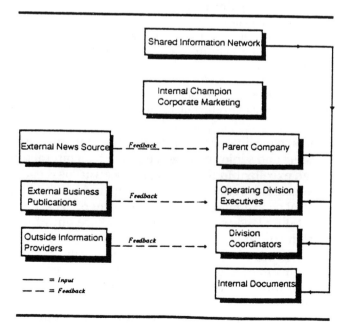

Figure 2. Optimum shared information network.

RESOURCE REQUIREMENTS

There is no doubt that these systems require at least one central coordinator. This position is responsible for the following tasks:

- procurement of data sources (working with outside suppliers and internal suppliers of information),
- maintenance of the database,
- coordination of the feedback process,
- end-user training, and
- future growth enhancements to the network.

In addition to these administrative and maintenance-based duties, the central coordinator must develop and nurture a reasonable level of awareness in peers and upper management. There are several ways the central coordinator may increase awareness. One way is to develop an in-house promotional effort. This may include brochures, promotional flyers, or even interoffice memos that are distributed to intended users of the system and highlight the benefits of the system. The coordinator should emphasize the benefits most suited to the user's needs. They might include the following:

- The system is simple to master and is user friendly, even to users who are not very computer literate.
- The system will dramatically reduce duplication of effort and reduce or eliminate the need for external news sources or publications.
- The system encourages information sharing and discourages information hoarding.
- The system systematically monitors competition.
- The system provides synthesis and analysis and contains the information that is most relevant to the activities of the organization.

The central coordinator may set up actual demonstrations of the system for peers and senior management. Such an interactive process should give an excellent indication whether awareness can be turned into acceptance. It also should result in some kind of feedback report that the central coordinator gives to management. These demonstrations should take place when all the "bugs" are out of the system.

In addition to developing an awareness level, the coordinator must also be a good salesperson of the system. Unless the users are aware of the information product and service offerings and enhancements to the system, they are dealing with a "blind spot." In some cases, two or more administrative people may be required to assist the central coordinator in large shared information networks, particularly those that are global in scope.

HOW TO MEASURE THE EFFECTIVENESS OF THE NETWORK

According to Citibank, its system "brings the efficiencies of a flat organization without Citibank being one" (*Business Week Newsletter*, 1988). These benefits, the ability to quantify productivity savings, block a competitor's moves, or bring a product to market quicker, illustrate the effectiveness of the system. There should be a thorough semiannual review of a network, rather than a quarterly review, to allow a time frame long enough to pinpoint tangible benefits or savings. Typically, such a review entails the use of hard copy questionnaires or personal interviews.

For organizations that have developed an intelligence network, the effectiveness of the network can be measured by answering the following questions:

- Are the goals and potential benefits of the network well communicated?
- Does the network have support from top management and several key functional areas (for instance, field sales, market research)?
- Can the network be modified or adjusted as the objectives and goals of the organization change?
- Are the people involved in the development or ongoing maintenance of the network motivated? Do they generate new ideas?
- Does the network effectively and efficiently gather and disseminate intelligence?
- Does the network provide pertinent information that can be transformed into actionable decision making?
- Does the network contain built-in measures for obtaining feedback?
- Are there provisions for reviewing and evaluating the network on a systematic basis?

PITFALLS

One pitfall of an intelligence network is failure of users to limit the amount of information that is loaded into the system; some people have the urge to integrate way too much information. Another pitfall can open up if the system initially involves too many groups or users at once. The execution of these systems is important. A phased development, both in terms of information content and end-user involvement, is recommended. Also, if the system is not being used, find out why. Perhaps another route, as indicated by the following company's story, might be more successful.

An Integrated Electronic and Hard Copy Network

A corporate librarian from a midsize integrated services digital network equipment firm wants to develop a hard copy information tool that is channeled to key executives of the organization. Given the size of the company (fewer than 1,000 employees), communication is not a critical factor. In this approach, the main challenge is to gather and digest information from hundreds of external sources, with limited resources. The librarian realizes that building an electronic information network is unnecessary, and from a budgetary perspective, impossible. What is needed, however, is a device that communicates external environmental intelligence to key executives.

The librarian realizes that a hard copy reporting system or newsletter might be more appropriate. Even so, the librarian clearly maps out a schematic or blueprint of the hard copy reporting system. The schematic defines the purpose of the system, notes the intended users, and provides a mechanism for continuous feedback. The newsletter or hard copy reporting system, however, can still contain the same information elements as an electronic network.

The information obtained from such a newsletter may be obtained from daily publications, industry-specific or trade publications, and from the field (sales representatives). Typically, sources would be included as part of the newsletter because many readers might want to refer to the original article. Such a newsletter may be set up for distribution on a weekly, biweekly, or even monthly basis. In some cases, an intelligence newsletter may be updated on a daily basis.

• • •

The first step in developing a shared information network is to approach your colleagues about the concept. Overall, the concept may involve input from various departments, including marketing research, information systems, finance, corporate library, or even the legal department. The key factor for you to discuss is the impact of a shared information network within your organization. You may want to schedule a one-hour meeting to brainstorm what the schematic would look like. The more departments involved in the conceptual/planning phase, the more successful the system will be. Use the topics that have been discussed in this article as the agenda for the meeting. Keep in mind these key questions:

- Why develop a shared information network?
- Is there a system already in place?
- What are the critical information needs of our organization?
- What are our critical lines of business?
- What should the network look like?
- Who are the users?

- Who will be responsible?
- What are the potential pitfalls?
- What budgetary questions are there?

For any phased process, such as the development of a shared information network, meetings that attempt to answer these questions are critical to the success of the network. Through communication and cooperation, corporate departments can build an effective network that benefits them and the company.

REFERENCES

Lewis, B. Letter to the author, 14 July 1989.
Onalfo, J. Letter to the author, 2 August 1989.
The Business Week Newsletter for Information Executives. April 27, 1988. New York: McGraw-Hill.

Information Politics

Thomas H. Davenport, Robert G. Eccles, and Laurence Prusak

"Information is not innocent."
—James March (1983)[1]

During the past decade, many firms have concluded that information is one of their most critical business resources and that broadening information access and usage and enhancing its quality are key to improving business performance. The "information-based organization," the "knowledge-based enterprise," and the "learning organization," forecasted by management experts, all require a free flow of information around the firm.[2] The computers and communications networks that manipulate and transmit information become more powerful each year. Yet the rhetoric and technology of information management have far outpaced the ability of people to understand and agree on what information they need and then to share it.

Today, in fact, the information-based organization is largely a fantasy. All of the writers on information-based organizations must speak hypothetically, in the abstract, or in the future tense. Despite forty years of the Information Revolution in business, most managers still tell us that they cannot get the information they need to run their own units or functions. As a recent article by the CEO of a shoe company put it: "On one of my first days on the job, I asked for a copy of every report used in management. The next day, twenty-three of them appeared on my desk. I didn't understand them. . . . Each area's reports were Greek to the other areas, and all of them were Greek to me."[3] A more accurate metaphor might be that these reports each came from a different city-state—Athens, Sparta, Corinth, Thebes, and Peloponnesus—each part of the organization but a separate political domain with its own culture, leaders, and even vocabulary.

We have studied information management approaches in more than twenty-five companies over the past two years. Many of their efforts to create information-based organizations — or even to implement significant information management initiatives — have failed or are on the path to failure. The primary reason is that the companies did not manage the politics of information. Either the initiative was inappropriate for the firm's overall political culture, or politics were treated as peripheral rather than integral to the initiative. Only when information politics are viewed as a natural aspect of organizational life and consciously managed will true information-based organizations emerge.

Furthermore, a good argument can be made — and there is increasing evidence for it — that as information becomes the basis for organizational structure and function, politics will increasingly come into play. In the most information-oriented companies we studied, people were least likely to share information freely, as perceived by these companies' managers. As people's jobs and roles become defined by the unique information they hold, they may be less likely to share that information — viewing it as a source of power and indispensability — rather than more so. When information is the primary unit of organizational currency, we should not expect its owners to give it away.[4]

This assertion directly contradicts several academic and popular concepts about how widespread information technology will affect organizations. These thinkers have hypothesized that as organizations make widespread use of information technology, information will flow freely and quickly eliminate hierarchy. Mention is rarely made in such accounts of the specter of information politics.[5] Although this optimistic view has widespread appeal, it is not what we see today in companies.

When owners of key information resist sharing it either outright or, more commonly, through bureaucratic maneuvers, they are often dismissed as unfair or opportunistic. Yet they may have quite legitimate reasons for withholding the information. Political behavior regarding information should be viewed not as irrational or inappropriate but as a normal response to certain organizational situations. Valid differences in interpretation of information, for example, may lead to apparently intransigent behavior. At an electronics company we once worked with, the marketing organizations for direct and indirect channels could never agree on what constituted a sale. Getting the product to the end-customer was direct marketing's sale; getting it to the distributor, even though it might return eventually, was how the indirect group wanted to measure success. When the indirect channel was the dominant one for the company, this group's view of sales prevailed. Later, as more product moved directly to buyers, end-customer sales became the official definition. In information politics, might makes right. As a result of losing influence, however, the indirect group wanted to create its own sales databases and reports. Political disputes of this type will often arise when there is no consensus around the business's information needs.

One reason the stakes are so high in information politics is that more than information is at stake. In order to arrive at a common definition of information requirements, organizations must often address not just the information they use, but the business practices and processes that generate the information. Most firms have not recognized the linkages between processes and information, but there are a few exceptions. At a fast-growing specialty manufacturer, CEO-appointed information "czars" are responsible for ensuring consistency in the information-generating activities of their areas. For example, the order-processing czar mandated common companywide practices for assigning customer and product numbers, recognizing revenue, and determining contract prices. At IBM, eighteen key business processes (e.g., "customer fulfillment") are being redesigned to build a new information infrastructure. Out of each new process will come information on its performance — how long it takes, how much it costs, how satisfied the customer is with it — as well as the more traditional results-oriented information such as sales and profitability. At Dow Chemical, managers believe there must be common financial processes around the world in order to create common measures of financial performance.

The overall organizational climate is also a powerful influence on information politics.[6] Unfortunately, the very factors that make free information flow most desirable and necessary also make it less likely. An organization that is highly unstable and operating in an uncertain business, in which employees are uncertain about their job security and place in the hierarchy, needs as much information as possible about the environment and its own performance. Yet this type of organization is most likely to engender information politics that inhibit sharing.

Our purpose is to help companies understand information politics and manage them. In the next section, we classify the major models of information politics we have seen in client companies and firms we have studied. Following that, we present a set of approaches to managing information politics at both a strategic and a day-to-day level.

MODELS OF INFORMATION POLITICS

We have identified five information models (or, to continue the political metaphor, "states") that are representative of the practices we have observed (see Table 1). Three of these, technocratic utopianism, anarchy, and feudalism, are less effective than the other two, monarchy and federalism.[7] After we define each model, we will evaluate their relative effectiveness along the dimensions of information quality, efficiency, commonality, and access.

Any organization is likely to have proponents for more than one of these models. Sometimes the models conflict, and sometimes one model predominates. Table 2 shows the distribution of models among the companies we studied. The first step in managing information more effectively and realistically is explicitly recognizing these existing models and then choosing a single desired state. Maintaining multiple models is confusing and consumes scarce resources. Once a model has been selected, an organization can manage the daily politics of information, just as an alderman manages a ward.

Technocratic Utopianism

Many companies have a strong bias toward approaching information management from a technological perspective. This approach eschews information politics, assuming that politics are an aberrant form of behavior. It is usually driven by a firm's information systems (IS) professionals, who see themselves as the custodians, if not the own-

Table 1. Models of Information Politics

Technocratic Utopianism	A heavily technical approach to information management stressing categorization and modeling of an organization's full information assets, with heavy reliance on emerging technologies.
Anarchy	The absence of any overall information management policy, leaving individuals to obtain and manage their own information.
Feudalism	The management of information by individual business units or functions, which define their own information needs and report only limited information to the overall corporation.
Monarchy	The definition of information categories and reporting structures by the firm's leaders, who may or may not share the information willingly after collecting it.
Federalism	An approach to information management based on consensus and negotiation on the organization's key information elements and reporting structures.

Table 2. Models Observed in Research Sites

25 Companies Studied	Federalism	Monarchy	Technocratic Utopianism	Anarchy	Feudalism
Chemicals					
Company A			✓		✓
Company B	✓	✓			
Company C	✓		✓		
Computers					
Company A	✓			✓	✓
Company B	✓		✓		
Consumer Goods					
Company A			✓		✓
Company B					✓
Direct Marketing		✓			
Electronics					
Company A					✓
Company B					✓
Entertainment					✓
Financial Services		✓		✓	✓
Gas Transmission		✓			
Information Services					
Company A			✓		
Company B	✓				✓
Insurance					
Company A		✓	✓		
Company B	✓				✓
Company C					✓
Medical Supplies					
Company A			✓		
Company B	✓				✓
Office Products	✓		✓		
European Office Products			✓		
Software					
Company A		✓		✓	
Company B				✓	
Specialty Manufacturing	✓				
Total	8	7	9	4	12

ers, of the firm's information. Their technological efforts to alleviate information problems often involve a considerable amount of detailed planning and revolve around modeling and efficient use of corporate data. Their goal is to plan a technology infrastructure that can deliver information to each individual's desktop and then to build databases with the correct structure to store this information without redundancy. Some technical efforts around information management are reasonable; however, when the technological approach to information predominates, the company's model of information management can be described as technocratic utopianism.

Although neither the IS professionals nor the users may be consciously creating a technocratic utopia, there is an underlying assumption that technology will resolve all problems and that organizational and political issues are nonexistent or unmanageable. In fact, information itself — its content, use, and implications for managing — receives little attention in this model. The focus is instead on the technologies used to manipulate the information.

We found technocratic utopianism, either by itself or alongside another model, in almost a third of the firms we analyzed. The model usually coexists, however uneasily, with other models; in fact, the technocratic utopian model is often held by a small group of technologists supported by many technical journals, consultants, and technology vendors. While the technologists plan a utopia around the free flow of information, the senior executives for whom they work usually ignore, or are ignorant of, their efforts. Because these technical models are difficult for nontechnologists to understand, managers outside the IS function are rarely active participants. If a technocratic utopia is the only political model, it is probably because senior managers have abdicated their roles in selecting and managing information.

Technocratic utopians often have three factors in common: they focus heavily on information modeling and categorization; they highly value emerging hardware and software technologies; and they attempt to address an organization's entire information inventory.

A key emphasis in most technocratic utopias is information modeling and categorization. Once a unit of information is represented in an "entity-relationship model" or a "data-flow diagram," all problems in managing it have been solved, according to the extreme utopians. They consider such modeling and categorization a key aspect of the engineering of information (indeed, "information engineering" is an established discipline within the IS profession). In this ideal world, information flows like water, and the only task is to construct appropriate canals, aqueducts, and dams in order for information to flow freely to those who need it. Information sometimes feels as common in organizations as water; since it is so plentiful, there is a natural instinct to try to channel it rather than drown in it.

Information engineering is important, of course, but the political aspects cannot be neglected. Information may flow like water, but in the real world even water doesn't flow without political assistance. Those knowledgeable about the back-room politics involved in bringing water to Los Angeles or about Robert Moses's political steamrolling in New York's water management will understand the role of politics in managing a "natural" resource like information.[8]

Technologists also frequently assert that new forms of hardware and software are the keys to information success. Executives often hear that they will get the information they need "when our new relational database system is installed" or "when our new network is complete." The coming panacea for many organizations is object-oriented technologies, in which information is combined with application functions in reusable modules. Too often, however, when the silver bullet arrives it does not have the intended effect. No technology has yet been invented to convince unwilling managers to share information or even to use it. In fact, we would argue that technology vendors suffer from the same political forces as do data model-ers. The failure of the "diskless workstation" to thrive in the marketplace may well be due to individuals' reluctance to lose control of their information.

Finally, utopians focus on all information throughout the corporation — at least all that can be captured by a computer. A common example is the creation of an "enterprise model" — a structured inventory and categorization of all data elements used throughout the firm. Such modeling exercises often take years and yield vast amounts of detail. Although their purpose is often to eliminate redundant data storage, they often yield little real business value. Several MIT researchers have chronicled their failure.[9] Like most utopias, they lead to nowhere (or, in Samuel Butler's famous utopian novel, *Erewhon* — nowhere almost backwards).

Technocratic utopians assume that managing information is an exercise without passion. Their rallying cry is an uninspiring, "Data is a corporate asset." They believe, consciously or unconsciously, that information's value for business decisions is not only very high but also self-evident. They assume that employees who possess information useful to others will share it willingly. They assume that information itself is valueless, or at least that its value is the same to all organizational members. If they are conscious of the relationship between information access and hierarchy, they assume that those high in the hierarchy would not restrict the flow of information for any reason other than corporate security. These assumptions resemble human behavior found only in utopias.

Anarchy

Some firms have no prevailing political information model and exist in a state of anarchy. Rarely do organizations consciously choose this state, in which individuals fend for their own information needs. Information anarchy usually emerges when more centralized approaches to information management break down or when no key executive realizes the importance of common information. Information anarchy was made possible — and much more dangerous — by the introduction and rapid growth of the personal computer. Suddenly individuals and small departments could manage their own databases, tailoring their own reports to their own needs at any time and at minimal cost.

Although several firms we researched have allowed anarchy to survive, we found only one firm that had consciously chosen it. This software firm had previously tried to develop an overall information management structure by asking key managers what information they needed to run the business. When the firm could not achieve consensus, it determined that a bottom-up structured exchange of documents across its network, using a new software technology developed for this purpose, would yield all of the required information. Even here, however, an alternative information model flourished in some quarters; as one senior executive put it, "I get all the information I need in breakfast meetings with the CEO."

The long-term shortcomings of information anarchy are obvious. Technologists might worry that so much redundant information processing and storage is inefficient, but anarchy has more serious shortcomings. When everyone has his or her own database, the numbers for revenues, costs, customer order levels, and so on will diverge in databases throughout the company. Although anarchy is seldom chosen consciously, its effects are not uncommon; we know of several firms in which it was the source of late or inaccurate quarterly earnings reports. A firm cannot survive for long with such information discrepancies. The desire for information that leads to anarchy should quickly be harnessed into a more organized political model.

Feudalism

The political model we most often encountered was feudalism. In a feudal model, individual executives and their departments generally control information acquisition, storage, distribution, and analysis.[10] These powerful executives determine what information will be collected within their realms, how it will be interpreted, and in what format it will be reported to the "king" or CEO. They can also decide what measures are used to understand performance as well as what "language," by which we mean a common vocabulary, is used within the realm. Different realms often end up with different languages, and the subsequent fragmenting of information authority diminishes the power of the entire enterprise — just as the growth of powerful noblemen and their entourages inhibited the king's power in medieval times.

Feudal actions diminish the central authority's power to make informed decisions for the common good. Key measures of the enterprise's health often are not collected, reported, or even considered beyond roll-up of financial outcomes, further diminishing the central authority's power. Corporatewide performance is of interest only to those within corporate headquarters, and its indicators may poorly reflect what is actually happening around the firm.

Feudalism flourishes, of course, in environments of strong divisional autonomy. When divisions have their own strategies, products, and customers, it is almost inevitable that their information needs will differ. Furthermore, they may also be reluctant to fully disclose potentially negative information at the corporate level.

At a major consumer electronics firm's U.S. subsidiary, the feudalism was quite overt. The firm was organized along product lines; product division heads were informally referred to as "barons." Each had his or her own financial reporting system, with only the most limited amounts of data shared with the subsidiary head. The latter executive eventually brought in consultants to give a seminar on the value of common data and systems — all, the last we heard, to no avail.

At a large consumer goods firm organized by distribution channel, each channel had its own measures of performance that it thought were important. This information autonomy had prevailed for years and was tolerated because the firm had long been profitable using any set of measures. A new CEO arrived at a time when profits were down, and he felt he had no way to manage across the entire firm. He mandated the development of a common information architecture. Unfortunately, the IS group charged with this initiative began to create a technocratic utopia. We suspect that the feudal culture will eventually prevail.

We have also seen a few examples of functional feudalism, in which financial and operational functions have their own information architectures and cannot achieve consensus on what should be monitored and how. In one high-technology manufacturing firm, for example, the quality function head created an executive information system that reported on operational performance and quality data. The IS director, and the CFO to whom he reported, strenuously opposed the system, arguing that the firm's traditional financially oriented reporting approach should be the only one. The quality-oriented system was building adherents (and product quality) until the quality director left for a summer vacation. When he returned, he found that the IS head and CFO had enlisted sufficient support from the other executives to shut down the system. The battle over which type of system will eventually predominate is still raging.

Despite these battles in feudal environments, some degree of cooperation can emerge. Powerful executives can create strategic alliances to share information or establish a common network or architecture, just as feudal lords banded together to build a road or common defense wall, go to war, or plan a marriage for mutual enrichment — although such communal efforts rarely include all of the lords. It is also possible that, as in Renaissance times, the proliferation of patrons will encourage innovation and creativity within each realm — for example, the development of a particularly useful quality information system by one division.

Monarchy

The most practical solution to the problems inherent in the feudal model is to impose an information monarchy. The CEO, or someone empowered by the chief executive, dictates the rules for how information will be managed. Power is centralized, and departments and divisions have substantially less autonomy regarding information policies.

Much depends on the approach the "monarch" takes to managing the realm's information. A more benign monarch (or enlightened despot, as they were called in the eighteenth century) will tilt toward freer access and distribution of key information and may attempt to rationalize and standardize the parameters used to measure the state's health and wealth. This top-down model may be most appropriate for firms that have difficulty achieving consensus across business units.

The rapidly growing specialty manufacturer mentioned above is an example. The CEO, who felt that information flow was critical to developing a flexible organization, decreed a policy of "common information" to bring about access to consistent information by all who needed it. His appointment of czars to define and implement common information policies reflected his belief in the importance of information management issues. Currently efforts are underway to embed this decree into a set of business practices and a technical architecture. This top-down approach is an example of enlightened monarchy at its best, since the action was taken not in response to a specific crisis but as a well considered response to a broad organizational objective.

A progressive further step is a constitutional monarchy. Constitutional monarchy can evolve directly from feudalism or from the more despotic forms of monarchy. It is established by a document that states the monarch's limitations, the subjects' rights, and the law's authority. As a model for information management, this means that dominion is established over what information is collected, in what form, by whom, and for what ends. The chart of accounts becomes the realm's Magna Carta ("great charter"), a document establishing rules that will be enforced by processes and enabled by an information technology platform. A common vocabulary is developed so that the information's meaning is consistent and has integrity throughout the firm. The financial functions at both Digital and Dow Chemical are establishing constitutional monarchies for financial information, with strong support from the CEOs.

We have seen several firms in which the installation of an executive information system (EIS) was the occasion for an attempt at constitutional monarchy. The CEO is usually considered the primary user of such a system, although some attempt is usually made to solicit the information requirements of other executives. The exercise of building consensus on the system's content can help to build a constitutional monarchy. However, the effort is not always successful. At one insurance company we studied, an EIS intended for the entire senior management team was never used seriously by anyone other than the CEO. Other executives were concerned about how their units would fare under close analysis, and kept their own feudal information sources.

One drawback to any information monarchy is the simple fact of mortality. When a monarch dies or is overthrown, new governments can be imposed. Likewise, retirement or turnover of CEOs and senior executives can open the door to very different approaches to information, even in the most constitutional of monarchies. Cultures and traditions take years to solidify in an enterprise. In one high-tech manufacturing firm, the founder CEO's retirement led to information anarchy for many years; only now is the firm beginning to establish a more structured environment. The short reigns of most monarchs bodes poorly for the growth of persistent information traditions.

Federalism

The final information state, federalism, also has a number of desirable features, and in today's business environment, it is the preferred model in most circumstances. Its distinguishing feature is the use of negotiation to bring potentially competing and noncooperating parties together. Federalism most explicitly recognizes the importance of politics, without casting it in pejorative terms. In contrast, technocratic utopianism ignores politics, anarchy is politics run amok, feudalism involves destructive politics, and monarchy attempts to eliminate politics through a strong central authority. Federalism treats politics as a necessary and legitimate activity by which people with different interests work out among themselves a collective purpose and means for achieving it.

Firms that adopt or evolve into this model typically have strong central leadership and a culture that encourages cooperation and learning. However, it takes tough negotiating and a politically astute information manager to make the federalist model work. Such an information manager needs to have the CEO's support (although not too much support, or a monarchy emerges) as well as the trust and support of the "lords and barons" who run the divisions. He or she needs to understand the value of information itself as well as of the technology that stores, manipulates, and distributes it. Such skills are not widely distributed throughout organizations, even (or perhaps especially) among IS executives.

An executive who has this perspective can then use cooperative information resources to create a shared information vision. Each realm contracts with the executive and with other realms to cede some of its information assets in return for helping to create a greater whole. This is a genuine leveraging of a firm's knowledge base.

At IBM, the former head of corporate information services, Larry Ford, concluded that the firm needed to manage information in a dramatically new way. Ford and his organization produced an information strategy that focused on the value that information can bring to all of IBM. The strategy was refined and ratified by all of the senior executives, and now Ford, his staff, and the divisional IS executives have gone out into the field to negotiate with senior managers about sharing their information with others in the company. "Would you share your product quality data with the service organization? How about sales?" Eventually all the important information will be in easy-to-access "data warehouses." Information management at IBM has become very personal politics, like the ward politician campaigning door to door.

Of course, the politician has only so much time to ring doorbells. A division may have hundreds of important data elements that need to be shared. IBM is finding that the time to educate and persuade information owners of their responsibilities is the biggest constraint to implementing a federalist model. Ford's departure from IBM to head a software firm may also place the federalist initiative at risk.

MANAGING INFORMATION POLITICS

Given these options for building an information policy, how do firms begin to effectively manage information? The first step is to select the preferred information mode, as discussed in the next section. Following that, we present other principles of politically astute information management, including matching information politics to organizational culture, practicing technological realism, electing the right information politicians, and avoiding empire-building.

Select an Information State. The first step in managing information politics is figuring out which models people in the firm hold, which model currently predominates, which is most desirable, and how to achieve it. As we have noted, adopting multiple models will needlessly consume scarce resources and will confuse both information managers and users. Therefore, a firm should choose one model and move continually toward it, however long it takes.

We believe that there are only two viable choices among the five models: monarchy and federalism. In a business culture that celebrates empowerment and widespread participation, federalism is preferable, but it is harder to achieve and takes more time. Federalism requires managers to negotiate with each other in good faith while avoiding the temptation to use and withhold information destructively. Most firms we know of profess a desire to move toward a federalist model. But a firm that has difficulty getting consensus from its management team on other issues may find that federalism is impossible; a benevolent monarchy may be almost as effective and easier to implement.

Table 3 summarizes our assessments of the five political models along four dimensions: (1) commonality of vocabulary and meaning; (2) degree of access to important information; (3) quality of information — that is, its currency, relevance, and accuracy; and (4) efficiency of information management. These dimensions can be useful for evaluating a firm's current model and its effectiveness.

Commonality refers to having a set of terms, categories, and data elements that carry the same meaning throughout the enterprise. The desirability of common discourse may appear obvious, but in our experience it does not exist in many large firms. Even the definition of what a "sale" is can be variously interpreted by different divisions, to say nothing of more ambiguous terms such as "quality," "performance," and "improvement."[11]

The degree of information access is another good indicator of political culture. Many firms proclaim that all employees should have the information they need to do their work well. However, in making the choices about who actually needs what information, firms are making political decisions, whether or not they acknowledge it. The technocratic utopians focus less on what information is accessed by whom and more on the mechanisms of distribution.

In many ways the quality of information is the most important of these indicators. Information quality is achieved through detailed attention to its integrity, accuracy, currency, interpretability, and

Table 3. Ranking Alternative Models of Information Politics

	Federalism	Monarchy	Technocratic Utopianism	Anarchy	Feudalism
Commonality of Vocabulary	5	5	3	1	1
Access to Information	5	2	3	4	1
Quality of Information	3	2	1	2	2
Efficiency of Information Management	3	5	3	1	3
Total	16	14	10	8	7

Key   5=high   3=moderate   1=low

overall value. As with other types of products, the quality of information is best judged by its customers. Even companies that declare themselves as firmly in the Information Age, however, rarely have measures or assessments of their information's quality.

Efficiency is often the objective of technologists who wish to minimize redundant data storage. The incredible improvements in price-performance ratios for data storage technologies have reduced this issue's importance somewhat. However, there is still the human factor. Multiple measures of the same item take time to analyze and synthesize. Effective management requires focusing on a few key performance indicators. Computers and disk drives may be able to handle information overload, but people still suffer from it.

Federalism has the potential to be effective on all four dimensions of information management. A common vocabulary emerges through negotiations between levels and units. This makes possible the widespread access and distribution of meaningful information, which is then used for the benefit of the whole enterprise. Federalism strikes a balance between the unintegrated independence of the feudal baronies and the undifferentiated units under monarchy. Although satisfying all constituencies may require gathering more information than is absolutely necessary (hence decreasing efficiency), and the necessary compromises may reduce quality, federalism scores higher in the minds of the managers we interviewed than any other model.

Because federalism explicitly acknowledges the important positive role that information politics can play, it is apt to be the most effective model for companies that rely on individual initiative for generating collective action. This is most likely to be the case for companies operating in complex and rapidly changing competitive environments, which create a high level of uncertainty. The federalist approach supports both autonomy and coordination. Accomplishing it, of course, requires negotiating skills and the willingness of managers to take the time to negotiate. Not all companies have executives with the ability or the commitment to do this. The temptation always exists to look to a strong monarch to resolve the endless negotiations by fiat, to fall prey once more to the alluring utopian vision painted by the technologists, to fall back into a nasty and brutish condition of feudal conflict, or to dissolve into the chaos of anarchy. Firms may want to pursue alternative models, in case feudalism fails. In fact, as Table 2 shows, many of the firms pursuing federalism were also pursuing other models, either consciously or implicitly as a backup strategy. Sooner or later it is obviously best to settle on one model, though most firms find this difficult.

An information monarchy solves some of the problems of managing information throughout the enterprise. A strong, top-down approach ensures that a common language — in both vocabulary and meaning — underlies the information generated. Little unnecessary information is collected or distributed, guaranteeing a high level of efficiency. The monarch and his or her ministers mandate and oversee the right processes to generate the right information to be used in the right way — all enhancing information quality, at least as they perceive it. These advantages, however, are often gained at the expense of information access. It is the rare monarch who has enough democratic ideals to make information as broadly available as in a federalist state.

Technocratic utopianism focuses on using information technology to dramatically improve data distribution. Efficiency is high, at least in terms of a lack of data redundancy. Information access is also relatively high, at least for technologically oriented users. Because technocratic utopians do not concern themselves with the processes that produce information, the quality of information remains low. Further, the quality of information usage is inhibited by technocratic efforts such as complex data modeling that are often not understood or appreciated by line managers. As a result, the information produced by computer systems and the information actually used to manage the company are decoupled. Although this model scores high in principle, many of these initiatives fail. Commonality, access, and efficiency in a failed utopian scheme may actually be as low as in feudalism or even lower.

Although few executives would consciously adopt anarchy, it is not the lowest-scoring model. Commonality and efficiency are the lowest possible, of course, but at least individuals have easy access to the data they need. The customer controls information, thus its quality is likely to be high — unless the customer is an executive trying to take an organizationwide perspective.

Feudalism is the least effective political model along these dimensions. The existence of strong, independent, and often warring fiefdoms prevents the development of a common vocabulary and shared meaning. The feudal lords restrict access to and distribution of information under their authority. Feudalism gets only middling marks for quality; it may be high for individual divisions, but it is low from the corporate perspective. Finally, because some information is duplicated around the organization, efficiency is also only moderate. Feudalism is the least desirable yet the most common state in the organizations we researched; when more difficult and effective models fail, it is easy to fall back into the feudal state.

The key in managing information politics is to know which political model is currently in ascendance within the firm and to which the organization should be moving. Most firms we know of profess a desire to move toward a federalist model, while currently operating in a feudal or technocratic utopian environment. But a firm that has difficulty getting consensus from its management team on other issues may find that information federalism is impossible; a benevolent monarchy may be almost as effective.

Match Information Politics to Your Organizational Culture. It is no accident that democracy emerged in eighteenth-century America, a sprawling continent with vast resources and an ethic of independence and self-sufficiency. Similarly, a firm's culture must be conducive to participative information management and free information flow before they will happen. Put another way, information flow does not make an organizational culture less hierarchical and more open; rather, democratic cultures make possible democratic information flows. When faxes were flying to and from pre-Tiananmen China, some observers argued that the free flow of information was leading to a more open society; now that the faxes and those who faxed them are silent, we know that the causal relationship was in the other direction.

Information policies, we have found, are among the last things to change in an organization changing its culture. We have never seen increased information flow leading to elimination of a management layer or a greater willingness to share information. When these latter changes happen, they happen for reasons unrelated to information: restructurings, tighter cost control, external events (e.g., the 1970s' oil shocks or the current banking crisis), and so forth. Several companies, however, state that their new organization could not have survived without new information policies. Phillips Petroleum, for example, radically reduced its management ranks after a raider-forced restructuring. A new information policy was the key to its functioning.[12]

We observed this relationship between organizational culture and information politics in two computer companies. One firm was a fast-growing personal computer (PC) manufacturer when we studied it; since then, its growth has slackened. The other firm was a large manufacturer of several types of computers that was experiencing financial problems when we visited it. Their cultures seemed similar at first glance; they both had tried to develop cultures in which information was shared freely throughout their organizations with little regard to level or function. However, two key aspects of their cultures — their organizational structures and their relative financial success — had led to radically different information politics.

The PC firm had a traditional functional structure. According to the executives and employees we interviewed, information flowed relatively freely in the company. The firm had an explicit ethic of open communications, stressing early notification of problems and a "don't shoot the messenger" response. As a key U.S. executive stated, "Someone in international can request any piece of data and ask us to explain it. Allowing others access to information requires a lot of trust, but that trust seems to exist here." However, the firm is beginning to face more difficult competitive conditions, as PCs increasingly become commoditized. In more difficult times, with new management, the open information environment may not persist.

The other firm had a "networked" organization, with ad hoc teams assembling to address specific tasks. This structure, which made the firm flexible and responsive, also seemed to hinder the flow of important information. Several managers we interviewed reported that hoarding of valuable information was common. The ad hoc teams often resisted sharing their unique information. The managers we interviewed speculated that this was because a team that shares its information fully may lose its reason to exist. This is particularly true during the economically difficult times now facing the company. If an organizational structure is defined by information nodes, then those who freely surrender information may lose their place in the structure. Put more broadly, in the information-based organization, information becomes the primary medium of value and exchange, and who would give it away for free?

How do you know when your culture is right for more democratic information politics? There are a number of indicators. We have noticed, for example, that companies that successfully implement quality programs have to deal with many of the same issues affecting information flow. They have to empower front-line workers to make decisions, work cross-functionally to improve processes, and remove as much as possible the use of fear as a motivator. Similarly, companies highly attuned to customer satisfaction must be able to deal with negative results in a positive fashion — a trait highly necessary in an information democracy.

Not surprisingly, in an era of mergers, acquisitions, and global management, most large organizations have multiple political cultures. A newly acquired firm may resist adopting the information-sharing norms of its acquirer (or even, as seen in *Barbarians at the Gate*, of its potential acquirers attempting to perform due diligence).[13] Poorly performing divisions will rarely be as enthusiastic about new information reporting initiatives as long-term strong performers. And geographic differences affecting the willingness to share information are legendary; how many times has it been uttered, "We're having problems getting data from our French subsidiary."

Practice Technological Realism. Although technology will not lead us to an information utopia, there are still important technological factors to consider. Information engineering should be highly focused, information should be in units that managers can understand and negotiate with, and technology platforms should be as common as possible.

Previously we pointed out the folly of trying to engineer an organization's entire information inventory. We (and other researchers) believe that focused, less ambitious information management objectives are more likely to succeed, given that the volume of information in corporations is too great to be rigorously categorized and engineered.[14] This is particularly true in a federalist environment, in which each key information element will require substantial negotiations. Information management efforts must be directed at only those information elements that are essential to implementing strategy and to running the business day to day. At IBM, for example, the firm's internal information strategy focuses primarily on customer and market information and secondarily on process quality information.[15] Although this approach includes a great deal of data, it also excludes a considerable amount.

It is also important to acknowledge that not all information will be managed through technological means, just as most of the water around us does not run through our water meters. Only about 5 percent to 10 percent of the information in most firms is in electronic form. According to a recent study of information use by managers, even computer-based data are often preceded by word-of-mouth renditions of the same information.[16] The verbal and visual information that informs all of us is not totally unmanageable, but it cannot be modeled and categorized through technological means.

Companies may also find it useful in negotiating on information to use a larger unit of information than the data element. Most managers do not think in such narrow terms: as one executive said, "Don't give me all the molecules; tell me the key compounds they can form." A more relevant unit of information may be the document — form, report, or memo. Technologists must concern themselves with the data elements that appear on documents, but managers will normally be happy not to delve below the document level in developing a common information language. Xerox, having designated itself "The Document Company," is beginning to explore how business processes can be supported through documents.[17]

A key aspect of making information more widely available, ineffective technocratic utopias to the contrary, is the nature of the information technology platform. Specifically, technology for widespread information use must be common, easily used, and interconnectable.[18] Technological realists recognize that their computers may not be best for all applications, but they meet the basic needs. Common, standardized technology is essential if the same information is to be presented in the same way all around the company. Aetna Life & Casualty, American Airlines, Du Pont, IBM, and a large consumer products firm are all initiating efforts to build and operate a common platform for information distribution. This may seem obvious, but few companies can send a piece of data to all their workstations without considerable machinations to address different products, protocols, and other technical particulars. These companies are discovering that the same federalist approach required for achieving consensus on information meaning is also required to achieve consensus on a standard technology platform.[19]

Elect the Right Information Politicians. Along with having a suitable political culture and technology environment, companies desiring to change their information politics must elect (or otherwise get into office) the right information politicians. We find that the information politician role — not the owner of information but the manager with primary responsibility for facilitating its effective use — is still up for grabs in many companies, despite some pretenders to the throne. In one fast-growing software company, for example, problems with information flow were widespread, but no one below the CEO took any ownership of the problem.[20] One would assume that CIOs would own this domain, but until now they have not necessarily been the best choice.

Until recently, most CIOs were selected for technical acumen rather than political skills. Few would have embarked on initiatives to improve the way information — not just information technology — is used and managed. Only a few IS function heads have the political clout to persuade powerful barons to share their information for the good of the entire kingdom. Still, this is changing. At companies such as IBM, Xerox, Kodak, and Merrill Lynch, recent CIOs have been fast-track executives with records of managing important nontechnology aspects of the business. If these nontechnical managers can master the considerable technical challenges in creating an information infrastructure, they will likely have the skills and influence to bring about a political environment in which the information can be shared and used.

The CFO is another candidate for information politician. Most CFOs, however, are solely associated with financial information. In order to take on broader responsibility for information management, they must at a minimum convince operational executives of their ability to understand and manage operational performance information. We have found a few CFOs with the sincere desire to do this but have seen no examples of a CFO becoming a successful information politician.

The CEO is perhaps best positioned to lobby for a particular information environment; indeed, in an information monarchy, the CEO is the only politician who counts. In more democratic environments, such as federalism, the CEO must appreciate the importance of information and communicate it throughout the firm. The time demands of day-to-day information negotiation may require that the CEO delegate political authority to other managers.

Like real politicians, information politicians must be good at both charismatics and organization. They must be able to persuade both individuals and the masses of the importance of information management and the correctness of the chosen political model. They must also organize collections of "advance agents" and "ward heelers" to work every day at building coalitions, influencing opinion leaders, and swaying recalcitrant members of the electorate.

Avoid Building Information Empires. Because information is such a powerful tool, federalist organizations will inherently resist or distrust managers who try to build an empire by controlling information. Concentration of all responsibility for collecting, maintaining, and interpreting information in one person, regardless of position, is too much power in any organization with democratic leanings. In fact, the concept of information ownership is antithetical to federalist information management. Rather, companies should institute the concept of information stewardship — responsibility for ensuring data quality — with ownership by the corporation at large. Stewardship of information, again perhaps at the document level rather than for individual data elements, should be assigned widely throughout the organization.

The IS organization should be particularly careful to avoid building an information empire. It may already wield considerable power by virtue of its technical custody of information. We have observed organizations that cede control over information to this "independent" third party, assuming that it will not use information for political gain. But the IS function may have its own interests to advance, its own kingdom to build.

For example, at a major direct marketing firm, nontechnical executives were intimidated by technology, and control over the firm's sixty-million-name database was ceded to IS. As a result, access to the database had to be on terms acceptable to IS. This often meant denial and delay to managers wishing to exploit the database for valid business purposes. IS built a proprietary database management system, further reinforcing the walls around the database. When the CEO himself was denied a report, the IS head was deposed and replaced by a trusted nontechnical associate of the CEO. Yet because he could not understand the technology, he could not dismantle the walls around the data. A new IS vice president was brought in from outside the company with an explicit mandate to open up the empire.

CONCLUSION

Explicitly recognizing the politics of information and managing them constructively is a difficult, complex, and time-consuming task. It will not happen by itself, nor will the problem go away. Effectively managing information politics requires a shift in organizational culture; new technology and even new executives alone are not enough to make this happen. Information management must become something that all managers care about and most managers participate in. They must view information as important to their success and be willing to spend time and energy negotiating to meet their information needs. As in real democracies, democratic information models like federalism require informed participation of all organizational citizens.

Unless the politics of information are identified and managed, companies will not move into the Information Age. Information will not be shared freely nor used effectively by decision makers. No amount of data modeling, no number of relational databases, and no invocation of "the information-based organization" will bring about a new political order of information. Rather, it will take what politics always take: negotiation, influence-exercising, back-room deals, coalition-building, and occasionally even war. If information is truly to become the most valued commodity in the businesses of the future, we cannot expect to acquire it without an occasional struggle.

NOTES

1. March, J. G. 1988. *Decisions and Organizations*. Cambridge, MA: Basil Blackwell.
2. For example: Scott Morton, M. S. 1991. *The Corporation of the 1900s: Information Technology and Organizational Transformation.* New York: Oxford University Press. Keen, P. G. W. 1991. *Shaping the Future: Business Design Through Information Technology.* Boston, MA: Harvard Business School Press. Vincent, D. R. 1990. *The Information-Based Corporation: Stakeholder Economics and the Technology Investment.* Homewood, IL: Dow Jones-Irwin.

3. Thorbeck, J. 1991. The turnaround value of values. *Harvard Business Review* (Jan/Feb): 52-62.
4. Pfeffer, J. 1986. *Power in Organizations.* New York: Harper Business.
5. See articles in McGowan, W. G., ed. 1991. *Revolution in Real-Time: Managing Information Technology in the 1900s.* Boston, MA: Harvard Business School Press. A notable example to the apolitical perspective is found in Markus, M. L. 1983. Power, politics, and MIS implementation. *Communications of the ACM* 26(6): 434-444.
6. March, J. G. The business firm as a political coalition. In *Decisions and Organizations.* Cambridge, MA: Basil Blackwell.
7. A term similar to "technocratic utopianism" has been defined, without reference to information management, by Howard P. Segal. See: Segal, H. P. 1985. *Technological Utopianism in American Culture.* Chicago: University of Chicago Press.
8. See Caro, R. A. 1975. *The Power Broker: Robert Moses and the Fall of New York.* New York: Random House; and *Chinatown,* the film.
9. See Goodhue, D. L., L. Kirsch, J. A. Quillard, and M. Wybo. 1990. Strategic Data Planning: Lessons from the Field. Working paper No. 215, October 1990, MIT Sloan School of Management, Center for Information Systems Research; and Goodhue, D. L., J. A. Quillard, and J. F. Rockart. 1988. Managing the data resource: A contingency perspective. *MIS Quaterly* (September): 373-392.
10. Some interesting examples of feudalism, again largely outside the information management context, are described in: Pfeffer, J. 1991. *Managing With Power.* Boston, MA: Harvard Business School.
11. Some of the reasons for these discrepancies are described in: McKinnon, S. M., and W. J. Bruns, Jr. 1992. *The Information Mosaic.* Boston, MA: Harvard Business School Press.
12. Applegate, L. M., and C. S. Osborn. 1988. *Philips 66 Company: Executive Information System.* Boston, MA: Harvard Business School.
13. Burrough, B., and J. Helyar. 1990. *Barbarians at the Gate.* New York: Harper & Row.
14. See Goodhue et al. (1988) and Goodhue et al. (1990).
15. Using Information Strategically: A Road Map for the 90s. Information and Telecommunications Systems, IBM Corporation, November 15, 1990.
16. McKinnon and Bruns (1992).
17. See the proceedings volume from the Xerox Document Symposium, March 10-11, 1992. Xerox Corporation, Stanford, Connecticut.
18. Sproull, L., and S. Kiesler. 1991. *Connections: New Ways of Working in the Networked Organization.* Cambridge, MA: MIT Press.
19. See Linder, J., and D. Stoddard. 1986. *Aetna Life & Casualty: Corporate Technology Planning.* 9-187-037. Boston, MA: Harvard Business School.
20. Gladstone, J., and N. Nohria. 1991. *Symantec.* N9-491-010 Revised February 4, 1991. Boston, MA: Harvard Business School.

Additional Readings
Part IV: Strategies
for Managing Information

Brumm, E.K. 1990. Chief information officers in service and industrial organizations. *Information Management Review* 5(3): 31-45.

Coombs, R.E., and J.D. Moorhead. 1992. *The Competitive Intelligence Handbook*. Metuchen, NJ: Scarecrow Press.

Cronin, B. 1992. Intelligence management systems for intelligent corporations. In *The Intelligent Corporation*, eds. J. Sigurdson, and Y. Tagerud, 143-159. London: Taylor Graham.

Cronin, B. 1992. What is social about social intelligence? In *From Information Management to Social Intelligence*, eds. B. Cronin and N. Tudor-Silovic, 103-110. London: Aslib.

Cronin, B., ed. 1992. *Information Management: From Strategies to Action*, vol. 2. London: Aslib.

Cronin, B., ed. 1986. *Information Management: From Strategies to Action*, vol. 1. London: Aslib.

Cronin, B., and E. Davenport. 1991. *Elements of Information Management*. Metuchen, NJ: Scarecrow Press.

Cropley, J. 1992. The practice of intelligence: Adding value. *The Intelligent Enterprise* 1(1): 25.

Davenport, T. 1992. *Process Innovation: Reengineering Work Through Information Technology*. Boston: Harvard Business School Press.

Hammer, M., and J. Champy. 1993. *Reengineering the Corporation*. New York: Harper Business.

Hamrefors, S. 1992. Practical implementation of business intelligence services in business organizations. In *The Intelligent Corporation*, eds. J. Sigurdson and Y. Tagerud, 115-129. London: Taylor Graham.

Horton, Jr., F.W., and C.W. Burke. 1988. *InfoMap: A Complete Guide to Discovering Corporate Information Resources*. New York: Prentice Hall.

Keyes, J. 1993. *Infotrends: The Competitive Use of Information*. New York: McGraw-Hill.

Lagerstam, Catharina. 1990. The theory of business intelligence: The intelligence process. In *The Knowledge Industries*, eds. B. Cronin and N. Tudor-Silovic, 59-68. London: Aslib.

Marchand, D. 1985. Information management: Strategies and tools in transition. *Information Management Review* 1(1): 27-34.

Marchand, D., and F.W. Horton, Jr. 1986. *Infotrends: Profiting from Your Information Resources.* New York: John Wiley & Sons.

Martin, J.S. 1992. Building an information resource center for competitive intelligence. *Online Review* 16(6): 379-389.

McGee, J., and L. Prusak. 1993. *Managing Information Strategically.* New York: John Wiley & Sons.

McKinnon, S.J., and W.J. Bruns. 1992. *The Information Mosaic.* Boston: Harvard Business School Press.

Meyer, H.E. 1991. *Real-World Intelligence: Organized Information for Executives.* 2nd ed. New York: Grove Weidenfeld.

Porter, M. 1985. *Competitive Advantage: Creating and Sustaining Performance.* New York: Free Press.

Porter, M. 1980. *Competitive Strategy: Techniques for Analyzing Industries and Competitors.* New York: Free Press.

Roszak, T. 1994. *The Cult of Information.* 2nd ed. Berkeley, CA: University of California Press.

Rowley, J. 1992. Current awareness or competitive intelligence: A review of the options. *Aslib Proceedings* 44(11/12): 367-372.

Schwartz, P. 1991. *The Art of the Long View: Planning for the Future in an Uncertain World.* New York: Doubleday.

Synnott, W.R. 1987. The emerging chief information officer. *Information Management Review* 3(1): 21-36.

Taylor, R. 1986. *Value-Added Processes in Information Systems.* Norwood, NJ: Ablex Publishing Corporation.

V
Assessing the Value
of Information

V
Assessing the Value of Information

INTRODUCTION

The problem of establishing the value of information has confounded economists and information scientists for many years. On the one hand, definitions of value have proved elusive as scholars have sought to differentiate among such varied concepts as apparent value, consequential value, exchange value, dollar value, social value, and use value. On the other, definitions of information have been equally problematic as theorists have grappled with separating information message or content from information process or delivery and both of these from information context or use. They have had to cope with the consequences of interpreting information as a resource but one with special attributes that prevent it from conforming to the accepted norms of economic behavior. As the study of the creation, control, flow, dissemination, and use of information has evolved and matured, sophisticated models and frameworks have been developed to explain some of these complexities.

In his article, Michael Koenig analyzes literature that deals with assessing the value of information from three different perspectives. The first uses quantitative techniques such as cost-benefit analysis to calculate the cost of providing information relative to the benefits or value derived from it. While the magnitudes of the effects tend to vary across studies, the findings are consistent in demonstrating that investment in information services generates handsome returns. The second set of literature examines the information environment of productive organizations. Regardless of whether the studies undertaken were in library and information science, management, economics, or sociology, they all confirm that the more productive and innovative organizations are characterized by the free flow of information into, out of, and within the company, and the high priority given to information access by senior managers. The third and concluding view presented concerns the characteristics of productive information workers. Here, too, findings across studies are consistent in showing that more productive individuals have greater access to and make more use of information. Koenig's review provides some comfort to those seeking to promote and garner support for their information services.

Gaining such support from senior decision makers is critical for the survival of information services and systems. As budgets shrink and costs undergo closer scrutiny, it becomes imperative for information managers to be able to demonstrate the value of their processes, products, services, and systems to senior managers in terms that are meaningful to them. The two remaining articles present techniques and evidence that can be used to convince decision makers that the benefits resulting from the information center of the organization substantially outweigh the costs of maintaining it. It stands to reason that before providing information, staff must first determine the types of information managers need and value most. Perceptions about the value and benefit sought from information services may differ between users and providers. To determine the priorities of organizational users, Marianne Broadbent describes the use of an instrument called Priority and Performance Evaluation (PAPE). The input from PAPE facilitated development of a set of information service options which could be ranked and used to assess the performance of the service on those factors which respondents identified as being most meaningful to them. Once critical products and services have been identified, the financial costs of provision need to be determined. Broadbent demonstrates the application of cost-benefit analysis to a current awareness service to help choose between several different modes of providing service.

Readers who require empirical evidence to support their claims regarding the value of information and information centers to senior managers will find it in the work of Jose-Marie Griffiths and Donald W. King. These researchers are arguably the most experienced consultants and prolific writers in the area of evaluation of information and information centers. In the course of nearly 300 projects carried out over the past 20 years, they have devised, tested, and refined measures, models, and methods to assess the performance, effectiveness, cost and benefit of information provision in public and private sector organizations. Typically, they show that professionals spend a substantial amount of time acquiring, reading, and using information. They calculate the costs in dollar savings, timeliness, quality, and productivity that would be incurred if the services of a corporate information center were not available. Their findings across organizations and professional groups such as engineers, scientists, lawyers, and administrators are remarkably consistent and impressive. They provide persuasive data to convince even hardened skeptics of the value of information.

Many consultants, scholars, and researchers have taken up the challenge to assess the value of information. The Additional Readings list some of the more notable efforts.

The Importance
of Information Services
for Productivity
"Under-recognized"
and Under-invested

Michael Koenig

INTRODUCTION

There is a significant amount of work addressing the relationship of
library and information services to the productivity of the organizations they support. The impact of that work has been very modest,
however. One reason for the lack of impact is that the work is very
scattered, and has appeared, as a glance at the list of references to
this article will indicate, in relatively obscure places. Much of the work
has appeared in technical reports little noticed by the business and
professional community, and a good chunk of it—some of the best—
has appeared in proprietary consulting reports which are not in the
public domain at all. The most thorough review of this literature is
a recent chapter in *Annual Review of Information Science and Technology* by Koenig (1990); a previous chapter in 1982 by Griffiths on
the "Value of Information and Related Systems, Products, and Services," though now slightly dated, is also very relevant.

There are also three other reviews of interest. Two, by Bearman
et al., (1986) and by Cronin and Gudim (1986), discuss the importance
of the problem, but do not discuss specific results; one by Bawden

Reprinted from *Special Libraries*, v. 83, no. 4 (Fall 1992), pp. 199-210, © by Special Libraries Association.

(1986) looks specifically at the topic of information systems and creativity, and pulls together a very disparate literature.

STUDIES ATTEMPTING TO CALCULATE THE VALUE OF INFORMATION SERVICES

One way of looking at the relationship of information services and productivity is to attempt to derive a value for the information services.

What is perhaps the seminal work on attempting to value and evaluate the effect of providing information services was conducted by Margaret Graham and her colleagues at the Exxon Research Center in the mid-1970s. Not atypical for work in this field, it appeared first in an internal technical report, but was fortunately picked up by Eugene Jackson for his *Special Librarianship, A New Reader* (1980). However, the fact that it never appeared in the sort of venue, the journal literature, where one would expect to see important new findings, was a major missed opportunity.

The findings were new and dramatic. The study built on previous research in user studies but was novel in its attempt to extrapolate and quantify the effect the services provided. The study participants (Exxon researchers) logged information-impacted events on 20 randomly selected days. The participants reported that 62% of those events were beneficial, and in 2% of the cases they were able to estimate the value of the benefit quantitatively. By extrapolating from only that 2%, and assigning no value to the remaining 60% of the impacts that were beneficial but not quantifiable, and subtracting the cost of the researcher's time spent in gathering information from the benefits, the authors concluded that the observable benefits were 11 times greater than the cost of providing external literature information services to the Exxon research community. One can conclude this is a lower bound for the benefits, based as it is on only a small percentage of the beneficial outcomes.

A much larger study, using similar techniques, was conducted in the late 1970s on NASA's information services. This study was conducted on a much broader scale than the one at Exxon. A stratified sampling procedure was used to elucidate data about the use and impact of seven different NASA information products and services. Respondents were asked three basic questions: 1) what was the nature of the consequent utility (termed ''application mode'') of the use of the information source? (Responses to question 1 were classified as: 0—not relevant or no application; 1—information use only; 2—improved products or processes; 3—new products or processes.); 2) (if the response was application mode 2 or 3) what were the estimated benefits likely to be achieved or costs to be saved?; and 3) what was the probability of accomplishing those benefits or cost savings? For each of the seven services the study reports: the probability for "application modes" 2 and 3, the unit cost (to NASA) for the information transaction, the cost to the user. and the expected net benefit (likely benefit X probability) per transaction.

Unfortunately, the study did not aggregate the data and failed to draw the salient conclusions that could and should have been drawn. Working from the published data, the aggregate data can be extrapolated as follows: The cost to NASA of providing the information service over the five-year period 1971-1976 was $14.3 million ($2.9 million per year) and the expected benefit was $191 million ($28 million per year), while the time expended by the user was valued at $82 million ($16.5 million per year). The ratio between expected benefits and NASA costs is 13:1. The author, Mogavero (1979), recommends that the user cost be subtracted from the expected benefit in calculating a cost-benefit ratio (the same technique as that used in the Exxon study). Thus,

$$\text{Cost-Benefit Ratio} = \frac{\text{Gross Estimated Benefit - Gross User Cost}}{\text{NASA Production Cost}}$$

Calculated this way, the cost-benefit ratio is 7.6 to 1.

While not quite so dramatic as the Exxon results, this result is still compelling. Note that the methodology which asks for both the anticipated benefit and the likelihood of achieving that benefit (in effect a deflator index), is a cautious and conservative one.

One can argue that the formula used is not the appropriate one, that from the organization's perspective, the salient ratio is that between benefit and cost (benefit foregone). (See the article by Bickner (1983) for further discussion of this point). That is, from the organization's perspective, the formula should be:

$$\text{Cost-Benefit Ratio} = \frac{\text{Gross Estimated Benefit}}{\text{NASA Production Cost + Gross User Cost}}$$

which yields:

$$\frac{\$191 \text{ million}}{\$14.3 \text{ million} + \$82 \text{ million}} \qquad \text{or } 1.98$$

as the ratio (effectively two to one) of benefit to cost. Note the very dramatic internal ratio of user expended cost of accessing information to the cost of providing information services, a ratio of almost 6 to 1. This implies that there is substantial opportunity for systems or service enhancements that diminish user costs and thereby enhance the cost benefit ratio. It also points out that the nominal cost of providing information services is only the tip of the iceberg. In this case, for every dollar expended in providing information services, another six dollars are spent by the user in using those services.

Using a related methodology Mason & Sassone (1978), also in the late 1970s, analyzed the operations of an information analysis center (IAC). In this technique the investigators, working with the users, tried to estimate only the employee's time saved and then assigned value by calculating the burdened salary cost of the employee's time. This technique was applied to an unidentified IAC, and the net present value of the time saved exceeded the net present value of the invested resources and operating cost by 4%.

The costing techniques are more rigorous and sophisticated than most because the present value of invested resources is included as well as operating costs. Mason and Sassone call this technique a "lower bound cost benefit" because the calculations are based solely on the user's time and costs, and no attempt is made to estimate either any larger benefits to the organization or any societal benefits. If the transaction saves $500 of the researcher's time compared with getting the information in some other fashion, but also results in $50,000 worth of benefits or savings, then the utility of the transaction is calculated as merely $500, not $50,000. Even with such stringent limitations, looking only at the cost of alternative processes for gathering information, not at the benefit provided by the information, the center shows a positive net present value.

Valuation methodologies of this general type have been most fully developed and most widely applied by King Research, Inc. (Griffiths and King 1990, 1988, 1985; King et al. 1984, 1982, 1981; Roderer et al. 1983; King and Roderer 1978; Griffiths 1978). Some of the studies involve government agencies and the reports are to some degree in the public domain and thus accessible though generally obscure; the bulk have been done for private corporations, are proprietary, and are accessible if at all only via personal contacts. Thus their work, though very important, is generally little known, particularly to the general business community outside of professional information circles.

First, the methodology (Griffiths and King 1990, 1988; King and Roderer 1978) analyzes the value of the information services to the organization in terms of the value of the time (as measured by salary and overhead) that the users are willing to expend on those services. This is taken as an indication of the organization's willingness to pay for the services. With this methodology the cost to the user, as indicated by time the user spends in accessing information, is treated as an indicator of implicit value rather than as a debit to savings or value achieved as in the three studies above. To be sure, such a measure is an indicator of the motivation to seek information, but as King points out (King et al. 1981), it seems to be fairly constant across organizations and therefore not likely to be very sensitive to the quality of service provided. In five different organizations studied, the following ratios were reported:

Ratios of Willingness to Pay (measured in terms of user professionals' time) to Nominal Cost of Providing Information Services:

Institution	Ratio
Major Diversified Chemicals Company (Griffiths 1987)	2.5 to 1
Major Diversified Chemicals Company B (Griffiths & King 1990)	4.3 to 1
Major Electronics and Communications Company (King et al.)	4.4 to 1
Major Public Utility (Griffiths & King 1988)	19 to 1
U.S. Department of Energy (King et al. 1982)	26 to 1

The spread of ratios is very wide, an order of magnitude in fact, but in all cases the value of the service as measured by the time users were willing to spend using it was very substantial. If, as King points out, the time information workers spend seeking information is relatively constant across different organizations, then the numbers above may also serve as an indicator of the intensity of the information services provided, the lower the ratio the more intense the information services provided. Note that Poppel (1982) in his study of managers in business organizations reports a very similar (21% as opposed to 25%) proportion of time spent in information seeking.

Second, value is attached to the information services by calculating the additional cost that would be incurred if there were no in-house information service and the documents had to be obtained elsewhere. The values calculated for this approach were:

Ratios of Cost to Use Alternative Services to the Nominal Cost of Providing Information Services:

Institutions	Ratio
Major Diversified Chemicals Company A (Griffiths 1987)	2.6 to 1
Major Diversified Chemicals Company B (Griffiths & King 1990)	2.7 to 1
Major Electronics and Communications Company (King et al.)	3.6 to 1
Major Public Utility (Griffiths & King 1988)	8 to 1

Again, the ratios are all highly favorable.

Thirdly, based on the observations that professionals tend to spend a relatively fixed proportion of their time seeking information and reading (a homeostatic function?), the methodology calculates the number of readings that would have to be foregone by the requirement to spend more time seeking information if no inhouse information service were available. From this figure one can derive a value of the savings (or research cost avoidance) that would be lost or incurred if the library or information center did not exist. Knowledge workers surveyed at each institution estimate the savings (or benefit) achieved by reading. However, these estimates are applied only to the transactions foregone, not to all transactions.

The intermediary results from a number of studies are summarized by Griffiths and King (1990) as:

Proportion of readings at which various levels of savings (benefit) are reported to be achieved:

Savings($)	Proportion(%)
0	73.9
1-11	12.5
11-100	3.9
101-1,000	4.2
1,001-10,000	3.4
>10,000	2.1

Calculated over the various studies, Griffiths & King (1988) report the following data for the value of reading an item:

$385	for reading a journal article
$1,160	for reading a book
$706	for reading an internal technical document

The value calculated at specific institutions for this approach were:

Ratios of Research Cost Avoidance to the Nominal Cost of Providing Information Services:

Institutions	Ratio
Major Diversified Chemicals Company A (Griffiths 1987)	4.8 to 1
Major Diversified Chemicals Company B (Griffiths & King 1990)	14 to 1
Major Electronics and Communications Company (King et al.)	16 to 1
Major Public Utility (Griffiths & King 1988)	17 to 1
US Department of Energy (King et al. 1982)	25 to 1

King Research also examined the value of the Energy Data Base (EDB) of the U.S. Department of Energy (DOE) (King et al. 1984).

The apparent value—the burdened salary cost of the time spent using the database—was approximately $500 million, out of a total research budget of $5.8 billion (including principal users of the database such as contractors, not just DOE). Estimated total savings attributed to those readings were approximately $13 billion. Thus:

Generation of + Information	Information Processing and Use	Future Savings to DOE Scientists
$5.3 billion	$500 million	$13 billion

can be intepreted as an investment of $5.8 billion, yielding a return on investment of approximately 2.2 to 1.

Using the research-cost avoidancc approach discussed above, assuming that there were to be no energy databases, there would be a loss of over 300,000 searches and almost 2.5 million readings (a value equivalant to $3 billion). If the current R&D budget is $5.8 billion, then without the EDB, an R&D budget of $8.8 billion would theoretically be required to maintain the same level of output. That is equivalent to saying that the EDB increases organizational productivity by 52%.

Griffiths & King (1985) estimate that, if one extrapolates these techniques broadly, the readings by all scientists and engineers in the United States resulted in savings of about $300 billion for the year 1984 alone. They admit this figure sounds enormous, but ask what could scientists and engineers accomplish without access to information? They calculate that the actual time value that scientists and engineers spend in reading exceeds $20 billion per year, based on an average burdened salary, which is in effect a ratio of 15 to 1 for benefit to cost invested in reading.

The calculation of cost-benefit figures is a complex and disputatious exercise, of rather more subtlety than is often realized. The article by Bickner on "Concepts of Economic Cost; (1983) is an excellent analysis of the issues and of some of the fallacies to avoid. The calculation of cost benefit figures where a principal commodity is information, a commodity particularly ill addressed by conventional economies, is even more fraught with peril.

The caveat above notwithstanding, the magnitude of the effects reported in these studies is quite striking, as is the very high degree of their consistency, both across different techniques and across different cases. This creates a high degree of confidence that the findings are not mere artifacts, but that they reflect a genuine phenomenon.

ECONOMETRIC CALCULATIONS

A few attempts have been made to calculate the overall effect of information as a factor in industrial productivity. Perhaps the first of these was the use by Hayes & Erickson (Hayes and Erickson 1982) of the Cobb-Douglas production function to estimate the value added by information services. In the basic Cobb-Douglas formula, the value of goals and services sold is calculated to be the product of a constant times the values of different inputs, labor, capitol, etc., each raised to a different power (exponent). The exponents are solved for by seeing which exponents best fit a number of separate cases. In the Hayes and Erickson formulation, the value added (V) in manufacturing industries is a function of labor (L), capital (K), purchase of information services (I), and purchase of other intermediate goods and services (X), and takes the form:

$$V = AL^a K^b I^c X^d, \text{ or}$$

$$\log V = \text{Log } A + a \text{ Log } L + b \log K + c \log I + d \log X$$

(where A, a, b, c, d are constants). Braunstein (1985) developed this approach further, arguing that the standard Cobb-Douglas production function is too specific, that it inappropriately requires that the substitutability between each pair of factors be constant and equal to 1. Braunstein substitutes the "constant elasticity of substitution" (CES) and the "translog" production functions, both of which permit elasticities other than 1. The marginal product of information estimated by the Cobb-Douglas function was 2.54, with Hayes and Erickson's 1972 data, and 2.50 as calculated by Braunstein with 1980 data. The CES function yielded a marginal product of information between 2.43 and 2.92, and the translog function yielded values between 2.34 to 3.67. There is striking consistency in these results, Braunstein argues, and they indicate substantial underinvestment in the purchase of information.

Also striking is the similarity of these numbers to the 2.2 to 1 value for the return on information investment calculated by King Research, Inc., in their analysis of the value of the Energy Data Base (King and Roderer 1978), and the 1.98 to 1 reported by Mogavero in his analysis of NASA's information services (Mogavero 1978), values which were derived in an entirely independent fashion.

CHARACTERISTICS OF THE INFORMATION ENVIRONMENT IN PRODUCTIVE ORGANIZATIONS

While they do not directly address the question of value and degree of under-investment, there have been a number of studies of characteristics of productive companies. These studies shed a great deal of light on the relationship between information services and organizational productivity; a very consistent thread is the importance of information access and information services.

Orpen (1985) examined productivity in R&D intensive electronics/instrumentation organizations and analyzed the behavior of research managers as perceived by the research staff. He found that in the more productive organizations (as defined by rates of growth and return on assets) the managers were perceived to be significantly more characterized by the following three behaviors: 1) they routed literature and references to scientific and technical staff; 2) they directed their staff to use scientific and technical information (STI) and to purchase STI services; and 3) they encouraged publication of results and supported professional visits and continuing education.

Equally striking was the finding that managerial behavior not directly concerned with information, such as planning future work changes, initiating personnel changes, hiring exemplars, or altering hiring and promotion policies, did not differentiate between the "high-performance" and the "low-performance" companies. In short information-related behavior strongly tended to discriminate between "high-performance" and "low-performance" companies, while non information-related behavior did not—a distinction that, interestingly enough, Orpen did not make.

In reviewing the corpus of work on R&D innovation, Goldhar, et al. (1976) conclude that there are six characteristics of environments that are conducive to technological innovations. Of the six, four are clearly related to the information environment—specifically: 1) easy access to information by individuals; 2) free flow of information both into and out of the organizations; 3) rewards for sharing, seeking, and using "new" externally developed information sources; and 4) encouragement of mobility and interpersonal contacts. The other two characteristics are rewards for taking risks and for accepting and adapting to change These findings and their implicit prioritization (in Goldhar's ordering, 1, 2, 3, & 6, that is the top three of Goldhar's six factors are all information related factors) are striking in that except for the work of Allen (Allen 1977, 1970, 1964), who found that more productive teams and individuals had more diverse information contacts outside the project team, none of the work reviewed by Goldhar comes from the traditional areas of information science. or communications; it comes almost entirely from the literature of economics and management. And like Orpen, Goidhar fails to make much of the predominance of information related factors.

A consistent macrotheme in this literature is that of the link between productivity and diversity of information contacts. Koenig (1990, 1983a, 1983b, 1982, 1975) has studied the relationship between research productivity and the information environment, using the pharmaceutical industry as the setting. A gross measure of productivity can be calculated simply as the number of approved new drugs per research dollar expended. That output measure is refined further by weighting it in regard to: 1) whether the FDA regards the drug as an important therapeutic advance, 2) the drug's chemical novelty, and 3) the filing company's patent position with regard to the drug, and indication of where the bulk of the research was done. Research productivity, thus measured, differs greatly among large pharmaceutical companies (Koenig 1983b). In comparing the information environment of the more-productive companies with the less-productive, the former are characterized by (Koenig and Gans 1975):

- Greater openness to outside information;
- Somewhat less concern with protecting proprietary information;
- Geater information systems development effort;
- Greater end-user use of information systems and more encouragement of browsing and serendipity;
- Greater technical and subject sophistication of the information services staff; and
- Relative unobtrusiveness of managerial structure and status indicators in the R&D environment.

To the degree that data were available, there did not seem to be any significant distinction between the more versus the less productive companies in terms of the extent of resources expended on information services (as measured by the number of information center staff).

These findings (above) are a part of a larger body of literature that finds that contact with external information sources and diversity of information sources are key factors in successful innovation. Project Sappho (Scientific Activity Predictor from Patterns with Heuristic Origins) conducted by the University of Sussex (1972) deliberately studied failures as well as successes. Twenty-nine "pairs" (one success and one failure) of innovation attempts in a similar industry segment were analyzed to determine what led to success. One of the five major conclusions was that "successful innovators make more effective use of outside technology and scientific advice, even though they perform more of the work in-house. They have better contacts with the scientific community, not necessarily in general, but in the specific areas concerned."

After reviewing a number of studies on innovation, principally from the management literature, Utterback (1974, 1971) concluded, "In general, it appears that the greater the degree of communications between the firm and its environment at each stage of the process of innovation, other factors being equal, the more effective the firm will be in generating, developing, and implementing new technology" (Utterback 1971). Wolek & Griffith (1974) reviewed the sociologically-oriented literature on this topic and came to substantially the same conclusion. McConnell, writing on how to improve productivity from an operational standpoint, and reviewing the literature in a less formal fashion, remarks: "Information flow, through both formal and informal networks, should be full and free—up, down, and across the organization. This required continuous effort and attention. . . . The more open and free communication is in the organization, the greater will be productivity" (McConnell 1980).

Kanter (1983, 1982) conducted an extension survey of innovations initiated by middle managers. From her findings, she made six major recommendations for structuring organizations to support creativity. The second recommendation was: "a free and somewhat random flow of information" (Kanter 1982). She further reports that to accomplish productive changes, a manager needs "information, resources, and support" (Kanter 1982), in that order.

When examining the literature about what characterizes productive organizations, it is clear that not only does a consistent theme emerge of greater openness toward and greater access to information, both internal and external, but that information access related factors emerge in positions of very high priority in comparison to other factors under management control. Also striking, and very corroboratory in its implications is the fact that these findings are consistent whether the investigator or the literature received is from the areas of library and information science, management science and economics, or sociology.

CHARACTERISTICS OF PRODUCTIVE INFORMATION WORKERS

There is also a large body of literature on the characteristics of productive information workers, and the findings are quite consistant with and complementary to those above. King Research (Griffiths and King 1990), in evaluating information use at Oak Ridge National Laboratories has documented a significant and positive relationship between the productivity of professionals and the amount of time spent in reading. Several indicators were used to measure productivity: number of formal records (i.e., of research, of project management), number of formal publications, number of proposals or research plans, number of formal oral presentations, and number of times the professionals were consulted for advice. All of these indicators were found to be positively correlated with the amount of reading done.

Mondschein (1990) studied the productivity of researchers in several major corporations, as measured by publishing activity, vis-a-vis their use of automated current-awareness services (SDI or selective dissemination of information). He found that scientists who use SDI frequently appear to be more productive than their colleagues who either do not use such services or use them only infrequently. Further, the productive researchers were characterized by their use of a wider variety of information sources, particularly by the extent of their efforts to stay current and by their use of patent information sources.

Ginman (1988) in studying the information use of CEOs, observes a very different information style for CEOs in companies in the revival phase as compared with those in the stagnation phase. The former are more extroverted in their information use style, and have an information culture that is characterized by greater width and depth, with greater use of external information sources and greater ability to pinpoint and recall specific items of information input, such as specific authors, articles, etc.

Chakrabarti & Rubenstein (1976), in studying NASA innovations adopted by industry, conclude that quality of information as perceived by the recipient is a major factor in the adoption of innovations. This is, of course, an extension to the high-tech environment of the classic work by Rogers (1983) on innovation and change agentry (use of agents who deliberately introduce beneficial change), most of which was done in relatively low-tech situations, and is consistent with Rogers' findings.

Johnston & Gibbons (1975) examined the characteristics of information that contributed to the resolution of technical problems with some 30 ongoing innovations in British industry. They found that 1) information obtained from the literature contributed as much as information obtained from personal contact; 2) different sources were selectively used to acquire different types of information; and 3) a wide range of information sources is important.

The studies reported above are typical of the larger body of research findings. The consistent theme is that more productive individuals make greater access to and greater use of information services.

CONCLUSION

There is an extensive literature that indicates very strongly that access to information is a very critical component of the productivity of information workers and consequently the productivity of the information dependent organization employing those persons. This phenomenon is generally recognized, but its comparative importance is still "under-recognized," even ill-recognized in the very literature that reports the findings (see particularly the discussion above of the work by Orpen (1985) and Goldhar). More importantly, there is an emerging body of research findings, emerging in very scattered locations, but perhaps now approaching some critical mass in size that quite consistently indicates that information-dependent organizations under-invest in information services and that to maximize their productivity, those organizations should substantially increase their investment in information services.

The agenda before the information profession is obvious:

- We need more research on the relationship between the information environment and organizational productivity.
- We need to integrate and disseminate the increasing body of knowledge we do have on the subject.

The importance of organizational productivity and productivity enhancement is well understood and almost totally accepted; the importance of the information environment and of information services to productivity is only beginning to be understood and is very much "under-recognized." Recent work by Matarazzo (1990) documents the general lack of awareness of managers about the real contributions made by libraries and information centers. We need to change that state of affairs.

REFERENCES

Albrecht, T. L., and V. A. Ropp. 1984. Communicating about innovation in networks of three U.S. organizations. *Journal of Communication* 34(3): 78-91.

Allen, T. J. 1977. *Managing The Flow of Technology: Technology Transfer and the Dissemination of Technological Information Within the R&D Organization.* Cambridge, MA: MIT Press.

Allen, T. J. 1970. Roles in technical communications networks. In *Communication Among Scientists and Engineers,* eds. E. Carnot and D. K. Pollock. Lexington, MA: Heath Lexington Books.

Allen, T. J. 1964. *The Utilization of Information Sources during R&D*

Proposal Preparation. Cambridge, MA: MIT Press. (MIT Alfred P. Sloan School of Management working paper no. 97-64).

Bawden, D. 1986. Information systems and the stimulation of creativity. *Journal of Information Science* 12(5): 203-216.

Bearman, T. C., P. Guynup, and S. N. Milevski. 1986. Information and productivity. *Journal of the American Society for Information Science* 36(6): 369-375.

Bickner, R. E. 1983. Concepts of economic cost. In *Key Papers in the Economics of Information Systems*, eds. D.W. King, N.K. Roderer, and H.A. Olsen, 107-146. White Plains, NY: Knowledge Industry Publications for the American Society for Information Science.

Braunstein, Y. M. 1985. Information as a factor of production: Substitutability and productivity. *Information Society* 3(3): 261-273.

Chakrabarti, A. K., and A. H. Rubenstein. 1976. Interorganization transfer of technology: A study of adoption of NASA innovations. *IEEE Transactions on Engineering Management* EM-23(1): 20-34.

Cronin, B., and M. Gudim. 1986. Information and productivity: A review of research. *International Journal of Information Management* 6(2): 203-216.

Ginman, M. 1988. Information culture and business performance. *IATUL Quarterly* 2(2): 93-106.

Goldhar, J. D., L. K. Bragaw, and J. J. Schwartz. 1976. Information flows, management styles, and technological innovation. *IEEE Transactions on Engineering Management* EM-23(1): 51-61.

Griffiths, J. M. 1987. Proprietary Report, presented at a research seminar, June 1987.

Griffiths, J. M. 1982. The value of information and related systems, products and services. In *Annual Review of Information Science and Technology*, vol. 17, ed. M.E. Williams, 269-284. White Plains, New York: Knowledge Industry Publications for the American Society for Information Science.

Griffiths, J. M., and W. D. King. 1990. *A Manual on the Evaluation of Information Centers and Services.* Oak Ridge, TN: King Research.

Griffiths, J. M., and W. D. King. 1988. *An Information Audit of Public Service Electric and Gas Company Libraries and Information Resources: Executive Summary and Conclusions.* Rockville, MD: King Research.

Griffiths, J. M., and W. D. King. 1985. *The Contribution Libraries Make to Organizational Productivity.* Rockville, MD: King Research. OCLC:16389522. Available by permission from King Research, PO Box 572, Oak Ridge, TN 37831.

Hayes, R. M., and T. Erickson. 1982. Added value as a function of purchases of information services. *Information Society* 1(4): 307-338.

Johnston, R., and M. Gibbons. 1975. Characteristics of information usage in technical innovation. *IEEE Transactions on Engineering Management* EM-22(1): 27-34.

Kanter, R. M. 1983. *The Change Masters: Innovations for Productivity in the American Corporation.* New York: Simon and Schuster.

Kanter, R. M. 1982. The middle manager as innovator. *Harvard Business Review* 60(4): 95-105.

King, W. D., and J. M. Griffiths. 1988. Evaluating the effectiveness of information use. In *Evaluating the Effectiveness of Information Centers and Services,* 1:1-1:5. Material to support a lecture series presented under the sponsorship of the North Atlantic Treaty Organization, Advisory Group for Aerospace Research and Development (AGARD), Technical Information Panel and the Consultant and Exchange Programme; September 5-6, 8-9, 12-13, 1988; Luxembourg; Athens, Greece; Lisbon, Portugal; Neuilly-sur-Seine, France: AGARD.

King, W. D., J. M. Griffiths, E. A. Sweet, and R. R. Wiederkehr. 1984. *A Study of the Value of Information and the Effect on Value of Intermediary Organizations, Timeliness of Services and Products, and Comprehensiveness of the EDB.* Rockville, MD: King Research. NTIS:DE85003670; OCLC:11712088; DOE:NMB-1078.

King, W. D., J. M. Griffiths, N. K. Roderer, and R. R. Wiederkehr. 1982. *Value of the Energy Data Base.* Rockville, MD: King Research. NTIS:DE82014250; OCLC:9004666; DOE:OR11232-1.

King, W. D., D. O. McDonald, and N. K. Roderer. 1981. *Scientific Journals in the United States: Their Production, Use, and Economics.* Stroudsburg, PA: Hutchinson Ross.

King, W. D., and N. K. Roderer. 1979. Information transfer cost/benefit analysis. In *Information and Industry: Proceedings of the North Atlantic Treaty Organization, Advisory Group for Aerospace Research and Development (AGARD), Technical Information Panel's Specialists' Meeting; October 18-19, 1987; Paris, France,* 8:1-8:10. Neuilly-sur-Seine, France: AGARD.

King, W. D., J. M. Griffiths, L. W. Lannow, and H. M. Kurtz. n.d. Study of the Use and Value of Library Network Services. Proprietary Report prepared by King Research.

Koenig, M. E. 1983b. A bibliometric analysis of pharmaceutical research. *Research Policy* 12(1): 15-36.

Koenig, M. E. 1983a. Bibliometric indicators versus expert opinion in assessing research performance. *Journal of the American Society for Information Science* 34(2): 136-145.

Koenig, M. E. 1982. Determinants of expert judgement of research performance. *Scientometrics* 4(5): 361-378.

Koenig, M. E. 1990a. The information and library environment and the productivity of research. *Inspel* 24(4): 157-167.

Koenig, M. E. 1990b. Information services and downstream productivity. In *Annual Review of Information Science and Technology,* vol. 17, ed. M.E. Williams, 55-86. White Plains, New York: Knowledge Industry Publications for the American Society for Information Science.

Koenig, M. E. 1975. The productivity of research effort in the U.S. pharmaceutical industry. *Research Policy* 4(4): 331-349.

Mason, R. M., and P. G. Sassone. 1978. A lower bound cost benefit model for information services. *Information Processing and Management* 14(2): 71-83.

Matarazzo, J. M., L. Prusak, and M. R. Gauthier. 1990. *Valuing Corporate Libraries: A Survey of Senior Managers.* Washington, DC: Special Libraries Association in cooperation with Temple, Barker & Sloane.

McConnell, J. D. 1980. Productivity improvements in research and development and engineering in the United States. *Society of Research Administrators Journal* 12(2): 5-14.

Mogavero, L. N. 1979. Transferring technology to industry through information. In *Information and Industry: Proceedings of the North Atlantic Treaty Organization, Advisory Group for Aerospace Research and Development (AGARD), Technical Information Panel's Specialists' Meeting: October 18-19, 1978; Paris, France,* 14:1-14:6. Neuilly-sur-Seine, France: AGARD.

Mondschein, L. G. 1990. SDI use and productivity in the corporate research environment. *Special Libraries* 81(4): 265-279.

Orpen, C. 1985. The effect of managerial distribution of scientific and technical information on company performance. *R&D Management* 15(4): 305-308.

Pelz, D. C., and F. M. Andrews. 1969. Diversity in research. In *The R&D Game: Technical Men, Technical Management, and Research Productivity,* ed. D. Allison, 73-89. Cambridge, MA: MIT Press.

Pelz, D. C., and F. M. Andrews. 1966. *Scientists in Organizations: Productive Climates for Research and Development.* New York: Wiley.

Poppel, H. L. 1982. Who needs the office of the future? *Harvard Business Review* 60(6): 146-155.

Roderer, N. K., D. W. King, and S. E. Brouard. 1983. *The Use and Value of Defense Technical Information Center Products and Services.* Rockville, MD: King Research. OCLC:12987688, 11599947.

Rogers, E. M. 1983. *Diffusion of Innovations.* 3rd ed. New York: Free Press.

Shilling, C. W., and J. S. Bernard. 1964. *Informal Communications Among Bioscientists, Part II.* Washington, DC: George Washington University. (Biological Science Communications Project Report no. 16A)

University of Sussex. Science Policy Research Unit. 1972. Success and Failure in Industrial Innovation. Report on Project Sappho. London, England: Center for the Study of Industrial Innovation.

Utterback, J. M. 1974. Innovation in industry and the diffusion of technology. *Science* 15; 183(4125): 620-626.

Utterback, J. M. 1971. The process of technological innovation within the firm. *Academy of Management Journal* 14(March): 75-88.

Weil, B. H. 1980. Benefits from research use of the published literature at the Exxon Research Center. In *Special Librarianship: A New Reader,* ed. E.B. Jackson, 586-594. Metuchen, NJ: Scarecrow Press.

Wolek, F. W., and B. C. Griffith. 1974. Policy and informal communication in applied science and technology. *Science Studies* 4(4): 411-420.

Demonstrating Information Service Value to Your Organization

Marianne Broadbent

THE NATURE OF THE CHALLENGE

Developments in the technology of online information are enabling more ready access to a wider range of sources in increasingly client specific forms and formats. Many senior managers intuitively recognise the importance of such services. However, they are often frustrated in their attempts to link these with the core business of their organisation, despite the best efforts of information professionals.

Information professionals require a clear understanding of the range of outcomes and benefits which are important to both senior management and users in the organisations. Traditional evaluation approaches developed by librarians and information scientists emphasise techniques which provide necessary indicators of output and operational efficiency. These need to be complemented by techniques which seek to identify the benefits of those information services to the organisation in terms which have meaning to both managers and users.

This paper addresses the challenge of demonstrating the value of information services and ways to meet this challenge. Two practical evaluation techniques which bridge the gap between those used by senior managers and those with which information service managers are comfortable are outlined. The first technique, Priority

Reprinted from *Online Information 92: 16th International Online Information Meeting Proceedings London 8-10 December 1992*. Learned Information, Oxford, pp. 65-83 with permission.

and Performance Evaluation (PAPE), builds on Critical Success Factor (CSF) methodology. This is complemented by a form of cost-benefit analysis applied, in this instance, to online profile and current awareness services.

These techniques were developed as part of a project to identify the value of information and library services. The project, referred to in this paper as the Value Study, was funded by three organisations who sought simple and effective techniques which could be applied by information service managers in their own organisations [see Broadbent & Lofgren (1991) for full details including literature analysis, progress of the study and instruments]. The techniques have been successfully trialled and applied in organisations. They form part of a management approach for information professionals which focuses on the value they and their services add to their organisation. This paper concludes with observations about effective information management practices from a sustained series of recent applied research and consulting assignments.

INFORMATION SERVICE VALUE

Despite the rhetoric of the strategic significance of information and information services to organisations, information costing and value are acknowledged as being 'difficult' (Orna 1990) and 'underdeveloped fields' (Burk and Horton 1987). Traditionally, information activities have been viewed as non-productive overheads because of the lack of understanding about the role and importance of information in managerial and firm performance. Defining productivity in the information arena is very difficult when compared to the productivity in production processes (Koenig 1990). As information and its management becomes a major activity, the question of value becomes critical as the costs become apparent and pervasive (Taylor 1982). Hale (1991) argues that as the proportion of organisational resources devoted to information functions increases, these functions can no longer be treated as unallocated costs.

In many instances the products and services of information centres and library units have a less identifiable connection to the mainstream of a business or government enterprise than even information systems and technology groups. In these latter areas, there is now a burgeoning literature identifying the business value of information technology (for example Carlson and McNurlin 1989; Keen 1991; Sassone and Schaffer 1978; Strassmann 1990; Weill 1990).

We should not underestimate the complexity of the issues involved in identifying the value of services and products based on the importance and use of the information content itself. The major reason that many information professionals, and their managers, experience problems in identifying the value of their products and services is that this, in itself, is an extremely difficult challenge.

In the information system and services field, three generic approaches to evaluation or identifying value have been described by Ahituv (1989): the normative approach, the realistic value approach and the perceived (subjective) value approach. The normative approach requires rigorous modeling and precise measurability of all factors and is based on a set of assumptions which do not usually apply in real situations. The conditions for such an approach can rarely be met in the information or management fields.

The realistic value approach seeks to measure the effect of information access and use on the performance of decision makers and the outcomes from their decisions. This may require that performance be measured and compared before and after the introduction of a new information service. Again, this is rarely feasible. It is usually impossible to isolate the impact on performance of the information system or service to the exclusion of other intervening variables.

The perceived value approach is based on subjective evaluation performed by users of an information system or service. The underlying premise is that users can recognise the benefits they gain from a system and are capable of transforming these into ranking scales and/or monetary terms. A feasible and practical approach is to seek 'the perception of users of the changes that have taken place in the way they work and their assessment of whether these changes have been beneficial or detrimental' (Ahituv 1990, 320).

In the Value Study we drew on Ahituv's perceived value approach and took it one step further by adding the perceptions of management. A significant flaw in the evaluation approaches used in many previous information systems and services areas has been that only some of the stakeholders have been included in the evaluation process. While user studies have featured extensively in both the literature and practice of information and library services, the perspective of senior managers has often been missing.

As our remit was to develop simple and useful organisationally-relevant techniques, we took a pragmatic approach to identifying the benefit or worth of information services and products, based on a judgement of what was important to key stakeholders. Our focus was on priorities, performance and benefits provided by information services and information products, rather than on the value of information *per se*. (The latter area is discussed in the Value Study report, Broadbent and Lofgren 1991).

STAKEHOLDER PERSPECTIVES ON VALUE

An information services group can be evaluated from many different dimensions: as an organizational group or unit and through its component parts such as personnel, products and services, resources and systems. These dimensions can be assessed from multiple stakeholder perspectives: the information service unit (ISU) management and staff, the manager(s) to whom the ISU reports and other managers to whom it relates, and the users and potential users of ISU products and services.

The inclusion of multiple stakeholder perspectives is essential in any process which seeks to go beyond what Eason (1988) has referred to as technical system performance. A complicating factor for ISUs is that there are not necessarily any formal linkages in organisations between these three stakeholder groups. Funding decisions can be made by a management process which does not take into account the views of users of a service. There might be no communication loop by which users provide direct input to management decisions. This is more likely to be the situation where the ISU manager has not been actively assembling such information as part of an on-going evaluation process. The missing components of the communication triad in Figure 1 are often a significant factor in the frustration expressed by senior managers in trying to identify the organisational benefit provided by their ISU.

Links between management and users are essential in ensuring an informed management perspective on the performance of the ISU. Those links will not exist unless the ISU manager actively facilitates them. The Priority and Performance Evaluation and the cost-benefit techniques outlined in this paper provide avenues to develop and enhance those links.

PRIORITY AND PERFORMANCE EVALUATION

Priority and Performance Evaluation (PAPE) seeks quantitative and qualitative input from managers, users and ISU staff about the areas in which the ISU should be directing its major efforts, together with an assessment of the current performance of the ISU in those areas. This provides input and feedback on the type of value or benefit sought from the ISU by management and users. It may indicate differing perceptions which require resolution, in order for the ISU to focus its efforts in areas where the organisational stakeholders perceive that they gain maximum benefit. The output from this approach facilitates the development of a series of well-grounded Critical Success

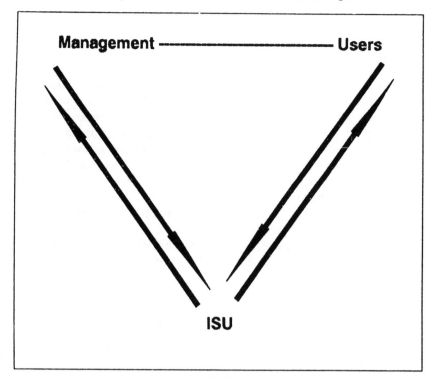

Figure 1. Communication triad.

Factors (CSFs) for the ISU as viewed by the major organisational stakeholders.

The PAPE technique draws on the methodology of CFS analysis (Daniel 1961; Herget and Hensler 1991; Rockart 1979; Rockart and Bullen 1986). PAPE is presented as a standard evaluation method in German information systems literature and is reported to work well in business environments (Heinrich and Burgholzer 1987; Lehner 1990). A form of this technique is used by IBM Australia to assess client perceptions of their priority and performance. Though Bryson (1990) makes mention of the use of Critical Success Factors, we were not aware of any published application of the PAPE technique in the information services or library fields.

Our aim was to adapt the PAPE technique to the ISU context and to assess whether it could be meaningfully applied. The service units in which we trialled the technique were the national information resource centre of an Australia-wide government business enterprise and the library and information service of a Victorian government agency. Both were relatively large units. Their combined budgets were over $A9 million and they employed over 50 staff.

The starting point for a PAPE is a list of result areas which describe desirable features of the ISU. We developed a generic list of result areas from managers of Special Libraries and Information Centres across Australia. Those included in the survey were either office-holders in the Australian Library and Information Association or had attended a workshop on identifying the value of online services. Forty-three potential indicators were identified and ranked in this manner. ISU staff in the two participating organisations then selected and adapted 21 (agency) and 19 (enterprise) of these from the top 25. Those selected by the agency are listed in Figure 2.

In other situations, a beginning list of result areas can be drawn up by ISU staff and then discussed with a small group of key stakeholders. Participation of relevant staff from outside the ISU is essential in finalizing a list of appropriate result areas.

In each organization, the PAPE evaluation form was four pages long. The first page provided an explanation and introduction to par-

---

a. Access to databases (online and CD-ROM)
b. Application of advanced management and planning methods within Library Services
c. Competence and qualifications of ISU staff
d. Current awareness service (CAS bulletin)
e. Gaining top management support for ISU
f. Image of ISU and its staff within the department
g. Inter-library loan service
h. Service area convenience (physical layout, lighting, equipment, facilities for reading, etc.)
i. Physical proximity of ISU or branch unit
j. Procedures for user feedback to ISU staff
k. Promotion and marketing of the ISU and its services and products
m. Provision of up-to-date books, journals and other information sources
n. Quality of information service and products (reliability, currency, etc.)
o. Quality of ISU staff assistance and support to users
p. Range of material in collection (e.g., subject areas covered)
q. Regular communication between ISU and management
r. Servicing all sections of the department
s. Timely delivery of products and services
t. Understanding of users' information needs
u. Use of state-of-the-art technology by the ISU

Figure 2. Agency PAPE result areas.

ticipants — details of the participant's position, workplace and, where appropriate, the branch of the ISU on which the participants primarily relied for their work. This gave essential information about the constituency of the stakeholder (manager, type of user or ISU staff member) together with the level and nature of their position.

The second and third pages constitute the essence of the PAPE. Extracts from sample pages of the form used in the enterprise are in Figure 3. Question 1 asks what priority the ISU should give each of the result areas. Question 2 seeks a response as to how well the ISU performs in each of those areas. In each situation, participants mark the area on a Likert scale from 1 through 7. For each result area and for each stakeholder group, the scores are then totalled and averaged. It is these averages which are then compared in any combination that is required.

For analysis purposes, each result area was given an alphabetical letter, as in Figure 2 above. To avoid response set answers, we mixed the order of the result areas for Question 2. For example, the

QUESTION 1:
In your opinion, what priority should the ISU give each of the following:
Please circle the number that best gives an indication of your assessment.

	Low priority					Very high priority		DON'T KNOW
<———————————————————————————————————>								
Availability and accessibility of Information Centre staff	1	2	3	4	5	6	7	N
Procedures for feedback to Information Centre staff	1	2	3	4	5	6	7	N
Promotion and marketing of the Information Centre and its services and products	1	2	3	4	5	6	7	N
Quality of information services and products — accuracy	1	2	3	4	5	6	7	N

QUESTION 2:
In your opinion, how well does the ISU perform in each of the following areas?
Please circle the number that best gives an indication of your assessment.

	Very poorly					Excellently		DON'T KNOW
<———————————————————————————————————>								
Quality of information services and products — accuracy	1	2	3	4	5	6	7	N
Procedures for feedback to Information Centre staff	1	2	3	4	5	6	7	N
Availability and accessibility of Information Centre staff	1	2	3	4	5	6	7	N
Quality of information services and products — timeliness	1	2	3	4	5	6	7	N

Figure 3. Extract of sample PAPE response form.

Agency result areas for Question were identified from 'a' through to 'u' and retained this identification, regardless of their position on the form, in the analysis of Question 2. The forms given to participants, though, had no such identification.

In each of the organisations in the Value Study we sought 100 participants. The choice of stakeholder groups was decided by the ISUs and management to achieve specific evaluation purposes. In the agency, there was particular interest in evaluating service to dispersed user sites, some of which were more than 300 kilometres from the head office of the agency and its ISU. Conditions for technical and professional staff and, perhaps, their perceptions of ISU service could differ substantially according to location. In the enterprise, senior ISU staff decided on surveying a sample of professional staff and administrators within one division of the organisation.

Response rates for return of the form were very high: 86% in the agency and 83% in the enterprise. An important factor in this achievement was the personal delivery of the forms, where practicable, by ISU staff prepared to answer questions about the evaluation.

After reviewing a number of statistical packages, we decided to analyse the results of the survey using a standard spreadsheet package, Excel (Version 3). This package (and others which are similar) is commonly used in organisations for general management purposes and thus would be more readily available to ISU managers than statistical packages. Graphical representations of the data are also possible and instructions for these are in the Value Study Report.

It is important to note here that the analysis can be done manually and does not require the use of a software package. A spreadsheet or statistical package is particularly useful for large samples (over about 30 participants) and to produce charts and graphs of the results. In the following section we present a portion of the results from the agency.

SAMPLE RESULTS FROM THE AGENCY PRIORITY AND PERFORMANCE EVALUATION

Presenting some results from application of the PAPE in the agency enables illustration of what can be done using the technique. We have selected results in two areas: first, to compare priority and performance assessments from the stakeholder groups of users and management; and, second, using a matrix, to identify result areas which require special attention — that is, where the priority is high but the

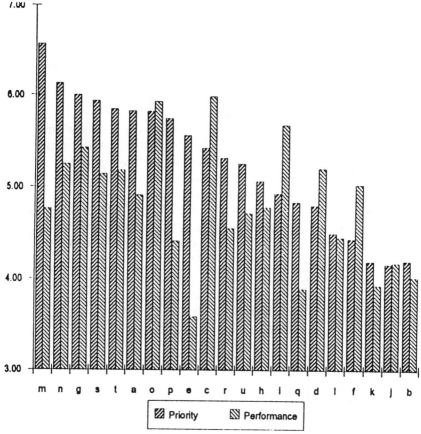

Figure 4. User and management perceptions of agency priority and performance.

performance low. These result areas then provide the basis for future Critical Success Factors for the ISU.

The first display, Figure 4, ranks the result areas for the agency in order of priority as seen by user and management respondents (excluding ISU staff). Some marked differences are readily apparent between priority and performance assessments. The two highest priority areas were **m**-Provision of up-to-date books, journals and other information services and **n**-Quality of information services and products, including reliability, answering, etc. The difference between the priority and performance levels in the first of these is particularly marked, as it is for areas **p**-Range of material in the collection and **e**-Gaining top management support for the service. This should alert management to a likely need for improved performances in these particular areas.

Not only differences between priority and performance are of interest here, but also the ranking order by priority assessments. Within the agency the area given the highest priority related to the currency of books and journals, while the lowest was the application of 'advanced management and planning methods'. The overall pattern of priority assessments was similar in the enterprise: timeliness, currency, and accuracy of information services and products was considered most important. In the Value Study, similar analyses was undertaken to compare the priorities and perceptions of many other combinations, such as users at different sites, and professionals *vis-à-vis* administrative and managerial staff.

The second display, Figure 5, presents this information in another form to assist in identifying future Critical Success Factors. The bottom right corner labelled 'Killer' contains result areas which are high

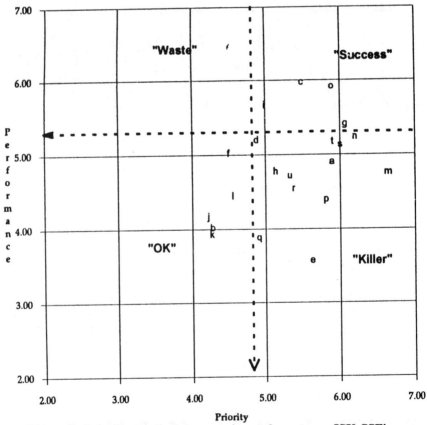

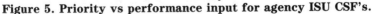

Figure 5. Priority vs performance input for agency ISU CSF's.

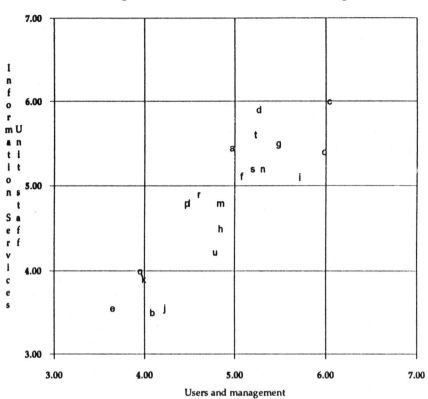

Figure 6. ISU vs user and management perceptions of priority.

in priority yet low in performance. These areas are those which provide the basis for future ISU CSFs requiring the greatest ISU management attention. In the agency, areas **e** and **m** are apparent.

The third display, Figure 6, illustrates how priority assessments by ISU staff (y-axis) compare with priority assessments by users and management (x-axis). Here, the ideal result is a spread which approximates a 45 degree diagonal line pointing towards the upper right-hand corner of the chart. Such an outcome would indicate that there is full agreement between ISU staff and users and managers on what the priorities of the ISU should be. It is clear that there are some differences. Similar analyses can be done for comparison of perceptions of performance and for different stakeholder groups.

The PAPE technique is systematic yet flexible. A wider or more limited range of activities, resources, services and products can be evaluated, as well as the unit or department as a whole, depending on the purpose of the evaluation. Similarly the sample of users and management respondents can be extensive or limited.

For any organisation, the results primarily have a diagnostic value: areas of strength and weakness are identified, and can be ranked in priority order for management consideration and action. They may require consideration and interpretation as to the reasons for some of the results in order that appropriate action can be taken.

The PAPE technique fits squarely within the perceived value approach outlined above. Other techniques are required to provide a more detailed evaluation of particular ISU products and services. An application of cost-benefit analysis can provide the basis for one such approach.

COST-BENEFIT ANALYSIS AND INFORMATION SYSTEMS AND SERVICES

Cost-benefit analysis is a generic term embracing a wide range of evaluation procedures. In simple terms, cost-benefit analysis involves estimating the extent to which the benefits of a product or service outweigh its cost. Central to the notion of cost-benefit analysis of a product, project or service is the perspective of management on the nature of benefits sought in the light of organisational goals (Horngren and Foster 1991, 8).

The field of cost-benefit analysis developed from the economic justification of public works (Sassone and Schaffer 1978). However, its discussion in recent managerial accounting texts is often from a more narrow perspective with costs as cash outflows and benefits as cash inflows. In most ISU service areas, however, such calculations, in monetary terms, are difficult and arbitrary.

The essential challenges in applying cost-benefit techniques to information systems and services are threefold:

(1) The costs and benefits do not usually occur within a comparable timeframe (Parker 1982). Costs are often immediate and tangible, while benefits are frequently long term, uncertain and intangible (Sassone 1988).
(2) Benefits, such as more timely information, improved organisational planning, faster decision-making and the ability to investigate a number of alternatives, are highly dependent on subjective judgements. Their conversion into monetary terms is highly suspect.
(3) There might be little agreement within an organization about the nature and measurement of costs and benefits (Parker et al. 1988). This is particularly likely to be the case in emergent areas, such as the development of sophisticated information systems products and services.

Senn (1990) argues in favour of the importance of determining benefits on the basis of what the system can do to keep managers informed: the value of the systems should be judged according to the users' perceptions rather than according to actual cost structure. In other fields too, such as manufacturing, traditional approaches to cost justification do not acknowledge appropriate arguments for investments in strategic or infrastructure systems (Samson et al. 1991).

Specific concerns about the applications of narrow criteria for quantitative cost-benefit techniques in the information and library services field focus on:

(1) The user's use of material (Lancaster 1977). This is not under the control of the ISU. Thus Lancaster suggested that the provider should be evaluated only on its delivery of documents to users when needed.

(2) The user's willingness to purchase an information service as an indication of the value placed on it (Flowerdew and Whitehead 1974). But the price paid for such a service does not reveal the full benefit of the service to the purchaser.

(3) The lack of a control group against which to judge the benefits of an information service (White 1985).

In the ISU area, some significant work has been reported by King and Griffiths (1984, 1991). Their approach is based on the premise that the primary work activities of professionals require that they obtain work-related information from the ISU, usually in the form of documentation.

In undertaking a form of cost-benefit analysis for ISU products, we drew in part on Sassone's cost-displacement/avoidance and cost-effectiveness categories (1988), and on elements of the 'higher order effects' impact of information service provision from the work of King and Griffiths (particularly 1991). We placed these in a relatively simple cost-benefit framework suitable for application by an ISU or business manager. In this approach, costs and benefits are addressed in terms which management finds appropriate. These could be a combination of quantitative (including monetary) and qualitative concerns in the context of providing, not providing an alternative provision for, an information product.

ISU PRODUCT COST-BENEFIT TECHNIQUE

We examined two different forms of Current Awareness services (CAS), one in each of the participating organisations. A list of seven cost elements for providing a CAS was developed from the literature, expertise and input from the agency and the enterprise. These seven cost elements are summarised as ISU staff time, user time to use the product, cost of information resources used, cost of materials and services in the physical production of the product, hardware and software usage, the cost of providing services stimulated by the product and archival maintenance of the product.

Eight benefit elements were identified and grouped into three categories. First, Category A benefits, were cost savings and cost avoidance of the users' time. Second, Category B benefits, were the cost of alternative products and services. The third, Category C benefits, were the impact and usefulness of the information to the organisation. Category C benefits included improved organisational products and services, increased range of organisational options, more timely information, project time saved and pertinent competitor intelligence input.

Each of these benefit areas is dependent on the subjective assessments of stakeholders, particularly users. Some quantitative and qualitative estimates can be made for categories A and B. Apart from specific instances, assessment of category C benefits is usually limited to qualitative comments.

In the Value Study we used a cost-finding approach to estimate costs over the previous twelve-month period. Costs which changed over that time, such as salaries, were held constant in the analysis. For the purposes of this exercise, benefits too were assumed to have occurred in the same time period. It was acknowledged that these are usually deferred and likely to occur over a more extended period.

The process of estimating benefit areas required considerable involvement of users as well as managers. We sought two forms of input from users on the benefits of the current awareness products they received. First, ten users in each organisation were asked to complete a CAS Response Form, and nine responded. This form was finalised only after being reviewed by management. The form sought to link the nature of the users' work, their critical information needs and their use of the product. This provided data in relation to each of the Category A and B benefits elements and some of the Category C elements.

The conference method was used as a second source of input in the enterprise. The user group was asked to bring their completed forms to a round-table discussion with the research team. This session reviewed the benefit elements and surfaced further critical instances where the provision of information, through the ISU product, made a difference to the user's work performance. In many situations, such instances go unreported and the organisation is unaware of the impact of not providing the product.

A selection of the results of the cost-benefit analysis for the profiling service provided by the resource centre of the government business enterprise follows. Some of the figures have been adjusted to assist in confidentiality. The quantitative figures present results with similar magnitude to those in the enterprise. We used the higher end for cost estimates and more conservative estimations for benefits. The worksheets refer essentially to category A and B benefits. These are followed by a summary of the Category C benefits as seen by users.

COST-BENEFIT ANLAYSIS FOR A PROFILING PRODUCT

The government business enterprise provided a profile-based current awareness service, referred to as PROFILES in the Value Study. This product was developed from database searches of external sources, principally those on DIALOG. The ISU produced over 75 different PROFILES each month for user groups throughout the organisation. The PROFILES were reviewed at least once a year for appropriateness, relevance and recall. Each PROFILE was used by between one and 21 individuals. The users were involved in applied research and consultancy in a wide range of technically oriented areas.

The summary worksheet developed for the costing of the PROFILES is presented in Figure 7. The full worksheets, including the derivation of all costs, can be found in the Value Study report. The enterprise had a standard approach to costing research technical staff ($A115 000 per year) and administration staff, which included the ISU ($A65 000). These figures included salary, oncosts, overhead and infrastructure costs. Our experience is that most organizations have figures such as these. They are usually about twice the average salary of workers in the particular grouping.

The total cost of the PROFILES was estimated at $727 210. This figure is for additional resources required by the ISU to offer this product: user time to use the product, the external costs for the searching time, a notional cost for equipment, the cost of providing the ISU services which this product stimulates and a notional portion of the serials collection allocation. ISU staff costs accounted for $124 500, user time $435 789 and the serials collection amount was $127 290. It is the user time which constitutes the largest cost and these figures have the widest margin for error.

Two cost-benefit scenarios are summarised in this paper. The first is for a situation where the PROFILES are no longer provided and users have to undertake the activity themselves. The second scenario

WORKSHEET 1: Costing of PROFILES —
                        Additional resources required plus portion of serials budget

A. STAFF TIME/GEN COSTS — ISU		$53,300
SDI Prep/Production:		
P1 Librarian	$52,000	
P3 Training	$1,300	
B. OTHER STAFF/USER TIME		$435,789
Time to use product:		
User hrs		
x Cost per hour	$435,789	
C. COST OF INFO RESOURCES USED		$29,600
External dbases searches:		
DIALOG quarterly updates	$15,200	
Database Alerting Services	$14,400	
D. COST OF MATERIALS, SERVICES		
Reprodn costs — negligible		
E. HARDWARE, SOFTWARE COSTS		$2,000
Portion of NIRC IT costs	$2,000	
F. SERVICES COSTS STIM'D BY PROFILES		$79,221
Document Delivery-Staff costs		
AO2 Allocation	$32,500	
P1 ILL Librarian	$39,000	
Document Deliver-Direct costs		
Australian ILL	$1,360	
British ILL + others	$5,281	
Telex costs pa	$1,080	
G. SERIALS COLLECTION ALLOCATION		$127,290
Portion of serials budget as per G in Assumptions	$127,290	
TOTAL COSTS		$727,201

Figure 7. Costing of the PROFILES.

presents a situation where the PROFILE preparation and document delivery is outsourced to a commercial provider.

Scenario 1: PROFILES are not provided

The first cost-benefit analysis was for the situation where the PRO-FILES product is not offered and the users have to undertake the activity themselves. Figure 8 presents these benefit elements. Users indicated that the PROFILES saved them 5 to 10 hours per week. They could not complete their jobs without access to the latest relevant literature. We used an even lower estimate of 3 hours per week for each week. The cost-benefit of PROFILE production in this situation was 1:26, with an annual saving to the enterprise of nearly $17 million. While this seems remarkably high, the enterprise staff and management considered this a reasonable reflection of the value provided by the PROFILES in their competitive environment.

The above figures were complemented by comments solicited

WORKSHEET 2: PROFILES not provided. Users have to undertake the activity themselves

A. COST ESTIMATES OF USERS' TIME		$8,748,000
Assumptions:		
No. of users	750	
Cost per user hour	$81	
Yearly hrs saved per user:		
3 hrs pw for 48 weeks	144	
B. OPPORTUNITY COSTS OF USER'S TIME		$8,748,000
As for (A) above		
TOTAL		$17,496,000
C. COST-BENEFIT RATIO		
Total cost of providing the service		$674,864
Cost of user's time to do it themselves,		
including user opportunity costs		$17,496,000
Cost-benefit ratio		1:26
Saving each year		$16,821,136

Figure 8. Quantitative benefits of PROFILES 1: Users undertake the activity themselves.

from PROFILE users through the Response Form. Users identified the qualitative benefits of the product in four areas: saving of time, better quality work, better informed work and avoidance of other costs. Some quotes from replies to the User Response Form were:

1) *Saving of time.* Current trends would be much more difficult to obtain; Would require a lot more of my time; Enabled faster initiation of a project which has widespread impact across Australia; We would need to spend a much longer time reading journals; It could cost me substantially more time; Provides contact names which saves time and clarifies ideas; Especially important in getting into new research areas; Avoids time taken by re-inventing the wheel.
(2) *Better quality of work.* Reading would be limited to mainstream journals only and thus work would be blinkered; We would not be able to give comprehensive advice to clients; Without PROFILES I would fall behind in what is happening in my field; Better able to indicate to clients our approach is in line with international practice; Quality of work performed would be lower without PROFILES.
(3) *Better informed.* Enables me to understand directions of industry; Without PROFILES we would miss articles, especially of journals not in the ISU; We would be only partially informed about technology developments.
(4) *Avoidance of other costs.* More literature searches and bibliographies would be needed.

Seventy percent of users indicated that the availability of PROFILES had made a significant difference to their work performance. Examples of specific instances cited from the users' responses included:

Ideas seen in a paper initiated a project here. The results from this work has had widespread impact across Australia.

My PROFILE provided a contact name. Able to discuss results in relation to performance testing of products. Saved time. Able to better clarify our ideas and indicate to our clients that our approach was in line with other organisations.

Recent document enabled the organisation to inform the appropriate people of alternatives to an environmentally unsound product.

Users could name the most recent document they had obtained as a result of reading a PROFILE and indicate its relevance to their work performance and output. During the conference session, users indicated that completing the Response Form had made them realise how important and essential the PROFILES were to their own work and that of the enterprise. They could not envisage meeting their work responsibilities without this product.

Subsequent use of this technique in later consulting work consistently identified very positive quantitative cost-benefit ratios and powerful statements by users about the impact of services such as PROFILES and other current awareness and document delivery services by ISUs. It is the combination of the quantitative worksheets together with the qualitative statements about impact on work performance which were important to senior managers.

Scenario 2 : Outsourcing of PROFILE preparation and document delivery

A second quantitative benefit costing involved continuation of the PROFILES, but through outsourcing both the development of PROFILES and document delivery requests arising from those PROFILES. This is summarised in Figure 9. Cost estimates were received from commercially-based services. These were averaged at $A25 for a request which could be met within Australia and $A38 for a request which had to be sent outside Australia. The most likely outsource providers would be the commercial arm of academic libraries of which there are at least two currently active in Melbourne (where the enterprise was located). Because of the specialist nature of the enterprise serials collection, an estimate was made that 10% of the titles which it held were not readily available elsewhere in Australia.

When the notional allocation of the serials budget is included in the ISU costings, there appears to be little difference in quantitative terms between providing the service inhouse and purchasing it externally. However, users indicated three qualitative aspects of PROFILES which need to be considered in any such decision: the impor-

WORKSHEET 3: Outsourcing of PROFILES and Document Delivery

A. EXTERNAL PREPARATION OF PROFILES		$111,000
For 75 PROFILES per year		
PROFILES set-ups (75 × $400)	$30,000	
Running of PROFILES		
75 × $1080 pa	$81,000	
B. OTHER STAFF/USER TIME		$435,789
Time to use product:		
User hrs × cost per hour	$435,789	
C. SERVICES COSTS STIM'D BY PROFILES		$189,266
Requests avail in Aust	968	
90% of 1075		
Cost per request	$25	
Overseas requests	547	
440 + 10% of 1075		
Cost per overseas request		
Total	$43,466	
Staff liaison with provider		
75 PROFILES, 2 hrs × 12, $81 ph	$145,800	
TOTAL COSTS		$736,055
D. COST-BENEFIT RATIO CALCULATIONS		
ISU vs. External PROFILE development and document delivery		
Differences in costings (including costs of serials):		
a. ISU staff and materials (A,C,E,F from Worksheet 1)		$164,121
b. Use of the Serials colln (G from Worksheet 1)		$127,290
Total		$291,411
c. Cost of external provision		$300,266
Cost-benefit ratio		1:1.103
Saving each year		$8,855
Differences in costings: 2 (excluding costs of serials):		
a. ISU staff and materials (A,C,E,F from Worksheet 1)		$164,121
c. Cost of external provision		$300,266
Cost-benefit ratio		1:1.83
Saving each year		$136,145

Figure 9. Quantitative benefits of PROFILES 2: Outsourcing PROFILES and document delivery.

tance of speed, ISU staff familiarity with their work, and considerations of confidentiality. At the same time, in such a large ISU there are significant implications and possible consequences of any large scale outsourced document delivery.

The enterprise currently meets 56% of requests generated by the PROFILES from its own collection. Because of the specialist nature of their collection, the proportion of these which would be readily available from one external source is limited. Thus there would be time delays while these were sought from libraries within or external to Australia.

A second factor raised by users is that the provision of the PROFILES and document delivery service inhouse means that the ISU staff become very well acquainted with the needs of their users. This characteristic is highly valued by both users and management in this organisation. The ISU staff indicated that this knowledge results in more informed collection management decisions.

A further negative referred to, where the enterprise used another agency to provide document delivery, was that this could give their competitors greater access points for information about current research and development activities. The enterprise has both local and international competitors and, in certain key areas, confidentiality is critical.

From an industry viewpoint, if a large ISU decided to outsource the major component of its document delivery to save the costs of subscribing to serials, this could be seen as an abuse of industry interlending (ILL) agreements. Such action would have industry-wide implications, as ILL arrangements would still be the basis for outsourced service. In the Australian context, these are based on the premise that each organisation meets the major portion of its users' needs from their own collection and contributes to the total national information resource. A large enterprise, or its outsource provider, which was not perceived to operate in this manner might find its document delivery arrangements with agencies such as academic, state and the National Library subject to review. Industry discussions of the outsourced scenario have not precluded the possibility that these institutions would raise their costs significantly to be much more than marginal rates. The costings in Figure 9 would thus be substantially increased.

REVIEWING THE COST-BENEFIT TECHNIQUE

The examples from the large government business enterprise provide some indication of the cost-effectiveness of the PROFILE product. While the costings are loose, the combination of both quantitative and qualitative data provides a reasonably informed picture of alternate courses of action. Labour costs comprise the major components of such products. Thus it is crucial to be able to convey the nature of the value added by the ISU staff working on such products and the relevance, to the organisation, of the output of users who exploit the product.

The reaction of management in both organisations in the Value Study to the technique outlined above was very positive. The looseness of the quantitative data was acknowledged, but it was seen to provide some indicators of the costs and benefits of the products. The technique was consistent with, and added to, other organisational processes. In the government agency, senior management indicated that the analyses provided them with much more detailed information about costs and benefits than they had gleaned in several previous extensive evaluations. In the enterprise, senior staff were keen to apply the approach to their current and planned new ISU products.

In both organisations, the process of discussing costs and benefits with groups of users and management was found to be particularly valuable to ISU staff. It provided further insights for all stakeholders on expectations of value and the role played by particular ISU products in the work of technical, professional and managerial staff. The importance of the expertise of information professionals was reinforced.

DEMONSTRATING VALUE AND THE PERCEPTIONS OF VALUE

Information professionals and ISUs provide economies of scale in providing resources and services to more than one person or group in the organisation. Perhaps more importantly is what Keen (1991) refers to as 'economies of expertise'. ISUs and their staff provide economies of expertise in information delivery which can be utilized by different groups within the organisation. This ISU benefit is underemphasised in both the literature and practice of information delivery.

The rationale for the recruitment of information professionals and for ISUs is that these provide access to information needed by an organisation in a cost-effective manner. The groups served by such units in business, industrial and government sectors are usually professional, technical and managerial staff who require timely and well-targetted products and services.

However, it is not adequate merely to provide good information services which are appreciated by users. The critical requirements for information professionals are twofold: first that they add value to their organisation's products, processes and services; and second, that they are able to demonstrate that added value in business and management terms. The two techniques outlined in this paper assist in linking information activities to organisational outcomes and demonstrating the value and benefits of information services to management.

The implementation of Priority and Performance Evaluation can assist an ISU manager to identify areas requiring further attention. The perceptions of priority and performance of both managers and users can be assessed against those of the ISU staff. Mediocre performance in key areas can be pinpointed and resources and attention redirected to critical product, services and resources.

This can be complemented by a cost-benefit analysis of particular products and services. Such an analysis can identify, in broad terms, the financial costs and benefits of alternate ways of providing a product, or the costs and benefits of not providing a certain product. This includes qualitative evidence sought from users concerning the impact of providing the product in a variety of ways.

In our experience of evaluation of different types of services and systems, the interaction which takes place as part of the process is at least as important as the product or report at the end of that process. On-going evaluation, aimed at improvement in service and changes to policies and resource allocation, is central to good management in any enterprise. Information professionals should expect to be regularly evaluated in ways which make sense to their host organisation. In any case, it is usually far more productive to initiate the evaluation process, and thus have a major say in the ground rules and shape of the evaluation, than to wait for it to 'be done' to you.

While providing quality information products and services is difficult, even that is not, on its own, sufficient. The perception of responsiveness and quality are essential ingredients in good information service management. This requires well-focused and on-going evaluation which demonstrates value to the organisation in ways which are pertinent to management. This activity is usually seen as an indicator of a competent and confident professional manager who understands the business of the organisation and his or her role in adding value to that organisation's outcomes.

A MANAGEMENT PERSPECTIVE

Over the past five years the author has been responsible for information systems and services research and for consulting activities which have involved interviewing over 100 senior managers and receiving written input from nearly 1000 other managers and professionals from over a dozen government, not-for-profit and private sector firms. My base since early 1991 has been in a leading national business school as Director of one of Australia's two Strategic Management Centres. This has provided a further perspective on the type of approaches to identifying information service value which are likely to be successful with management, together with perceptions of effective and ineffective information service managers.

Many managers still lack a basic understanding of the rationale for and benefits provided by information professionals and ISUs. This is as simple as not realising that the major rationale for an ISU is to provide cost-effective services and resources which are able to anticipate and meet information needs. It includes the fact that most services and products in corporate environments are provided to professional, technical and managerial staff whose expertise is not in information finding, and whose time is usually more expensive than those who specialise in information delivery. Information professionals have expertise in information delivery which draws on an understanding of the needs of key users and expertise about sources of information and its appropriate packaging. They can find and deliver information sources more quickly than their users, thus saving the organisation the scarce resources of time and money.

In some instances we have seen ISUs which have undertaken considerable work in surveying users. However, the users at whom the bulk of the service is directed are not the key users the ISU should be seeking to satisfy. They might be a marginalised group whose needs and work is not highly valued by the organisation. Serving these users well does not impress senior management.

There has been an increased emphasis in performance measurement in all types of information systems and services areas. This is both necessary and laudable. However, ISU managers have to make sure that they are measuring outputs and outcomes which key stakeholders regard as important. Very few ISUs provide the organisation's management with the type of priority, performance and benefit information which have any meaning in terms of the organisation's business focus.

Effective information service managers can usually readily answer the following ten questions in relation to their host organisation:

(1) What are the mission, the values and the Critical Success Factors for my organisation?
(2) What is the business of this organisation and what is its strategic orientation in that business?
(3) What is the nature of the strategy formation process in this organisation, who participates in it and where is it documented?
(4) Who are the key decision makers in this organisation and how often do they receive an ISU product?

(5) What are the core business drivers of this firm/government agency?
(6) How do the services and products of the ISU relate to each of these business drivers?
(7) What are the information service and product priorities of the key stakeholders in this organisation?
(8) What is the perception of performance for high priority information services and products of the key stakeholders in this organisation?
(9) What are the real costs to the organisation of each of the ISU products we provide?
(10) What are the quantitative and qualitative benefits to the organisation of each of the ISU products we provide?

Knowing the answers to the first five questions is an essential ingredient in generating the answers to the last five.

Effective information service managers do not wait to be told the answers to the first five questions. If they do not know the answers they go and find out. The fact that an information professional actually knows enough to be asking these questions is generally regarded very favourably. Finding out these answers is seen as an expected and entirely reasonable part of their job. These ten questions provide an agenda for demonstrating information service value to your organization.

ACKNOWLEDGMENTS

Sections of this paper draw on the work of Hans Lofgren, Research Associate for the research study 'Identfying the Value of Information Services' for which the author was Chief Investigator. Full details of that study can be found in Broadbent and Lofgren (1991). The author would like to acknowledge and thank the three organisations which funded that study: ACLIS (Australian Council for Library and Information Services), TELECOM and CIRCIT (Centre for International Research in Communications and Information Technologies).

Dr Marianne Broadbent
Key Centre for Strategic Management
Graduate School of Management
University of Melbourne
200 Leicester Street
Carlton
VIC 3053
Australia
Tel: +61 (3) 349 8180
Fax: +61 (3) 349 8133
E-mail: Broadbent%gsmstaff%unimelb@muwaye.ucs.unimelb.edu.au

REFERENCES

Ahituv, N. 1989. Assessing the value of information: Problems and approaches. In *Proceedings of the Tenth International Conference on Information Systems*, 4-6 December, 315-325. Boston, MA.

Broadbent, M., and H. Lofgren. 1991. *Priorities, Performance and Benefits: An Exploratory Study of Library and Information Units.* Canberra, Australia: ACLIS and CIRCIT.

Bryson, J. 1990. *Effective Library and Information Centre Management.* Aldershot, England: Gower.

Burk, C., and F.W. Horton. 1987. *Infomap: A Complete Guide to Discovering Your Corporate Information Resources.* Englewood Cliffs, NJ: Prentice Hall.

Carlson, W.N., and B.C. McNurlin. 1989. Measuring the Value of Information Systems, I/S Analyzer Special Report. United Communications Group. (Available from UCG, 4550 Montgomery Ave., Suite 700N, Bethseda, MD 20814-3382, USA.)

Daniel, R.D. 1961. Management information crisis. *Harvard Business Review* (Sept/Oct).

Eason, K. 1988. *Information Technology and Organisational Change.* London: Taylor & Francis.

Flowerdew, A.D., and C.M. Whitehead. 1974. Cost Effectiveness and Cost/Benefit Analysis in Information Science, OSTI Report 5206, London School of Economics and Political Science, London.

Griffiths, J.M., and D. King.1991. *The Evaluation of Information Centres and Services.* France: North Atlantic Treaty Organisation Advisory Group for Aerospace Research Development, AGARD.

Hale, E. 1991. Assessing the Value of Information. Master of Business (Information Technology) Thesis, RMIT.

Heinrich, L.J., and P. Burgholzer. 1987. *Informations management: Planung, Uberwachung und Steuerung der Informations-Infrastruktur,* Olderburg, Munchen.

Herget, J., and S. Hensler. 1991. Erfolgsfaktoren der Informationsvermittlung. Teil 1: Theoretische Grundlagen und methodische Konzepte. Konstanz: FG Informationwissenschaft, Universitat Konstanz. (Manuscript).

Horngren, C.T., and G. Foster. 1991. *Cost Accounting.* Englewood Cliffs, NJ: Prentice Hall.

Keen, P.G. 1991. *Shaping the Future: Business Design through Information Technology.* Cambridge, MA: Harvard Business School Press.

King, D.W., et al. 1984. A study of the value of information and the effect on value of intermediary organizations, timeliness of services and products, and comprehensiveness of the Energy Data Base. In *The Value of Libraries as an Intermediary Information Service,* Volume 1. Oakridge, TN: Office of Scientific and Technical Information, U.S. Department of Energy.

King, D.W., and J.M. Griffiths. 1991. Five years' research: New pieces of the information puzzle. *Bulletin of the American Society for Information Science* 17(2): 11-15.

Koenig, M.E. 1990. Information services and downstream productivity. *ARIST* 25: 55-86.

Lancaster, F.W. 1977. *The Measurement and Evaluation of Library Services.* Washington, DC: Information Resources Press.

Lehner, F. 1990. Die Erfogsfaktoren-Analyse als Instrument des Informationsmanagemenets: Erfahrungen bei der prakitischen Anwendung. In *Pragmatische Aspekte beim Entwurf und Betrieb von Informationssystemen: Proceedings des 1 Internationalen Symposiums fur Informationswissenschaft,* 465-477. Konstanz, Germany: Universitatverlag Konstanz.

Orna, E. 1990. *Practical Information Policies: How to Manage Information Flow in Organisations.* Aldershot, England: Gower.

Parker, M.M. 1982. Enterprise information analysis: Cost-benefit analysis and the data-managed system. *IBM Systems Journal* 21(1): 108-123.

Parker, M.M., R.J. Benson, and H.E. Trainor. *Information Economics: Linking Business Performance to Information Technology.* Englewood Cliffs, NJ: Prentice Hall.

Rockart, J.G. 1979. Chief executives define their own data needs. *Harvard Business Review* (March/April): 81-93.

Rockart, J.F., and C. Bullen, eds. 1986. *The Rise of Managerial Computing.* Homewood, IL: Dow-Jones Irwin.

Samson, D., K. Langfield-Smith, and P. McBride. 1991. The alignment of management accounting with manufacturing priorities: A strategic perspective. *Australian Accounting Review* 1(1): 29-40.

Sassone, P. 1988. A survey of cost-benefit methodologies for information systems. *Project Appraisal* 73-83. Surrey: Beech Tree Publishing.

Sassone, P., and W.A. Schaffer. 1978. *Cost-Benefit Analysis: A Handbook.* New York: Academic Press.

Senn, J.A. 1990. *Information Systems in Management.* Belmont, CA: Wadsworth.

Strassmann, P.A. 1990. *The Business Value of Computers.* New Canaan, CT: Information Economics.

Taylor, R.S. 1982. Information and productivity: On defining information output (I). *Social Science Information Studies* 2: 131-138.

Weill, P. 1990. *Do Computers Pay Off? A Study of Information Technology Investment and Manufacturing Performance.* Washington, DC: International Center for Information Technologies.

White, H.S. 1985. Cost benefit analysis and other fun and games. *Library Journal* 15(Feb): 118-121.

The Value
of Information Centers

Jose-Marie Griffiths and Donald W. King

INTRODUCTION

In this chapter, we explore ways to assess the value of information centers. Below, we briefly discuss the rationale that we have used in assessing value of services. In particular, value is assessed from three perspectives: what users are willing to pay, how much more it would cost users to get information if the services were not available, and the extent to which the services achieve cost savings for the users. Then we analyze the value of the information centers in providing journals, books and internal reports. We also assess the value of online bibliographic searching and Current Awareness Bulletins, since they are particularly important services. The value of information centers is found to be substantial, regardless of the perspective from which the evaluation is performed.

VALUE OF INFORMATION CENTER COLLECTION

There are three levels that are considered in assessing the contribution that an information center makes to the value of information. Information centers are not inexpensive. Typically, organizations spend an average of between $500 and $1,500 per professional in their organization. On behalf of the organization, the center pays for expensive journals, books and other materials. Acquiring, processing,

"The original version of this material was first published by the Advisory Group for Aerospace Research and Development, North Atlantic Treaty Organisation (AGARD/NATO), in AGARDograph 310 'A Manual on the Evaluation of Information Centers and Services' in 1991."

maintaining and distributing these materials in a timely way is very labor-intensive. Furthermore, information centers provide a range of other services such as reference, online searching, translation, and so on. There needs to be a clear demonstration of a favorable return on this investment.

The first question that comes to mind is whether the price paid for center materials and services has a concomitant value. The lowest bound for assessing this value is from the perspective of the readers. What are they willing to pay for this information? One can readily measure what they do pay, recognizing that they might pay more if they had to. Time of professionals is a scarce resource. Professionals must decide how to utilize their time in order to be most productive. Engineers, scientists, lawyers, administrators, and so on, devote a substantial amount of their time to getting, reading and using information found in documents such as journals, books, internal documents, patents, and so on. Their decision to use their scarce time for information seeking and reading is a strong indication of the value they place on information. The total time (and the dollar amount represented by this time) spent on information provided by an information center is an indicator of the value of the center. In organizations, this value tends to be on the order of several times that of the cost to the information centers in purchasing and providing these materials.

Of course, the information could be obtained by the professionals from other sources. They could subscribe to journals or purchase books themselves. Then they would lose potential savings achieved by sharing these materials. They could use another source, such as an academic library, but that involves substantial professional time required to identify, locate and get access to these other sources. They could order materials from document delivery services, publishers or elsewhere, but that assumes an ability of professionals to identify needed information then locate where it is and acquire it. Furthermore, if all professionals relied on academic, public or other libraries, these libraries would soon stop making their collections available because of the enormous cost and possible denial of access to their own primary patrons. In fact, this trend has already begun at some academic institutions in the U.S. The point is that having a nearby library in the parent organizations saves their professionals considerable time and money.

About two-thirds of the cost savings achieved by information centers involves professional time. We have observed, over the years, that professionals tend to spend a relatively constant proportion of their time in getting and reading information. The amount of time they spend may shift from accessing to reading or vice versa, but the total seems not to vary much. With this in mind, we developed a rationale for determining what would happen if professionals had to rely entirely on non-information center sources (i.e., if there were no center). We assume that there would be less reading because more time would be required for identifying, locating and acquiring information from other sources. Therefore, the potential benefits derived from readings that are lost would not be achieved. Such benefits, include savings (in time, equipment, etc.) derived from information and improvements in quality of work, timeliness of work output, and so on. Such lost benefits are what we consider the highest order of value of the information center services. This value, compared with the cost of centers, is substantial. The savings alone are typically found to be on the order of 10 to 20 times the total cost of the center services.

Determining the extent to which services contribute to the value of information is achieved using the following rationale:

- The number of readings that are made from materials provided by the information center is first determined.
- The amount of time that the professionals spend in identifying, locating, obtaining, accessing and reading the materials provided by the center is estimated. This is what the professionals are "willing to pay" for these materials.
- Then assume that center services are not available to the professionals. If they are not available, the professionals would have to get their journals, books, etc. from alternative sources such as personally subscribing, using other office collections, going to an external library, contacting a colleague to get materials, and so on. Even assuming the least expensive and timeconsuming alternative, we find that professionals must spend more of their time getting access to the information and that additional costs are involved as well.
- The additional amount of time and other costs required by professionals is estimated. This is the second level of the value of the information center.
- It is assumed that professionals spend a given amount of time in information seeking and reading. Because they would have to spend more time if center services were not available, they would read less and, therefore, lose savings, timeliness, quality, productivity, etc., resulting from lost readings.
- The dollar savings, quality, timeliness, productivity, etc., that are lost by not having the center available are considered to be the third type of value of these services.

THE VALUE OF JOURNAL ARTICLES PROVIDED BY INFORMATION CENTERS

In this example, professionals from the organization surveyed are estimated to read about 600,000 journal articles per year. About 196,000 of these readings are from journals provided by the information center (from copies located at the center, journal routing, etc).

The approximate professional time required for identifying, gaining access to and reading journal articles obtained from the center is estimated as given in Table 1 for all article readings from the center journal copies.

The estimated total amount of time professionals spend identifying and gaining access to journal articles provided by the information center is about 38,500 hours per year or about 11.7 minutes (0.195 hours) per article read. Adding to that the amount of time spent read-

Table 1. Amount of Time Spent per Year in Identifying, Locating, Obtaining and Photocopying Journal Articles Obtained from Information Center by Organization Professionals

Activity	Avg. Time Per Reading (minutes)	Total Amount of Time per Year (000 hours)
Professional's Time		
Going to center	3.7	12.2
Identify article	1.4	4.6
Locate article	3.4	11.2
Obtain article	0.2	2.6
Photograph article	2.4	7.9
Total	11.7	38.5
Someone Else's Time		
Going to center	2.1	6.9
Identify article	1.4	4.6
Locate article	1.4	4.6
Obtain article	1.3	4.3
Photograph article	0.8	2.6
Total	7.0	23.0

SOURCE: King Research, Inc. Survey of Professionals

ing (0.7 hours for journal readings from center copies), it is estimated that the total time spent is about 175,700 hours per year or $6.7 million for the professionals (assuming an average hourly wage of $38.13). Adding to that the costs of the time of others and other costs ($2.20 and $0.80 per article read or a total of $588,000) yields a total of $7.3 million.

The average current cost of these readings of journals provided by the center is $37.20. This is a minimum that professionals are "willing to pay" for these materials and, as such, the amount is a lower bound on the value of journal articles provided by the center. Typical average additional costs to the center of purchasing and processing subscriptions and conducting online searches are estimated to be about $12.00 per reading. Thus, the ratio of center costs ($12.00) to this value of information ($37.20) is about three to one.

There are two ways that we have studied the methods and costs of obtaining journal articles from alternative sources (i.e., other than the center). The first involves observing from national surveys which explore how scientists and engineers get their articles when they have no library available (e.g., when they are employed by small businesses). We determined the approximate amount of time spent identifying, locating and getting information from the other sources. For the second method, we also asked professionals to indicate (1) how they would obtain the information (not necessarily the journal article, if another source such as a colleague or consultant was less expensive) from the least expensive alternative, and (2) how much additional costs (above the current cost) would be required in terms of: (1) their time; (2) the time of others (e,g., secretary, technician, etc.); and (3) other costs, such as subscription to a journal, etc.

The process began by determining whether the professionals knew about the information reported (or discussed) in the most recent article read, prior to their reading about it. About 68 percent of the readings involved new information. The readers were asked how they would get the articles, if the information center could not be used. About four percent of the professionals said they would not obtain the article or information. Of the readings in which the information was not new, the information would most frequently be obtained from a colleague or other source.

The average additional costs (i.e., how much more it would cost over current costs) of using the least expensive alternative source for journal articles (if the center were not available) are summarized as given in Table 2.

The average cost to professionals for the alternative sources of journal article readings is $75.60 per reading (including current costs plus additional cost of the alternative). This average cost of alternative sources includes the following components of cost:

	Avg. Current Costs	Avg. Costs of Alternatives	Avg. Difference ($)
Professionals time	$34.20	$64.90	$30.70
Time of others	$ 2.20	$12.40	$10.20
Other costs	$ 0.80	$ 1.10	$ 0.30
Total	$37.20	$78.40	$41.20

Table 2. Amount of Additional Time It would Take in Identifying, Locating, Obtaining and Photocopying Journal Articles if Organization Professionals Did Not Have an Information Center

Activity	Avg. Time Per Reading (minutes)	Total Amount of Time Per Year (000 hours)
Professional's Time		
Going to center	28.3	92.4
Identify article	8.3	27.1
Locate article	6.3	8.2
Obtain article	4.2	13.4
Photograph article	1.1	3.6
Total	48.2	157.5
Someone Else's Time		
Going to center	9.1	29.7
Identify article	12.1	39.5
Locate article	5.4	17.6
Obtain article	4.2	13.7
Photograph article	1.1	3.6
Total	31.9	104.2

SOURCE: King Research, Inc. Survey of Professionals

The total cost of alternative sources to the information center is about $8.1 million (i.e., $41.20 times 196,000 readings of journal articles provided by the center). This amount is the second estimate of the value of the information center.

A third way to look at the value of the center in providing access to journals is to consider that professionals seem to spend a relatively fixed amount of time in information seeking and reading (based on national data collected by us and others over 25 years). If we assume that this is true for professionals in this example, they would have less time for this activity (i.e., obtaining and reading articles) if the center were not available (or did not exist). The total time the professionals spend identifying, gaining access to and reading journal articles (accessed though the center service) is 175,500 hours. The additional time necessary to obtain articles previously provided by the center (if the services were not available) is about 157,500 hours, thus a new average time per article read is 1.7 hours per reading (i.e., 333,000 hours divided by 196,000 readings). Dividing this into the constant hours devoted by professionals to this activity (175,500 hours) yields 103,200 readings. Therefore, about 92,800 readings would be lost to professionals (i.e., 196,000 minus 103,200). Assume average loss in savings attributable to reading journal articles is $450 or 11.8 professional hours per reading. Total loss would be $842 million or 1.1 million hours of professional time. Thus, their productivity would be affected. In addition to lost savings in time, the lost readings would also have some effect on quality, timeliness and other work performance factors as well.

THE VALUE OF BOOKS PROVIDED BY THE INFORMATION CENTER

Professionals in the example organization have 520,000 readings from books per year of which 124,000 of these readings are from books provided by the center. The approximate amount of professional time spent reading books provided by the center is estimated to be about 1.7 hours spent reading and 0.35 hours spent identifying, locating and getting the books (Table 3).

The total time spent by professionals on identifying and accessing the center-provided books is about 43,300 hours. The total time, including reading, is about 253,800 hours. The amount professionals pay in terms of their own time getting access to and reading books is about $9.7 million (i.e., the minimum value to them).

About 75 percent of the readings of books provided by the center involved books containing information whose existence was known prior to reading. About 72 percent of the time the respondents indicated the information could have been obtained elsewhere, such as from an external library (30%), a colleague, consultant, etc., (26%), they would have bought it (12%) or the professionals' own collec-

Table 3. Amount of Time Spent in Identifying, Locating, Obtaining and Photocopying Books Obtained from the Information Center by Organization Professionals

Activity	Avg. Time Per Reading (minutes)	Total Amount of Time (000 hours)
Professional's Time		
Going to center	8.1	16.7
Identify book	3.6	7.4
Locate book	3.1	6.4
Obtain book	2.1	4.3
Photography book	3.9	8.1
Total	20.8	43.0
Someone Else's Time		
Going to center	4.0	8.3
Identify book	1.8	3.7
Locate book	1.2	2.5
Obtain book	1.1	2.3
Photography book	1.7	3.5
Total	9.8	20.3

SOURCE: King Research, Inc. Survey of Professionals

tion (4%). Even though professionals know about the information most of the time, the cost of locating and acquiring it is expensive. These costs are summarized as follows in Table 4.

The average cost per reading books currently obtained through the center and by using alternatives is as follows:

	Avg. Current Costs	Avg. Costs of Alternatives	Avg. Difference ($)
Professionals time	$ 78.40	$103.50	$25.10
Time of others	$ 3.10	$ 10.50	$ 7.40
Other costs	$ 15.60	$ 18.70	$ 3.10
Total	$ 97.10	$132.70	$35.60

Thus, the total cost of alternatives to the information center is $4.4 million, (i.e., 124,000 times $35.60).

Table 4. Amount of Additional Time It would Take in Identifying, Locating, Obtaining and Photocopying Books if Organization Professionals Did Not Have the Information

Activity	Avg. Time Per Reading (minutes)	Total Amount of Time per Year (000 hours)
Professional's Time		
Going to center	17.2	35.5
Identify book	5.8	12.0
Locate book	6.4	13.2
Obtain book	5.2	10.7
Photograph book	4.8	9.9
Total	39.4	81.4
Someone Else's Time		
Going to center	11.5	23.8
Identify book	2.9	6.0
Locate book	3.0	6.2
Obtain book	2.9	6.0
Photograph book	2.9	6.0
Total	23.2	47.9

SOURCE: King Research, Inc. Survey of Professionals

Finally, the additional costs to professionals (in their time) for obtaining the book-related information are about 81,400 hours, or a new total of about 338,200 hours for 124,000 readings. Taking this additional cost into account results in a new average hours per reading (2.7 hours per reading). In order to maintain a constant total 256,800 hours, the number of readings would be 95,100 instead of 124,000 readings. Therefore, 28,900 readings would be lost. The value of these lost readings represents the potential savings in time and equipment (i.e., $690 or 18.1 hours of professional time per reading) as well as improved quality and timeliness of work that would have been achieved. Converted to professional time, this comes to about 523,100 hours. The total value calculated in this manner is $20 million (i.e., 28,900 readings that are lost times $690 in savings per reading).

THE VALUE OF INTERNAL DOCUMENTS PROVIDED BY THE INFORMATION CENTER

Professionals read about 360,000 internal documents of which 158,000 are through documents obtained at the information center. The professionals are estimated to spend an average of about 1.0 hour (per reading) in reading internal documents and 0.31 hour in identifying, locating and getting the documents to read. The latter estimates are subdivided as shown in Table 5.

Table 5. Amount of Time Spent in Identifying, Locating, Obtaining and Photocopying Internal Documents Obtained from the Information Center by Organization Professionals

Activity	Avg. Time Per Reading (minutes)	Total Amount of Time per Year (000 hours)
Professional's Time		
Going to center	4.3	11.3
Identify internal documents	4.4	11.6
Locate internal documents	1.5	4.0
Obtain internal documents	7.9	20.8
Photograph internal documents	0.7	1.8
Total	18.8	49.5
Someone Else's Time		
Going to center	2.8	7.4
Identify internal documents	1.6	4.2
Locate internal documents	1.7	4.5
Obtain internal documents	2.0	5.3
Photograph internal documents	0.9	2.4
Total	9.0	23.8

SOURCE: King Research, Inc. Survey of Professionals

The estimated time spent by professionals in identifying, locating, obtaining and reading documents provided by the center is 207,000 hours (i.e., 158,000 readings times 1.31 hours per reading). Thus, the "willingness to pay" value is $7.9 million.

The information found in read internal documents was known by the readers for 53 percent of the readings. They indicated that some would not have obtained the document or information, if the center was not available (24%). Most of them would get it from a colleague (47%), an alternate library (23%) or elsewhere (5%).

The average additional costs of obtaining internal documents or information found in them from alternative sources to the center are given in Table 6.

The average cost for using alternative sources is $12.00 per reading as shown below.

	Avg. Current Costs	Avg. Costs of Alternatives	Avg. Difference ($)
Professionals time	$50.10	$60.30	$10.20
Time of others	$ 2.90	$ 4.20	$ 1.30
Other costs	$ 0.90	$ 1.40	$ 0.50
Total	$53.90	$65.90	$12.00

The total cost of using alternatives for the 158,000 readings of internal documents is $1.9 million.

A total of 42,000 hours of additional professionals' time would be involved in using alternative sources. Thus, a total of 249,000 hours would be required to obtain and read 158,000 documents — or 1.58 hours per reading. If the professionals continue to spend 207,000 hours with these documents, they would be able to read 131,000 at 1.58 hours per reading. This means they would lose about 27,000 readings. Savings for these 27,000 readings is estimated to be $1,210 a piece (on the average) or a total of $33 million. In terms of professionals' time this value is 850,000 hours.

VALUE OF OTHER SERVICES

The value of searches performed by the information center staff is how much more it would cost to do the searches if there were no center staff available to search. We find that about 19 percent of the searches would not have been done. Over four-fifths of the searches would have been delegated to someone else on the professional's staff; 12 percent would have been obtained from an external library; and 20 percent, called a knowledgeable colleague or used a contractor or online service. The cost of using alternative means of searching is estimated to be about $240 *more* than is currently spent on the searches (about $110). Most of this additional cost is

Table 6. Amount of Additional Time It would take in Identifying, Locating, Obtaining and Photocopying Internal Documents If Organization Professionals Did Not Have the Information Center

Activity	Avg. Time Per Reading (minutes)	Total Amount of Time per Year (000 hours)
Professional's Time		
Going to center	7.0	18.4
Identify internal documents	1.6	4.2
Locate internal documents	3.4	9.0
Obtain internal documents	2.6	6.8
Photograph internal documents	1.4	3.7
Total	16.0	42.1
Someone Else's Time		
Going to center		
Identify internal documents	1.2	3.2
Locate internal documents	1.2	3.2
Obtain internal documents	1.2	3.2
Photograph internal documents	0.5	1.3
Total	4.1	10.9

SOURCE: King Research, Inc. Survey of Professionals

in terms of the users' time ($59), but some of it is in the additional cost to purchase a search ($21), someone else's time ($8) or other expense ($22). Thus all told, it would cost the organization about $1.1 million more to conduct the searches without the benefit of the center staff.

The users of Current Awareness Bulletins indicated a number of ways in which they benefitted by having the last Current Awareness Bulletin as follows:

- Identified needed sources that they probably would not have identified otherwise   58%
- Identified needed sources sooner than they could have otherwise   29%
- Saved them or their staff time in identifying needed documents   21%

They indicated it would require an average of about 3.4 hours of their time or their staffs' time to identify needed documents themselves.

If the Current Awareness Bulletin was not provided to the professionals, the users would have identified the needed sources in the following manner:

- They could not have done it   59%
- Department circulation/routing   17%
- They would have conducted an online search   9%
- They would have delegated an online record   8%
- Other means   8%

The cost of using the other source is estimated to be about $57 per use of the Bulletins. This cost of alternative sources is derived from:

- Using their own time $34.00
- Using the time of others $12.00
- Cost of purchasing a search service $10.60
- Telephone calls and other $ 0.30

TOTAL VALUE OF THE INFORMATION CENTER

As indicated above, the value of the information center services can be assessed from three perspectives: what users are willing to pay (in terms of their time and effort) for information provided by the center, what it would cost them to use alternative sources for obtaining the information, and what savings (or research cost avoidance) would be lost if the center did not exist. Rough estimates for these three perspectives of value are given below.

The return-on-information of this cost is substantial, regardless of how one views value. That is, the return is:

- 4.3 to one in terms of willingness to pay,
- 2.5 to one in terms of cost to use alternative sources, and
- 15 to one in terms of research cost avoidance (savings).

These returns are impressive indeed.

Table 7. The Value of Information Center Services from Three Perspectives and By Source of Reading

	Willingness to Pay	Cost to Use Alternative Sources	Cost Avoidance by Savings
Journals	$ 7.3 million	$8.1 million	$42 million
Books	$ 9.7 million	$4.4 million	$20 million
Internal documents	$ 7.9 million	$1.9 million	$33 million
Online searching	$ 1.5 million	$1.1 million	—
Current Awareness Bulletins	$ 0.2 million	$0.7 million	—
Total	$26.6 million	$15.3 million	$ 95 million

SOURCE: King Research, Inc.

RESOURCES

Allen, T. J. 1977. *Managing the Flow of Technology: Technology Transfer and the Dissemination of Technological Information Within the R&D Organization.* Cambridge, MA: MIT Press.

American Psychological Association. n.d. *Project on Scientific Information Exchange in Psychology,* vol. 2: PB-169 005, vol. 3: PB-182 962. Washington, DC: American Psychological Association.

Griffiths, J. M., and D. W. King. 1990. *Keys to Success: Performance Indicators For Public Libraries.* Library Information Series, No. 18. UK: Office of Arts and Libraries, Her Majesty's Stationary Office.

Johnson, R. M. 1974. Trade-off analysis of consumer values. *Journal of Marketing Research* 11(May): 121-127.

King, W. D., and E. C. Bryant. 1971. *Evaluation of Information Services and Products.* Washington, DC: Information Resources Press.

King, D. W., and J. M. Griffiths. 1988. Evaluating the effectiveness of information use. In *Evaluating the Effectiveness of Information Centers and Services.* AGARD (Advisory Group for Aerospace Research & Development) Lecture Series No. 160 presented in Luxembourg 5-6 September 1988, Athens, Greece 8-9 September 1988, Lisbon, Portugal 12-13 September 1988. NATO. AGARD-LS-160.

King, D. W., and J. M. Griffiths. n.d. *Special Libraries and Information Services - Increasing the Information Edge.* Oak Ridge, TN: Information Frontiers Publications.

King, D. W., D. McDonald, and N. K. Roderer. 1981. *Scientific Journals in the United States: Their Production, Use, and Economics.* New York: Academic Press.

Lord Kelvin. 1977. Lecture to the Institution of Civil Engineers. In *Scientific Quotations: The Harvest of a Quiet Eye*. New York: Crane Russack.

NSF Grants to Develop Statistical Indicators of Scientific and Technical Communication in the US. 1977/78; 1984/85.

Palmour, V. E., M. C. Bellassai, and N. V. Dewath. 1980. *A Planning Process For Public Libraries*. Chicago, IL: American Library Association.

Rosenberg, P. 1985. *Cost Finding For Public Libraries: A Manager's Handbook*. Chicago, IL: American Library Association.

Additional Readings
Part V: Assessing
the Value of Information

Arrow, K. J. 1979. The economics of information. In *The Computer Age: A Twenty-Year View*, eds. M. L. Dertouzos, and J. Moses, 307-317. Cambridge, MA: MIT Press.

Bates, B. J. 1988. Information as an economic good: Sources of individual and social value. In *The Political Economy of Information*, eds. V. Mosco, and J. Wasko, 76-94. Madison, WI: The University of Wisconsin Press.

Bearman, T. C., P. Guynup, and S. N. Milevski. 1985. Information and productivity. *Journal of the American Society For Information Science* 36(6): 369-375.

Black, S. H., and D. A. Marchand. 1982. Assessing the value of information in organizations: A challenge for the 1980s. *Information Society* 1(3): 191-225.

Bookstein, A. 1981. An economic model of library service. *Library Quarterly* 51(4): 410-428.

Braunstein, Y. M. 1985. Information as a factor of production: Substitutability and productivity. *Information Society* 3(3): 261-273.

Chick, M. J. 1990. Information value and cost measures for use as management tools. In *Information: A Strategy For Economic Growth*, 19-36. Washington, DC: Special Libraries Association.

Cronin, B., and M. Gudim. 1986. Information and productivity: A review of research. *International Journal of Information Management* 6(2): 85-101.

Drake, M. A. 1987. Value of the information professional: Cost/benefit analysis. In *President's Task Force on the Value of the Information Professional, June 1987*. Washington, DC: Special Libraries Association.

Griffiths, J.M. 1982. The value of information and related systems, products and services. In *Annual Review of Information Science and Technology*, ed. M. E. Williams, 269-284. New York: Knowledge Industry for American Society for Information Science.

Griffiths, J. M., and D. W. King. 1993. *Special Libraries: Increasing the Information Edge*. Washington, DC: Special Libraries Association.

Griffiths, J.M., and D. W. King. 1990. *A Manual on the Evaluation of Information Centers and Services.* Neuilly sur Seine, France: AGARD. (AGARDograph No. 310) [Available in the US from American Institute of Aeronautics and Astronautics, Technical Information Service, 555 West 57th Street, Suite 1200, New York, NY 10019.]

Harmon, G. 1984. The measurement of information. *Information Processing and Management* 20(1-2): 193-198.

Hayes, R. M., and J. Becker. 1984. Cost accounting in libraries. In *Costing and the Economics of Library and Information Services,* 7-25. London: Aslib.

Hayes, R. M., and T. Erickson. 1982. Added value as a function of purchases of information services. *Information Society* 1(4): 307-339.

Kantor, P. B. 1989. Library cost analysis. *Library Trends* 38(Fall): 171-188.

Koenig, M. E. 1990. Information services and downstream productivity. In *Annual Review of Information Science and Technology,* vol. 25, ed. M. E. Williams, 145-172. NY: Elsevier Science Publishers B.V. for the American Society for Information Science.

Lamberton, D. M. 1984. The economics of information and organization. In *Annual Review of Information Science and Technology,* vol. 19, ed. M. E. Williams, 3-30. White Plains, NY: Knowledge Industry Publications, for the American Society for Information Science.

Machlup, F. 1980. Knowledge: Its creation, distribution, and economic significance. In *Knowledge and Knowledge Production.* Princeton, NJ: Princeton University Press.

Machlup, F. 1979. Uses, value and benefits of knowledge. *Knowledge: Creation, Diffusion, Utilization* 1(1):62-81.

Magrill, R. M. 1985. Evaluation by type of library. *Library Trends* 33(Winter): 267-295.

Manning, H. 1987. The corporate librarian: Great return on investment. In *President's Task Force on the Value of the Information Professional, June 1987.* Washington, DC: Special Libraries Association.

Marshall, J. G. 1993. *The Impact of the Special Library on Corporate Decision-Making.* Final Report to the Special Libraries Association. Washington, DC: Special Libraries Association.

Matarazzo, J. M., L. Prusak, and M. R. Gauthier. 1990. *Valuing corporate libraries: A survey of senior managers.* Washington, DC: Special Libraries Association in cooperation with Temple, Barker, & Sloan.

McClure, C. R., and B. Reifsnyder. 1984. Performance measures for corporate information centers. *Special Libraries* 75: 193-204.

Porat, M.U., and M.R. Rubin. 1977. *The Information Economy.* Washington, DC: US Department of Commerce, Government Printing Office.

Prusak, L., and J. Matarazzo. 1992. *Information Management and Japanese Success.* Washington, DC: Special Libraries Association.

Repo, A. J. 1987. Economics of information. In *Annual Review of Information Science and Technology,* vol. 22, ed. M. E. Williams, 3-35. Amsterdam, The Netherlands: Elsevier Science for the American Society of Information Science.

Rubin, M. R. 1990. The size and shape of the information economy: An historical overview. In *Information: A Strategy For Economic Growth*. Washington, DC: Special Libraries Association.

Strassmann, P. A. 1985. *Information payoff: The transformation of work in the electronic age*. New York: Free Press.

Taylor, R. S. 1986. *Value-Added Processes in Information Systems*. Norwood, NJ: Ablex.

Valuing Special Libraries and Information Centers: An SLA Information Kit. 1993. Washington, DC: Special Libraries Association.

Van House, N. A. 1984. Research on the economics of libraries. *Library Trends* 32(4): 407-423.

Varlejs, J., ed. 1982. *The Economics of Information*. London, England: McFarland & Company.

Woodsworth, A., and J. F. Williams II. 1993. *Managing the Economics of Owning, Leasing and Contracting Out Information Services*. Brookfield, VT: Ashgate.

VI
Information Without Boundaries

VI
Information Without Boundaries

INTRODUCTION

Originally, this part of the book was to be devoted to articles that represented the very best examples of information management practices. Being from a Faculty of Information Studies, we hoped that these articles would show information specialists playing a prominent role in achieving the goals, influencing the decisions, and contributing significantly toward the productivity of their organizations. We sought exemplary articles that would demonstrate how information specialists were at the forefront in anticipating the needs of their managers, supplying them with relevant, synthesized, and analyzed information using the appropriate internal and external, personal and impersonal, local and far-flung sources regardless of the technologies involved. We were convinced that information specialists had the knowledge and skills to satisfy even the most information-hungry organizations. The problem, then, was simply to find a few articles to confirm our convictions.

After extensive and repeated manual and online reviews of the literature, discussions with colleagues, consultants, and other experts, we finally acknowledged that our quest for the perfect articles demonstrating information specialists spearheading the information services of their organizations was a futile one. We found few articles devoted to an organization-wide view of information management. What we did find were many brief descriptions of a particular aspect of an information service, and numerous hortatory pieces suggesting what information professionals ought to do to become more valued members of their organization. In some cases, the most intriguing material appeared in proprietary consultants' reports or other sources that were not readily reproducible. We also found that the practice of information management in some parts of Asia and Europe was more advanced than in Canada and the U.S. and that in the case of Europe, especially Britain and Scandinavia, these practices were extensively documented in the open literature. In the end, we consoled ourselves with the realization that had there been an abundance of articles describing exemplary practices, the need for this book might not have been as urgent.

Although we are still convinced that information specialists have the potential to play a central role in managing information in organizations, we have also come to realize that there are still deterrents to overcome before that bright future is realized. The constraints or boundaries that act as inhibitors are attitudinal, geographical, organizational, professional, and technological.

For too long, information specialists have been isolated both literally and figuratively from the critical policy and decision making processes of the organization. Too many still operate in a reactive mode, gathering, conserving, and storing information. Today's organizations, forced to review the necessity of all functional areas, require professionals to be proactive, accountable, and team players. It is no longer enough to have the largest, most current collection or provide access to commercially available online services or networks. Organizations want their information to be analyzed, synthesized, and customized and to contribute directly to their productivity and profitability. Information specialists are expected to work as active partners with other information professionals such as data analysts, systems designers, hardware and software engineers as well as professionals in research and development, planning, and marketing to ensure that the information environment of the organization is fully integrated with the mission and ultimate success of the firm. Many librarians are already performing in this mode and achieving unprecedented recognition and awards. For others, a change in attitude will be needed.

In addition to attitudinal changes, information specialists will also need to expand their geographical horizons. The xenophobic tendency of North Americans to disregard developments in managing information beyond our shores cannot be justified. There is much to learn from organizations in Asia and Europe who have used advanced information management strategies to become formidable competitors in the global marketplace.

In North America, many organizational barriers remain to be breached. Too few decision makers and senior managers really appreciate the need for planned, integrated, networked information management. Nor is the relationship between information and innovation, information and productivity, or information and profitability fully understood or supported. For their part, information specialists must be prepared to function at all levels of the organization, contributing to information needs across functions, processes, and even countries as required.

Successful information specialists will embrace new technologies as indispensable tools that enable them to create, organize, and deliver information in innovative ways. They will go beyond existing databases to shape systems and networks that become a critical part of the intelligence of the organization.

Last, as professionals, information specialists will use their wide-ranging skills and knowledge to provide vision and direction to the other professionals working with information and to the organization as a whole.

The first article, by Tom Davenport and Larry Prusak, reinforces many of these views and extends them further. They too contend that too many librarians continue to view the library as a warehouse or an expertise centre when they should be operating as overseers of a multi-media network providing access to internal and external, personal and impersonal sources. They urge librarians to align themselves with others in the organization skilled in both information content issues and the infrastructure of information provision. In their view the library as a physical entity may well become unnecessary whereas the roles of librarians may indeed expand to become more important than ever before. They go on to outline how this may be achieved.

According to the experts, few western companies have truly embraced the notion of information management as a vital component of business success. Rather, it is the Japanese who have recognized the interrelationships between information and competitiveness and have closely tied the role of information systems and services to the achievement of corporate business strategies. B. Bowonder and T. Miyake have written one of the few articles that describes in detail the internal operations of a major Japanese company. They analyze the process whereby Nippon Steel Corporation, the world's biggest steel manufacturer, creates and sustains competitiveness through information management. They show how the company uses environmental scanning and analysis, multilevel information systems, information accumulation, horizontal information flow structures, organizational learning, information fusion and concurrent engineering to integrate functions, centralize control, decentralize decision making, build competence, and foster new business development. They illustrate how the strategic applications of IS and IT combine to transform Nippon Steel from a resource-based to a knowledge-based industry that can maintain its pre-eminent position in the global marketplace. The Japanese example of information management that is totally integrated into the operations of the firm is indeed impressive. However, as the authors point out, it has taken years to evolve to its present form and relies on a business culture that emphasizes team work, information sharing, and achieving harmony between information management strategies and those of the corporation as a whole.

In the west, it is the highly competitive, research-intensive industries such as the financial services firms and the drug manufacturers that have developed sophisticated models of information provision. The role of the information professional in providing competitor intelligence to the pharmaceutical industry in Britain is described in the article by Bijel H. Desai and David Bawden. They interviewed the managers of information units in ten companies to determine the place of Competitor Intelligence in the units' activities; the importance of CI to the organization; the way CI is provided; the sources used; how the value of CI is measured; whether CI is integrated with other information systems; and the extent to which technology is used in providing CI. The comments of the managers as they chronicle their successes and frustrations make compelling reading for information professionals struggling to provide actionable intelligence to the diverse user groups in their organization.

What becomes clear from the literature is that managing the information requirements of organizations has acquired a new urgency as firms compete in a global environment. Information needs are complex and the skills required range across professional domains that have previously been quite distinct. James E. Herring, the author of the last article in this volume, argues that effective information management in the future will necessitate a convergence of professions. By analyzing advertisements for jobs in healthcare information management, he provides persuasive evidence to prove that qualified candidates will have to combine knowledge and skills in information analysis, information resources, information storage and retrieval, information technology, systems analysis, and strategic management. For those who have the requisite expertise, the future is indeed bright.

Further visions of the directions in which information management in general and libraries in particular are likely to go as we approach the 21st century are included in the Additional Readings.

"Blow up the corporate library"

Thomas H. Davenport and Laurence Prusak

INTRODUCTION

The information age is clearly upon us. Academics, consultants, and managers state that information is a critical competitive weapon, that information can transform organizational structures and processes, and that we are all now in the information business. By every measure, including the proliferation of information sources and expenditures for information, the generation and use of information is growing. Management experts such as Peter Drucker and Tom Peters, and Kodama and Nonaka in Japan, consistently trumpet the importance of information use and effective information management.

These, then, should be halcyon days for libraries as the keepers and distributors of information. What function would be better positioned to understand information requirements, distribute information to the right employees and locations, and determine the structure of the 'corporate memory'? Surely not information systems functions; they are still largely concerned with technology, despite the presumptuous title of chief information officer.

Libraries do play an important role in some firms, particularly in research and information-intensive organizations such as pharmaceuticals, investment banks and consulting. They are significant cost centres at many large firms. There are at least 20 000 professionai librarians working in corporate or government libraries, as well as another 50 000 non-professionals. Almost all major (and many smaller) corporations have a library, or library-like functions, as do most major government agencies. Several very large firms have library organizations with as many as 50 distinct units. While it is difficult

This article was first published in the *International Journal of Information Management*, Vol. 13, Issue 6, December 1993, pp. 405-412, and is reproduced here with the permission of Butterworth-Heinemann, Oxford, UK.

to determine what information is specifically bought by libraries, it is estimated that corporate libraries collectively spend 1.7 billion dollars annually.

Yet corporate libraries in the USA have largely been left behind by the information revolution. They have performed relatively narrow functions, mainly associated with identifying and acquiring information, and have not become integrated into the major organizational processes for managing information. Most of them operate on obsolete storage-based models of information management. They have little influence and their employees are often in dead-end careers. Though in many organizations the head of information technology reports to the chief executive officer, to argue that a librarian should do so would be unprecedented. Even though librarians often know more about 'information' than any other staff professionals, few if any have received the title of chief information officer.

It would be easy to say, "blow up the library", and indeed library budgets are often among the first to be cut during hard times (Matarazzo 1981). But libraries and librarians have a high degree of potential value. They often know, better than anyone else in the firm, what information is needed for specific projects, and how to facilitate the effective delivery of that information. Unlike their counterparts in the information systems function, they have chosen to focus on information, rather than technology. Finally, some of the 'library' functions we have studied in other parts of the world — particularly in Japan — provide a valuable model for how libraries can fully achieve their potential (Matarazzo and Prusak 1992). We are therefore arguing that libraries should be blown up in a positive sense— that their mission, function and scope should be significantly expanded, and perhaps combined with other information functions in the firm. All that needs to be detonated is the physical library, the low-level box on the organizational chart, and the stereotypes of librarians more concerned with books than business needs.

WHAT'S WRONG WITH LIBRARIES TODAY

Despite their potential key role in the 'information age', corporate libraries today have many problems. They are poorly understood even by their own managers, and are based on an obsolete model of information provision. They are usually not well integrated with either the businesses they serve or other information-oriented functions. As a result, the value they deliver is often unclear, and in any case less than what is possible.

Libraries are not well understood by those who manage them.

About 40 percent report to general administration functions whose managers rarely know, or care much about, information provisioning. Out of 165 corporate libraries surveyed in a previous study, only three reported to a person who had any professional experience in running the library (Prusak, Matarazzo and Gauthier 1990). Libraries that report to specific functions such as marketing, planning, or R&D are better represented with management; however, they usually serve only their host functions well, developing materials primarily relevant to single functions. And while this has obvious value for these functions, there is no leveraging of sources.

The corporate library developed and grew in the 1920s and 1930s, when print-based resources were predominant, and was based on the model of the public library. The goal was to obtain as many physical volumes — books — as possible on the assumption that someday someone would want to use each one ('a book for every patron' was a common library mission statement). Library policies focused not on how to ensure that information resources were used, but rather on ensuring that they did not leave the premises illicitly. Librarian skill development focused on acquisition, storage, and classification of printed materials, and distribution of them on request. This is essentially a *warehouse* model of information provision. Yet potential users of the information not only had little idea what was in the information warehouse; they also frequently lacked an understanding of why they should even take a look.

As books began to be supplemented by a panoply of less voluminous and structured sources, in more sophisticated organizations the model of information provision did change somewhat. Instead of warehousing books, this new model of the library warehoused people—specifically subject matter experts. Such an *expertise centre* model assumed that employees requiring information on a topic would simply seek out a content expert in a library unit dedicated to a particular topic, e.g., competitive information or information about microelectronics. But this model neglected the fact that most of the people in an organization with subject-matter expertise are not information professionals. Expertise centres are clearly an improvement over the warehouse model, but they do not go far enough in distributing information around an organization.

Furthermore, no real rethinking of either the warehouse or expertise centre models took place when computers entered the library, or when users got access to desktop computers and all-pervasive networks. The improvement from storing CD-ROMs in the warehouse rather than books is one of marginal efficiency, not effectiveness. Though schools of librarianship, or information science, have taught computer skills and advocated more active roles for many years, actual practice in most firms has not changed significantly.

There has also been little integration or even cooperation between libraries and other information-oriented functions. Librarians collect, categorize and store largely textual information; information systems groups focus on largely quantitative or transactional information, and rarely do the twain meet. If an executive wanted to find out more about a customer or competitor who shows up in the latest weekly printout or terminal display, he or she must go to an entirely different source for the information, using different protocols for expressing the information requirement and accessing the source. Only in precious few organizations, such as some universities, firms with strong R&D functions, and financial service firms, for example, have librarians and information technology executives begun to seriously collaborate. Other information-oriented groups, e.g. market researchers, executive assistants, and finance, have also not generally been closely aligned with libraries.

A focus on information content is of great potential value to any organization. Yet librarians have focused on functional efficiency and the profession of being corporate librarians. They often know little beyond the information content needs about the businesses they serve, and are thus unable to suggest ways to make more effective use of information within those businesses. They spend their time not living with information users, but maintaining the stacks. It should also be pointed out that information systems professionals are also often as poorly integrated into the businesses they serve, but they are making faster strides in the right direction than librarians are.

Without this intimate knowledge of the business, neither librarians nor most of their information systems counterparts have been able to focus on actively determining the broad information needs of managers and employees and providing that information in a useful format. As a result, librarians and IS managers are often hard pressed to prove or demonstrate the value of their functions. Because of their distance from the usage of information, putting a value on the information itself is virtually impossible.

Librarians have also declined to try to influence or shape information behaviour, or how employees identify, use and share information. Attempts at outreach programmes often involve teaching employees how to best use the facilities rather than how to solve information problems, or how information can create product and service value. This absence of focus forms a critical gap for many firms, since no other information-oriented function has assumed it either.

As is perhaps obvious by now, the problems of libraries are not only structural and historical. They are also at least partially attributable to librarians themselves. Though there are many exceptions, the typical library professional does not relish the hurly-burly of business. As several librarians have told us, 'we librarians prefer books to people'. Few students would enter library schools in order to get on 'the fast track'. Though such reticence has its attractions, it hinders the effective use of information by business people who sorely need it.

Of course, the fault lies not only with librarians, but also with managers who do not value information in the first place, and who are proud of their ability to act on uninformed intuition. We would argue more generally that the American business culture does not place a high value on acquiring and using information. An indication of this problem is the guilt many managers feel when they are seen reading a book or a journal at their desks. This behaviour is much more the norm in Europe and Japan, where we have observed senior executives actually *reading* at their desks or in the library, with no apparent shame. Perhaps this cultural problem will be eased by the growth of computerized information sources; our culture's love for technology generally attaches much less of a stigma to staring at a cathode ray tube.

OUT OF THE WAREHOUSE

It is time for a new model of the corporate library and the librarian. The warehouse concept must be blown up; librarians, or rather information managers, must view themselves not as warehouse custodians, or even as providers of centralized expertise, but rather as overseers of a multi-media network (see the Appendix, Table 1). They must be concerned with the structure and quality of the content that goes out over the network (programming), in what format it is distributed (media selection), to what audience it is directed (broadcasting vs. narrowcasting), and how the receiver's behaviour changes

Table 1. Models of information provision

Model	Primary objective	Mode of operation
Warehouse	Control and storage of printed matter	Limited information distribution; establishment of formal systems
Expertise centre	Provide access to human experts and their information sources	Reliance on information professionals; some value added to information
Network	Connect providers and users of information	Computer-based multi-media networks with pointers to human sources

in response to the content (advertising response). However, just as television networks do not produce all of the programmes they broadcast, the role of the information network executive in firms should be to encourage wide participation in information creation and dissemination. Broadly speaking, the role of the information professional becomes the establishment of connections between those who have information, and those who want it.

The library itself must be viewed as a virtual information network. The network should be multinodal, with eventually more nodes than there are employees. Several Japanese firms, including Mitsubishi, Nomura, and Dai-Ichi Pharmaceuticals, already have substantial technical and business information networks in place. These well-designed networks provide access to internal and external textual and quantitative information, and will eventually allow access by virtually all employees. In the USA several firms have developed, or are developing, broad networks for employee conferencing and information access. The firms include Barclays and Chemical Bank (Rothstein, Stoddard and Applegate 1992), IBM, American Airlines (Anderson and McKenney 1992), and several professional services firms. These networks serve both a communications and an information function ; some percentage of the materials on them will eventually become part of the 'corporate memory'.

For the technical and employee networks to be effectively combined, someone must devote considerable effort to structuring the information, deciding what should be discarded or saved, and educating the organization on how to use them. Some of the new technologies for information exchange, including Lotus Notes and NCR's Cooperation, are much more amenable to the provision of document-oriented information than previous technologies. However, no technologies currently available can decide what information should go onto the network, how different information bases should be structured, and what information is worth keeping around. We are likely to need humans for such activities over the next few decades. Librarians are the most likely candidates for these roles, if they take up the challenge. If no one accepts the roles, the technical networks firms build for information exchange are likely to be severely underleveraged, as was the case at one professional services firm where only information systems people were involved in implementation (Orlikowski 1992).

This is not to imply that computer networks are the only vehicle for information networking. Librarians must be creative about the media used to help employees achieve 'current awareness,' as it is called in the profession. This might involve arranging seminars, broadcasts over corporate video networks, or disseminating audio tapes for drive-time listening. At NEC, a large Japanese firm, researchers are asked to create posters about their research work, which are then hung on corridor walls for passers-by to study. Finally, there will probably always be a role for the human 'information assistant,' who knows what information is needed by an executive, how to get it, and how to summarize and interpret it. These positions are expensive, but as long as senior managers have a greater need for information than they have time to obtain and digest it, they will continue to be valuable. Due to budget cuts, many of these information assistants are no longer around. In the September MIE meeting, Bob Eccles said he had to either teach 20 percent more or lose his business analysts. Ed Hann of NCR said they have already lost their analysts. Those people not adept at gathering information take time away from their job to collect information.

Under the network model, book-banning, never an activity favored by librarians, must come into vogue. Though we love books as much as anyone, they are often inefficient vehicles for the dissemination of information in corporations. They have more information than most managers need for ad hoc requests and they are difficult to copy and distribute. Even technical journals contain much information that is not useful to an individual reader, and also have copyright problems. On the other hand, on-line databases and CD-ROMs already contain most of the information that managers need day-to-day. Many publishers of books and journals are experimenting with unbundling of printed materials and with publishing them in electronic form. Even periodicals' clearinghouses, which manage lists of magazine and journal subscriptions for corporate libraries, are also addressing this issue. Information managers should work with these firms to try to speed their development efforts. The token copy of Michael Porter's *Competitive Strategy* can remain on managerial bookshelves, but the real use of information awaits new media and new approaches.

With a decreasing emphasis on books and shelves, there should be much less of a need for the library as a place. While having a physical location for printed materials can be logistically beneficial, it does more harm than good. Librarians should attempt to place printed materials on credenzas and in briefcases, not in the stacks. Browsing, which happens rarely anyway in our book-averse culture, should be facilitated over networks. When we visit the new firms who do maintain attractive reading rooms, we rarely find people using them. And librarians themselves should be found not among books, but among users (either actual or potential) of information. At one contract research firm, for example, there is a kiosk equipped with an information professional and an array of printed and electronic sources in each technical area.

Corporate librarians and information systems managers should align more closely. Better yet, those employees who are skilled at information content issues — not only librarians but also some information systems professionals, business analysts, and functional specialists — should align with each other, and providers of technological infrastructure in both camps can join together in a separate organization. The problem with folding them all into one information organization is two-fold. First, librarians and data centre operators have little in common in terms of knowledge and responsibility. Secondly, many organizations might fear the idea of a single functional entity with responsibility for all aspects of information management. If information is truly power, a united information function might prove to be powerful. Perhaps the appropriate model is similar to that in the current US telecommunications industry, in which some firms (e.g., regional Bell operating companies, AT&T) have concentrated on network infrastructure, and others (Dun & Bradstreet, McGraw-Hill, Dow Jones) have focused on content. Alliances between these two worlds are desirable and becoming common, but no one firm seems able to master both.

As Peter Drucker has noted, we have only begun to understand how managers and organizations use information. There is a great need for understanding of how people use and value information — how they gather it, share it, act (or not act) on it, and dispose of it — and under what conditions it should be supplied, including preferred medium and source. The combination of all of this detail would yield a true information architecture, with flows, nodes, inputs, outputs, transformations, and usage patterns. Previous versions of information architecture have been much too granular, technical, and detailed to be of much use; future versions should be created not at the data element or entity level, but at the level of bounded information — often in the form of a document. Again, no one is better positioned than librarians to pursue and act on these issues; they deal frequently with information requirements and documents.

The librarians or information managers in tomorrow's organization must realize that people, not printed or electronic sources, are the most valuable information asset in any organization. Legions of annual reports say that 'the experience and knowledge of our people is our most valuable asset,' yet firms do little or nothing to capitalize on or provide access to this asset. The modern librarian will catalogue not only printed materials or even knowledgeable information professionals, but also that Jane Smith is working on a sales force compensation project, and that Joe Bloggs knows a lot about the metallurgical properties of wheel bearings. When another division or a customer calls to find out this sort of information, they will

Table 2. Requirements for tomorrow's information professionals

1. Get out of the library, and into the business
2. Actively assess who needs information, and who has it — then help them to connect
3. Focus on multiple media, and how they can be exploited using tomorrow's technologies
4. Develop an alliance with the more user-oriented IS personnel
5. Don't assume that technology will replace humans in information provision
6. Develop an architecture of information
7. Work with external providers to develop more useful vehicles for information
8. Emphasize usage of information materials over control

finally have a place to go. Several of the firms we have worked with already feel that this is a valid role for librarians; at one telecommunications firm, for example, librarians were referred to as 'human PBXs' because of their ability to make connections between people requiring information and people possessing it.

All these changes will undoubtedly seem daunting to information professionals (they are summarized in Table 2). They do comprise a radical shift in how people provide information throughout organizations. Better, however, to transform these information jobs than to lose them entirely. The old model of librarians guarding the stacks from information users, or of researchers and executives browsing in comfortable reading rooms, will never be appropriate again.

IMPLICATIONS AND CONCLUSION

As we can see, librarians have their work cut out for them. There are many potential roles to be performed for which they are well-suited. All the more shameful that they continue working in the passive, low-status environment that characterizes most corporate libraries today. Some of today's librarians may find it difficult to make the transition to network executives, and for virtually all this is a transition that will take a number of years. The combination of information functions, and the blending of different types of information skills, will make the necessary cultural changes more possible.

Of course, the issues described here are bigger than the library. What we are talking about is, in fact, a larger set of issues around information management. Whether computer people, librarians, market researchers, or outsourcers provide these services is not really important. That they are ultimately provided in an effective form is what really matters.

It may also be clear that the ideas presented here, because they represent incremental functionality, will require incremental resources. Some current information-oriented activities, such as purchasing the same information multiple times across the organization, spending time in searching for information (about 11 per cent of total work time, according to one recent study of 200 executives) (Accountemps 1992), and buying information for the warehouse that never gets used, can be streamlined or eliminated through better information management. But the information revolution won't come for free. We must be willing to invest in the management of information that helps us make better products, decisions, and customer relationships. What makes this even more expensive is that once someone has been provided with good information, he or she often just wants more. When the information is germane and well-packaged, there is no such thing as information overload (Bruns and McKinnon 1992).

The library was created at a time when information access and usage was a more leisurely activity. We might want to return to those days, but they have not been present for a long time in the corporations we study and work with. To adapt to current and future information environments, radical changes must be undertaken in corporate libraries. Ironically, if they are not begun soon, libraries, and those who focus on content rather than computers, may become extinct in the information age.

REFERENCES

Accountemps. 1992. Survey conducted by Accountemps and reported in *Information Week*, 47.

Anderson, E., and J. McKenney. 1992. American Airlines: The Inter-AAct Project (A) & (B). Harvard Business School Report No. N9-193-013/4, Boston, MA.

Bruns, W., and S. McKinnon. 1992. *The Information Mosaic*. Boston, MA: Harvard Business School Press. The authors find little evidence of information overload among manufacturing executives, even though the information received is often of poor quality.

Matarazzo, J. 1981. *Closing the Corporate Library: Case Studies on the Decision-Making Process*. New York: Special Library Association.

Matarazzo, J., and L. Prusak. 1992. Information Management and Japanese Success. Special Report, Ernst & Young's Center for Information Technology and Strategy, Boston, MA.

Orlikowski, W. 1992. Learning from Notes: Organizational Issues in Groupware Implementation. CISR working paper 241, MIT Center for Information Systems Research.

Prusak, L., J. Matarazzo, and M. Gauthier. 1990. *Value Corporate Libraries: A Survey of Senior Managers.* Washington, DC: Special Libraries.

Rothstein, P., D. Stoddard, and L. Applegate. 1992. Chemical Banking Corporation—Developing a Communications Infrastructure for the Corporate Systems Division. Harvard Business School Report No. N1-192-103, Boston, MA.

Creating and Sustaining Competitiveness: Information Strategies of Nippon Steel Corporation

B. Bowonder and T. Miyake

INTRODUCTION

The role of information, information systems and information technology in creating and sustaining competitiveness has been highlighted by a variety of researchers as well as practitioners, and computer integrated management has been identified as the next competitive breakthrough (Wilmont 1988). Intense business competition among firms has made information a critical strategic variable. New information system strategies can provide a competitive edge to many firms. Similarly, new information technology can provide new business and strategic opportunities, as well as knowledge-based systems (Davenport and Short 1990); knowledge engineering is changing the information environment all over the globe. Information technology has tremendous integration and unification potential (Cash and Konsynski 1986) in organizations and it is all pervasive. Globalization, strategic alliances, unification of Europe and privatization of business are some of the trends which are intensifying the international competition in manufacturing and services (Figure 1), and this has implications for information management. The marginal utility of strategic information is increasing and will continue to do so as the global

This article was first published in the *International Journal of Information Management*, Vol. 12, Issue 1, March 1992, pp. 33-56, and is reproduced here with the permission of Butterworth-Heinemann, Oxford, UK.

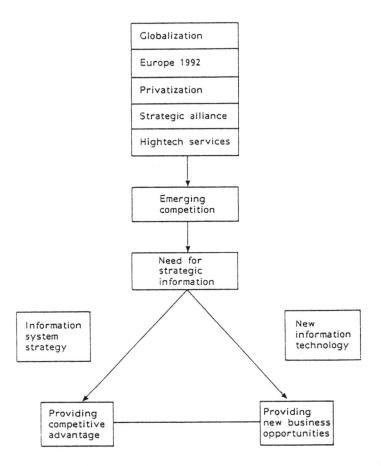

Figure 1. Emerging global trends and information technology interactions.

competitive trend intensifies and the triad power is consolidated (Hamilton 1990). This paper is an analysis of the process of creating and sustaining competitiveness through information management by Nippon Steel Corporation of Japan. The first section gives a framework linking information management and the process of sustaining competitiveness. The second section deals with information management and its strategic dimension at Nippon Steel Corporation. The third section analyses the strategies adopted by Nippon Steel Corporation to create new business opportunities and to move from the business of steel to that of information technology. The last section deals with the lessons that can be derived from the experience of Nippon Steel Corporation in the field of information management.

INFORMATION MANAGEMENT AND COMPETITIVENESS

The strategic dimension of information management has been brought out clearly in a number of studies. It involves information technology as well as information generation and the use of information in an organization (Cronin, Cavaye, and Davenport 1988). Information management results in two strategic options, namely information system (IS) strategy and information technology (IT) strategy. Both these will provide ways for creating and sustaining competitiveness. Earl has identified four potential applications for information management (Earl 1988):

- enabling potential of new technology;
- pursuing competitive advantage;
- identifying and achieving new IT business; and
- changing the basis of IS and IT.

This is conceptually represented in Figure 2. According to Hamilton (1990), technology facilitates new options in two ways: by opening windows and creating options, and by creating new businesses and expanding options; IS and IT do both these. IS is helping to redraw

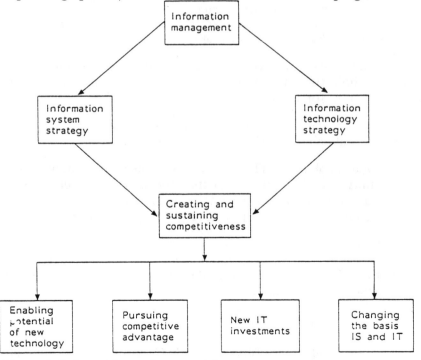

Figure 2. Information and competitiveness.

the competitive boundaries and is increasingly becoming a strategic weapon (Cash and Konsynski 1986).

In this paper a framework is proposed which can help in analysing the process of creating and sustaining competitiveness, through the use of information systems and information technology strategy. To analyse how information systems and information technology influence competitiveness, the authors propose a framework (Figure 3) which extends Porter's model for creating and sustaining the competitiveness (Porter 1990). It can be seen that Nippon Steel Corporation has used a variety of strategies for creating and sustaining competitiveness. For each element of the 'Competition diamond' proposed by Porter (1990), there are a variety of reinforcing factors. The various elements of information strategy which facilitate competitiveness are identified in Figure 4.

Information systems and technology facilitate competitiveness in a variety of ways. The factor conditions (competitive advantages arising out of human resources, physical resources, knowledge resources, capital resources, and infrastructure)

- Facilitate productivity improvements through computerized quality inspection and control.
- Permit better optimization and control.
- Support quick information exchange through networking.
- Allow for large-scale storage of information.

Information system (IS) strategies and information technology (IT) strategies help firms in a variety of ways with respect to demand related factors for products or services:

- precise understanding of the market dynamics; and
- stimulation of IT business or activities in the firm.

Developing capability in IT will help the firms by providing options for diversification in developing competence in new emerging business areas, in related and supporting industries.

The fourth factor which facilitates competitiveness involves:

- the firm's strategy towards IS and IT;
- strategy to increase cooperation and information exchange; and
- strategy to jump ahead of rivals through better anticipatory, forward-looking, scanning systems.

Information management can facilitate the achievement of major business goals, such as quality, productivity. flexibility and adaptability. Some of the specific strategies which facilitated the creation and sustenance of competitiveness at Nippon Steel Corporation are:

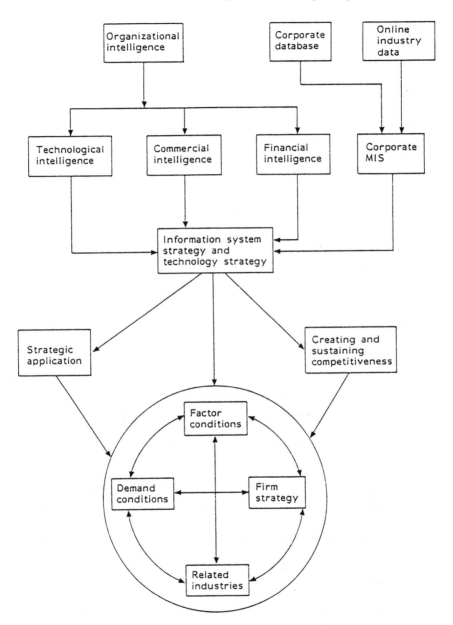

Figure 3. Interrelationships between information and competitiveness

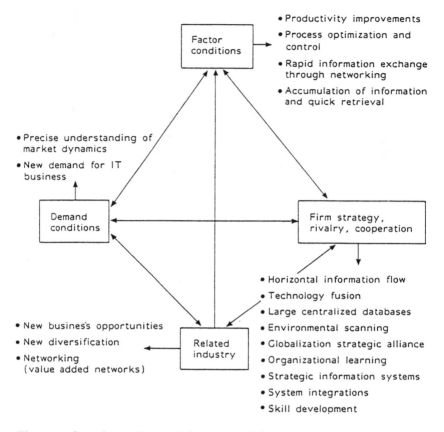

Figure 4. Creating and sustaining competitiveness applying Porter's model

- horizontal information flow structures as well as managerial controls as opposed to vertical information flow structures widely used in Western firms;
- large centralized database at headquarters networked to various units;
- continuous and regular environmental scanning or technology monitoring;
- technology fusion through combination of various technologies (example is integration of neural network technology with fuzzy process control technology);
- globalization and strategic alliances (Nippon Steel Corporation and Hitachi have collaborated for developing Factory automation computers);
- organizational learning by which an enterprise is able to observe, assess and act upon stimuli which are either internal or external to the organization in cumulative, interactive and purposeful ways;

- by having strategic information systems at the corporate level; and
- intensive skill development in the use of IS and IT strategies, and developing new IT business.

With this framework in mind, we examine first the competence-building process at Nippon Steel Corporation in IS and IT. Then we analyse the process of information management at Nippon Steel so as to derive lessons for creating and sustaining competitiveness through the use of IS and IT. Because of the emerging technological changes the boundary which divided IS and IT is vanishing.

IS AND IT AT NIPPON STEEL CORPORATION

Nippon Steel Corporation is the largest steel manufacturing firm in the world (International Iron and Steel Institute 1990). Its IT experience began with the application of process control computers in 1972. It started with the concept 'learning by doing.' It integrated continuous casting and rolling into one integrated process (Editor 1985b). The conventional process takes 12 days for casting and rolling as a sequence. In comparison, the integrated process, covering casting, electrolytic cleaning, annealing, cooling, temper rolling and finishing is completed in one day; it requires 72 per cent fewer operators and the process yield is 60 per cent higher (Editor 1985b). Sensing the success achieved in integrating the processes, intensive use of computerization was attempted in the form of improvement of control over product size and shape accuracies through the use of process control computers, and computerized machine condition monitoring and diagnostics. In the hot rolling process, computerized gauge control and computerized width control was achieved. The organizational learning philosophy was learning by doing (developing new computerized systems) and learning by using new computerized systems through implementation and continuous improvements.

As IT applications in process control evolved, Nippon Steel Corporation implemented a multilevel information system in 1984. This system is called Nippon Steel Iron Making Control and Data Exchange System (NICE) (Editor 1984). The objectives of this computerized operations data processing system are speedy data exchange; improved data analysis; and improved ironmaking operation control through the establishment of a company-wide integrated network. The system will help Nippon Steel Corporation in three ways:

- stable production of high quality products;
- reducing manufacturing costs; and
- enhancing technical competitiveness.

The system links Nippon Steel's head office computer with eight steelworks' computers and with steelworks' plant terminals and two research labs' terminals by means of a combination of public communication circuits and dedicated circuits for online data transmission as shown in Figure 5. NICE includes such features and a 600 MB operations database containing ironmaking operating data. The NICE database can handle 1500 line items of data covering virtually every aspect of ironmaking including blast furnace operations, sintering and coking operations (Editor 1984). Data are collected online and can be stored for each piece of equipment on an ongoing basis on the basis of hour, shift, day, ten-day period and month, for a period of one to ten years. The NICE system has such functions as interactive graphic display, editing of periodical reports and output in hard copy formats. Terminal operators can simulate operational conditions and create interactive graphic displays of all data for purposes of analysis, comparison and monitoring. This has helped Nippon Steel to enhance its competitiveness through improved operational control and information exchange.

In 1987, Nippon Steel Corporation implemented operation of its Nippon Steel Information Network System (NS-INS), an advanced telecommunication system shown in Figure 6 (Editor 1987). NS-INS is a company-wide system that links the 23 offices all across Japan using high-speed digital circuits provided by Nippon Telegraph and Telephone Corporation. NS-INS is a multimedia system which enables integrated communications through telephone, facsimile, data and image communication. Nippon Steel's introduction of new communications systems as a multiple mail system, an eight-station teleconferencing system, and a personal computer communications system has opened the way to the implementation of wide area office automation to support its diversified new business. The information system strategy helped Nippon Steel in the rapid implementation of its multiple business strategy through the use of advanced information technology.

Foreseeing the future potential of telecom networking, Nippon Steel proceeded with the introduction of integrated services digital network for the entire telecommunications system. This system was designed to provide a digital communication system that will realize a digital end-to-end system throughout the company. To this end, Nippon Steel has been using large-scale installations of multimedia multiplexing equipment and advanced digital PBXs which incorporate line-sharing functions in order to improve the quality of the company's telecommunications and its communications processing capability and expandability. The objective of the operation, maintenance and integration of the NS-INS system is that it will contribute to the

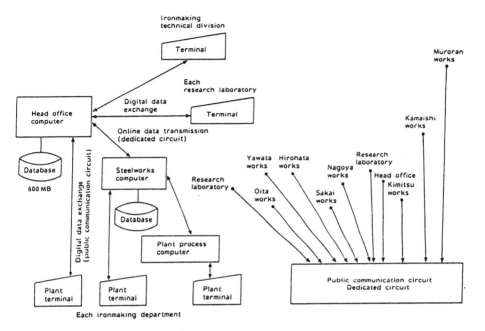

Figure 5. Nippon Steel ironmaking information and data exchange system.

acquisition of new business opportunities in information telecommunication operations which can link computer and telecommunication networks.

Learning by doing and learning by using have helped Nippon Steel to develop new business opportunities and to facilitate continuous upgrading of the operating systems, by using feedback information. Forward-looking implementation, operation and maintenance of the integrated digital services network gave Nippon Steel the confidence to enter the IT business.

The next section analyses how the Nippon Steel Corporation used its IT and IS experience for sustaining and creating competitiveness.

IS AND IT STRATEGIES FOR SUSTAINING COMPETITIVENESS

IS and IT can help corporations in creating and sustaining competitiveness in a number of ways:

- improving the efficiency of manufacturing operations;
- providing information for quick decision making and managerial control;

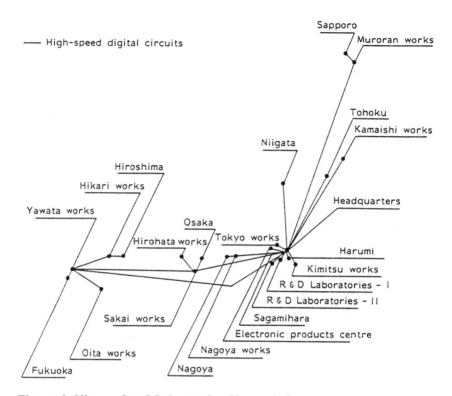

Figure 6. Nippon Steel Information Network System

- facilitating the development of new business opportunities;
- real time process optimization;
- developing competence in emerging technologies ahead of others.

A summary of how IS and IT strategies can help in creating and sustaining competitiveness is shown in Table 1.

Subsequent to the intensive use of IS and IT in the form of databases, computerized operational control systems, management information systems and networking, in 1986 Nippon Steel Corporation decided to branch out into electronics by diversifying its business activities for the purpose of consolidating its strategy of multiple business and maintaining Nippon Steel's position as a world class manufacturer by selecting two major activities namely computing and electronic equipment. In computers using the internal experience, Nippon Steel Corporation will produce and market super minicomputers jointly with a US manufacturer. The strategy will be to develop not only through its own technology development efforts, but to carry out joint research with, and introduce technologies from,

Table 1. IS and IT strategy and applications

Application	Information system strategy	Information technology strategy
Manufacturing, operations	Data exchange and data storage	Online controls, distributed data processing
Learning, training and simulation	Implementing MIS	Learning by doing and using
Decision making	Quick management response	Up-to-date information, large databases
Competence building	Operating and maintaining MIS and networks	Linking computers and communication systems
New business development	IS services	Value-added networks, factory automation

outside organizations and also to take advantage of opportunities to form joint ventures and carry out corporate take-overs to establish electronics/communications as a major pillar of its multiple business management (Nippon Steel Corporation 1989, Editor 1990a).

In May 1987, Nippon Steel Corporation announced its multiple management plan for doubling its turnover by 1995 to 4000 billion yen. It also announced the formation of separate divisions to handle information and communication technology. On 1 April 1988 Nippon Steel established four new information and communications systems companies (Editor 1988). This move, which is a part of Nippon Steel's aggressive multiple business strategy, will allow the company to make use of the IS and IT competence it had accumulated in its steelmaking business. The four information and communication systems companies started in 1988 were:

- Nippon Steel Information and Communication Systems Inc was established by spinning off Nippon Steel Corporation's Computer and Communication System Division and amalgamating it with Nippon Steel Computer systems Co Ltd. This will concentrate on developing and providing remote computing services, and other value-added services.

- Nippon Steel and Information System Service Corporation, a joint venture with IBM Japan Ltd, will concentrate on overall system services including both hardware and software with a primary focus on the development of smaller computer systems.
- Nittetsu Hitachi Systems Engineering Inc, a joint venture with Hitachi Ltd, was set up to develop and market office automation systems and factory automation systems linking multifunction workstations to mainframe host computers.
- NCI Systems Integration Inc works on systems integration for large-scale systems ordered by customers, or rather system development and integration.

Nippon Steel introduced information system technologies in its steel-making operations ranging from business administration to production and shipping control. The company diversification into Information Systems and Information Technology was based on its wide-ranging experience in development and application of systems and hardware and software technologies. As a creative integrator, and as an innovative supplier, Nippon Steel is developing new business coupling its own assets with external strengths through original development, establishment of new firms and capital participation in or business ties with other companies (Nippon Steel Corporation 1989).

Nippon Steel Corporation has developed new business relating to information technology through a variety of competences, namely:

- Systems integration: The company developed competence for constructing comprehensive and integrated systems of very high level through an effective combination of project management and system integration covering a variety of functions (finance, operations, distribution and transportation).
- Information processing services: The company provides computation services requiring high level know how and resale of circuits. Nippon Steel offers CAD/CAM and value-added communications services through NS-INS. The company provides extensive information services for research, study, education and consulting.
- Software development: Nippon Steel markets multipurpose software packages and develops large-scale systems to meet specific customer needs and also trains people using computer-aided instruction.
- Marketing of value-added computers: Nippon Steel satisfies diverse user-specific needs by applying Nippon Steel's system development capabilities with special reference to use of small and medium size computer systems. Also, Nippon Steel markets Nippon Sun Microsystems Workstations. Nippon Steel is planning to extend business into network integration, marketing minisupercomputers to microcomputers.
- Communication systems planning: In collaboration with the GTX Cor-

poration of the USA, which has the most advanced technology in the computer graphics field, Nippon Steel manufactures and sells the revolutionary automatic drawing and recognition systems.

- Database management: In collaboration with Tau Engineering Inc, NSC is moving into the market for information retrieval and database systems as well as image processing.
- Factory automation: Nippon develops and markets factory automation systems.
- Construction: Nippon Steel undertakes planning, design and construction of high technology resort facilities and intelligent buildings.

The basic elements of information management used by Nippon Steel Corporation are outlined in the following sections.

ENVIRONMENTAL SCANNING AND ANALYSIS

The most critical aspect of information management is continuous environmental monitoring or scanning to reduce environmental uncertainty. Environmental scanning and analysis consists of four stages:

- scanning the environment to detect warning signals;
- monitoring specific environmental trends;
- forecasting the future direction of environmental changes; and
- assessing current and future environmental changes for their organizational implications (Narayanan and Fahey 1987).

For anticipating changes, reducing surprises and taking advantage of new opportunities, information 'scanning, screening, processing, analysis and synthesis' are attempted. Japanese firms emphasize scanning (Tatsuno 1990), which is the most crucial step in information management. Scanning is an input to a comprehensive organizational intelligence system consisting of business, commercial, financial and technological intelligence (Matsuda 1988). Since the scanning is done through a variety of channels such as trading houses, subsidiaries, foreign offices and banks, the overall cost is low. From the transaction cost approach, the overheads for scanning are spread over a large organizational base and government agencies; for example, MITI and JETRO supplement the information scanning and are mutually supportive (Johnson 1982). Intensive environmental scanning has helped Nippon Steel to initiate strategic action for developing new business.

MULTILEVEL INFORMATION SYSTEMS

Nippon Steel has three information systems catering to a wide variety of requirements:

- corporate level business and market information;
- plant level operation and control information; and
- R&D and technical design and engineering data and specifications.

Each of these information systems caters to various aspects of the steel business; the last system is purely for engineering and technical information.

The Japan Iron and Steel Federation (JISF) has a Japan Iron and Steel Information System (Figure 7) to cater for the needs of industry level information (Editor 1985a). This is a complex information system interlinked to all the major steel manufacturing firms. This is accessible to all JISF members. Japan is probably the only country to have an industry level information system operated by an industry consortium. Japanese firms consider information sharing as positive in terms of cooperation.

INFORMATION ACCUMULATION

Another characteristic of Nippon Steel's information management strategy is information accumulation through databases, and the continuous processing and sharing of information with various operating units and functional divisions. Initiated in 1986, information support systems form part of Nippon Steel's basic strategies (Figure 8) for achieving multiple business policy:

- strengthen the total capabilities of the Nippon Steel Group;
- increase comprehensive technological capabilities;
- develop human resources policies for supporting multiple business;
- promote policies regarding information systems; and
- promote global policies.

Information management forms the core of Nippon Steel Corporation's capability building strategy as shown in Figure 8 (Editor 1990b). Long-term commitment to the use and development of corporate information systems have synergistic effects on the various capabilities. Japanese firms use three information strategies for this accumulation: experience looping, design looping and concept crossing (Maruyama 1985). The nature of work organization is a major determinant of IT implementation (Jellis 1988) and, in the Japanese

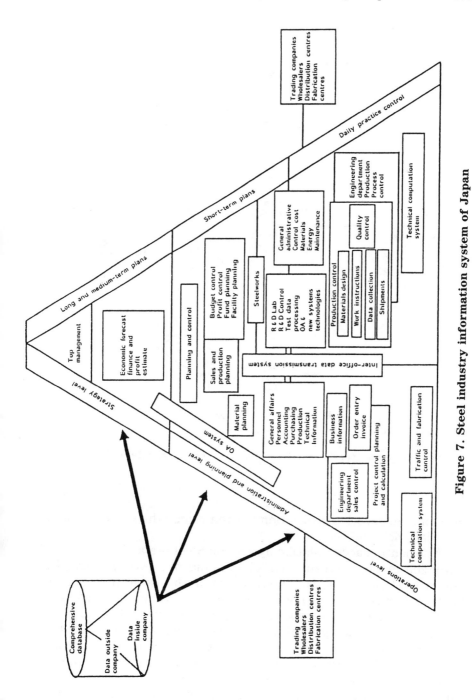

Figure 7. Steel industry information system of Japan

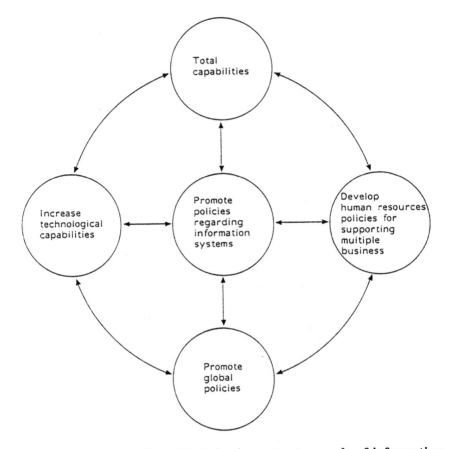

Figure 8. Nippon Steel's multiple business strategy: role of information systems.

environment, work organization has reinforced the information accumulation.

Information accumulation by Nippon Steel — starting from computerized process control, artificial intelligence (AI) systems (Nippon Steel Corporation was the first firm in the world to use AI for blast furnace control), corporate databases and information networking — has helped the company to diversify from steel making into information technology. Information accumulation and utilization were facilitated by technology flow structures, technology fusion and organizational learning and their synergistic interaction. Various Japanese information management strategies are interactive in nature resulting in mutual reinforcement (Bowonder and Miyake 1991, 1988, 1990).

HORIZONTAL INFORMATION FLOW STRUCTURES

One of the major differences between western firms and Japanese firms is the structure of information flow. American firms are characterized by vertical information flow structures (Arrow 1985) and systems, which is more economic but slow to respond to environmental changes (Aoki 1986). Japanese organizations mostly use horizontal information systems and are characterized by some amount of information processing redundancy but quick responsiveness (Aoki 1988). Horizontal information flow structures — in the form of multifunctional new product teams, new start-up ventures, quality circles, 'Kaizen' (continuous production process improvement schemes), multifunctional technology transfer teams and job rotation — facilitate information accumulation. For example, there is more interaction between design engineers and plant engineers at the early phase of design and it is often difficult to say where the phase of prototype fabrication and testing actually starts (Aoki 1990). Horizontal information flow structures facilitate organizational learning processes; result in information or technology fusion; provide for immediate feedback; and stimulate functional integration.

ORGANIZATIONAL LEARNING

Organizations are learning systems (Jellis 1988) involving two aspects — technology and people involved in learning. Organizational learning is defined as the ability of an enterprise to observe, assess and act upon stimuli which are either internal or external to the organization in cumulative, interactive and purposeful ways (Argyris and Schon 1978; Meyers 1990). The nature and dynamics of people and technology interaction will determine the speed of learning. Nonaka has shown that organizational learning has been a key element of Japanese information management, which is facilitated by other complimentary Japanese management practices, such as quality circles, Kaizen, job rotation, etc. (Nonaka 1990) Nippon Steel Corporation used a variety of elements for information management practices which have resulted in new innovations and business diversifications based on these innovations. It is an interactive process and the elements are linked. Some of the major elements used by Nippon Steel are:

- continuous scanning of technology trends;
- fusing different technologies;
- job rotation;

- innovation task force;
- start up of independent new business subsidiaries;
- facilitating information exchange through networking;
- industry online information systems; and
- promoting strategic partnerships.

The process of technology assimilation, organizational learning systems and building core competence in new technologies and then moving into subsidiaries is schematically presented in Figure 9. This is the Japanese style of information management starting from environmental scanning and ending up with new business development.

INFORMATION FUSION

Another characteristic feature of information management in Japanese firms is fusing information to generate newer innovative options. By fusing information from two different fields new combinations or creative options are developed. This can also be termed horizontal transfer of technological information resulting in innovations. Hamilton has termed this as creating new businesses and expanding options (Hamilton 1990). One example of technology fusion is the use of Fuzzy Control Systems in cold rolling mills in steel plants.

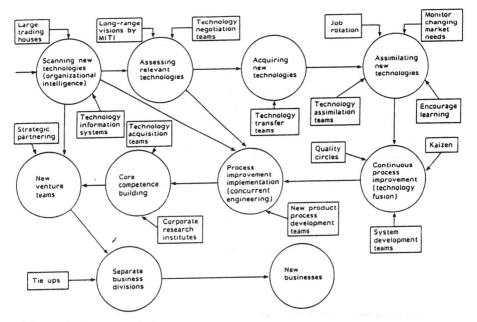

Figure 9. Japanese information system and information management.

Nippon Steel developed competence in cold strip rolling mill technology. Through environmental scanning, when Nippon Steel recognized the potential of fuzzy control systems, it incorporated and installed a fuzzy control technology based cold rolling mill. The linking of competence through fusion of information is also facilitated by horizontal information flow and organizational learning systems. Kodama has termed this process technology fusion (Kodama 1990, 1986). Figure 10 shows how fusion or interlinking of competence occurred in the case of Nippon Steel Corporation.

CONCURRENT ENGINEERING

The adoption of new information technologies, such as

- digital data control,
- online process control,
- online quality control,
- real-time process monitoring,
- computer-aided design and
- networking of process units,

has speeded up the development cycle. This has necessitated intense integration of such functions as design, engineering, manufacturing and marketing. New information technologies facilitate better centralized control but at the same time decentralized decision making (Applegate, Cash, and Mills 1988). The new process is called concurrent engineering or simultaneous engineering, or simultaneous design in which improvements in design, engineering, and production and technology upgrading are instantaneous and information exchange is continuous. Feedback loops of development processes or, more generally speaking, horizontal coordination among various organizational units are more intense yet tend to be more informal in

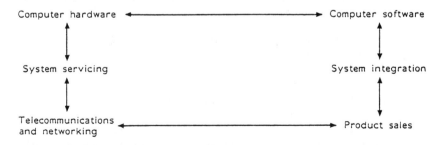

Figure 10. Interlinking competences.

the Japanese firms (Aoki 1990). The information management strategy of Nippon Steel has been interactive and synergistic (as shown in Figure 11), giving rise to rapid new business development, through technological innovations.

NEW BUSINESS DEVELOPMENT

The most important aspect of information management at Nippon Steel is the conversion of capabilities into core competence in manufacturing and then developing new business in these new segments. For this, Nippon Steel Corporation initiates tie-ups with firms having the required specific capabilities or core competence. Information technology is accelerating business process redesign through the development of newer capabilities (Davenport and Short 1990). Information acquisition and assimilation through tie-up has a lower transaction cost, in comparison with indigenous or internal generation. Here the strategy of Nippon Steel is to go in for non-steel business for up to 40 per cent of its revenue by 1995. Information technology strategy and information system strategy together have helped Nippon Steel to diversify so as to create and sustain competitiveness.

CONCLUSIONS

Nippon Steel Corporation has used a combination of information management strategies for:

- sustaining competitiveness in existing business segments (steel);
- creating competitiveness by developing new business segments (IT);
- continuously creating new information technology related equipment/machinery for various segments (IT); and
- conceptualizing, developing, implementing and networking management information systems (MIS) and developing competence in emerging technological areas.

The success of the information management strategy of Nippon Steel Corporation, can be stated as the capability for:

- scanning new information;
- identifying new business opportunities for IT;
- rapid information assimilation through organizational learning;
- information fusion for generating new innovations;
- intensive use of information through learning by doing and learning by using;

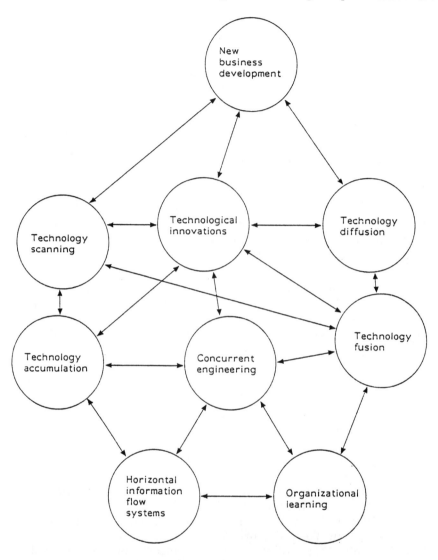

Figure 11. Elements of information management strategy and new business development.

- building competence for achieving new business through tie-ups and rapid commercial utilization of already available technologies; and
- highly forward looking and interactive information management strategy at the firm level.

This analysis brings out clearly that information management strategies and overall corporate strategies need to be harmonized if full potential of IT and IS is to be realized. Some of the imperatives which are clearly discernible are:

- need to have rigorous organizational learning system which can scan, assess and utilize information on new technologies with a view to seeking new business opportunities;
- commitment to develop and use full potential of IT and IS;
- horizontal information flow systems for quick assimilation of new information as well as organizational information accumulation; and
- ability to rapidly innovate through concurrent engineering.

Nippon Steel's change-over, from a "resource-based industry" to "knowledge-based industry" is in consonance with the Japanese national objective of "informationalization of society." Rapid diffusion of new technologies in an organization requires institutionalization and systematization of functional integration or coordination. Japanese innovation strategy and business strategy are isomorphous in terms of functional coordination, continuous scanning for new ideas, and continuous opportunity seeking through design looping, concept crossing and experience looping. Finally, Japanese management practices, work organization and intense team working spirit have facilitated the rapid diffusion and utilization of information management as well as its continuous upgrading to higher levels of decision making and its culmination as multiple business strategies.

REFERENCES

Applegate, L.M., J.L. Cash, and D.Q. Mills. 1988. Information technology and tomorrow's manager. *Harvard Business Review* 66(6): 128-136.

Aoki, M. 1990. Toward an economic model of the Japanese firm. *Journal of Economic Literature* 28: 1-27.

Aoki, M. 1988. *Information, Incentives and Bargaining in the Japanese Economy.* New York: Cambridge University Press.

Aoki, M. 1986. Horizontal versus vertical information structure of the firm. *American Economic Review* 76: 1971-1983.

Argyris, C., and D.A. Schon. 1978. *Organizational Learning.* Wokingham: Addison-Wesley.

Arrow, K.J. 1985. The information structure of the firm. *American Economic Review Proceedings* 75: 303-307.

Bowonder, B., and T. Miyake. 1991. Industrial competitiveness: An analysis of the Japanese electronics industry. *Science and Public Policy* 18: 93-110.

Bowonder, B., and T. Miyake. 1990. Technology and industrial competitiveness. *Futures* 22: 21-45.

Bowonder, B., and T. Miyake. 1988. Technology at industry level: A case study of the steel industry in India and Japan. *Science and Public Policy* 15: 246-269.

Cash, J.I., and B.R. Konsynski. 1986. IS redraws competitive boundaries. *Harvard Business Review* 64(3): 134-142.

Cronin, B. 1988. Value chains, pogo sticks, and competitive edge. *Aslib Proceedings* 40: 217-228.

Cronin, B., A. Cavaye, and L. Davenport. 1988. Competitive edge and information technology. *International Journal of Information Management* 8: 179-187.

Davenport, T.H., and J.E. Short. 1990. The new industrial engineering: Information technology and business process redesign. *Sloan Management Review* 29(3): 11-27.

Earl, M. 1988. IT and strategic advantage. In *Information Management,* ed. M. Earl, 33-53. Oxford: Clarendon.

Editor. 1990a. Basic policy of new comprehensive medium management plan looks to the 21st century. *Nippon Steel News* 221: 2.

Editor. 1990b. Nippon Steel establishes new base for electronics and information operations. *Nippon Steel News* 220: 1-2.

Editor. 1988. Nippon Steel starts four new information and communication companies. *Nippon Steel News* 208: 1.

Editor. 1987. Advanced communication system goes into operation. *Nippon Steel News* 205: 1-2.

Editor. 1985a. JISF calls for information oriented steel industry to be more so. *Nippon Steel News* 185: 2.

Editor. 1985b. Leading technologies at Nippon Steel. *Nippon Steel News* 185: 5-6.

Editor. 1984. On-line ironmaking control system links head office and eight works. *Nippon Steel News* 169: 1-3.

Fleck, J., J. Webster, and R. Williams. 1990. Dynamics of information technology implementation. *Futures* 22: 618-640.

Hamilton, W. F. 1990. *The Dynamics of Technology and Strategy. European Journal of Operations Research.* 47: 141-152.

Huber, G.P. 1990. A theory of the effects of advanced information technologies. *Academy of Management Review* 15: 47-71.

International Iron and Steel Institute. 1990. *World Steel in Figures: 1990.* Brussels: IISI.

Ives, B., and G.P. Learmouth. 1984. The information system as a competitive weapon. *Communications of the ACM* 27: 1193-1201.

Jackson, C. 1989. Building a competitive advantage through information technology. *Long Range Planning* 22(4): 22-39.

Jellis, J. 1988. Information management. *International Journal of Information Management* 8: 35-42.

Johnson, C. 1982. *MITI and the Japanese Miracle.* Stanford, CA: Stanford University Press.

Kodama, F. 1990. Japanese innovations in mechatronics. In *Measuring the Dynamics of Technological Changes,* ed. J. Sigurdson, 40-53. London: Frances Pinter.

Kodama, F. 1986. Japanese innovation in mechatronics. *Science and Public Policy* 13: 44-51.

Magee, J.F. 1985. What information technology has in store for managers. *Sloan Management Review* 24: 45-49.

Maruyama, M. 1985. Experience looping, design looping and concept crossing. *Futures* 17: 385-399.

Matsuda, T. 1988. OR/MS in interaction with and benefit from Japanese organizational intelligence. *Omega* 16: 233-241.

McFarlan, E.W., J.L. McKenney, and P. Pyburn. 1983. The information archipelago: Plotting a course. *Harvard Business Review* 61: 145-156.

Meyers, P.W. 1990. Non-linear learning in large technological firms. *Research Policy* 19: 97-115.

Narayanan, V.K., and L. Fahey. 1987. Environmental analysis for strategy formulation. In *Strategic Planning and Management*, eds. W.R. King, and D.I. Cleland, 147-175. New York: Van Nostrand Reinhold.

Nippon Steel Corporation. 1989. Nippon Steel Corporation, Tokyo.

Nonaka, I. 1990. Managing globalization as a self renewing process. In *Managing the Global Firm*, eds. D.A. Barlett, Y. Doz, and G. Hedlund, 69-94. London: Routledge.

Porter, M. 1990. *Competitive Advantage of Nations*. New York: Macmillan.

Porter, M., and V. Millar.1986. How information gives you competitive advantage. *Harvard Business Review* 64(4): 149-160.

Stark, J. 1990. *Competitive Manufacturing Through Information Technology*. New York: Van Nostrand Reinhold.

Tatsuno, S.M. 1990. *Created in Japan*. New York: Harper & Row.

Wightman, D.W. 1987. Competitive advantage through information technology. *Journal of General Management* 12(4): 36-47.

Wijnhoven, A.B., and D.A. Wassenaar. 1990. Impact of information technology on organizations. *International Journal of Information Management* 10: 35-53.

Wilmont, R. 1988. Computer integrated management: The next competitive breakthrough. *Long Range Planning* 21(6): 65-80.

Competitor Intelligence in the Pharmaceutical Industry: The Role of the Information Professional

Bijel H. Desai and David Bawden

INTRODUCTION

> "He who knows himself and his enemy always wins. He who knows himself but not his enemy sometimes wins and sometimes loses. He who does not know himself nor his enemy always loses"
> (Sun Tzu, quoted in Scrip, 8).

> "A company unaware of its rival's intentions will soon find the war over before it has the chance to lift its sales sword"
> (J.J. Hutton 1989)

The concept of Competitor Intelligence (hereafter CI) as a strategic tool has been recognised in military situations for many years and business theorists such as Michael Porter have, more recently, begun to propose the advantages of systematic CI for enhancing corporate decision-making, gaining the competitive edge and increasing commercial success in the business environment. Much has been written about CI in general (e.g., Attanasio 1989; Fuld 1991, 1988; Cronin and Davenport 1988) but empirical studies of CI practice are much fewer (e.g., Gelb 1991; Ghoshal and Westney 1991).

The aim of this study was to investigate the principles and prac-

This article was first published in the *Journal of Information Science*, Vol 19, No 5, 1993, pp 327-338, and is reproduced here with the permission of Elsevier Science B.V., Amsterdam, The Netherlands.

tice of CI, and in particular the role of formal information services and of the information professional, in the specific context of the research-based pharmaceutical industry; one of the most competitive and information intensive of business environments.

After a general introduction to CI, the study is reported in two sections. The first provides a description of the information sources available (for CI in the pharmaceutical context. The second describes a survey of CI provision in ten British pharmaceutical companies, in order to give an understanding of current practice.

COMPETITOR INTELLIGENCE

Competitor Intelligence may also be known as corporate research, corporate intelligence, company tracking, market intelligence, and commercial espionage (Englade 1989). Whatever the name, its purpose is to "formalise information for tactical and strategic management" (Attanasio 1989), and "to help executives channel resources into the critical areas of business operations" (Kelly 1985).

As Herring (1988) states:

> "intelligence is hard to define because it is both a product and a process. The product is actionable in formation; the process is the systematic means of acquiring, evaluating and producing that actionable information".

Competitor Intelligence may help a business in several ways: in making strategic decisions and plans, "[stimulating] strategic thinking and behaviour" (Creer 1989); in developing its resources; in directing innovation and change; and in entering into new ventures. It should specifically help to identify competitors in the marketplace, track and assess their market thrusts, products, strengths and weaknesses, with consequent identification of marketing opportunities (Ghoshal and Westney 1991; Herring 1988). It should act as an early warning system: preventing surprises, and identifying threats, changes and opportunities in time for action to be taken. It has a forecasting component, providing predictions on how external forces will disrupt or enhance business plans, and reducing uncertainty (Creer 1989; Cronin 1988). Finally, CI makes a major contribution to organisational learning, teaching lessons about the marketplace which may be of use in the future.

It is generally held that CI is of most value to "top management," however this may be defined; although in practice its application may be rather more widespread. Attanasio (1989) for example, identifies several groups within an organisation who may be aided by such intelligence, including directors, general management, specialised subunits of a business, e.g. R & D, and marketing.

Exactly what information comes within the scope of CI is a matter for debate, and is likely to be interpreted differently in different environments. A survey of 158 companies (Eisenhart 1989) indicated the following types of material to be useful components of CI (expressed as percentages):

Pricing 99
Strategic plans 95
Key customers 94
Sales statistics 94
Market share changes 90
Manufacturing costs 88

Several key areas of information about competitors were identified as particularly relevant: customer details; distribution policies; sales, marketing and advertising strategies; details of financial status, and organisational and operational structures; strategic plans; R & D plans, spending, new results; patent and trademark situation and developments.

A concept closely tied up with CI is that of the Intelligence Cycle. As Creer (1989) clearly puts it:

> the fundamental role of intelligence is to forecast the intentions and capabilities of external market forces which may influence business decisions or opportunities. To arrive at such an end point requires a logical sequence of actions and analyses known as the intelligence cycle.

The Intelligence Cycle can be defined as the process component of intelligence and it has four distinct stages (Creer 1989; Hutton 1989). The first, *direction* is the essential first step: a user-driven determination of what information is required, and for what purpose, and what resources may be assigned to it.

The second stage is *collection*. "[The] collection of raw data has to be systematically addressed and planned . . . [one must] identify potentially relevant information sources and form an assessment of their reliability, probable accuracy and cost effectiveness" (Creer 1989). In devising a "network of sensing mechanisms" to monitor and gather competitor information, soft information, rumour, hearsay, etc., may be as significant as harder, factual information. Sources are many and varied, and may include formal information sources (printed and computerized), human sources, reverse engineering (whereby a competitor's products are examined to establish information not available otherwise), and (most controversially) industrial espionage.

The third stage is *processing*. "Gathering data is half of the task. It doesn't become intelligence until the bits of data are compiled and analysed ... when you look at these pieces of data and say — hey there's a pattern here, then it's intelligence" (Fuld 1991). Data is raw, unconnected pieces of knowledge" and processing is the "intellectual process whereby raw data is sifted, evaluated and upgraded into intelligence" (Creer 1989).

Hutton (1989), describes processing as the "Intelligence Service", which itself has four stages, or processes: organising, synthesising, judging and deciding.

Organising — the grouping, classifying, formatting and displaying of data to create information.

Synthesizing — the systematic selection of information to create knowledge with grouping, classifying, interpreting and compressing of information.

Judging — the critical selection and evaluation of information in relation to decisions needed to be made. This results in intelligence (useful knowledge). It involves "presenting arguments, matching needs and problems, estimating advantages and disadvantages, structuring and compilating [sic]" information.

Deciding — assessing the decision to be made in terms of the intelligence found — involves matching goals, compromising, bargaining, choosing alternatives, consulting experts.

Processing and analytical methods are very varied: they may include multivariate analysis techniques, such as cluster analysis, and business analysis methodologies, such as SWOT (Strengths, Weaknesses, Opportunities, Threats). Herring (1988) points out the need for "experienced, responsible" analysts to standardise and interpret information to prevent it misleading those who will act on it.

The fourth stage is *dissemination*, involving provision of intelligence to those able to make best use of it, and feedback to ensure that the intelligence is of the right type and quality.

COMPETITOR INTELLIGENCE SYSTEMS

The Competitor Intelligence function, as with any other information service function, may be achieved by means of discrete and autonomous activities and procedures. But, again as with other information functions, there are likely to be gains in effectiveness and efficiency if these activities and procedures are integrated within a CI system. This in turn may well be subsumed within a wider corporate information system.

Competitor Intelligence systems are also known by other names: Intelligence Programs (Fuld 1991); Business Intelligence Systems (Herring 1988); Competitor Analysis Systems (Ghoshal and Westney 1991) Strategic Information Systems (Cronin and Davenport 1988). All amount, in essence, to the same thing: the "systematic approach to intelligence collection, analysis, and use" (Herring 1988)

> An organised Competitor (Intelligence) system acts like an interlinked radar grid that constantly monitors competitor activity, filters the raw information picked up by external and internal sources, processes it for strategic significance and efficiently communicates actionable intelligence to those who need it" (Ghoshal and Westney 1991)

Creer identifies several distinct benefits stemming from an integrated CI system: *synergy* — the bringing together of information scattered throughout the organisation, resulting in more efficient use; *discrimination* — filtering and directing information to minimise the risk of information overload; *confidence* — of users in information quality; *timeliness* — directing the right information to get to the right person at the right time; *completeness* — fully exploiting a wide range of sources to give a fuller picture; *objectivity* — allowing management to make decisions on a basis of fact rather than opinion.

According to Fuld (1991), successful CI systems encompass three key concepts: *reality* — systems are built around the actuality of the organisation's situation and information state, rather than being based on a theoretical, or ideal, model; *time* — adequate time is given for systems to be set up, to grow and mature, and to be operated effectively, without unrealistic pressure for instant results; *knowledge* — staff are made aware of the importance of information, and given incentives to contribute to the collection process, and to make use of intelligence, and organisational expertise is consciously united.

Cronin and Davenport (1988) give another definition of success, coupled with a warning. An organisation may have several different information systems, but they must be compatible, integrated and networked for an integrated CI function to succeed.

It will be clear from the above discussion that CI is a demanding function, requiring high quality access to a range of sources of different types. It will also be clear that, although there is some consensus, the specifics of how a CI functions should be organised are by no means self-evident. We shall now consider the kinds of sources available to support this function in the pharmaceutical context.

COMPETITOR INTELLIGENCE IN THE PHARMACEUTICAL INDUSTRY

The research-based pharmaceutical industry is well-known as being one of the most information intensive industries, arguably the most information intensive, involving as it does many scientific, medical and commercial disciplines, and generating very large amounts of data from its own program (Haygarth Jackson 1987; Scott 1988; Pay 1991).

It is, furthermore, an industry which spends very large amounts on research and development, and recoups correspondingly large amounts in revenue. Revenue may, however, be largely, or entirely, dependent on a very small number of products, and may be drastically affected by the introduction of competitor products. It is therefore not surprising that CI assumes considerable importance in this industry. As Creer puts it:

"The pharmaceutical industry is distinguished from many other industrial sectors by the vast amount of information about events in the marketplace which is available to it ... the systematic and effective employment of such information in direct support of decision making is thus becoming increasingly important as a factor offering competitive advantage within the industry" (Creer 1989).

The significance of CI for the pharmaceutical industry is expounded, inter alia, by Fuld (1988, 1993), Esposito and Gilmont (1991), Tyson (1989) and Kukobo (1991). Snow describes its importance for the health service industry, which has strong similarities to pharmaceuticals (Snow 1989).

For obvious reasons, pharmaceutical companies tend not to publicise details of their CI activities. However, it has been put on record that several companies have developed formal CI systems, and that there is a trend for this function to extend beyond the simple product oriented form of intelligence to encompass details of factors such as research activities, competitor strategies, financial situation, and so on, as noted earlier in the discussion of criteria for CI (Creer 1989; Edwards 1992).

SOURCES OF PHARMACEUTICAL COMPETITOR INTELLIGENCE

It is generally held that 90-95% of the information sought is freely available if only one knows where to look (Tyson 1989, Ljungberg 1983). The key is the integration of information from many sources (Fuld 1992, 1993, Edwards 1992).

As with any form of CI, the sources likely to be of value in a pharmaceutical context are many and varied, encompassing both formal and informal, hard and soft. Since the pharmaceutical environment requires a mix of scientific, medical and commercial information, the sources are correspondingly diverse. The range of sources has increased markedly in recent years, with a more investigative trade press, more extensive company reporting, more data available from drug stocks analysts, and an increasing number of medical and other conferences, and of online databases (Scrip).

In general terms, for pharmaceuticals as for other sectors, sources for CI may be categorised as formal and informal. Formal sources include both printed and computerised information services, which would normally come within the remit of a library and information service; whereas informal sources, essentially people-oriented, would not. We will now look at each of these categories in more detail.

FORMAL SOURCES FOR PHARMACEUTICAL COMPETITOR INTELLIGENCE

Potentially useful sources are numerous and diverse. A fuller description is given elsewhere (Desai 1992), and other writings deal with this aspect (Ojala 1989); so a brief summary, covering the more important examples only, is given here. Sources are categorised in a five-fold division, according to their perceived usefulness in CI and it is noted that this categorisation is far from exact, and that there will be considerable overlap. The categories are: current awareness; sales figures; general company information; product information; and R&D information.

It is worth noting that there is a number of abstracting and indexing services, available as printed indexes, online databases and CD-ROM files, which can be applied to pharmaceutical competitor intelligence, generally for checking background and trends. They include: *International Pharmaceutical Abstracts* and *IMS American Pharmaceutical News Index* (for all pharmaceutical aspects); *Medline* and *Embase* (particularly for clinical data); *Biosis* (especially for conference coverage where new developments are often disclosed for the first time); *CAS* (for chemical information of products in early development stages); and *Predicast's Prompt* (for commercial aspects, especially management, organisational structure, sales and marketing).

Patents are also useful for both product and for company information, and are, in general, an under-rated source for CI.

''Many consider patent databases to be loaded with devilish pitfalls and snares for the unwary. Yet to ignore totally the patent files is to overlook a potentially valuable source of competitor information'' (Ojala 1989).

Patent analysis can be used to provide both technical and techno-commercial CI, by means ranging from simple analysis of contents, to statistical analysis by time and by technology (Desai 1992). Patent information may be found in the general scientific databases, and in specialist files such as those of *Derwent* and *Inpadoc,* and may by analysed by general purpose software, or by specific systems such as Derwent's *PatStat* (Eisenschitz 1990).

Current awareness

The main sources here are: newspapers; journals; specialised newsletters; and online databases.

Of newspapers, *Financial Times, Wall Street Journal, New York Times, Japan Economic Journal, Guardian,* and *Reuters News Service* are particularly important for business and financial information, and strategic developments. Major advances in drugs are also reported but one must be cautious of newspaper inaccuracy and bias. ''Scientific newspapers'', such as *Science* and *Nature* may also be useful for product current awareness. Major medical journals such as the *Lancet, British Medical Journal, Journal of the American Medical Association,* and *New England Journal of Medicine,* may contain details of clinical trial results (although these tend to be announced initially at conferences), and general company and product news. Pharmaceutical journals, such as *Chemist and Druggist,* are useful for product launches, changes in pricing policy, changes in formulae and product withdrawals. Specialised newsletters of importance in this area include *Scrip,* often described as the most important single source for general pharmaceutical industry news, and *IMS Marketletter,* covering similar ground to *Scrip,* but with a more strongly sales orientation. *Adis Inpharma* contains clinical trial results of new and existing products and its *Literature Monitoring Service* reviews clinical trial data in specific therapeutic areas.

Generally, formal information systems for current awareness in this area seem to be heavily reliant on scanning paper products. Online databases may be of some value, at least as backup, while the constantly updated online news services, such as *Textline,* may be valuable.

Sales figures

Some sales information may be gleaned from the current awareness
sources noted above, or from general business databases, or obtained
directly from company annual reports. There are also specific sources
for this area, particularly the services and databases of IMS.

General company information

This category includes information such as: competitors' present and
future plans; marketing strategies and strategic focus; sales potential; sales outlets; market share; profitability; R&D activity areas; expenditure; suppliers; promotional spending; investments; acquisition
plans; licensing agreements; financial resources and resource allocations; share prices; company image; corporate ownership; internal structure, etc.

Principal sources include: company annual reports; stockbroker
and health care financial analysts' reports; market research reports
(particularly those from firms specialising in the pharmaceutical sector); and investment analysts reports (again particularly those from
pharmaceutical specialists).

There are also secondary information services from which such
information can be obtained; some are specifically pharmaceutical,
while some cover broader areas. Business databases, such as *Dun
and Bradstreet's Duns Financial Records Plus, ICC's British Company Financial Datasheets,* and *Datastream* provide general company information. The *Investext* and *ICC International Business
Research* databases contain full text analysts' reports.

Pharma Marketing Service (online database from Datastar) covers
pharmaceutical marketing information, while the *EPHMRA* European
Pharmaceutical Market Research database also contains market
research information but references to company and product names
are removed. In addition to these reports there are other sources of
company information, specific to pharmaceuticals, both in printed
and computerised form, particularly those from the specialist producers, PJB and IMS.

Product information

Much information on pharmaceutical products is contained in the
manufacturers' data sheets, which are compiled, in the UK, by the
Association of the British Pharmaceutical Industry, in its *Data Sheet
Compendium.* Standard reference works, such as *Martindale's Ex-*

tra Pharmacopeia produced by the Royal Pharmaceutical Society of Great Britain, also contain general product information. Again, there are sector-specific information sources from specialised producers, PJB, Adis and IMS, in both printed and electronic form.

Conferences, and their proceedings, are often a source of primary information disclosure on new products. While it is necessary to be present to receive this information for current awareness purposes, conference proceedings databases may be useful background sources.

Advertisements of launched products, may also be informative in a non-technical sense. The page positioning size of advertisement and frequency of appearance can indicate how much money a company is spending on a product which in turn can give an indication as to how important they regard the product to be. This, of course, necessitates scanning printed medical journals, newsletters and magazines.

R&D information

Key sources in this area are sector-specific products. They are typified by *PJB Pharmaprojects* and *IMS Drug Licence Opportunities*, both of which update and compile information on research in progress, patent and licensing situation, etc. Some of the services noted under the Current Awareness heading also give useful R&D information.

Informal sources for pharmaceutical Competitor Intelligence. It is very clear that informal sources are, in general, as important as, if not more important than, formal sources in provision of CI. In the case of pharmaceuticals, the array of formal sources is much broader and deeper than for most other sectors, but even here informal sources are of great value.

Sales representatives are generally regarded as key sources of CI (Kelly 1985; Eisenhart 1989) because of their ability to obtain immediate feedback from customers — doctors and pharmacists in this case.

Company staff, in whatever capacity, are often able to obtain "snippets" of information from colleagues, or even competitors, particularly in the context of attendance at conferences, exhibitions and visits. Given the relatively small and specialised pharmaceutical arena, this could be expected to be a particularly important source.

External experts and consultants are also likely to be major sources of intelligence, particularly at the "soft" end.

It is clear from the discussion above, that the research-based pharmaceutical industry appears to be provided with a range of sources of many kinds, which should be applicable to provision of an integrated CI service. The importance of the integration of sources, from a specifically pharmaceutical viewpoint, has been noted (Edwards 1992). The industry study, which will now be described. set out to determine how these resources were being used in practice.

THE SURVEY RESULTS

The aim of this survey was to investigate how CI activities are carried out in practice, within the research-based pharmaceutical industry within Britain, with particular emphasis on the role of the information professional and information department. Specifically, the study aimed to establish:

1. Information unit background and place of CI.
2. Definition of CI and its importance to the organisation.
3. Way in which CI is provided.
4. Sources used.
5. Feedback and measurement of value.
6. Integration with other information systems.
7. Use of IT.

Semi-structured interviews were carried out, with personnel at 10 pharmaceutical companies. The interviewees were all at manager/section head level within information units, and directly involved with the provision of CI. Full details of the interview methodology, interview transcripts, and detailed results, are given elsewhere (Desai 1992). Here, we present an outline of the result only in sufficient detail to bring out the main points. The results are structured under the seven headings noted above.

Information unit background and place of Competitor Intelligence

The units had various titles (Commercial Information Service, Strategic and Medical Intelligence Unit, Information Resources Department, Information Services Department, Research Information Centre, etc), and varying places within the organisational structure. 5 units were attached to the R&D Division; 2 to the Finance Division; one each to Intellectual Property, Medical and Human Health Divisions respectively. Although all units were involved in CI provision, only one unit was dedicated specifically to this task. The remainder was involved in many other tasks, depending on their place within the organisation, providing scientific, medical, and/or commercial information, and library and/or documentation services, as appropriate.

The sole unit entirely dedicated to the provision of CI had been set up a year previously, to provide a "focus group" to work on this kind of intelligence, and thereby enhance decision making in senior management.

Definition of Competitor Intelligence
and its importance to the organisation

All the units understood CI in broad terms, and essentially those described earlier, albeit expressed in specifically pharmaceutical terms of new chemical entities and therapeutic classes. Its importance was generally seen to be in the "conventional" terms of maintaining competitive advantage and market share, avoiding threats, and aiding better decision making. Two aspects possibly of particular importance in the pharmaceutical environment were brought out; getting new ideas for research, and shortening development times and costs.

The importance of "soft" information was emphasised: "intelligence is not always hard facts, it can be soft data or gossip. It can be assumptions based on past performance of a company or sector."

Some comments made by staff of the various units are illuminating in setting these aspects in context.

One unit (which was dedicated to CI provision) stated that there was a strong possibility that it may expand in the future if demand for CI continues to rise. It also commented that due to lack of forward planning by senior management, requests for information often came in with short deadlines which made it difficult to give comprehensive coverage of information. The quality of response would improve if management allowed more time for answers to be prepared.

Another unit admitted that CI is "seen as a minor thing" in its company. Interest in it is increasing but it is "still a minor part of our work."

Another comment that "CI is an important area but is costly" i.e. in terms of staff, information cost. "It is an area a lot of people would like to develop but need to justify its cost". There is a tendency to "look at cost rather than value".

A comment made by one unit, but echoed by others, is that "even if you have all the resources, it is still difficult to get information" especially about research campaigns in the early stages, while another typical comment was "we think it [CI] is important .. it has a part to play in decision-making, [but] paying too much attention to other people can be paralysing''.

Ways in which Competitor Intelligence is provided

A considerable variation in the frequency of CI queries was found. Eight of the units reported that they received CI enquiries "regularly" or "frequently" with between 10-40% of their enquiries being related to CI. The sole unit dedicated to CI provision reported as many as 10 in-depth CI enquiries per week, in contrast with another unit, which received them "occasionally", typically one per month. General comments were that many CI enquiries were not necessarily phrased as such, and that there was considerable variation according to the activities of the user groups, e.g. particularly high during the time when marketing groups were formulating long-term plans.

Three units stated that they provided CI fairly regularly and reactively though there was some proactive provision by means of current awareness bulletins including CI. Four units stated that they provided CI regularly both reactively and proactively through SDI and bulletins. One unit provided only irregular ad-hoc information, whilst another provided regular CI to its Marketing Department both reactively and proactively, and ad-hoc reactive CI to other departments.

Apart from one unit which stated that it did not always have the resources for providing in-depth, extensive CI, all the other units reported that they "occasionally" or "sometimes" provided such intelligence to particular projects. Examples included: identifying the current indications and potential indications of particular drug classes; identifying current competitor status, growth, joint ventures, products, estimates of sales (for merger potential); producing in-depth studies of new potential therapeutic areas; producing full competitor profiles.

Six units indicated that they had staff specialising in the CI function; in the other 4, all staff dealt with such information; one of the latter indicated that it wished to develop specialists in the future.

Two units indicated that their staff were involved in information analysis, evaluation and recommendations, including provision of "impact statements" on CI; the others restricted themselves to provision of "raw" information. One unit commented on the need for staff to be "credible" and "technically competent" in order for their judgements and recommendations to be accepted by clients, in an area in which the client is already an expert.

Asked about types of enquiries, 5 units received mainly R&D enquiries. Four received R&D or product enquiries and indicated that company, sales or market enquiries were dealt with by the Marketing or Market Research departments. One unit dealt primarily with company-oriented enquiries. Examples of enquiries are given elsewhere (Desai 1992), as are examples of matching of enquiry to client group and ultimate use. Particularly telling, in the latter context, were comments that "one expects that this is what they use it for ... they don't always say", and the information is used for their own purpose ... we don't always ask".

All units used a combination of oral, written and electronic means of delivering CI information. Only one unit made wide use of electronic transmission, by e-mailing downloaded material with annotations. The remainder cited problems of the availability and compatability of IT systems as well as user resistance, to wide use of electronic delivery, although 2 of these saw distinct advantages in developing this capability.

Sources used

All units indicated some use of both online and hardcopy sources in varying proportion. One unit invariably scanned hardcopy sources first before going online, whilst another hardly ever used hardcopy. The most frequently used sources for particular types of query are listed in Table 1; a fuller account is given elsewhere (Desai 1992).

Four units made some use of patents, but usage was fairly limited and mainly for product information, although one unit used patents for "strategic purposes". Six units did not use patents, of which 5 indicated that there were other information departments in the company that dealt with patent information; one of these also stated that it did not use patents because it dealt only with information on products at the post marketing stage.

Only 2 units reported any use of sales representatives, though both of these considered that this source of information would increase in importance in the future; one regarded representatives as "a much under-used source of information". Three units reported use of general contact, including independent information consultants, internal and external experts, and "colleagues working in the opposite companies".

In-house databases were used by 4 units, one of which had a database dedicated to CI, constructed from scanning key printed sources, including *Scrip* and *Marketletter*. Of the other 3, one had a database containing details of own and competitors' products, one a database

Table 1. Main sources used.

Sales figures
- IMS MIDAS service
- Brokers/investment analysts reports

Product portfolios
- IMS Product Monographs
- Data sheet compendium and drug lists

R & D portfolios
- IMS Drug Licensing Opportunities
- Pharmaprojects

Market information
- PJB Scrip
- IMS Marketletter

Company information
- Annual/broker/investment analysts reports
- PJB Scrip
- IMS Marketletter
- Predicast's Prompt
- Dun & Bradstreet Services

Economic data
- Datastream

Medical information
- Medline
- Excerpta Medica

Press sources
- Financial Times

Patents information
- Current Patents Fast Alert
- Patents Previews

Note: IMSBASE, the database covering many IMS publications, was frequently mentioned for most categories.

containing adverse drug reaction data, and one a database with *Pharmaprojects* and *Scrip* abstracts.

Six units indicated that they maintained discrete files of competitor information, 2 in electronic and hardcopy form, one a database of "competitor profiles" and one within a general CI database, and 4 as hardcopy only, in the form of cuttings files, "company boxes" of key press and journal articles, etc. The 4 units which did not keep such discrete files, nonetheless had access to annual reports, and similar material.

Seven units indicated that they would never go to an outside information source for CI material. Their reasons included: availability of all necessary information in-house; need to maintain confidentiality; distrust of competence of outside consultants for specialised enquiries.

Three units did occasionally make use of outside sources. Their reasons were: need for particular expertise; pressure of work or staff shortage. Examples of sources used are: HERTIS; London Business School; SRIS Japanese Information Service.

Feedback and measurement of value

Three units had formalised feedback mechanisms, with the clients' opinions sought on the value and relevance of the information provided for each enquiry, and a continuing dialogue on progress for major projects. One of these is seeking to implement a formal quality control mechanism.

Five units had informal feedback procedures, with varying degrees of proactivity, and a dissatisfaction with techniques such as surveys, questionnaires and other "objective" methods. A typical comment was "as far as we know, they are quite happy ... we give up to date information speedily ... therefore there is no need to ask on the impact of the information ... we don't need to measure it".

Two units had no feedback mechanisms at all, though one of these proposed to implement a procedure shortly.

Integration with other information systems

All units stated, as might have been expected, that there were either definitely other departments (not necessarily information departments) in the company either in the UK or abroad which may be handling CI (or at least they suspected that there were other departments but were not sure of their existence or activities). These departments included: Scientific Information Unit (providing Patent and R & D CI); Market, Product and Corporate Strategy Departments; Corporate Planning and Market Research Departments; Public Affairs Group and Medical Information Department, all providing different types of CI.

Three units stated that CI provision was a centralised activity, at least in the UK whilst the other 7 stated that provision was decentralised. In general, all operated independently though there was some degree of informal information integration between the different departments providing CI within the company. Comments included that there is: "co-operation" between departments; sharing of information on an in-house database or accessibility to another department's database; daily contact between departments via e-mail; "team work between the teams". A clear implication was that information from disparate sources is often integrated, whether from choice or necessity, by the client.

Use of IT

All units commented on how important IT, in some respect, was to their work, including CI as much as other functions.

The problems of systems incompatibility in a large organisation were universally mentioned, together with the efforts which have had to be made to rationalise the different systems and standardise the technology so that information could become shareable, "effectively managed" and that "economic use" is made of it. The difficulties in the general use of e-mail, regarded by most as a valuable tool, were noted above.

The main uses of IT noted — access to external and corporate databases, local data compilation, and report preparation — do not appear to differ greatly from the norm in any information function. The lack of emphasis on IT for information analysis, often held to be vital for CI, may be explained by the tendency of most units to pass on information "as is".

DISCUSSION OF SURVEY RESULTS

In many respects, the results of this survey tend to confirm, at least in terms of best practice, the remarks made about CI in general above. The definitions, and statements of the importance and advantages of CI given by the interviewees echoed those already noted: gaining a competitive edge, saving time and money, enhancing decision making, etc. It is worth noting, however, that most of these pharmaceutical units took an unusually wide view of CI: thus the R&D information units did not define CI solely in R&D terms, but included concepts such as company culture, corporate activities, finance, etc. This indicates that they understood CI to be more than just the areas in which they were involved. One company even defined CI in terms of the Intelligence Cycle, showing that they saw CI to be a process and not just a product.

Though all units surveyed provided CI, most had functions in addition to CI provision, with only one unit solely concerning itself with CI. Not surprisingly, this unit had the clearest plans to expand, should the demand for CI continue to increase, and also showed the most advanced CI techniques and standards. For the rest, CI functions showed a wide diversity of practice and resource, with little uniformity of provision between different units, even where these shared a similar title, and apparently similar remit. It would, however, be wrong to assume that those companies which did not have a prominent CI function in the unit surveyed here necessarily undervalued or underused CI, since the results indicate that some of these had other units in the company also active in the CI area.

Though many units frequently and regularly received CI requests, most provided CI only reactively, indicating perhaps that the company to which they were attached did not regard CI as important enough to warrant proactive provision. Where proactive provision was occurring it was effected mainly via current awareness services not dedicated to CI. This could potentially be a dangerous practice because, as Fuld (1991) points out, if CI is not collected proactively, small but critical competitor changes over time, which could influence decisions, could be overlooked.

The provision of CI for major company projects indicates a recognition of the importance of CI, especially if key corporate decisions are to be made as a result of the project initiative. However, not all units provided regular project-oriented CI indicating that possibly key decisions were being made without a full knowledge of competitor activities.

The presence of staff denoted as CI specialists in some, though by no means all, units indicates that CI provision is seen, to some extent, as a specialised aspect of information work. This merits a fuller investigation, although exact definitions of the role are made problematic by the extent to which client users play a major part in evaluating and integrating intelligence. The need for "experienced, competent, responsible, trained" analysts to standardise and interpret the data, to control dissemination and to ensure that information reaches the critical decision makers without misleading them has been made (Herring 1988), and the role of the information professional in meeting these needs deserves further study.

There is a clear correlation between the place of the unit in the organisational structure, and the types of information and enquiries handled. There is further a clear proliferation of units handling CI throughout the organisation, and a consequent need for co-ordination and integration, which does not appear to be fully resolved in all cases. It may be that the necessity for a clear delineation between the research and marketing functions is one partial explanation, although this was not mentioned by any respondent. This is clearly an important aspect of overall information resource management within the organisation.

The three main client groups, correlated with use of CI, were: R & D and clinical research staff, using CI to further specific research activities; managers and team leaders, using CI essentially for project planning and management; senior management, using CI for strategic planning. It is worth noting that three aspects of CI claimed to be of equal importance (Gelb 1991, Ghoshal and Westney 1991) — i.e. self-improvement/organisational learning, legitimisation/justification, and benchmarking — did not emerge as significant for this survey, nor did the particular contribution of CI to management decision-making.

In terms of sources, it has to be said that there seemed to be a reliance on the traditional tools of the information professional — journals, newsletters, and printed/electronic data sources. The main sources seem to be very much those outlined earlier in this paper as the most likely to be valuable. Three specific sources appear to be rather underused. Sales representatives, generally held to be a major source of CI, were not much used here, though it may be that their information would be directly channelled through a marketing department, and (hopefully) integrated at some point. Patents information might have been expected to be more widely used, especially in an R&D setting. External expertise is also not sought as widely as might have been expected, for a variety of not entirely convincing reasons.

Despite the advocacy of senior figures in the pharmaceutical world for the desirability of the monitoring and profiling of competitors, and for the integration of information from disparate sources (Edwards 1992), the majority of those surveyed here relied upon traditional externally generated information sources. The one unit which had devised a series of computerised competitor profiles appeared to be uniquely aware of this aspect.

In IT terms, the units surveyed here seemed to share the situation of many information units, aware of the potential benefits of an electronic environment, but unable to move towards it, for both practical reasons of incompatible systems and for reasons of user resistance. It might have been thought that the CI area, with its potential for directly affecting both competitive position and strategic direction, would have been a major focus for development of IT application, and it is perhaps depressing to realise that this is not so. This is in sharp contrast to the view that provision of customisable and easy-to-use computer access to competitor intelligence is a crucial factor in the use of such information, particularly by senior management (Edwards 1992; Fuld 1992).

The feedback situation seems rather unsatisfactory, at least for those units who apparently make no real attempt to assess the value of what they do. This appears to be an area where an investigation of the value, both perceived and real, of an information service could be of particular value, both as an end in itself and as an example of the general problem of the assessment of the benefits of information services. In view of the comments of the cost of effective CI provision, noted above, such an investigation seems particularly appropriate.

Finally, we may note that one of the comments made by a respondent, on the potentially "paralysing" effect of some CI provision, is the first concrete suggestion we have seen to the effect that CI may actually be counter-productive, apart from a veiled remark in Gelb's study that "overreliance on competitive data may interfere with timely and consistent decisions" (Gelb 1991). This may be an aspect worthy of further investigation.

CONCLUSIONS

This study has indicated that the CI function is taken very seriously within the UK research-based 5 pharmaceutical industry, albeit with a range of very different structures and procedures. Overall, the sources and methods used, although there is a considerable range, remain largely those familiar to any information professional. Unconventional sources, even such hardy perennials as the patent literature, seem to be underused. The analysis, evaluation and integration of information is carried out in disparate ways, but more by end-users than information staff. Evaluation of effectiveness and benefits, and applications of information technology, are not well developed.

In view of the importance of this area, further studies are justified, to illuminate points raised by this investigation. These should concentrate on the specific points noted above, with CI being seen both as an important part of information resource management, and as an increasingly significant role for the information professional.

REFERENCES

Anonymous. Start analysing your competitors, companies urged. *Scrip* 990: 8.

Attanasio, D.R. 1989. The multiple benefits of competitor intelligence. *Journal of Business Strategy* (May/June): 16-19.

Creer, J. 1989. Business intelligence—relevance to the pharmaceutical industry. *Pharmaceutical Times* (Sept): 18-20.

Cronin, B. 1988. Strategic intelligence and competitive advantage. In *New Horizons for the Information Profession*, eds. L. Wood and G. Tseng, 3-22. London: Taylor Graham.

Cronin, B., and E. Davenport. 1988. Strategic information management: Forging the value chain. In *Post Professionalism: Transforming the Information Heartland,* 154-166. London: Taylor Graham.

Desai, B.H. 1992. Competitor Intelligence in the Pharmaceutical Industry. Unpublished MSc dissertation, City University, London.

Edwards, N. 1992. Healthy competition. *Which Computer* 15(12): 36-40.

Eisenhart, T. 1989. Competitive intelligence— where to go when you need to know. *Business Marketing* (Nov): 38-47.

Eisenschitz, T. 1990. Intellectual property. In *Information Sources in Pharmaceuticals,* ed. R. Pickering, 144-170. Bowker-Saur.

Englade, K.F. 1989. Competitor analysis comes in from the cold. *Across the Board* (April): 18-25.

Esposito, M.A., and E.R. Gilmont. 1991. Competitive intelligence: doing corporate homework. *Pharmaceutical Executive* 11: 68-74.

Fuld, L.M. 1993. Monitoring competitor intelligence. *Pharmaceutical Marketing* (March): 27-29.

Fuld, L.M. 1992. A tale of two intelligence systems. *Chief Information Officer Journal* 5(1): 5-10.

Fuld, L.M. 1991. A recipe for business intelligence success. *Journal of Business Strategy* (Jan/Feb): 12-17.

Fuld, L.M. 1988. *Monitoring the Competition.* New York: Wiley.

Gelb, D. et al. 1991 Competitive intelligence: Insights from executives. *Business Horizons* (Jan/Feb): 43-46.

Ghoshal, S., and D.E. Westney. 1991. Organizing competitor analysis systems. *Strategic Management Journal* 12: 17-31.

Haygarth Jackson, A.R. 1987. Pharmaceuticals—an information-based industry. *Aslib Proceedings* 39: 75-86.

Herring, J.P. 1988. Building a business intelligence system. *Journal of Business Strategy* (May/June): 4-9.

Hutton, J.J. 1989. Tales from the intelligence front. *Business Marketing* (November): 48-50.

Kelly, G. 1985. Marketing—keeping ahead of competitors. *Management Today* (UK) 3: 39-46.

Kukobo, A. 1991. Japanese competitor intelligence for R&D. *Research Technology Management* 34(5): 38-41.

Ljungberg, S. 1983. Intelligence service—a tool for decision makers. *International Forum for Information and Documentation* 8: 23-26.

Ojala, M. 1989. A patently obvious source for competitor intelligence: The patent literature. *Database* 12(4): 43-49.

Pay, S. 1991. Information provision in the pharmaceutical industry. *Aslib Information* 19: 81-82.

Scott, E. 1988. Corporate information in the pharmaceutical industry. In *New Horizons for the Information Profession,* eds. H. Dyer and G. Tseng, 53-67. London: Taylor Graham.

Snow, B. 1989. Competitive intelligence in the health device industry. *Online* 13(4): 107-114.

Tyson, T. 1989. Do you know what your competitors are up to? *Medical Marketing and Media* 24(4): 9-14.

Information Management— The Convergence of Professions

James E. Herring

INTRODUCTION

The term 'convergence of technologies' has become a much used (and abused?) phrase in the last 10-15 years. The term implies the coming together of a range of technologies, e.g., the computer, the telephone, the printer, to produce an added-value product. This article seeks to argue that information management can now be seen as the convergence of the knowledge and skills of a range of professions to produce new information professionals whose *raison d'être* is added-value services. Particular attention will be given to (a) recent literature on information management, (b) evidence of demand for information professionals, including a survey done for a recent validated BA Information Management and (c) an analysis of recently advertised posts for healthcare information professionals.

INFORMATION MANAGEMENT LITERATURE

Perhaps the most comprehensive review of information management in recent literature, is Lewis and Martin's *Information management: State of the art in the United Kingdom*. Lewis and Martin review definitions of information management, information resource management and information resources management and identify the key

This article was first published in the *Journal of Information Science*, Vol. 11 No. 2, June 1991, pp. 144-155, and is reproduced here with the permission of Butterworth-Heinemann, Oxford, UK.

features of information management as being '... integrative; content-oriented; organisation-wide; dynamic; strategic' (Lewis and Martin 1989).

The present author views information management as both a domain of knowledge and a career path for information professionals, culminating in the post of information manager, who would be a person with the status of a senior manager/executive in a company or organization with responsibility for the strategic, organization-wide management of information, information systems and information personnel. In practice, however, the term 'information manager' is already used for lower level posts in some organizations, e.g,, the National Health Service (see below). This does not detract from using the term to denote a person whose role is a strategic one in an organization. The term 'librarian,' for example, can refer to a person running a small public library or a person with professional status in a university.

Lewis and Martin cite examples of people involved in information management such as data processing managers, financial information coordinators, information technology managers, information consultants, information scientists and librarians. They also refer to North American research on posts such as Chief Information Officer and the growing acceptance of the concept of information management in the National Health Service. Lewis and Martin conclude that

> ... the management of information for strategic or competitive purposes ... is one particular aspect of information management which appears to be growing (Lewis and Martin 1989, 246).

Two recent articles by Wiggins (1988) and Picot (1989) add to the debate. Wiggins states that

> with technology having a major part in the structuring of and activities within organizations, professional staff from various disciplines and backgrounds are finding that their areas of specialization are no longer sacrosanct (Wiggins 1988, 5).

Examples included by Wiggins in an excellent pictorial diagram include IS strategy planner, database administrator, systems analyst, programmer, information scientist, information officer, librarian, records manager and archivist (Wiggins 1988, 6-7). Wiggins concludes that the terms 'information management' and 'information resource management' are here to stay and cites the changing role of Aslib (now the Association for Information Management) and the Institute of Information Scientists, which now recruits a wide range of information professionals as members (Wiggins 1988, 11).

Picot states boldly that

> Information shapes organizational, technical and personnel considerations, and at the same time provides a basis for developing corporate strategy (Picot 1989, 237).

Information management, Picot argues is no longer 'a fourth factor in production', but is 'the prime production factor' (Picot 1989, 238). Because of the changes in competitive business environment, Picot further argues that traditional management approaches will not be adequate to cope with the increasingly complex world of today's business activity, i.e.,

> what is needed is an innovative, *information-oriented* (this author's italics) corporate development plan that takes a global view of affairs and covers organizational structure, personnel and technology (Picot 1989, 240).

If the competitive world has changed and the company's strategies have changed, Picot argues that the roles of company personnel must also change. To be effective, companies must, Picot states, abandon the traditional compartmentalization of information activities and like a 'global' approach. The person appointed to oversee information-related activities (the information manager) would not only require skills in either O&M or data processing or telecommunications, but a combination of these. The key skills in information management, according to Picot, are strategic and not operational and are thus more concerned with establishing holistic information policies in companies, as opposed to choosing the right information systems.

Picot's stance would therefore tend to support the view of convergence in relation to the professional approaches to information management. It is becoming increasingly clear that a person who is, for example, a data processing manager, cannot become an information manager without adding to his/her range of skills and without synthesizing these skills under the umbrella of a strategic managerial approach.

The breaking down of traditional professional barriers can also be seen in the computing world. The organ of the British Computer Society, the *Computer Bulletin,* changed its subtitle from being a journal for 'computing professionals' to one for 'information systems professionals'. Is it too speculative to suggest that the word 'information management' will be introduced to replace 'information systems' in the next few years?

In a recent article in *Computer Bulletin,* Benyon-Davies reflects this changing attitude. Writing about systems analysts, he argues that

> ... the stereotypical computer studies student is generally regarded
> as a good technician but a poor communicator

and that future systems analysts will

> have to play a number of roles in any project — the technical expert,
> the socially aware investigator, the managerial consultant... (Benyon-
> Davies 1990, 21)

The implications of Benyon-Davies' argument are that informa-
tion/information technology specialisms are only relevant if accompanied by a range of other skills and that these 'other' skills include
noncomputing related aspects such as communication skills and
management skills. As will be seen below, knowledge and experience
of systems analysis is often seen as one of the key attributes of an
information manager in the healthcare world. It is the contention
of this author that in the future, systems analysts are likely to be
seen as a subset of the information management profession.

The debate on the role of information systems professionals has
been lively in recent issues of *Computer Bulletin*. For example, in
the May 1990 issue, a letter from Galliers, referring to recent articles
on 'hybrid managers' states that, while companies need to effectively
exploit IT to survive,

> ...they are faced with the twin problems of information systems staff
> with little appreciation of the needs of their business and management
> with scant appreciation of the opportunities (and limitations) of IT (Gal-
> liers 1990, 25).

In an article in the same issue, Skyme and Earl continue this theme,
stating that the new 'hybrid manager' requires, in addition to IT skills,
a range of management skills and that

> Of these, the 'soft' or 'social' skills feature time and time again with
> hybrid managers and personnel recruiters; with communications the
> most frequently cited. (Skyme and Earl 1990, 20).

It is interesting to note that both Skyme and Earl are associated with
the Oxford Institute of *Information Management* (this author's
italics).

The BCS debate is also commented on in *Computer Weekly*
(21.06.90), with the arresting headline of

> One track IT buffs won't travel far.

The report quotes Sue Ottley of BCS as stating that the 'IT person' tends to be less sociable than other professionals and this lack, particularly of communication skills, will be important in the future. The BCS report on 'hybrid managers' is summarized and the characteristics of the 'hybrid manager' include:

1. Business knowledge.
2. Organization-specific knowledge.
3. Interpersonal skills.
4. Communication skills.
5. Cognitive capabilities.
6. Personality traits and behaviour (*Computer Weekly* 1990, 6).

In the same issue of *Computer Weekly*, Earl (see above) is quoted as stating that, in relation to a new MBA course at the London Business School,

> My policy would be that each graduate must have as much training in information management as in financial and, personnel management. (*Computer Weekly* 1990, 86)

A similar debate is taking place in the business arena. Two recent articles by Meiklejohn in *Management Today* reflect the arguments seen in *Computer Bulletin*, only this time it is the *managers* who are urged to adopt IT skills. However, Meiklejohn argues strongly that it is the business skills of what he terms 'senior IT managers' that are most important when such people are being recruited and that

> . . . boards look around for someone whose management skills they can trust and also won't hide — wittingly or unwittingly — behind a barrier of jargon (Meiklejohn 1989, 137).

The implication here is that traditional computing professionals might well be guilty of hiding in such a manner.

In the second article, Meiklejohn cites Esso as a company where 'hybrid managers' have been successful and quotes Glenday, Esso's IT manager, as stating

> The biggest success factor is that people on both sides, information systems and line, manage the projects better (Meiklejohn 1990, 116).

Meiklejohn also cites British Airways who have an information management department. It is very interesting to note that Meiklejohn does not distinguish between Esso's IT department and British Airways' IM department, but regards both as doing the same ob.

Thus an examination of the literature — from related areas of information management, information technology and business — demonstrates that information management is demanding that traditional job barriers be broken down and that traditional job descriptions need to be rewritten. There is a convergence of skills and attitudes and, at the senior level in organizations, where the 'hybrid managers' are now in evidence, a convergence of professions.

EVIDENCE OF DEMAND

The demand for information professionals can be seen from recent studies which point to an expansion in the types and numbers of posts open to information management and information technology graduates and also to a shortage of graduates whose educational background is not only in information technology but includes communication and information management knowledge and skills. Buckroyd and Cornford predict a growth in demand for IT related staff of an *additional* 51 000 over the next five years. Using a less conservative model, they argue that the demand could be as high as 100 000. Buckroyd and Cornford also report that there is a trend away from employing only computer science graduates as systems staff; that

> There is a shift in job emphasis in IT departments towards 'user support roles' . . .;

and that employers are seeking graduates with IT knowledge and skills who also have an understanding of business issues and are good communicators (Buckroyd and Cornford 1988).

A parliamentary report, *First report from the Trade and Industry Committee: Information technology* confirms and expands on the above figures, stating that

> . . .the shortages are of the order of one tenth of the number of IT specialists at work.

The report also emphasizes the importance of the management of information technology in organizations and states that

> . . . preparations for professional qualifications . . . should embrace information management as a core activity (House of Commons 1988).

In the information field, reports by Angell and by Moore point to an expanding market for information managers. Angell states that the need for effective management of information and new technology in organizations is leading to a demand

> ... for a new kind of information worker, combining the qualities and skills of several different professions (Angell 1987)

Moore reports a 'dramatic' growth in new posts for information systems staff and for information analysts, concluding that there is now a

> ... significant employment market for information managers at tactical and strategic levels within the organization (Moore 1988).

In the national press, a similar picture of the changing nature of IT work and of potential staff shortages can be seen. The *Scotsman* (24.10.88) stated that 51 per cent of Scottish companies reported shortages of IT staff, while in *Observer Scotland* (04.06.89) the projected figure for 1992 was 55 per cent of companies. The move away from traditional computing posts is reported in the *Guardian* (14.03.89) in an article which states that

> As new technology becomes more integrated into Organizations, the emphasis is shifting to project management and interpersonal skills.

Computing (09.02.89) identifies a trend in higher education to respond to IT users' needs by producing people

> ... who concentrate on how IT is used in organizations and cover subjects like psychology, sociology and business skills, as well as systems design.

Thus there is overwhelming evidence of a growing demand for information professionals and, in many cases, there is a concurrent demand that these information professionals have a *range* of skills and aptitudes different from those of the traditional IT person. In a survey done by Queen Margaret College prior to the validation of the new BA Information Management degree, there was clear evidence of a growing demand for graduates from a multidisciplinary course which contains elements of information science, information technology, management, systems analysis, communications, psychology and sociology as well as specific vocational areas such as healthcare informatics, information management in government, information management in marketing and information management in libraries and information services. Of the respondents to a questionnaire, 94 per cent stated that the market for graduates of the proposed course would expand in the next ten years; 96 per cent either strongly agreed or agreed that the proposed course would be a useful foundation for information personnel in their organization. When asked if they would be likely to interview graduates from the course, 96 per cent said they would interview if the student had relevant experience and, perhaps more interestingly in relation to possible future shortages, 78 per cent said they would interview graduates with no experience. In making individual comments, one leading retail firm stated that the combination of elements in communication, management and IT skills (particularly systems analysis) would meet the needs of their future IT managers, while a government computer service department stressed the importance of information strategies and structured systems analysis and design methodology (SSADM), both of which feature strongly in year 3 of the BA Information Management.

The college's market research would therefore support the published findings on the strong demand for information personnel. It also corroborates the findings relating to the *type* of personnel firms and organizations wish to recruit and it is clear that such firms and organizations see a convergence in the knowledge and skills they consider necessary to meet future information and IT needs.

HEALTHCARE INFORMATION PROFESSIONALS

The healthcare services have recently been the subject of much debate in terms of accountability, efficiency and quality assurance. One consequence of this has been the widespread introduction of information technology in the area of management information systems. This has been accompanied by greater emphasis on the use of information for decision making at all levels; recognition of the need for coherent information strategies; greater emphasis on systems analysis and systems procurement; recognition of new training needs; and, most relevant in this context, the creation of new posts in information management, followed by the appointment to these posts of personnel with a variety of information and information technology backgrounds. It is interesting to note that the terms 'information management' and 'information manager' are now quite commonly used in healthcare.

A recent Department of Health report *Training for Information Management Staff* (1990) identified the key responsibilities of information managers in healthcare as to:

1. Develop and implement strategies to provide the information required to support the achievement of the business objectives of the health authority or the hospital.
2. Identify the systems required to meet these information requirements and determine the priorities for their introduction.
3. Specify in detail these systems and to coordinate their development or procurement and implementation.
4. Organize and manage the operational support required to maintain these information systems.
5. Provide and manage an information reporting and analysis service to support clinicians, operational managers and general managers.
6. Organize appropriate training and development for non-specialist managers and health professionals in the field of information and computing (Department of Health 1990, 3-4).

The report goes on to identify a range of skills which an information manager requires in order to carry out the wide range of responsibilities identified above. The skills identified are:

1. Business analysis.
2. Systems analysis and design.
3. Networks and communications.
4. Specific operational computing.
5. Information analysis.
6. Data management.
7. Project management.
8. Presentation, training and human interaction.
9. Data and information sources awareness (Department of Health 1990, 4).

From this list of skills, it is clear that healthcare authorities are seeking information managers who can cover a wide range of information related areas. It would seem unlikely that authorities could possibly attract managers with experience of *all* the above areas, but there is a clear expectation that the authorities are seeking managers who can promote the convergence of skills which the posts demand. The training initiative, which was the subject of the report, seeks to supplement the existing skills of managers, who may come from a variety of backgrounds. What is clear from the report is that there is a clear expectation that whatever specialist area the information manager may come from, s/he will develop into a strategic generalist, having knowledge, although not necessarily in-depth knowledge, of a number of different information and information technology areas.

To further discover the extent of the 'convergence' of skills in the healthcare information management field, a survey was carried

Table 1. Breakdown of information-related posts.

Director of information services/information manager	35
Information officer	31
Systems support/computing officer	18
Assistant information officer/information assistant	5
Information analyst	5
Senior information officer	4
Project manager	3
Data administration/audit officer	3
Information management training officer	2

out of all information-related posts advertised in the *Health Service Journal* during the period 1 September 1989 to 23 February 1990. The survey involved writing to personnel departments for job descriptions and other information sent to candidates. In total, 106 job descriptions were received. The breakdown of posts in terms of numbers is shown in Table 1.

Within each category, however, there was a wide range of job titles and it became clear, on reading the job descriptions, that the title 'information manager' was interpreted differently in different health authorities. In all cases where the title was 'director of information services', the job description corresponded to the definition of an information manager given above. Where the title 'information manager' was used, there was inconsistency in the level of seniority and responsibility given to this post in different authorities. The title was sometimes used for posts in individual hospitals, e.g., Watford General Hospital, but this post was similar to many of the information officer posts advertised in other authorities. Where 'information manager' was used in a post relating to a district or authority responsibility for information, then the title corresponded with the definition given above. Other titles which were used and which would fit the definition included information services manager, district information systems manager, research and information manager and information resource manager.

An analysis of the job descriptions identified a number of areas which were common to posts which had organization-wide responsibility for information and information technology and these areas correspond mostly to the training areas identified in the Department of Health report. The five main areas, in order of importance, which were identified were:

1. Information strategy.
2. Systems development.
3. Management information.
4. Training.
5. Liaison.

INFORMATION STRATEGY

In all senior posts, one of the main responsibilities was to produce, implement, develop and review the information strategy within the health authority, e.g., in South West Surrey Health Authority (HA),

> To be responsible for coordination of the production and implementation of a district information strategy.

For Northumberland HA's post of District Information Manager, the information sent to applicants stated that, under the heading 'Most challenging part of the job', the first requirement was

> To provide an information strategy by May 1990.

Under 'Key result areas' this was expanded to

> To produce an information strategy by May 1990 with emphasis on the different information needs relating to the core functions of the district health authority.

In the majority of job descriptions, it was clear that the term "information strategy" covered the production and use of information as well as the development of information technology. In some cases, the term "information strategy" specifically covered the services to be provided. In Scarborough HA's post of director of information services, the information strategy development should include

> the provision of a comprehensive management information and statistical service for the monitoring and planning of services,

as well as

> the effective and economic development of computer systems within and throughout the Authority.

The strategic planning role of the information manager is thus highlighted in the job descriptions analysed, as is the organization-wide responsibility for information and for systems.

SYSTEMS DEVELOPMENT

After information strategy design and implementation, the development and review of information systems was seen as the next prime task for the healthcare information manager. In many cases, this was seen as being directly linked to the information strategy in that the development and review of systems was seen as a major part of the implementation of the information strategy. Thus Rugby HA's district information services manager is expected

> To develop an information system according to the district's information strategy.

Information systems development and review was seen in the context especially of new information systems. In the accompanying information sent to applicants, there was almost always reference to systems being planned or investigated. For example, applicants for East Birmingham HA's district information services manager post were informed that

> There is intense activity in IT terms at present. In the immediate future, systems to support the resource management initiative must be acquired.

It was also interesting to note that in virtually all job descriptions for information managers, there was a statement at the end to the effect that, given the extensive organizational and technological changes taking place within the National Health Service (NHS), the job description would be reviewed periodically. The implication of this is that new developments in information technology could change the nature of the posts held in the future.

MANAGEMENT INFORMATION

The development and review of systems was seen in a variety of contexts, e.g., to produce statutory returns for the Department of Health or to provide information to clinicians, but the principal need identified was to provide effective management information. One of the 'key result areas' for Merton and Sutton's senior information manager's post is to develop systems

> . . . in order to provide information to support the needs of operational management.

Northumberland HA's district information manager will be expected to

> ... raise the awareness and consciousness of managers ... to the use
> of information in the decision-making process.

Sheffield HA's computing and information manager's job description
has a section on 'Information technology responsibilities' but a
separate section on 'Management information system responsibilities'. In the latter section, one of the duties is

> To be responsible for the overall development and operational resource
> management of ... information systems to meet the needs of senior
> managers and heads of department.

In the accompanying literature for applicants, many HAs stressed
the vital importance of management information to the HA's future.
In some instances, reference was made to national developments such
as the Korner reports (Winsor 1986) or to the White Paper *Working
for patients* (Department of Health 1989), both of which emphasize
effective management information as a prerequisite for overall effectiveness within the NHS. East Cumbria HA sent applicants extracts from their outline regional information strategy which
highlights the necessity for effective management information to be
provided to a variety of units and also includes a quotation from the
NHS Information Management Group:

> Management without information is a blind process.

TRAINING

The need to train users at all levels was also a feature of virtually
all information management posts analysed. Training was needed in
relation to both information and technology and it was encouraging
to see the number of job descriptions which highlighted the need to
train users not only how to use computers but also how to effectively use the information retrieved from information systems.

Rochdale HA's district manager of information and computing
is expected to

> Review existing knowledge of, and the need for, training in informa-
> tion technology in the district.

Merton and Sutton HA's senior information manager has to

> Plan and coordinate a computer users' group training programme to assist in the skills development of microcomputer users.

Scarborough HA's director of information services will

> In conjunction with the district training officer ... identify the training/development needs of managers and health professionals in the field of information and computing and establish programmes to meet these needs.

Northumberland HA's district information manager is expected to

> Train both managers and staff in the implementation of new information systems to the stage where they no longer need the support of the district information manager.

Thus considerable emphasis is put on the need to train staff in relation to new technology but *more* emphasis is put on the need for training in relation to the use of information. For example, in the case of Merton and Sutton HA's senior information manager, the following 'Key result area' precedes that seen above in relation to computer use training:

> To promote knowledge and use of information by providing inservice training and familiarization in information and statistics to all disciplines

Similarly, Cornwall and Isles of Scilly HA's unit information manager's job description notes the need

> To assist in developing information management training programmes for clinicians, managers and other priority groups.

Rugby HA's district information services manager is required

> To develop training programmes, in conjunction with the appropriate district officers, in training all grades of staff in the use of information.

Leicester HA's information support manager will

> Contribute to the unit training strategy by training clinicians and managers in the use and interpretation of clinical based activity data.

South West Hertfordshire HA's information manager is expected

> To educate users of information in the identification and use of information to manage resources and services.

It is interesting here to note the phrase 'To educate users' as this will be familiar to librarians in schools and in higher education in particular.

LIAISON

The healthcare information manager works in an environment where information is ubiquitous and where the volume of information produced can threaten to overwhelm the managers of resources and services related directly and indirectly to patient care. All the job descriptions of information managers implied that the information manager could not succeed by working independently but had to keep in close touch with other service managers in the healthcare services. In many cases, this was recognition that the information manager was part of the senior management team within an authority and clearly had a role to play as a *manager* as well as an information manager.

For example, South West Surrey HA's post of information manager is described as

> ... one of several senior posts reporting directly to the director of administration and planning ... The postholder will develop close working relationships with managers throughout the district, planning department colleagues and the department of public health in particular.

Lambeth, Southwark and Lewisham family practitioner committee's (FPC) manager of computing and information is one of five joint general managers within the FPC and under the heading 'Communications and working relationships' is expected to liaise with a wide range of managers and clinicians within the authority as well as with outside agencies such as

> Regional health authority liaison officers; district health authority commissioning officers; managers of directly managed units; managers of self governing trusts; and community health councils.

Bromsgrove and Redditch HA's information manager is seen as a key person in developing resource management in the authority and should

> Work with the unit management team on the development of resource management ... with the unit accountant ... on the development of adequate financial systems ... with the unit personnel manager ... to develop adequate manpower control and planning systems.

As well as the five main areas of responsibility for information managers identified in the analysis of job descriptions, the other most common areas were — the management of an information department; budget responsibilities; the evaluation of services; responsibility for compliance with the Data Protection Act; the analysis of information needs; and the provision of an information service. In all these areas, however, there was an implication that while the information manager might have ultimate responsibility, the day-to-day responsibility would lie with subordinate staff, e.g., information officers.

CONCLUSION

There would seem to be evidence from a range of sources that information management can now be seen as a developing profession in its own right and that this new profession represents the convergence of skills and knowledge of a range of other professions, plus the addition of conventional senior management skills which are recognized both in the public and private sector. From the evidence above, it is clear that information managers, particularly in the healthcare services, have wide responsibilities which call for a mixture of specialist and generalist knowledge and skills if they are to make a contribution to the *overall* management of their organizations.

Further research in this area could usefully identify what qualifications, knowledge and skills employers expect potential information managers to have; from which information and information technology areas information managers actually come from; and whether the previous post held by an information manager affects his/her management style on taking up such a senior post.

REFERENCES

Angell, C. 1987. *Information, New Technology and Manpower.* London: British Library.
Benyon-Davies, P. 1990. The behaviour of systems analysts. *Computer Bulletin* 2(2): 21.
Buckroyd, B., and D. Cornford. 1988. The IT skills crisis: The way ahead. National Computing Centre. *Computer Weekly.* June 21, 1990: 86, 6.
Department of Health. 1990. *Training for Information Management Staff.* London: Department of Health.
Department of Health. 1989. *Working for Patients.* London: HMSO.
Galliers, R.D. 1990. Letter to *Computer Bulletin* 2(4): 25.

House of Commons, Trade and Industry Committee. 1988. *First Report: Information Technology* Vol. 1. London: HMSO.

Lewis, D., and W. Martin. 1989. Information management: State of the art in the United Kingdom. *Aslib Proceedings* 41(7/8): 225-250.

Meiklejohn, I. 1990. Whole role for the hybrid. *Management Today* March: 116.

Meiklejohn, I. 1989. CIOs search for a role. *Management Today* September: 137.

Moore, N. 1988. *Information Intensive Management*. Birmingham Polytechnic/Aslib.

Picot, A. 1989. Information management - The science of solving problems. *International Journal of Information Managment* 9(4): 237-243.

Skyme, D.J., and M.J. Earl. 1990. Hybrid managers: What should you do? *Computer Bulletin* 2(4): 20.

Wiggins, R.E. 1988. A conceptual framework for information resources management. *International Journal of Information Management* 8(1): 5-11.

Winsor, P. 1986. *Introduction to Korner*. London: BJHC Books.

Additional Readings
Part VI: Information
without Boundaries

Blick, A.R. 1992. Information provision across national boundaries: Developing an information sciences department within a new multinational company. In *The Common Market for Information*, ed. M. Blake, 9-19. London, UK: Taylor Graham.

Brumm, E.K. 1990. Chief information officers in service and industrial organizations. *Information Management Review* 5(3): 31-45.

Dougherty, R. M., and C. Hughes. 1993. *Preferred Futures II: Charting the Paths*. Mountain View, CA: Research Libraries Group.

Dowlin, K. E. 1991. Public libraries in 2001. *Information Technology and Libraries* 10(4): 317-321.

Drabenstott, K. M. 1994. *Analytical Review of the Library of the Future*. Washington, DC: Council on Library Resources.

Drake, M. A. 1990. Georgia Institute of Technology. In *Campus Strategies for Libraries and Electronic Information*, ed. C. Arms, 157-175. Bedford, MA: Digital Press.

Eckert, A. 1992. Market analysis, competitive intelligence, and news: Desktop delivery at Digital Equipment Corporation. In *Online/CD-ROM '92 Conference Proceedings*, 63-67. Wilton, CT: Eight Bit Books.

Fuld, L.M. 1992. Achieving total quality through intelligence. *Long Range Planning* 25(1): 109-115.

Gapen, D. K. 1993. The virtual library: Knowledge, society, and the librarian. In *The Virtual Library: Visions and Realities*, ed. L.M. Saunders, 1-14. Westport, CT: Meckler.

Gorman, M. 1991. The academic library in the year 2001: Dream or nightmare or something in between. *Journal of Academic Librarianship* 17(1): 4-9.

Hedin, H. 1993. Business intelligence: Systematised intelligence activities in ten multinational companies. *The Journal of AGSI* (Association of Global Strategic Information) 3: 126-136.

Hoffman, M. M., et al. 1993. The rightpages service: An image-based electronic library. *Journal of the American Society for Information Science* 44(8): 446-452.

Hogeveen, E., and R. Jones. 1993. Paradox, paragon, or paralysis? Three organizations in 2005. *Special Libraries* 84(4): 220-225.

Horny, K. 1992. Digital technology: Implications for library planning. In *Advances in Librarianship*, vol. 16, ed. I. P. Godden, 107-126. San Diego, CA: Academic Press.

Horton, W., Jr. 1994. *Extending the Librarian's Domain: A Survey of Emerging Occupational Opportunities for Librarians and Information Professionals*. Washington, DC: Special Libraries Association.

Jackson, M. E. 1993. Document delivery over the Internet. *Online* 17(2): 14-21.

Kahn, R. E., and V. G. Cerf. 1988. *An Open Architecture for a Digital Library System and a Plan for its Development: The Digital Library Project; Volume 1: The World of Knowbots*. Washington, DC: Corporation for National Research Initiatives.

King, H. 1993. Walls around the electronic library. *The Electronic Library* 11(3): 165-174.

Landoni, M., N. Catenazzi, and F. Gibb. 1993. Hyper-books and visual-books in an electronic library. *Electronic Library* 11(3): 175-186.

Linder, J.C. 1992. Today a librarian, tomorrow a corporate intelligence professional. *Special Libraries* 83(3): 142-144.

Lynch, C. A. 1993. The transformation of scholarly communication and the role of the library in the age of networked information. *Serials Librarian* 23(3/4): 5-20.

Martin, J.S. 1992. Building an information resource center for competitive intelligence. *Online Review* 16(6): 379-389.

Meurisse, M. 1992. What is required from competitor analysis today? - and what part can online research play? In *Online Information '92*, ed. D.I. Raitt, 85-94. Oxford, UK: Learned Information.

Saunders, L. M. 1992. The virtual library today. *Library Administration and Management* 6(2): 66-70.

Seiler, L. H., and T. T. Suprenant. 1993. The virtual information center: Scholars and information in the twenty-first century. In *Libraries and the Future: Essays on the Library in the Twenty-First Century*, ed. F.W. Lancaster, 157-180. Binghampton, NY: The Haworth Press.

Spaulding, F. H. 1988. Special librarian to knowledge counsellor in the year 2006. *Special Libraries* 79(2): 83-91.

Strub, M.Z. 1994. Quality at warp speed: Reengineering at AT&T. *Bulletin of the American Society for Information Science* 20(4): 17-19.

Synott, W.R. 1987. The emerging chief information officer. *Information Management Review* 3(1): 21-35.

Vandenhende, J. 1993. The creation of a shared network for information within a multinational company. *The Journal of AGSI* (Association of Global Strategic Information) 1: 24-28.

Virtual libraries virtually here. 1993. *Searcher* 1(3): 18-19.

Von Wahlde, B., and N. Schiller. 1993. Creating the virtual library: Strategic issues. In *The Virtual Library: Visions and Realities*, ed. L.M. Saunders, 15-46. Westport, CT: Meckler.

About the Contributors

Ethel Auster is Professor, Faculty of Information Studies, University of Toronto, Toronto, Ontario.

Rachel Barker is Administrator, Sheffield Hallom University, Sheffield, UK.

David Bawden is Senior Lecturer, Department of Information Science, The City University, Northampton Square, London, UK.

David C. Bernhardt is Managing Consultant at Business Research Group, a Geneva-based competitive intelligence consulting and research firm.

B. Bowonder is BEL Chair Professor on Technology Management, Administrative Staff College of India, Bella Vista, Hyderabad, India.

Marianne Broadbent is Professor, Graduate School of Management, University of Melbourne, Melbourne, Australia.

Chun Wei Choo is Assistant Professor, Faculty of Information Studies, University of Toronto, Toronto, Ontario.

Blaise Cronin is Dean, Studies in Library and Information Science, Indiana University, Bloomington, Indiana.

Richard L. Daft is Professor, Department of Management, Vanderbilt University, Nashville, Tennessee.

Thomas H. Davenport is Professor, Graduate School of Business, University of Texas at Austin, Austin, Texas.

Robert G. Eccles is Professor, Graduate School of Business Administration, Harvard University, Boston, Massachusetts.

David Ellis is Senior Lecturer, Department of Information Studies, University of Sheffield, Sheffield, UK.

Patricia Fletcher is Assistant Professor, School of Information Studies, Syracuse University, Syracuse, New York.

Jose-Marie Griffiths is Professor and Director, Graduate School of Library and Information Science, University of Tennessee, Knoxville, Tennessee.

James E. Herring is Professor, Department of Communication and Information Studies, Queen Margaret College, Edinburgh, UK.

Forest Woody Horton, Jr. is a Consultant in Washington, DC.

Jeffrey Katzer is Professor, Information Studies, Syracuse University, Syracuse, New York.

Donald W. King is at King Research, Knoxville, Tennessee.

Michael Koenig is Dean, Graduate School of Library and Information Science, Rosary College, River Forest, Illinois.

Robert H. Lengel is Professor, Department of Management and Marketing, University of Texas at San Antonio, San Antonio, Texas.

T. Miyake is Expert on System Analysis, United Nations, ESCAP, Bangkok, Thailand.

Ruth C.T. Morris is Manager of Information Services, Corporate Technical Library, The Upjohn Company, Kalamazoo, Michigan.

Michael E. Porter is Professor, Graduate School of Business Administration, Harvard University, Boston, Massachusetts.

Laurence Prusak is a Principal, Center for Information Technology & Strategy, Ernst & Young, Boston, Massachusetts.

Ruth Stanat is founder and President of Strategic Intelligence Systems, Inc. (SIS).

Robert S. Taylor is Professor Emeritus, Information Studies, Syracuse University, Syracuse, New York.

Author Index

Personal names conform to the following code:
a = author of article included in volume
n = name cited in note or reference of article
r = name cited in additional reading
t = name mentioned in text of article

Abrams, E., 116t&n, 129n
Aburdene, P., 238n, 249n
Accountemps, 454n
Achleitner, H.K., 225n, 242n
Ackoff, R.L., 45n, 46t, 56n,
  105n, 129n, 183n, 184n, 210n,
  229t, 240t, 242n
Agnew, N.M., 242n
Agor, W.H., 234t, 242n, 271r
Aguilar, F.J., 104n, 129n, 178n,
  199t, 208t, 210n, 253n, 254t,
  269n, 258n, 259n, 271r
Ahituv, N., 395t&n, 417n
Aiken, M., 199n, 210n
Albrecht, T.L., 389n
Aldrich, H.E., 61r
Allan, P., 225n, 242n
Allen, B.L., 220t, 234t, 242n
Allen, R.W., 206n, 213n
Allen, Thomas J., 25t, 37n,
  100n, 101t&n, 104n, 106n,
  110t, 111n, 112t&n,113t&n,
  114n, 115n, 129t&n, 131n,
  144n, 157n, 163r, 199t, 211n,
  318t, 321n, 385t&n, 389n,
  432n
Allison, D., 392n
Almquist, Eric, 158n
Alter, S.L., 45n, 56n, 242n
American Psychological Associa-
  tion, 432n
Anderson, E., 450n, 454n

Anderson, J.C., 38n, 62r, 183n,
  214n, 249n
Andrews, F.M., 103n, 114n,
  133n, 392n
Angell, C., 509t&n, 518n
Anthony, R.N., 271r
Aoki, M., 473n, 476n, 478n
Applegate, L.M., 368n, 450n,
  455n, 475n, 478n
Argyris, C., 242n, 473n, 478n
Arms, C., 521r
Arrow, Kenneth J., 24t, 25t&n,
  37n, 172n, 211n, 435r, 473n,
  478n
Arthur, F., 56n
Attanasio, D.R., 481n, 482t&n,
  500n
Auster, Ethel, 169t, 253-270a,
  253n, 254n, 255n, 257n, 264n,
  269n, 271r
Avery, R.D., 115n, 131n
Avis, N., 213n
Azien, I., 182n, 211n

Balakrishnan, B., 159n
Baloff, N., 201n, 211n
Bar, J., 287t, 295n
Barker, R., 299-323a, 300t, 306t,
  321n
Barlett, D.A., 480n
Basek, J., 270n
Bates, B.J., 435r

525

Huber, G.P., 62r, 217n, 220n,
229n, 230t, 231t&n, 232t&n,
234n, 246n, 479n
Huberman, M., 102n, 132n
Huff, S.L., 43t, 59n
Hughes, C., 521r
Hurtubise, R., 44n, 57n
Hutton, J.J., 483n, 484t, 501n

International Iron and Steel In-
stitute, 463n, 479n
Isabella, L., 246n
Isenberg, D.J., 226t, 232t, 234t,
246n, 272r
Isensen, R.S., 111n, 134n
Ives, B., 479n

Jablin, F.M., 38n, 62r, 246n,
249n
Jackson, B. Bund, 51t, 52t, 53t,
57n
Jackson, C., 479n
Jackson, E.B., 392n
Jackson, M.E., 522r
Jacobson, T.L., 138n, 158n
Jagger, H., 311t, 323n
Jain, S.C., 254n, 269n
James, William, 154t, 159n
Janis, I.L., 230n, 246-247n
Jacques, E., 272r
Jauch, L.R., 256t, 269n
Jellis, J., 470n, 473n, 479n
Jequier, N., 291t&n, 296n
Johannes, J.R., 117n, 132n
Johnson, C., 469n, 479n
Johnson, R.M., 432n
Johnston, R., 388t, 390n
Jones, R., 522r
Judd, C.M., 257t, 269n

Kahn, R.E., 522r
Kahneman, D., 235n, 236n,
247n, 251n
Kanter, R.M., 225n, 228t&n,
247n, 272r, 387t&n, 390n,
391n
Kantor, P., 159n, 160n, 164r,
436r

Kaplan, R., 155n, 159n
Kaplan, R.E., 217n, 220t, 225n,
229n, 232t, 233n, 239n, 248n,
272r
Kaplan, S., 155n, 159n, 156t&n,
161n
Karlovac, M., 212n
Kasarda, J.D., 206n, 212n
Katz, E., 25t, 38n, 100n, 130n
Katz, R., 157n
Katzer, Jeffrey, 163r, 168t,
217-252a, 225n, 247n
Keegan, W.J., 178n, 199t&n,
200t, 208t, 212n, 254n, 258n,
259n, 269n
Keen, P.G., 46t, 47t, 55n, 57n,
234t, 248n, 367n, 394n, 413t,
417n
Kefalas, A.G., 178n, 198t, 199t,
200t, 212n
Kelly, G., 482n, 490n, 501n
Kendall, P.L., 257t, 270n
Kennedy-McGregor, M., 28t, 37n
Kerr, S., 249n
Keyes, J., 369r
Kidder, L.H., 269n
Kieffer, J.A., 117n, 132n
Kiesler, S., 62r, 247n, 368n
Kilman, R.H., 202n, 214n
Kim, S.K., 254n, 269n, 267t,
268t
Kimberley, J.R., 105n, 132n,
205n, 212n
King, D.N., 125t, 132n
King, Donald W., 374t, 390n,
392n, 405t, 417n, 419-433a,
422n, 424n, 426n, 427n, 428n,
430n, 432n, 435r, 436r
King, H., 522r
King, J.L., 50n, 58n
King, L.S., 121n, 122t, 123n,
127n, 132n
King, M., 119n, 135n
King, W.D., 380n, 381t&n,
382t&n, 383t, 384n, 387n,
391n, 432n
King, W.R., 44t, 45t, 58n, 480n
Kinnucan, M.T., 238n, 243n

Simon, Nora, 55n, 59n
Sims, Jr., H.P., 236n, 251n
Singh, J.V., 220n, 246n
Skivington, J., 208n, 214n
Skyme, D.J., 506t&n, 519n
Slocum, Jr., J.W., 246n
Slovic, P., 100n, 134n, 247n
Smith, E.R., 269n
Snow, B., 486t&n, 501n
Snyder, H.W., 159n
Soelberg, P.O., 251n
Sormunen, J., 269n
Spaulding, F.H., 522r
Spitalnic, R., 45n, 59n
Sprafke, S.A., 123n, 131n
Sproull, L.S., 7n, 37n, 62r, 247n, 368n
Srivastva, S., 252n, 272r
Stalker, G., 205t&n, 211n
Stambaugh, R.J., 104n, 130n
Stanat, Ruth, 279t, 325-345a
Stanton, M., 314t, 323n
Starbuck, W.H., 61r, 62r, 272r
Stark, J., 480n
Staw, B.M., 37n, 38n, 61r, 62r, 164r, 214n, 243n, 244n, 249n
Stead, B.A., 176n, 181t, 212n
Stewart, R., 225n, 251n, 272r
Stewart, T.A., 281n, 292n, 296n
Stinchcombe, A.L., 62r
Stinson, E.R., 124t, 134n
Stinson, J.A., 104n, 119n, 133n
Stoddard, D., 368n, 450n, 455n
Strassman, P.A., 49t, 54t, 59n, 238n, 251n, 281n, 296n, 394n, 418n, 437r
Strenski, J.B., 315n, 317t, 323n
Strub, M.Z., 522r
Suchman, L.A., 220t, 251n
Sullivan, Jr., C.H., 50n, 52n, 59n
Suprenant, T.T., 522r
Swanson, D.R., 161n, 287t&n, 296n
Swanson, E.B., 29t&n, 38n, 39n
Sweet, E.A., 391n
Swift, A.L., 116t
Synnott, W.R., 44n, 59n, 370r, 522r

Tagerud, Y., 281n, 369r
Taggart, W., 250n, 251n
Tague, J.M., 152n, 160n
Tai, C.H., 312t, 313t, 323n
Tatsuno, S.M., 469n, 480n
Taylor, R., 370r
Taylor, R.L., 114n, 134n
Taylor, R.N., 243n
Taylor, Robert S., 30t, 37n, 69t, 70t, 93-135a, 94n, 101n, 102t, 103n, 104n, 105n, 107n, 108t&n, 120n, 128n, 132n, 134n, 142t, 143t&n, 144t&n, 145t, 147t, 148t&n, 159n, 160n, 163r, 164r, 220t&n, 223n, 232t&n, 233t, 239n, 240n, 242n, 248n, 251n, 306t, 307n, 323n, 394n, 418n, 437r
Tegler, P., 149n, 159n
Theoret, A., 248n
Thomas, L., 134n
Thomas, P.S., 254n, 270n
Thompson, J.D., 23n, 39n, 62r, 178t, 202t, 214n, 233n, 251n
Thorbeck, J. 368n
Thorngate, W., 210t, 214n
Tichy, N.M., 236t, 251n
Time, 286n, 297n
Toffler, A., 291n, 297n
Tomita, K., 100n, 131n
Tomlinson, J.W., 225t&n, 226t, 243n
Trainor, H.E., 281n, 296n, 418n
Trevino, L.K., 271r
Trivison, D., 159n, 164r
Trow, D.B., 244n
Tseng, G., 500n, 501n
Tuden, A., 233n, 251n
Tudor-Silovic, N., 369r
Tushman, M.L., 63r, 114n, 129n, 134n, 172n, 184t, 198n, 201n, 202n, 214n, 215n, 217n, 251n
Tversky, A., 230t, 235n, 236n, 247n, 251n
Tyson, T., 486t&n, 501n

Subject Index

Page numbers in italics indicate information found in a figure or diagram.